Strength for the Journey: Soul, Mind, and Body

Cathy Tardif, RD, LDN

To Luke, Hannah and Evie,
May you find joy in the
journey every day of the year!
Hope you enjoy the book and
daily recipes!
Love,
Aunt Cathy

TRILOGY CHRISTIAN PUBLISHERS

TUSTIN, CA

Trilogy Christian Publishers
A Wholly Owned Subsidary of Trinity Broadcasting Network
2442 Michelle Drive
Tustin, CA 92780

Strength for the Journey: Soul, Mind, and Body

Rights Department, 2442 Michelle Drive, Tustin, CA 92780.

Trilogy Christian Publishing/TBN and colophon are trademarks of Trinity Broadcasting Network.

For information about special discounts for bulk purchases, please contact Trilogy Christian Publishing.

Trilogy Disclaimer: The views and content expressed in this book are those of the author and may not necessarily reflect the views and doctrine of Trilogy Christian Publishing or the Trinity Broadcasting Network.

Manufactured in the United States of America

10 9 8 7 6 5 4 3 2 1

Library of Congress Cataloging-in-Publication Data is available.

ISBN: 978-1-63769-608-8

E-ISBN: 978-1-63769-609-5

Dedication

Dedicated to my family, who bless me every day with their love. To my wonderful husband, Gil, my amazing children, Tim and Kristina, my beautiful grandchildren: Peyton, Tommy, Torrey, Micah, Marcus, and Sammy, to my lovely mom, Lucille, who is still going strong at ninety-five, and to my talented brother, Craig, who has written several books and inspired me to follow in his footsteps.

Introduction

Jesus taught Peter a very valuable lesson when He invited him to walk on water toward Him in the midst of a violent storm (Matthew 14:22-33). Peter was doing great until he took his eyes off of Jesus and started fearing the serious situation in which he found himself. Then he panicked and started sinking! That lesson is extremely valuable for us today as well. I pray this daily devotional book will help you keep your eyes on Jesus and give you strength for your journey to our heavenly home.

Helpful Hints for Making the Most of Your Daily Devotional Time:

1. The first section each day is called The Word of God to Guide Your Soul. This includes a Bible verse and prayer. The Word of God never returns void (Isaiah 55:11) but achieves the will of God, so starting your day with Scripture is the best way to put your day into God's hands. In addition to reading the Scripture verse selected for the day, take time to read the whole chapter the verse came from, so you have the verse in context. Scripture is one way God expresses His great love for you, so it is natural to respond to His love by expressing your love

and gratitude. The written prayer gets you started, but don't stop there. You are the best one to offer thanksgiving for your personal blessings.

2. The second section is called Music to Inspire Your Mind. God gives us glimpses of heaven here on earth through many ways, but I believe a very important way is through music. When was the last time you were feeling down, and some special music lifted you right up and gave you back your joy? I know music is very personal, so I've given you several choices, including contemporary Christian, classical, easy listening vocal, etc. I've also listed a hymn, as the poetry of hymns can be very beautiful, and we don't want to just let them fade into the past. Every song I've picked you can check out online. There is also a space for you to write down your own favorite inspirational music.

3. The final section is called Nutrition to Strengthen Your Body. You've nourished your soul and mind, so now it's time to nourish your body. This is important so you can be healthy and strong in order to fulfill God's will for your life. Nutrition can be very confusing since what is good or bad seems to change daily, but one thing we know for sure—most of us do not get our five or more recommended servings of fruits and vegetables daily. So, I've tried to share some fun vegetable, fruit, and other plant-based recipes to help you and your family meet that important goal.

May God bless you and your family on this pilgrimage through life, and may we praise Him together in our heavenly home for all eternity!

Resolve to Pursue God's Calling for Your Life

January 1

The Word of God to Guide Your Soul
"But one thing I do, forgetting those things which are behind and reaching forward to those things which are ahead, I press toward the goal for the prize of the upward call of God in Christ Jesus" (Philippians 3:13b-14).

> *Dear Lord, I love You and thank You for another year to follow You and serve others. In this New Year, send Your Holy Spirit to fill me with Your love, wisdom, patience, kindness, compassion, generosity, and forgiveness. Help me to let go of the past and follow Your will for my life. Grant me peace of mind and joy of spirit. Make me mindful of those less fortunate and willing to alleviate their suffering as I am able. Amen.*

Music to Inspire Your Mind
- Contemporary Christian "That Was Then, This Is Now" by Josh Wilson and Ben Glover, performed by Josh Wilson.

- Vocal "I Will Follow" by Chris Tomlin, Reuben Morgan, and Jason Ingram, performed by Chris Tomlin.
- Hymn "O God beyond All Praising"—Text: Michael Perry, Music: Gustav T. Holst, performed by the BJU Singers and Orchestra.
- Your music choice: _____

Nutrition to Strengthen Your Body

Slow Cooker Vegetarian Lasagna

- 1 jar (32 ounces) meatless spaghetti sauce (option: add extra flavor with 1 teaspoon each oregano and basil, ¼ teaspoon garlic powder)
- 9 thick lasagna noodles (bronze cut)
- 24 ounces reduced-fat ricotta or cottage cheese
- 2-3 cups chopped vegetables of choice (mushrooms, green pepper, onion, etc.)
- 1 package (10 ounces) frozen, chopped spinach, thawed, and drained well
- 2 cups (8 ounces) reduced-fat mozzarella cheese, shredded
- Nonstick olive oil cooking spray

Spray slow cooker with nonstick olive oil cooking spray. Spread ½ cup spaghetti sauce on the bottom to keep noodles from sticking. Break noodles so they fit and cover most of the bottom. Cover with ⅓ of the ricotta or cottage cheese, veggies, spinach, sauce, cheese, and end with noodles. Repeat layers two more times for a total of three layers. End with noodles on top and cover with a thin layer of sauce and a bit more shredded cheese. Cover and cook on high for 3 hours or low for 5-6 hours. Turn the slow cooker off and let the lasagna sit for at least one hour, allowing all the moisture to get soaked into the noodles. Depending on how long you let it sit, you can either scoop pieces out or cut with a knife.   8 servings

Find Strength in Quiet Time with God

January 2

The Word of God to Guide Your Soul
"For thus says the Lord GOD, the Holy One of Israel: 'In returning and rest you shall be saved; in quietness and confidence shall be your strength'" (Isaiah 30:15a).

> *Dear Lord, I love You and thank You for always being there to give me strength when I need it most. Help me to stay calm even among the storms of life, remembering You are in control and know the bigger plan for my life. When I get distracted and stressed, help me to think of You and the unconditional love You have for me. Send me Your Holy Spirit so I can pass Your love and peace along to others that I meet today. Amen.*

Music to Inspire Your Mind
- Contemporary Christian "You're Not Alone" by Meredith Andrews.
- Choral "Gaelic Blessing (Deep Peace)"—Text: Anonymous, Music: John Rutter, performed by Libera.

- Hymn "Be Still, My Soul (In You I Rest)"—Text: Katharina von Schlegel, Music: Jean Sibelius, additional lyrics and performed by Kari Jobe.
- Your music choice: _____

Nutrition to Strengthen Your Body

Sugar Snap Peas with a Salsa Twist

- 1 pound fresh or frozen sugar snap peas
- ½ cup vegetable broth or water
- 1 jar of your favorite salsa
- 1 cup reduced-fat sharp Cheddar cheese or other favorite cheese, shredded (optional)

In a 3-quart saucepan, bring the sugar snap peas and broth or water to a boil over high heat. Reduce heat to medium. Cover and cook for 3-4 minutes and drain. Place salsa in a microwave-safe container and warm for 30-45 seconds. Spoon salsa over peas, top with cheese (if desired), and serve immediately. (If using microwaved sugar snap peas, prepare as directed, drain, place in serving bowl, and then add warmed salsa and cheese.)

4 servings

Follow Your Savior's Lead

January 3

The Word of God to Guide Your Soul
"Now may the God of peace Himself sanctify you completely; and may your whole spirit, soul, and body be preserved blameless at the coming of our Lord Jesus Christ. He who calls you is faithful, who also will do it" (1 Thessalonians 5:23-24).

> *Dear Lord, I love You and thank you for Your faithfulness in sanctifying me completely and preserving me blameless until You come again. Send Your Holy Spirit to help me follow Your lead in living a holy life. Even if I lose sight of You today and get caught up in the stuff of life, I know You will never take Your eyes off of me. Lead all my loved ones and me to Your strong arms and loving embrace. Amen.*

Music to Inspire Your Mind
- Contemporary Christian "All the Way My Savior Leads Me"—Music: Robert Lowry, Text: Fanny J. Crosby, Arrangement and Additional Lyrics by Chris Tomlin and Matt Redman, performed by Chris Tomlin.

- Classical "The Prayer" by Carole Bayer Sager and David Foster, Italian lyric by Alberto Testa and Tony Renis, performed by Charlotte Church and Josh Groban.
- Hymn "Jesus, Lover of My Soul"—Text: Charles Wesley, Music: Simeon B. Marsh, performed by Michael Card.
- Your music choice: _____

Nutrition to Strengthen Your Body

Grilled Cheese, Tomato, and Spinach Sandwiches

- Margarine (olive-oil based), as needed
- 4 slices whole grain bread
- 2 slices reduced-fat cheese (your choice)
- 2 large slices tomato
- Baby spinach leaves

Spread margarine on one side of each slice of wholegrain bread and place one slice of cheese, one slice of tomato, and baby spinach leaves inside with margarine facing outside. In a large skillet, heat over medium heat until bread is golden brown and then turn and brown on the other side. Serve with favorite soup for a warm, winter meal.   2 Sandwiches

Worship the King with a Pure Heart

January 4

The Word of God to Guide Your Soul

"Oh come, let us worship and bow down; let us kneel before the LORD our Maker. For He is our God, and we are the people of His pasture, and the sheep of His hand" (Psalm 95:6-7).

> *Dear Lord, I love You and thank You for Your love and protection. As the wise men sacrificed much to seek You and worship You, help me to seek You and worship You throughout the coming day. Send Your Holy Spirit to give me a pure heart of worship and be a light to lead others to You. Amen.*

Music to Inspire Your Mind

- Contemporary Christian "Heart of Worship" by Matt Redman, performed by Matt Maher.
- Choral "Psalm 95" by Benjamin Britten, performed by University of Hawaii Choir.
- Hymn "O Worship the King"—Text: Robert Grant, Music: William Gardiner, performed by Chris Tomlin.

- Your music choice: _____

Nutrition to Strengthen Your Body

Vegetable and Egg Casserole

- 1 package (10.8 ounces) of frozen, mixed vegetables, cooked or microwaved, and drained
- ¼ cup sweet onion, finely chopped
- 6 eggs, hard-cooked, coarsely chopped (may only use egg whites, if desired)
- 1 can (10.5 ounces) cream of mushroom soup, condensed (lower in fat and sodium)
- ⅛ teaspoon garlic powder
- ⅛ teaspoon pepper
- ¼ cup reduced-fat Cheddar cheese
- ¼ cup shredded wheat, crushed
- Nonstick olive oil cooking spray

Preheat oven to 350 degrees. Spray 2-quart casserole with cooking spray. In a large bowl, combine vegetables, onion, eggs, soup, and seasonings. In a small bowl, toss crushed shredded wheat and cheese together. Sprinkle over casserole. Bake 30 minutes, uncovered.   6 servings

Ask for Wisdom in Understanding God's Will

January 5

The Word of God to Guide Your Soul
"See then that you walk circumspectly, not as fools but as wise, redeeming the time, because the days are evil. Therefore, do not be unwise, but understand what the will of the Lord is" (Ephesians 5:15-17).

> *Dear Lord, I love You and thank You for this day and all of the possibilities it holds. Send Your Holy Spirit to help me discern Your perfect will in all I say and do. Grant me wisdom and the ability to see all of Your miracles, both great and small. Help me to be aware of the needs of others, rather than just my own. Amen.*

Music to Inspire Your Mind
- Contemporary Christian "Power of Your Love" by Geoff Bullock, performed by Hillsong.
- Vocal "Thy Will" by Bernie Herms, Hillary Dawn Scott, and Emily Weisband, performed by Hillary Scott.

- Hymn "Take My Life and Let It Be Consecrated"—Text: Frances Havergal, Music: Henry Malan, performed by Chris Tomlin (arrangement and additional choruses by Chris Tomlin and Louie Giglio).
- Your music choice: _____

Nutrition to Strengthen Your Body

Honey-Glazed Carrots

- 1 package (16 ounces) fresh baby-cut carrots
- 1 tablespoon margarine (olive-oil based)
- 2 tablespoons light brown sugar
- 2 tablespoons honey
- 2 teaspoons cornstarch

In a small skillet, melt margarine over medium heat and add all other ingredients, except carrots. Put carrots in a microwave-safe casserole dish and top with margarine mixture. Cover and cook on high 10-12 minutes, stirring once after 5 minutes, until tender.   4 servings

Store Up True Treasure in Heaven

January 6

The Word of God to Guide Your Soul
"Do not lay up for yourselves treasures on earth, where moth and rust destroy and where thieves break in and steal; but lay up for yourselves treasures in heaven, where neither moth nor rust destroys and where thieves do not break in and steal. For where your treasure is, there your heart will be also" (Matthew 6:19-21).

> *Dear Lord, I love You and thank You for giving me Your Word to guide my life. Send Your Holy Spirit to help me keep a heavenly perspective today and stay focused on what really matters—the treasures that will bring me and others to eternal life with You. Amen.*

Music to Inspire Your Mind
- Contemporary Christian "Where I Belong" by Jason Ingram and Jason Roy, performed by Building 429.
- Vocal "Turn Your Eyes Upon Jesus (Look Up)" by Nichole Nordeman, Chris Stevens, and Matt Maher, performed by Nichole Nordeman.

- Hymn "Give Me Jesus"—Text and Music: Traditional Spiritual, performed by Danny Gokey.
- Your music choice: _____

Nutrition to Strengthen Your Body

Slow Cooker Vegetable and Bean Chili

- 2 tablespoons olive oil
- 1 cup sweet onion, chopped
- 1 cup green or red bell pepper (or ½ cup of each)
- 1 clove garlic, minced or $1/8$ teaspoon instant minced garlic
- 1 can (14.5 ounces) black beans, rinsed and drained
- 1 can (15.5 ounces) pinto beans, rinsed and drained
- 2 cans (16 ounces each) diced tomatoes
- 2 cups celery, chopped
- 1 cup carrot, chopped
- 1 teaspoon each chili powder, basil, and oregano
- ¼ teaspoon black pepper and thyme

In a large nonstick skillet, heat oil over medium-high heat. Add chopped onion, bell pepper, and garlic; cook and stir 5 minutes or until vegetables are tender. Spoon sauteed vegetables into a slow cooker. Add remaining ingredients in order listed and mix well. Cover and cook on low 5 to 6 hours or until celery and carrots are tender.   8 servings

Trust That God is Working in and Through You

January 7

The Word of God to Guide Your Soul

"Now to Him who is able to do exceedingly abundantly above all that we ask or think, according to the power that works in us, to Him be glory in the church by Christ Jesus to all generations, forever and ever. Amen" (Ephesians 3:20-21).

> *Dear Lord, I love You and thank You for helping me to put my trust in You instead of in myself or others. I put this day into Your hands and ask You to guide me every step of the way, for, without You and Your love, I would never have been created or able to accomplish anything of eternal worth. Amen.*

Music to Inspire Your Mind

- Contemporary Christian "God Is Able" by Ben Fielding and Reuben Morgan, performed by Hillsong.
- Vocal "Great Expectations" by Steven Curtis Chapman.

- Hymn "How Great Thou Art"—Text: Stuart K. Hine, Music: Swedish folk melody (adapted by Stuart K. Hine), performed by Sandi Patty.
- Your music choice: _____

Nutrition to Strengthen Your Body

Easy Cheesy Potatoes and Veggies

- 3 medium potatoes, cooked (microwave for 4 minutes, turning after 2 minutes) and sliced
- ½ cup coarsely chopped celery
- ½ cup coarsely chopped carrots
- 1 can (10 ¾ ounces) condensed Cheddar Cheese Soup (lower fat and sodium)
- 1 tablespoon prepared mustard
- Nonstick olive oil cooking spray

Preheat oven to 375 degrees. Spray a 9-inch square baking pan with nonstick olive oil cooking spray. Combine potatoes, celery, and carrots; place in pan. Blend cheese soup and mustard in a small mixing bowl; pour over vegetables. Bake for 30 minutes or until hot and bubbly. (This is a good recipe to use up leftover veggies as well. Just cut up and use in place of or in addition to the celery and carrots.)   6 servings

Look Forward to Your Heavenly Home

January 8

The Word of God to Guide Your Soul
"Blessed be the God and Father of our Lord Jesus Christ, who according to His abundant mercy has begotten us again to a living hope through the resurrection of Jesus Christ from the dead, to an inheritance incorruptible and undefiled and that does not fade away, reserved in heaven for you" (1 Peter 1:3-4).

> *Dear Lord, I love You and thank You for the promise of eternal life with You in heaven. When I get discouraged, help me to remember that I am the child of a King and have a great inheritance in store. Send Your Holy Spirit to give me and those I interact with today a glimpse of what that inheritance will offer—a life raised up by Your love, joy, and peace, now and forever. Amen.*

Music to Inspire Your Mind
- Contemporary Christian "Glorious Day (Living He Loved Me)" by John Chapman, Mark Hall, and Michael Bleecker, performed by Casting Crowns.

- Vocal "You Raise Me Up" by Rolf Lovland and Brendan Graham, performed by Josh Groban.
- Hymn "What a Day That Will Be"—Text and Music: Jim Hill, performed by Heritage Singers.
- Your music choice: _____

Nutrition to Strengthen Your Body

Asian Vegetable Medley

- 2 tablespoons olive oil
- 3-4 stalks of celery, sliced
- 1 small sweet onion, sliced
- 1 can (4 ounces) mushroom stems and pieces, drained
- 1 can (5 ounces) water chestnuts, drained and sliced
- 2 tablespoons slivered almonds
- 2 tablespoons reduced-sodium soy sauce

In a large nonstick skillet, heat oil over medium heat. Mix in the remaining ingredients. Cover and simmer over medium-low heat for 15 to 20 minutes or until celery is of desired doneness, stirring occasionally. Serve over brown rice.   4 servings

Celebrate Your Baptism

January 9

The Word of God to Guide Your Soul
"Therefore we were buried with Him through baptism into death, that just as Christ was raised from the dead by the glory of the Father, even so we also should walk in newness of life" (Romans 6:4).

> *Dear Lord, I love You and thank You for the gift of baptism, which makes me part of Your family forevermore. Help me to live out my baptism today by trusting in You at all times and by showing Your love to all I meet. Come, Holy Spirit, and help me to "walk in newness of life" and experience the true peace and happiness that can only be found in You. Amen.*

Music to Inspire Your Mind
- Contemporary Christian "Something in the Water" by Chris DeStefano, Brett James, and Carrie Underwood, performed by Carrie Underwood.
- Vocal "Wade in the Water"—Traditional African-American Spiritual, arranged and performed by Eva Cassidy.

- Hymn "Baptized in Water"—Text: Michael Saward, Music: Traditional Gaelic melody ("Morning Has Broken"), performed by Jubilate.
- Your music choice: _____

Nutrition to Strengthen Your Body

Greek Cucumber Boats

- 2 cucumbers
- 12 baby-cut carrots, cut in half, lengthwise
- 1 can or jar (2.25 ounces) sliced Black or Kalamata olives, drained
- Salt-free seasoning, as desired
- 4 ounces Feta cheese, crumbled

Preheat oven to 400 degrees. Cut 2 cucumbers in half lengthwise and scoop out the seeds. Place cucumbers on a foil-lined baking sheet. Top with carrots, olives, seasoning, and Feta cheese. Bake for 15-20 minutes or until softened.

4 servings

Renew Your Mind, Soul, and Body

January 10

The Word of God to Guide Your Soul

"And be renewed in the spirit of your mind, which was created according to God, in true righteousness and holiness" (Ephesians 4:23-24b).

> *Dear Lord, I love You and thank You for making all things new with the start of each day. Send Your Holy Spirit to help me follow You with a renewed mind, soul, and body. Guide me into all righteousness and holiness as I go through this day. I also pray for all those who do not know You that they would come to understand the unconditional love You have for each person You created. Amen.*

Music to Inspire Your Mind

- Contemporary Christian "Alive Again" by Matt Maher and Jason Ingram, performed by Matt Maher.
- Vocal "At the Feet of Jesus" by Steven Curtis Chapman.
- Hymn "Come, Thou Almighty King"—Text: Anonymous, Music: Felice de Giardini, performed by Mark Miller.

- Your music choice: _____

Nutrition to Strengthen Your Body

Brown Rice and Quinoa Veggie Pilaf

- 1 package (6.3 ounces) Brown Rice and Quinoa Pilaf (or other rice mixture of choice)
- 1 package (10 ounces) frozen peas and carrots, cooked or microwaved, and drained
- 1 package (10 ounces) frozen asparagus, cooked or microwaved, drained, and cut into 1-inch pieces
- ¼ cup reduced-fat sour cream

Prepare brown rice and quinoa mix according to package directions. Add cooked or microwaved vegetables to the rice mixture during the last 5 minutes of cooking. Just before serving, stir in sour cream.   4 servings

Wait with a Patient Heart

January 11

The Word of God to Guide Your Soul
"Therefore be patient, brethren, until the coming of the Lord. See how the farmer waits for the precious fruit of the earth, waiting patiently for it until it receives the early and latter rain. You also be patient. Establish your hearts, for the coming of the Lord is at hand" (James 5:7-8).

Dear Lord, I love You and thank You for Your perfect timing in my life. Help me to trust in You and have patience, even when Your answers to my prayers are delayed. Grant me strength today, and make my heart firm in faith, hope, and love as I follow Your will. Send Your Holy Spirit to make me aware of how others may need my help today. Amen.

Music to Inspire Your Mind
- Contemporary Christian "Everything in Its Time" by Corrinne May.
- Choral "You Were There" by Robert Prizeman, performed by Libera.

- Hymn "In His Time"—Text and Music: Diane Ball, performed by the Maranatha Singers.
- Your music choice: _____

Nutrition to Strengthen Your Body

Whole Wheat Veggie Pitas

- 2 whole wheat pitas
- 4 ounces reduced-fat Cheddar cheese or other favorite cheese
- 2 hard-boiled eggs, chopped (may only use egg whites, if desired)
- 1 cup baby spinach leaves
- 1 tomato, chopped
- ½ cup sunflower seeds
- Low-fat Italian dressing or other favorite dressing

Cut whole wheat pita bread in half to make pockets. Fill with the rest of the ingredients, distributed evenly among 4 pocket pitas. Get creative and come up with your own veggie fillings!

4 servings

Look to the Lord for Strength and Deliverance

January 12

The Word of God to Guide Your Soul

"But the salvation of the righteous is from the LORD; He is their strength in the time of trouble. And the LORD shall help them and deliver them; He shall deliver them from the wicked, and save them, because they trust in Him" (Psalm 37:39-40).

> *Dear Lord, I love You and thank You for always being by my side and protecting me, especially in times of trouble. Never let me get so distracted by the world that I forget to seek safety in Your arms. Help me remember today that You are my deliverer and strength. Send Your Holy Spirit to grant me boldness in sharing with others the beautiful comfort, peace, and joy they can find when they open their hearts to loving and trusting You. Amen.*

Music to Inspire Your Mind

- Contemporary Christian "My Deliverer" by Rich Mullins and Mitch McVicker, performed by The Ragamuffins.

- Vocal "I Look to You" by Robert Kelly, performed by Whitney Houston.
- Hymn "A Shield About Me"—Text: Donn Thomas, Music: Donn Thomas and Charles Williams, performed by The Maranatha! Singers.
- Your music choice: _____

Nutrition to Strengthen Your Body

Baked Sweet Potato Wedges

- 5 teaspoons olive oil
- 4 sweet potatoes
- ¼ teaspoon paprika
- ¼ teaspoon salt-free seasoning

Preheat oven to 400 degrees. Peel potatoes and slice lengthwise into quarters. Combine olive oil and paprika in a large bowl. Add potato wedges and stir to coat; place on foil-lined baking sheet. Bake 35-40 minutes, turning once halfway through bake time, or until tender. Lightly sprinkle with salt-free seasoning.

4 servings

Call on Your Heavenly Father

January 13

The Word of God to Guide Your Soul
"But as many as received Him, to them He gave the right to become children of God, to those who believe in His name: who were born, not of blood, nor of the will of the flesh, nor of the will of man, but of God" (John 1:12-13).

> *Dear Lord, I love You and thank You that I can call you Father and that You have adopted me as Your child. Remind me of Your love today when I'm feeling less than loved by others. Send Your Holy Spirit to help me lead more people into Your family today. Amen.*

Music to Inspire Your Mind
- Contemporary Christian "Child of God" by Kathryn Scott.
- Classical "The Lord's Prayer" by Albert Hay Malotte, performed by Andrea Bocelli.
- Hymn "Children of the Heavenly Father"—Text: Carolina Sandell Berg, Music: Traditional Swedish Melody, performed by the Concordia Choir.
- Your music choice: _____

Nutrition to Strengthen Your Body

Vegetable and Bean Bake

- 2 cans (14.5 ounces each) vegetable broth
- ¾ cup cream of wheat cereal (2½ minute cook time), uncooked
- ½ cup sweet onions, chopped
- ½ cup green peppers, chopped
- 2 eggs, lightly beaten, or ½ cup egg substitute
- 2 tablespoons grated Parmesan cheese
- 1 package (10 ounces) frozen broccoli and cauliflower (or any frozen vegetable combination, as desired)
- 2 cans (15.5 ounces each) white beans, drained and rinsed
- ½ teaspoon garlic powder
- ¼ cup reduced-fat Cheddar cheese, shredded
- Nonstick olive oil cooking spray

Preheat oven to 350 degrees. Microwave frozen vegetables according to package directions and drain. Bring broth to boil in a medium saucepan over medium-high heat. Gradually stir in cereal until well blended. Cook 4 minutes or until thickened, stirring constantly. Remove from heat and cool for 5 minutes. Stir in onions, green peppers, eggs, and Parmesan cheese; set aside. Spray 2-quart casserole with cooking spray, and combine vegetables, beans, and garlic powder in the casserole dish. Spoon cereal mixture evenly over vegetables and beans. Bake 25 minutes or until the cereal mixture is set. Sprinkle with Cheddar cheese and bake for an additional 5 minutes. Let rest for 5-10 minutes before serving.   6 servings

Have Hope in the Resurrection

January 14

The Word of God to Guide Your Soul

"But I do not want you to be ignorant, brethren, concerning those who have fallen asleep, lest you sorrow as others who have no hope. For if we believe that Jesus died and rose again, even so God will bring with Him those who sleep in Jesus" (1 Thessalonians 4:13-14).

> *Dear Lord, I love You and thank You for Your promise of resurrection and eternal life. Send Your Holy Spirit to grant me the virtue of faith in life everlasting so I will never "sorrow as others who have no hope" at the death of loved ones. Help me give comfort to those who are grieving so they can also have hope in Jesus, who died and rose for the salvation of all. Amen.*

Music to Inspire Your Mind

- Contemporary Christian "Resurrection Power" by Ryan Ellis, Ed Cash, and Tony Brown, performed by Chris Tomlin.

- Vocal "Christ Our Hope in Life and Death" by Keith Getty, Matt Boswell, Jordan Kauflin, Matt Merker, and Matt Papa, performed by Matt Papa, Keith Getty, and Kristyn Getty.
- Hymn "I Know That My Redeemer Lives"—Text: Samuel Medley, Music: Lewis D. Edwards, performed by Linda Rowberry, arranged by Michael R. Hicks.
- Your music choice: _____

Nutrition to Strengthen Your Body

Classy Corn Medley

- 1 package (10 ounces) frozen whole kernel corn
- ½ cup chopped celery
- 1 vegetable bouillon cube, crushed
- ⅓ cup water
- 1 can (4 ounces) sliced mushrooms, drained
- 1 medium tomato, cut in thin wedges
- Pepper and celery seed to taste (optional)

In a medium saucepan, combine corn, celery, bouillon cube, and water. Bring to a boil; cover and simmer 5 to 7 minutes, or until vegetables are tender. Stir in sliced mushrooms and tomato wedges; cover and heat through on low heat. Season to taste with pepper and celery seed, as desired.   6 servings

Keep Your Eyes on Jesus

January 15

The Word of God to Guide Your Soul
"And when Peter had come down out of the boat, he walked on the water to go to Jesus. But when he saw that the wind was boisterous, he was afraid; and beginning to sink he cried out, saying, 'Lord, save me!' And immediately Jesus stretched out His hand and caught him, and said to him, 'O you of little faith, why did you doubt?'" (Matthew 14:29-31).

> *Dear Lord, I love You and thank You for being there to catch me when I fall and doubt You. Help me to grow in trusting You more each day, even when I see waves crashing around me and circumstances looking very bleak. As I go through this day, show me how I can help others through the storms of life and assist them in turning to You for salvation and guidance. Amen.*

Music to Inspire Your Mind
- Contemporary Christian "Oceans (Where Feet May Fail)" by Matt Crocker, Joel Houston, and Salomon Ligtheim, performed by Hillsong United.

- Choral "The Storm Is Passing Over" by Charles Albert Tinley, performed by the Detroit Mass Choir.
- Hymn "You Are My Hiding Place"—Text and Music: Michael Ledner, performed by Selah.
- Your music choice: _____

Nutrition to Strengthen Your Body

Roasted Winter Vegetables

- 1 package (10 ounces) frozen Brussels sprouts
- 8 ounces fresh baby carrots
- 4 medium potatoes, peeled and cut into ½ inch cubes (may do part white and part sweet potatoes)
- ½ cup margarine (olive-oil based)
- 1 teaspoon dill weed
- 1 teaspoon parsley
- 2 garlic cloves, minced or ¼ teaspoon dried, minced garlic
- Nonstick olive oil cooking spray

Preheat oven to 375 degrees. Prepare Brussels sprouts according to package directions and drain. Spray a 9x13-inch baking dish with cooking spray. Place vegetables in the baking dish. In a small frying pan, melt margarine over medium heat; add seasonings and garlic. Drizzle over vegetables. Cover and bake for 40 to 50 minutes or until tender.   6 servings

Live in the Spirit

January 16

The Word of God to Guide Your Soul
"But the fruit of the Spirit is love, joy, peace, longsuffering, kindness, goodness, faithfulness, gentleness, self-control. Against such there is no law. If we live in the Spirit, let us also walk in the Spirit" (Galatians 5:22-23, 25).

> *Dear Lord, I love You and thank You for sending Your Holy Spirit to guide me and enable me to live a life pleasing to You. Help me receive Your Spirit anew today, and let the fruit of the Spirit grow and flourish in all I do and say. Amen.*

Music to Inspire Your Mind
- Contemporary Christian "Spirit of the Living God" by Audrey Assad.
- Choral "Veni Sancte Spiritus" by Wolfgang Mozart, performed by Hastings College Choir.
- Hymn "Spirit of God, Descend upon My Heart"—Text: George Croly, Music: Frederick C. Atkinson, performed by Sue Nixon with Walt Wagner.

- Your music choice: _____

Nutrition to Strengthen Your Body

Marinated Cucumber Salad

- 3 cups cucumbers, peeled and thinly sliced
- 1 medium green pepper, seeded and cut into rings
- ½ medium red onion, thinly sliced, separating rings
- 2 tablespoons olive oil
- 2 tablespoons lemon juice
- 2 tablespoons vinegar
- 1 teaspoon sugar
- ¼ teaspoon dill weed
- Dash of pepper
- Reduced-fat sour cream (optional)

In a large bowl, combine cucumbers, green pepper, and onion. In a small bowl, blend together oil, lemon juice, vinegar, sugar, and dill. Pour over vegetables; toss lightly. Cover and refrigerate for 1 hour. Toss lightly and serve over lettuce or baby spinach leaves. May also garnish with a teaspoonful of reduced-fat sour cream, as desired.   8 servings

Spread God's Healing Touch

January 17

The Word of God to Guide Your Soul
"He heals the brokenhearted and binds up their wounds. He counts the number of the stars; He calls them all by name. Great is our Lord, and mighty in power; His understanding is infinite" (Psalm 147:3-5).

> *Dear Lord, I love You and thank You for Your healing touch. You healed so many during Your ministry on earth, and You continue to heal, both physically and emotionally. Please come and bind up any open wounds I still suffer from and help me to be part of Your healing ministry today, perhaps by a kind word of encouragement for others along the way. Amen.*

Music to Inspire Your Mind
- Contemporary Christian "We Come to You" by Josh Blakesley.
- Vocal "Heal Us, Lord" by Liam Lawton.
- Hymn "He Touched Me"—Text and Music: William J. Gaither, performed by Elvis Presley.

- Your music choice: _____

Nutrition to Strengthen Your Body

Creamy Mashed Potato Casserole

- 4 medium potatoes, cooked and mashed with low-fat milk
- 4 ounces Neufchatel Cheese or favorite flavor of Laughing Cow Cheese
- 1 egg, lightly beaten, or ¼ cup egg substitute
- 2 tablespoons chopped sweet onion
- 1 tablespoon chopped parsley
- Paprika or Old Bay Seasoning, as desired
- Nonstick olive oil cooking spray

Preheat oven to 400 degrees. Combine mashed potatoes and cheese, beating until well blended. Stir in egg, onion, and parsley. Spray a 1½-quart casserole dish with cooking spray; spoon potato mixture into the dish and sprinkle with paprika or Old Bay Seasoning. Bake for 30 minutes or until heated through.   8 servings

Turn Often to Your Father in Prayer

January 18

The Word of God to Guide Your Soul
"But you, when you pray, go into your room, and when you have shut your door, pray to your Father who is in the secret place; and your Father who sees in secret will reward you openly" (Matthew 6:6).

> *Dear Lord, I love You and thank You for the gift of prayer and for the privilege of being able to come before You as Your child and friend. Help me to daily take time to pray, but also to listen to You in silence, apart from the distractions of the world. I pray now for all those who do not love You that they would come to know Your love and forgiveness. Amen.*

Music to Inspire Your Mind
- Contemporary Christian "I Turn to You" by Todd Smith and Chris Eaton, performed by Selah.
- Vocal "Warrior" by Steven Curtis Chapman.
- Hymn "Sweet Hour of Prayer"—Text: William Walford, Music: William Bradbury, performed by Casting Crowns.
- Your music choice: _____

Nutrition to Strengthen Your Body

Blueberry Oatmeal Muffins

- 1¾ cups quick or old-fashioned oats, uncooked
- 2 tablespoons firmly packed brown sugar
- 1 cup all-purpose flour (add an additional 2 tablespoons if using old-fashioned oats)
- ½ cup granulated sugar
- 1 tablespoon baking powder
- ¼ teaspoon salt (optional)
- 1 cup low-fat milk
- 1 egg, lightly beaten, or ¼ cup egg substitute
- 2 tablespoons olive oil
- 1 teaspoon grated lemon peel
- 1 teaspoon vanilla
- 1 cup fresh or frozen blueberries (do not thaw)

Preheat oven to 400 degrees. Line 12 medium muffin cups with paper baking cups. For topping, combine ¼ cup oats and brown sugar; set aside. Combine 1½ cups oats with remaining dry ingredients in a large bowl; mix well. In a small bowl, combine milk, egg, oil, lemon peel, and vanilla; mix well. Add to dry ingredients and stir just until moistened. Gently fold in berries. Fill muffin cups until almost full; sprinkle with topping. Bake 20-24 minutes or until light golden brown. Cool muffins in pan on rack for 5 minutes; remove from pan and serve warm. 1 dozen muffins

Be Christ's Hands and Voice

January 19

The Word of God to Guide Your Soul

"So Jesus said to them again, 'Peace to you! As the Father has sent me, I also send you.' And when He had said this, He breathed on them, and said to them, 'Receive the Holy Spirit'" (John 20:21-22).

> *Dear Lord, I love You and thank You for the gift of Your peace and the Holy Spirit to give me the strength to do Your work during my pilgrimage back to my heavenly home. Help me to follow up my prayers for others with action. Thank you for the opportunity to be Your hands, feet, and voice. Amen.*

Music to Inspire Your Mind
- Contemporary Christian "I Refuse" by Josh Wilson.
- Vocal "St. Theresa's Prayer" by John Michael Talbot.
- Hymn "I Love to Tell the Story"—Text: A. Catherine Hankey, Music: William G. Fischer, performed by Alan Jackson.
- Your music choice: _____

Nutrition to Strengthen Your Body

Quick and Easy Vegetable-Pasta Soup

- 2 tablespoons olive oil
- 1 medium sweet onion, diced
- 1 package (10.8 ounces) frozen mixed vegetables, your choice
- 2 cans (18.5 ounces each) light vegetable soup
- ½ cup broken spaghetti pieces (uncooked)

Heat oil in a large saucepan over medium heat. Add onion and vegetables to hot oil and saute, stirring occasionally, until lightly browned, for about 10 minutes. Add vegetable soup—heat to boiling over high heat. Add spaghetti pieces. Reduce heat to low, cover, and simmer for 20-30 minutes or until all vegetables and spaghetti pieces are tender. Stir occasionally.

4 servings

Enjoy the Fellowship of the Great I Am

January 20

The Word of God to Guide Your Soul
"And lo, I am with you always, even to the end of the age. Amen" (Matthew 28:20b).

> *Dear Lord, I love You and thank You for the promise that You are always with me. Send Your Holy Spirit to remind me I am never alone and the great "I am" is my best friend and King, forever guiding me and loving me. Let Your love shine through me to everyone I meet today, inspiring them to seek You as their Lord and King. Amen.*

Music to Inspire Your Mind
- Contemporary Christian "I Am" by Mark Schultz.
- Vocal "Great I Am" by Jared Anderson, performed by Phillips, Craig, and Dean.
- Hymn "Great Are You, Lord"—Text and Music: Steve and Vikki Cook, performed by Don Moen and Hosanna! Music.
- Your music choice: _____

Nutrition to Strengthen Your Body

Vegetarian Enchilada Casserole

- 1 medium sweet onion, chopped
- 1 tablespoon olive oil
- 2 cans (8 ounces each) tomato sauce
- 1 can (12 ounces) Mexicorn, drained
- 1 can (10 ounces) mild enchilada sauce
- ½ teaspoon chili powder
- ¼ teaspoon oregano
- 1 can (16 ounces) vegetarian refried beans
- 12 corn tortillas
- 6 ounces low-fat mozzarella cheese, shredded
- 1 cup shredded lettuce
- ½ cup fresh tomatoes, chopped
- Nonstick olive oil cooking spray

Preheat oven to 350 degrees. In a large skillet, brown onion in olive oil over medium-high heat until soft. Add tomato sauce, Mexicorn, enchilada sauce, and seasonings; mix well. Bring to a boil; reduce heat and simmer for 5 minutes. Stir in refried beans. Spray a 9x13-inch baking dish with cooking spray. Place 6 tortillas in the bottom. Spread half of the bean mixture over tortillas; sprinkle with ½ of the mozzarella cheese. Repeat layers of tortillas and mixture. Bake for 20 minutes. Sprinkle with remaining mozzarella cheese and bake for an additional 5 minutes. Garnish with lettuce and tomatoes.   8 servings

Soar Like an Eagle with Perseverance and Hope in the Lord

January 21

The Word of God to Guide Your Soul

"Have you not known? Have you not heard? The everlasting God, the Lord, the Creator of the ends of the earth, neither faints nor is weary. His understanding is unsearchable. He gives power to the weak, and to those who have no might He increases strength. But those who wait on the LORD shall renew their strength; they shall mount up with wings like eagles, they shall run and not be weary, they shall walk and not faint" (Isaiah 40:28-29, 31).

Dear Lord, I love You and thank You for the strength You give me to persevere as I journey through this life. Send Your Holy Spirit to help me trust You with all the trials and frustrations I may encounter today. Show me how to inspire my family and friends to love You more and to "mount up with wings like eagles." Amen.

Music to Inspire Your Mind

- Contemporary Christian "Soar" by Meredith Andrews, Mia Fieldes, and Seth Mosley, performed by Meredith Andrews.
- Vocal "Those Who Wait on the Lord" by Esther Mui.
- Hymn "On Eagle's Wings"—Text and Music: Michael Joncas, performed by Josh Groban.
- Your music choice: _____

Nutrition to Strengthen Your Body

Carrots, Potatoes, and Onions, Oh My!

- 4 medium potatoes, peeled and cubed
- 1 medium sweet onion, peeled and sliced
- 4 medium carrots, peeled and sliced
- 1 can (10¾ ounces) cream of potato condensed soup (reduced sodium and fat)
- Paprika
- Nonstick olive oil cooking spray

Preheat oven to 350 degrees. Spray an 8-inch square baking pan with cooking spray. Layer potatoes, then onions, then carrots. Combine soup with 1 soup-can of water. Pour over vegetables. Sprinkle with paprika. Bake, covered, for 30 minutes. Uncover and bake 30 minutes more or until vegetables are tender.

6 servings

Thank Jesus for His Constant Intercession

January 22

The Word of God to Guide Your Soul
"Therefore He is also able to save to the uttermost those who come to God through Him, since He always lives to make intercession for them" (Hebrews 7:25).

> *Dear Lord, I love You and thank You so much for dying for me and obtaining my salvation. It is only by Your sacrifice that someday I will be able to live with You, the angels, and the communion of saints, forever, in great joy and peace. Thank You for the assurance You are praying for me and that You care about every detail of my everyday life. Help me be an intercessor for others today, and let my life be an example of the abundant life You offer to all. Amen.*

Music to Inspire Your Mind
- Contemporary Christian "Lifesong" by Mark Hall, performed by Casting Crowns.

- Orchestral/Vocal "You'll Never Walk Alone"—Text: Oscar Hammerstein II, Music: Richard Rodgers, performed by Andre Rieu Orchestra and Vocalists.
- Hymn "My Jesus, I Love Thee"—Text: William R. Featherston, Music: Adoniroam J. Gordon, performed by Darlene Zschech (additional lyrics by Darlene Zschech).
- Your music choice: _____

Nutrition to Strengthen Your Body

Veggie Macaroni and Cheese

- 1 package (7.25 ounces) macaroni and cheese dinner with whole grain pasta
- 2 tablespoons olive oil
- 1 cup coarsely chopped fresh mushrooms or 1 can (4 ounces) sliced mushrooms, drained
- ½ medium green pepper, chopped
- ½ medium sweet onion, chopped
- ¾ cup sliced black olives, drained
- ¼ teaspoon dried, minced garlic

Prepare macaroni and cheese according to package directions (using olive oil-based margarine and nonfat milk). While pasta is cooking, saute vegetables and garlic in olive oil over medium-high heat in a large skillet until tender. Add vegetable mixture to cooked macaroni and cheese. Be creative and try other vegetables as well!   4 servings

Be Mindful of the Lord in All Your Ways

January 23

The Word of God to Guide Your Soul:

"Trust in the LORD with all your heart, and lean not on your own understanding; in all your ways acknowledge Him, and He shall direct your paths" (Proverbs 3:5-6).

> *Dear Lord, I love You and thank You for directing my "paths" today. Help me to know You are always with me and taking care of any problems I might face. When I start to worry, send Your Holy Spirit to remind me to trust in You and be mindful of Your will for my life. Let others see the peace and joy I have in knowing You. Amen.*

Music to Inspire Your Mind

- Contemporary Christian "Arms of Love" by Gary Chapman, Michael W. Smith, and Amy Grant, performed by Amy Grant.
- Choral "I Was There to Hear Your Borning Cry" by John Ylvisaker, performed by the St. Olaf Choir.

- Hymn "As the Deer"—Text and Music: Martin Nystrom, performed by the Maranatha Singers.
- Your music choice: _____

Nutrition to Strengthen Your Body

Italian Zucchini Squares

- 3 cups shredded zucchini
- ½ cup sweet onion, chopped
- 1 tablespoon olive oil
- 1¼ cups oats (quick or old-fashioned, uncooked)
- ¼ cup (1 ounce) shredded part-skim mozzarella cheese
- 1 egg or ¼ cup egg substitute
- ½ teaspoon basil or oregano
- ½ teaspoon salt-free seasoning
- ⅛ teaspoon pepper
- ⅓ cup tomato sauce
- Nonstick olive oil cooking spray

Preheat oven to 375 degrees. Spray an 8-inch square glass baking dish with cooking spray. Press zucchini between paper towels to remove excess moisture. In a small skillet, saute onion in oil over medium-high heat until tender; transfer to a large bowl. Add zucchini and remaining ingredients, except tomato sauce; mix well. Spread into prepared baking dish. Spread tomato sauce evenly over the top. Bake for 30 minutes or until heated through. Let sit for 5 minutes and cut into squares. 8 servings

Praise the Lord with Your Whole Heart

January 24

The Word of God to Guide Your Soul
"I will praise You, O LORD, with my whole heart; I will tell of all Your marvelous works. I will be glad and rejoice in You; I will sing praise to Your name, O Most High" (Psalm 9:1-2).

> *Dear Lord, I love You and thank You for the gift of beautiful music, which lifts me up and takes my mind to thoughts of You and sharing eternity with You in heaven someday. Whenever I feel discouraged today, help me think of hymns full of praise and worship to Your most Holy Name. Help me to share the song of Your love with others as often as possible. Amen.*

Music to Inspire Your Mind
- Contemporary Christian "Ever Be" by Chris Greeley, Kalley Heiligenthal, Bobby Strand, and Gabriel Wilson, performed by Aaron Shust.
- Orchestral "Symphony of Praise" by Paul Terracini, performed by Prague Symphony Orchestra.

- Hymn "Praise to the Lord, the Almighty"—Text: Joachim Neander, Music: Stralsund Gesangbuch, 1665, performed by Christy Nockels.
- Your music choice: _____

Nutrition to Strengthen Your Body

Cheese and Veggie Stuffed Potatoes

- 4 large baking potatoes
- 1 cup low-fat cottage cheese
- 2 tablespoons low-fat milk
- 2 tablespoons minced onion
- 2 tablespoons chopped green pepper (or other vegetable as desired—be creative!)
- ¼ teaspoon paprika

Scrub potatoes, remove blemishes, and poke several times with a fork. Place potatoes on a paper towel and microwave for 8 minutes, turning halfway through. Allow potatoes to cool enough to handle. Slice each potato in half, lengthwise. Using a spoon, scoop out pulp, leaving about ¼ inch thick shells, saving pulp. In a medium bowl, blend cheese, milk, onion, and green pepper. Add potato pulp; mix until light and fluffy. Fill potato halves with mixture. Sprinkle paprika over potatoes. Return to microwave for two minutes to reheat, if desired.   4 servings

Reach Out to Jesus for Healing

January 25

The Word of God to Guide Your Soul

"Now a leper came to Him, imploring Him, kneeling down to Him and saying to Him, 'If You are willing, You can make me clean.' Then Jesus, moved with compassion, stretched out His hand and touched him, and said to him, 'I am willing; be cleansed'" (Mark 1:40-41).

> *Dear Lord, I love You and thank You for Your healing touch in my life. Remind me to always turn to You when I'm hurting, rather than trying to comfort myself with the things of this world, for only through You is true and lasting healing. Grant me an opportunity to reach out to someone who is hurting today and show them Your compassionate love. Send Your Holy Spirit to guide me and give me courage. Amen.*

Music to Inspire Your Mind

- Contemporary Christian "When I'm With You" by Ben Calhoun, Josh Calhoun, Seth Mosely, performed by Citizen Way.

- Vocal "Touch of the Master's Hand"—Text: Myra Brooks Welch, Music: John Kramp, performed by Wayne Watson.
- Hymn "Just as I Am"—Text: Charlotte Elliott, Music: William Bradbury (additional music and lyrics by Travis Cottrell, David Moffitt, and Sue Smith), performed by Travis Cottrell.
- Your music choice: _____

Nutrition to Strengthen Your Body

Stir-Fried Vegetables

- 1 package (16 ounces) frozen broccoli and cauliflower florets (do not thaw)
- 2 teaspoons olive oil
- ½ cup lemon juice
- 1 cup vegetable broth
- 1 tablespoon reduced-sodium soy sauce
- 1 tablespoon grated lemon rind
- 1 clove garlic, minced, or ⅛ teaspoon dried, minced garlic
- 2 tablespoons cornstarch

In a medium saucepan, combine lemon juice, broth, soy sauce, lemon rind, and garlic; heat just to boiling. In a small bowl, combine cornstarch and 2 tablespoons of water. Gradually add to the broth, stirring constantly, until thickened. In a wok or heavy skillet, heat olive oil over medium heat. Add frozen cauliflower and broccoli and stir-fry for 5-7 minutes or until vegetables are crisp-tender. Remove from heat. Add sauce to vegetables and serve over brown rice.   4 servings

Reflect on How Much Jesus Loves You

January 26

The Word of God to Guide Your Soul
"For this reason I bow my knees to the Father of our Lord Jesus Christ, that Christ may dwell in your hearts through faith; that you, being rooted and grounded in love, may be able to comprehend with all the saints what is the width and length and depth and height—to know the love of Christ which passes knowledge; that you may be filled with all the fullness of God" (Ephesians 3:14, 17-19).

> *Dear Lord, I love You and thank You for loving me so much that You died for my salvation. Send Your Holy Spirit to help me truly understand "the width and length and depth and height" of Your love and to let that amazing love shine through me to everyone I meet today. When my thoughts turn negative or worry creeps in, remind me that Your love is all I need. Amen.*

Music to Inspire Your Mind
- Contemporary Christian "Jesus Loves Me" by Chris Tomlin, Reuben Morgan, and Ben Glover, performed by Chris Tomlin.

- Vocal "Morning Comes When You Call" by Anne Herring and Matthew Ward, performed by the 2nd Chapter of Acts.
- Hymn "O the Deep, Deep Love of Jesus"—Text: Samuel Trevor Francis, Music: Thomas J. Williams, performed by Selah.
- Your music choice: _____

Nutrition to Strengthen Your Body

Scrambled Eggs—Tuscany Style

- 2 tablespoons olive oil
- 1 medium sweet onion, peeled and chopped
- 1 red pepper, seeded and chopped
- 1 cup baby spinach leaves
- 1 can (14 ounces) diced tomatoes
- 6 eggs or 1½ cups egg substitute
- Salt-free seasoning, pepper, and basil to taste
- Grated Parmesan cheese

Heat oil over medium heat in a nonstick skillet. Saute the onions and red peppers for 5-6 minutes. Add spinach leaves and tomatoes; cook over low heat for 15 minutes. Meanwhile, whisk eggs in a bowl until well blended and stir in seasonings. Add egg mixture to vegetables and cook over medium heat, stirring constantly. Remove from heat as soon as eggs begin to set but are still moist; about 3 minutes. Sprinkle with Parmesan cheese and serve immediately.   4 servings

Remember to Count Your Blessings

January 27

The Word of God to Guide Your Soul

"Bless the Lord, O my soul; and all that is within me, bless His holy name! Bless the Lord, O my soul, and forget not all His benefits: who forgives all your iniquities, who heals all your diseases, who redeems your life from destruction, who crowns you with lovingkindness and tender mercies" (Psalm 103:1-4).

Dear Lord, I love You and thank You for all of Your blessings, too numerous to count! Send Your Holy Spirit to remind me to appreciate my blessings every day and "forget not all His benefits." I praise Your name with all the angels and saints for delivering my life "from destruction" and surrounding me "with lovingkindness and tender mercies." Show me how to share this Good News with others, so their days can be filled with Your love. Amen.

Music to Inspire Your Mind

- Contemporary Christian "Counting Every Blessing" by Gareth Gilkeson and Chris Llewellyn, performed by Rend Collective.
- Vocal "10,000 Reasons (Bless the Lord)" by Jonas Myrin and Matt Redman, performed by Matt Redman.
- Hymn "Praise My Soul, the King of Heaven"—Text: Henry F. Lyte, Music: John Goss, arranged and performed by Graham Kendrick and Martin Smith.
- Your music choice: _____

Nutrition to Strengthen Your Body

Tasty Vegetarian Burgers

- 2 cups cooked brown rice
- 1 can (16 ounces) kidney beans, rinsed and drained
- 2 tablespoons ketchup
- Seasonings: ½ teaspoon garlic powder, 1 teaspoon oregano, ¼ teaspoon thyme, ½ teaspoon basil
- Salt-free seasoning and pepper to taste
- ¼ cup finely chopped sweet onions
- ¼ cup finely chopped green peppers or pickles
- 2 tablespoons olive oil

Prepare brown rice according to package directions. In a large bowl, mix together beans, rice, ketchup, and spices. Mash beans well with a fork or potato masher. (Rice will still be lumpy.) Add in chopped onions and green peppers or pickles.

Divide mixture evenly and form into 8 burgers, about ½-inch thick. Keep hands slightly wet to avoid sticking. Heat olive oil in a large skillet over medium heat. Place burgers in the skillet and cook until browned on both sides, turning several times. Serve hot on multigrain buns with lettuce, tomato, and all your favorite burger condiments and toppings.   8 servings

Look for Guidance in the Word of God

January 28

The Word of God to Guide Your Soul

"Your word is a lamp to my feet and a light to my path. Your testimonies I have taken as a heritage forever, for they are the rejoicing of my heart" (Psalm 119:105, 111).

> *Dear Lord, I love You and thank You for Your Word that guides me and keeps me on the right path to eternal life with You. Send Your Holy Spirit to awaken the wonder and enthusiasm of reading and studying the Bible daily and to understand it with Your help. Grant me the opportunity to share Your word of hope with someone today. Amen.*

Music to Inspire Your Mind

- Contemporary Christian "Word of God Speak" by Bart Millard and Pete Kipley, performed by MercyMe.
- Vocal "Your Word" by Chris Davenport, performed by Hillsong Worship.

- Hymn "Thy Word"—Text: Amy Grant (based on Psalm 119:105), Music: Michael W. Smith, performed by Amy Grant and Michael W. Smith.
- Your music choice: _____

Nutrition to Strengthen Your Body

Greek Spinach and Cheese Squares

- 3 eggs or ¾ cup egg substitute
- 6 tablespoons flour (preferably whole wheat)
- 2 packages (10 ounces each) frozen, chopped spinach, cooked and drained
- 2 cups (16 ounces) reduced-fat cottage cheese
- 2 cups (8 ounces) reduced-fat sharp Cheddar cheese, grated
- ½ teaspoon salt-free seasoning
- 3 tablespoons wheat germ (optional)
- Nonstick olive oil cooking spray

Preheat oven to 350 degrees. Beat eggs and flour in a large bowl until smooth. Add the rest of the ingredients and mix well. Spray a 9x13-inch baking pan with nonstick cooking spray; pour in the spinach and cheese mixture, spreading out evenly. Sprinkle with wheat germ, if desired. Bake, uncovered, for 45 minutes. Let the dish rest for 5 minutes and cut into squares for serving. 8 servings

Hold Fast to Your Faith

January 29

The Word of God to Guide Your Soul

"Let us hold fast the confession of our hope without wavering, for He who promised is faithful" (Hebrews 10:23).

> *Dear Lord, I love You and thank You for Your promise of forgiveness and everlasting life. Help me always to stand up for You and never be afraid to share what I believe. When times get tough today and in the future, help me remember Your promise that You are always faithful. Send Your Holy Spirit to grant me courage and fortitude so I may always "hold fast" and never waver from my faith in You. Amen.*

Music to Inspire Your Mind

- Contemporary Christian "This Is What We Believe" by Aaron Shust and Jonathan Lee, performed by Aaron Shust.
- Vocal "I Pledge Allegiance to the Lamb" by Ray Boltz.
- Hymn "O Jesus, I Have Promised"—Text: John E. Bode, Music: Arthur H. Mann, performed by Scottish Festival Singers.
- Your music choice: _____

Nutrition to Strengthen Your Body

Sauteed Cabbage, Tomatoes, and Green Peppers

- 2 medium sweet onions, sliced
- 2 tablespoons olive oil
- 1 green pepper, cut into one-inch pieces
- 2 large tomatoes
- ½ medium head of green cabbage
- ½ teaspoon garlic powder
- Salt-free seasoning and pepper to taste

In a large skillet, saute onions in olive oil over medium heat for 3 minutes. Add green pepper; cover and cook for 5 minutes. Cut tomatoes into quarters and cabbage into 4 wedges; add to onion and green pepper. Mix in seasonings, cover, reduce heat to low, and simmer for about 15 minutes.   4 servings

Be Thankful You Are a Child of God

January 30

The Word of God to Guide Your Soul
"Behold what manner of love the Father has bestowed on us, that we should be called children of God! Therefore the world does not know us, because it did not know Him" (1 John 3:1).

> *Dear Lord, I love You and thank You for adopting me as Your child and loving me tenderly as my Father. Help me to remember I am part of an eternal family, and my home is really with You in heaven. Send Your Holy Spirit to help me bring others into Your family and show compassion to all, as they are my brothers and sisters. Amen.*

Music to Inspire Your Mind
- Contemporary Christian "Children of God" by Phil Wickham.
- Vocal "Child of God (Father, You're All I Need)" by Kathryn Scott.
- Hymn "Day by Day and with Each Passing Moment"—Text: Carolina Sandell Berg, Music: Oscar Ahnfelt, performed by Katherine Journey.

- Your music choice: _____

Nutrition to Strengthen Your Body

Slow Cooker Hearty Vegetable and Pinto Bean Stew

- 2 cans (15 ounces each) pinto beans, rinsed and drained
- 1 package (16 ounces) frozen green beans
- 2 cups cauliflower florets
- 1 cup sweet onion, chopped
- 1 cup baby carrots, cut in half crosswise
- 3 cups vegetable broth (reduced-sodium preferred)
- 2 teaspoons ground cumin
- ½ teaspoon garlic powder
- 1 teaspoon dill weed
- 1 bay leaf
- 1 can (15 ounces) chunky tomato sauce with garlic and herbs
- ½ cup dry-roasted peanuts

Place pinto beans in a slow cooker. Top with vegetables. Combine broth and seasonings in a large bowl and mix well. Pour mixture over beans and vegetables. Add bay leaf. Cover and cook on low for 9 to 11 hours. Mix in tomato sauce. Cover and cook on low for an additional 15 minutes. Divide stew into bowls and evenly sprinkle peanuts over each serving. 6 servings

Sing Praises to the Lord

January 31

The Word of God to Guide Your Soul:
"But I have trusted in Your mercy; my heart shall rejoice in Your salvation. I will sing to the LORD, because He has dealt bountifully with me" (Psalm 13:5-6).

> *Dear Lord, I love You and thank You for all of the amazing blessings You have given to me and those I love. Thank You for the love of family and friends, the beauty of nature, and most of all—Your faithfulness through the years. Even when I strayed from You, You never left me or gave up on me. Send Your Holy Spirit to help me "rejoice in Your salvation" and sing Your praises, no matter what this day or future days may bring. Amen.*

Music to Inspire Your Mind
- Contemporary Christian "I Could Sing of Your Love Forever" by Martin Smith, performed by Sonicflood (featuring Lisa Kimmey).
- Vocal "I Will Sing" by Matt Boswell and Michael Farren, performed by Matt Boswell.

- Hymn "I Sing the Mighty Power of God"—Text: Isaac Watts, Music: From Gesangbuch der Herzogl, Württemberg, 1784, performed by the Ball Brothers.
- Your music choice: _____

Nutrition to Strengthen Your Body

Broccoli Bake

- 2 packages (10 ounces each) frozen broccoli spears (microwaved and drained)
- 2 tablespoons margarine (olive-oil based)
- 1 cup low-fat milk
- 1 tablespoon lemon juice
- ½ teaspoon salt-free seasoning
- ½ teaspoon pepper
- 6 slices tomatoes
- 2½ tablespoons all-purpose flour
- 4 ounces (1 cup) of reduced-fat Cheddar cheese, shredded

Preheat oven to 350 degrees. In a medium saucepan, melt margarine over low heat. Add flour and stir until smooth; then add milk, stirring. Add cheese and stir until dissolved. Next, add lemon juice. Place cooked broccoli in a 2-quart casserole. Sprinkle with salt-free seasoning and pepper with tomato slices around the edge. Pour cheese sauce over the center and bake for 20 minutes until bubbly.   6 servings

Be Not Afraid

February 1

The Word of God to Guide Your Soul
"For He Himself has said, 'I will never leave you or forsake you.' So we may boldly say: 'The LORD is my helper; I will not fear. What can man do to me?'" (Hebrews 13:5b-6).

> *Dear Lord, I love You and thank You for never leaving me alone. Even when it's hard to know You're there, I have Your promise that You will never forsake me. Whenever fear creeps in, please send Your Holy Spirit to remind me that You are my helper, and I should not be afraid. Help me to comfort others with this assurance and remind them of Your faithfulness. Amen.*

Music to Inspire Your Mind
- Contemporary Christian "He Will Hold Me Fast" by Matthew Merker, performed by Keith and Kristyn Getty.
- Choral "Inscription of Hope" by Z. Randall Stroope, performed by the New Jersey Honor Choir.
- Hymn "We Rest on Thee"—Text: Edith Cherry, Music: Jean Sibelius, performed by Richard Jensen.

- Your music choice: _____

Nutrition to Strengthen Your Body

Sweet Potato Pancakes

- 2 sweet potatoes, baked and cooled (or 1 sweet potato and 1 white potato)
- 2 eggs or ½ cup egg substitute
- ⅛ teaspoon salt
- ¼ teaspoon ground cinnamon
- Nonstick olive oil cooking spray
- Applesauce (optional)

Scoop out sweet potatoes and place in a mixing bowl or blender. Add eggs, salt, and cinnamon. Mix or blend until smooth. Spray an 8-inch skillet with nonstick cooking spray and heat over medium-high heat. Drop ¼ cup of the potato mixture into the skillet and flatten slightly. Cook for 3 minutes; gently flip; cook for an additional three minutes or until golden brown. Serve with applesauce, if desired.   8 pancakes

Seek Shelter in the Lord

February 2

The Word of God to Guide Your Soul
"Be merciful to me, O God, be merciful to me! For my soul trusts in You; and in the shadow of Your wings I will make my refuge, until these calamities have passed by" (Psalm 57:1).

Dear Lord, I love You and thank You for providing refuge for me in the storms of life. Help me to praise You in all circumstances and know that You are in control. Send Your Holy Spirit when I start to despair and get discouraged. Help me turn to You—my Rock in whom I trust. I pray for all those who are going through the fiery trials of life, and I pray for the strength and wisdom to always be a comfort to them. Amen.

Music to Inspire Your Mind
- Contemporary Christian "Shelter" by Jordan Bailey, Michael Loy, Justin Mosteller, Joel Rousseau, Scott Cash, Jeremiah Homes, and Andrew Bergthold, performed by Carrollton.
- Vocal "Praise You in This Storm" by Mark Hall and Bernie Herms, performed by Casting Crowns.

- Hymn "I Have a Shelter"—Text and Music: Steve Cook, Vikki Cook, and Bob Kauflin, performed by Sovereign Grace.
- Your music choice: _____

Nutrition to Strengthen Your Body

Fiesta Vegetable Skillet Dish

- 2 tablespoons olive oil
- 1 cup baby carrots, cut in fourths
- ½ cup sweet onion, chopped
- 1 small zucchini, halved lengthwise, cut into ¼-inch-thick slices (¾ cup)
- 1 medium tomato, chopped
- 1 can (15.5 ounces) pinto beans, drained and rinsed
- 1 can (11 ounces) Mexicorn (whole kernel corn, red and green peppers), undrained
- 1 can (8 ounces) tomato sauce
- ½ cup mild, thick and chunky salsa (use medium or hot, if you like spicy foods)
- ¼ cup water
- 4 teaspoons taco seasoning mix (half of the 1¼-ounce package)
- 4 ounces (1 cup) reduced-fat sharp Cheddar cheese, shredded (or your favorite cheese)

In a large nonstick skillet, heat oil over medium heat. Add carrots and onion; cook and stir 8 to 10 minutes, or until vegetables are crisp-tender. Stir in all remaining ingredients, except cheese. Bring to a boil. Reduce heat to medium-low; cover and simmer 5 to 7 minutes, stirring once. Remove from heat. Sprinkle with cheese. Cover; let stand until cheese is melted.   6 servings

Know You Are Precious in God's Eyes

February 3

The Word of God to Guide Your Soul
"Since you were precious in My sight, you have been honored, and I have loved you; therefore I will give men for you, and people for your life. Everyone who is called by My name, whom I have created for My glory; I have formed him, yes, I have made him" (Isaiah 43:4, 7).

> *Dear Lord, I love You and thank You for creating me in Your image and having me in mind even before time began. Help me remember today that I am precious in Your eyes, especially when I feel rejected by those around me. Send Your Holy Spirit to help me reach out to others who might feel they are not important or loved. Amen.*

Music to Inspire Your Mind
- Contemporary Christian "He Knows My Name" by Francesca Battistelli, Mia Fieldes, and Seth Mosley, performed by Francesca Battistelli.
- Vocal "Fearfully and Wonderfully Made" by Matt Redman and Beth Redman, performed by Matt Redman.

- Hymn "Let All Things Now Living"—Text: Katherine Davis, Music: Traditional Welsh Melody, performed by Michael Card.
- Your music choice: _____

Nutrition to Strengthen Your Body

Heavenly Cauliflower Casserole

- 1¼ cups (8 ounces) orzo pasta, uncooked
- 2 packages (10 ounces each) frozen cauliflower florets
- 1 cup low-fat milk
- 2 eggs, beaten, or ½ cup egg substitute
- 2 cups (8 ounces) reduced-fat sharp Cheddar cheese, shredded
- ½ teaspoon onion powder
- ½ teaspoon salt-free seasoning
- ¼ teaspoon pepper
- Dash nutmeg
- Nonstick olive oil cooking spray

Preheat oven to 375 degrees. Cook orzo according to package directions and drain. Microwave cauliflower according to package directions, drain, and chop into bite-size pieces. In a large bowl, mix together orzo, cauliflower, milk, eggs, cheese, onion powder, salt-free seasoning, pepper, and nutmeg. Spray a 9x13-inch baking pan with cooking spray; spread mixture in pan. Bake for 30 to 35 minutes or until set. Let stand 10 minutes before serving.   6 servings

Lean on Jesus' Prayers and Everlasting Arms

February 4

The Word of God to Guide Your Soul
"I pray for them. I do not pray for the world but for those whom You have given Me, for they are Yours. Now I am no longer in the world, but these are in the world, and I come to You. Holy Father, keep through Your name those whom You have given Me, that they may be one as We are" (John 17:9, 11).

Dear Lord, I love You and thank You for thinking of me and praying for me, even while You still walked this earth. Thank you for keeping me close to You and gently bringing me back even when I get distracted by worldly pleasures and problems. Send Your Holy Spirit to remind me that You are my Strong Tower and refuge during this life, and I can always lean on Your everlasting arms. Help me to remind others that You are always with us, and You will never give up on us. Amen.

Music to Inspire Your Mind

- Contemporary Christian "Strong Tower" by Aaron Sprinkle, Marc Byrd, Jon Micah Sumrall, and Mark Lee, performed by Kutless.
- Choral "Always with You" by Takatsugu Muramatsu and Robert Prizeman, performed by Libera.
- Hymn "Leaning on the Everlasting Arms"—Text: Elisha A. Hoffman, Music: Anthony Showalter, performed by Alan Jackson.
- Your music choice: _____

Nutrition to Strengthen Your Body

Banana Yogurt Smoothie

- 1 8-ounce carton (1 cup) plain or fruited low-fat yogurt
- 1 medium ripe banana
- ½ cup orange juice, apple juice, or pineapple juice
- ¼ cup quick or old-fashioned oats, uncooked
- 1 tablespoon wheat germ
- 1 tablespoon honey
- ⅛ teaspoon nutmeg (optional)
- ½ cup crushed ice or 4 to 5 ice cubes

Place all ingredients in a blender or food processor. Blend on high speed for about 1 minute or until smooth.   2 servings

Bear with One Another and Forgive

February 5

The Word of God to Guide Your Soul
"Therefore, as the elect of God, holy and beloved, put on tender mercies, kindness, humility, meekness, longsuffering; bearing with one another, and forgiving one another, if anyone has a complaint against another; even as Christ forgave you, so you also must do" (Colossians 3:12-13).

> *Dear Lord, I love You and thank You for suffering and dying on the cross so that I might be forgiven. Thank You for Your limitless mercy and unconditional love. Help me to have a heart that forgives, as You have forgiven me. When someone cuts me off in traffic today or hurts my feelings, send Your Holy Spirit to help me forgive them and pray for them. Amen.*

Music to Inspire Your Mind
- Contemporary Christian "Family of God" by Seth Mosley and Mark Stuart, performed by Newsboys.
- Vocal "By Our Love" by Christy Nockels.

- Hymn "They'll Know We Are Christians"—Text and Music: Peter Scholtes, performed by For King and Country.
- Your music choice: _____

Nutrition to Strengthen Your Body

Corn and Cucumber Microwave Marvel

- 2 tablespoons margarine (olive-oil based)
- 2 tablespoons sliced green onion
- ½ teaspoon dried basil
- 1 cup frozen whole kernel corn
- 1 medium cucumber, peeled and chopped
- 1 tablespoon chopped pimiento
- ¼ teaspoon dry mustard
- ¼ teaspoon dill weed
- ⅛ teaspoon black pepper

Combine margarine, onion, and basil in a 1½-quart casserole and cover. Microwave on high for 2 minutes, or until onion is tender. Stir in remaining ingredients and cover. Microwave on high for 4-6 minutes, or until cucumber is tender, stirring every 2 minutes.   4 servings

Stay Close to Jesus in Times of Temptation

February 6

The Word of God to Guide Your Soul
"Therefore, in all things He had to be made like His brethren, that He might be a merciful and faithful High Priest in things pertaining to God, to make propitiation for the sins of the people. For in that He Himself has suffered, being tempted, He is able to aid those who are tempted" (Hebrews 2:17-18).

Dear Lord, I love You and thank You for leaving Your glorious heavenly home in order to experience the same trials and temptations that I face every day. Thank you for being there for me and understanding what I am going through. Send Your Holy Spirit to help me look to You for help and guidance and to offer that help and guidance to others who are also pilgrims on their way back home. Amen.

Music to Inspire Your Mind
- Contemporary Christian "Draw Me Close" by Kelly Carpenter, performed by Michael W. Smith.
- Choral "In Your Arms" by Tore W. Aas and Calvin Bridges, performed by the Oslo Gospel Choir.

- Hymn "What a Friend We Have in Jesus"—Text: Joseph M. Scriven, Music: Charles C. Converse, performed by Kathryn Scott.
- Your music choice: _____

Nutrition to Strengthen Your Body

Mixed Vegetable Casserole

- 2 packages (16 ounces each) frozen, mixed vegetables (your choice), thawed and drained
- 1 cup (4 ounces) reduced-fat Cheddar cheese, shredded (or other cheese of your choice)
- 1 can (2.8 ounces) French fried onions
- 1 can (11 ounces) condensed Cheddar cheese soup (reduced fat and sodium)
- ½ cup low-fat sour cream
- ¼ cup low-fat milk
- ½ teaspoon oregano
- ½ teaspoon basil
- Salt-free seasoning and pepper to taste

Preheat oven to 375 degrees. In a 9x13-inch baking dish, combine vegetables, ½ cup cheese, and ½ can of onions. In a mixing bowl, combine soup, sour cream, milk, and seasonings; pour evenly over vegetables and stir until well mixed. Bake, covered, for 40 minutes. Top with remaining cheese and onions; bake, uncovered, another 5 minutes. 8 servings

Rejoice in the Lord

February 7

The Word of God to Guide Your Soul
"Rejoice in the LORD, O you righteous! For praise from the upright is beautiful. Praise the LORD with the harp; make melody to Him with an instrument of ten strings. Sing to Him a new song; play skillfully with a shout of joy" (Psalm 33:1-3).

> *Dear Lord, I love You and thank You for surrounding me with Your love. Help me to rejoice in You no matter what may happen today and to find joy in the loving surprises You send my way. Keep my eyes fixed on You, and fill me with Your Holy Spirit. I also pray for all the people I meet today that they will encounter You through me and feel the love and joy that can come only from You. Amen.*

Music to Inspire Your Mind
- Contemporary Christian "(Never Gonna) Steal My Joy" by Sam Mizell and Matthew West, performed by Mandisa.
- Vocal "Great Are You Lord" by David Leonard, Jason Ingram, and Leslie Jordan, performed by Casting Crowns.

- Hymn "Rejoice the Lord Is King"—Text: Charles Wesley, Music: John Darwall, performed by Tommy Walker.
- Your music choice: _____

Nutrition to Strengthen Your Body

Simply Pinto Beans and Spanish Rice

- 1 box (6 ⅞ ounces) Spanish rice mix
- 1 can (16 ounces) diced tomatoes
- ½ cup diced green bell pepper
- ¼ teaspoon cumin
- 1 can (15-16 ounces) pinto beans, rinsed and drained

Follow package directions to prepare Spanish rice in a large frying pan. Before covering with a lid, add green pepper and cumin. When rice is cooked, stir in beans and heat for 5 minutes.   6 servings

Rest in the Lord's Love

February 8

The Word of God to Guide Your Soul
"The Lord has appeared of old to me, saying: 'Yes, I have loved you with an everlasting love; therefore with lovingkindness I have drawn you'" (Jeremiah 31:3).

> *Dear Lord, I love You and thank You for Your unconditional and faithful love that never changes or lets me go. Thank you for Your mercy when I stray and let my anxieties and worries take over. Send Your Holy Spirit to always guide my thoughts to You so I have the strength and awareness to point others to Your love and mercy on this day. Amen.*

Music to Inspire Your Mind
- Contemporary Christian "Nobody Loves Me Like You" by Ed Cash and Scott Cash, performed by Chris Tomlin.
- Vocal "God Loves You" by Wayne Kirkpatrick and Mark Heimermann, performed by Jaci Velasquez.
- Hymn "O Love That Will Not Let Me Go"—Text: George Matheson, Music: Albert L. Peace, performed by Chris Rice.
- Your music choice: _____

Nutrition to Strengthen Your Body

Quick Asian Medley

- 1 package (10 ounces) frozen Asian vegetables (plain, no sauce added)
- 2 tablespoons reduced-sodium soy sauce
- 1 teaspoon sugar
- ½ teaspoon sesame seed
- 1 clove garlic, minced, or ⅛ teaspoon dried, minced garlic
- 1 cup fresh bean sprouts
- 8 cherry tomatoes, cut in half lengthwise

Microwave vegetables in a 2-quart casserole according to package directions and drain. Add the rest of the ingredients and mix well. Microwave at high for 1 to 2 minutes longer, or until bean sprouts are tender-crisp.   4 servings

Praise God for All Your Blessings

February 9

The Word of God to Guide Your Soul
"Every good gift and every perfect gift is from above, and comes down from the Father of lights, with whom there is no variation or shadow of turning" (James 1:17).

> *Dear Lord, I love You and thank You for all of the gifts and blessings You have given me. Thank You for the light You bring into my life and into this world of darkness. Send Your Holy Spirit to help me remain thankful throughout this day, and remind me to express gratitude to my family, friends, and co-workers for all they do for me. Amen.*

Music to Inspire Your Mind
- Contemporary Christian "Shout to the Lord" by Darlene Zschech.
- Vocal "That's Where the Joy Comes From" by John Elliott, performed by Steve Green.
- Hymn "Doxology (Praise God from Whom All Blessings Flow)"—Text: Thomas Ken, Music: Attributed to Louis

Bourgeois, additional lyrics and music by Phil Wickham, performed by Phil Wickham.

- Your music choice: _____

Nutrition to Strengthen Your Body

Savory Zucchini and Couscous

- 1 medium zucchini, cut into 2-inch strips
- 2 tablespoons sliced green onion
- 1 tablespoon parsley
- 2 tablespoons reduced-sodium soy sauce
- 2 tablespoons white wine or water
- Dash garlic powder
- Dash ground ginger
- ½ cup uncooked couscous
- ½ cup water
- 1 tablespoon margarine (olive-oil based)

In a 1½-quart casserole, stir together zucchini, onion, parsley, soy sauce, wine or water, garlic powder, and ginger. Cover and microwave at high for 2 to 3 minutes. Stir in remaining ingredients and re-cover. Microwave on high for an additional 2½ to 4 minutes, or until mixture boils. Let stand, covered, for 3 minutes. Toss lightly and serve.   4 servings

Declare the Lord's Wondrous Deeds

February 10

The Word of God to Guide Your Soul
"And those who know Your name will put their trust in You; for You, LORD, have not forsaken those who seek You. Sing praises to the LORD, who dwells in Zion! Declare His deeds among the people" (Psalm 9:10-11).

> *Dear Lord, I love You and thank You for calling me to follow You. I thank You for the gift of breath to be able to praise Your name in the beautiful times and in the most difficult of times. I praise You for the gift of music to help me express my gratitude for all You have done for me and for how much You love me. Send Your Holy Spirit to me today to help others see the joy You give me that could be theirs as well. Amen.*

Music to Inspire Your Mind
- Contemporary Christian "May the Peoples Praise You" by Keith Getty, Kristyn Getty, David Zimmer, Stuart Townend, and Ed Cash, performed by Keith and Kristyn Getty.

- Choral "Ever We Praise You" by Liam Lawton and Chris de Silva, performed by Liam Lawton and Chris de Silva and Choir.
- Hymn "Lord, I Lift Your Name on High"—Text and Music: Rick Founds, performed by Hillsong.
- Your music choice: _____

Nutrition to Strengthen Your Body

Red Potato "Hash" Browns

- 2 tablespoons olive oil
- 3½ cups red potatoes, cubed and cooked
- 1 small sweet onion, chopped
- 1 small red or green pepper, diced
- ¼ teaspoon thyme or rosemary
- ¼ teaspoon salt-free seasoning
- ⅛ teaspoon pepper

Heat olive oil in a large skillet over medium heat. Add all ingredients. Stirring occasionally, cook 8 to 10 minutes or until lightly browned and tender.   6 servings

Rejoice in the Lord's Endless Mercy

February 11

The Word of God to Guide Your Soul
"For He who is mighty has done great things for me, and holy is His name. And His mercy is on those who fear Him from generation to generation" (Luke 1:49-50).

> *Dear Lord, I love You and thank You for doing "great things for me." Send Your Holy Spirit to help me always rejoice in Your endless mercy and faithfulness. Bless my family, friends, and all whom I encounter today. Open their hearts to rejoice in Your amazing mercy as well. Amen.*

Music to Inspire Your Mind
- Contemporary Christian "Exceeding Joy" by Miriam Webster, performed by Hillsong.
- Vocal "Mercy" by Mark Hall, Omega Levine, Sam De Long, and Tauese Tofa, performed by Casting Crowns.
- Hymn "Holy Is His Name"—Text: based on Luke 1:46-55, Music: John Michael Talbot, performed by John Michael Talbot.

- Your music choice: _____

Nutrition to Strengthen Your Body

Mediterranean Bean and Vegetable Casserole

- 2 teaspoons olive oil
- 2 cloves garlic, minced (or ¼ teaspoon dried, minced garlic)
- 1 cup sweet onions, chopped
- 2 cups sliced mushrooms or 8-ounce can of sliced mushrooms, drained
- 1 can (14.5 ounces) chopped tomatoes, drained (reserve liquid)
- 1 tablespoon cornstarch
- 1 teaspoon each basil and oregano
- 2 cans (16 ounces each) Great Northern beans or Cannellini beans, rinsed and drained
- 3 tablespoons pitted black olives, thinly sliced
- Nonstick olive oil cooking spray

Preheat oven to 350 degrees. Heat olive oil in a large skillet over medium heat. Saute garlic and onions for 5 minutes, stirring frequently. Add mushrooms and continue to saute and stir for 5 more minutes. Add tomatoes. In a small bowl, combine tomato liquid and cornstarch, stirring until dissolved. Add to skillet along with basil and oregano. Cook and stir until mixture comes to a boil. Continue to cook and stir for 2 to 3 minutes. Remove skillet from heat and add beans and olives. Mix well.

Spray a 1½-quart casserole with cooking spray. Spoon mixture into prepared casserole. Cover and bake for 40 minutes. Serve over brown rice or couscous. (Leftovers can be spooned into pita breads and heated.)   6 servings

Ask God for Strength and Courage

February 12

The Word of God to Guide Your Soul
"O God, You are more awesome than Your holy places. The God of Israel is He who gives strength and power to His people. Blessed be God!" (Psalm 68:35).

Dear Lord, I love You and thank You for giving me the strength to get through whatever this day has in store. Help me to rest in You no matter what happens and to trust You above all else. Send Your Holy Spirit to empower me to be Your witness to the world and help others grow in their love for You. Amen.

Music to Inspire Your Mind
- Contemporary Christian "Confidence" by Matt Armstrong, Chris Rohman, Dustin Lolli, and Ethan Hulse and performed by Sanctus Real.
- Vocal "Strong Enough" by Matthew West.
- Hymn "God of Grace and God of Glory"—Text: Harry Emerson Fosdick, Music: John Hughes, performed by Concordia Publishing House Choir.

- Your music choice: _____

Nutrition to Strengthen Your Body

Spinach-Stuffed Manicotti

- 8 ounces manicotti, uncooked
- 1 package (10 ounces) frozen chopped spinach, thawed and well drained
- 2 cups (8 ounces) reduced-fat mozzarella cheese, shredded
- 1 cup low-fat cottage cheese
- 1 egg or ¼ cup egg substitute
- ½ teaspoon garlic powder
- ¼ teaspoon pepper
- 3½ cups (32-ounce jar) meatless spaghetti sauce

Preheat oven to 375 degrees. Cook manicotti according to package directions and drain. (To keep manicotti from sticking together, cool in a single layer on wax paper or aluminum foil.) In a mixing bowl, combine remaining ingredients, except spaghetti sauce, and spoon into manicotti. Spread a thin layer of spaghetti sauce on the bottom of a 13x9-inch baking pan. Arrange filled manicotti in a single layer over sauce and cover with remaining sauce. Cover with aluminum foil; bake for 35 minutes or until hot and bubbly. Let the dish rest for 5 minutes and serve.   8 servings

Follow the Way of Love

February 13

The Word of God to Guide Your Soul

"In this the love of God was manifested toward us, that God has sent His only begotten Son into the world, that we might live through Him. In this is love, not that we loved God, but that He loved us and sent his Son to be the propitiation for our sins" (1 John 4:9-10).

> *Dear Lord, I love You and thank You for how much You love me. Your love is beyond my understanding; it is so unconditional, merciful, and everlasting. Send Your Holy Spirit to help me love You more each day and to love my family, friends, and all I meet with the same lavish love You give me. Amen.*

Music to Inspire Your Mind

- Contemporary Christian "My Savior, My God" by Aaron Shust.
- Vocal "First Love" by Reuben Morgan, Chris Tomlin, and Martin Smith, performed by Chris Tomlin (featuring Kim Walker-Smith).

- Hymn "The Love of God"—Text and Music: Frederick M. Lehman, performed by Mercy Me.
- Your music choice: _____

Nutrition to Strengthen Your Body

Saucy Green Beans and Potatoes

- 3 medium potatoes, peeled and cubed
- 1 teaspoon salt-free seasoning
- ¼ teaspoon oregano
- 1 package (10 ounces) frozen French-style green beans
- 2 teaspoons cornstarch

In a large saucepan, cook potatoes with seasonings in 1-inch of water, covered, for 15 minutes. Add green beans and cook 5 to 10 minutes more, or until vegetables are tender. Drain, reserving ¾ cup cooking liquid, and set vegetables aside. In a cup, blend cornstarch with 1 tablespoon cold water; stir into reserved liquid. Cook, stirring until thickened, about 2 minutes. Add potatoes and green beans back, stir and reheat over medium-low heat.   4 servings

Abide in God's Perfect Love

February 14

The Word of God to Guide Your Soul
"And we have known and believed the love that God has for us. God is love, and he who abides in love abides in God, and God in him. Love has been perfected among us in this: that we have boldness in the day of judgment; because as He is, so are we in this world. There is no fear in love; but perfect love casts out fear, because fear involves torment. But he who fears has not been made perfect in love. We love Him because He first loved us" (1 John 4:16-19).

> *Dear Lord, I love You and thank You for this beautiful promise of Your love. Whenever I am fearful, send Your Holy Spirit to remind me of Your perfect love, which casts out all fear. Help me to love others today, as You have loved me. Amen.*

Music to Inspire Your Mind
- Contemporary Christian "One Thing Remains" by Brian Johnson, Jeremy Riddle, and Christa Black, performed by Kristian Stanfill.

- Vocal "You Are My Hiding Place" by Michael Ledner, performed by Selah.
- Hymn "I Love You, Lord"—Text and Music: Matt Maher, performed by Matt Maher.
- Your music choice: _____

Nutrition to Strengthen Your Body

Valentine Strawberry Breakfast Surprise

- Whole grain bread
- Reduced-fat regular or strawberry cream cheese
- Strawberries, quartered and cut into small pieces

Toast bread and use a heart cookie cutter to make heart shapes. Spread with cream cheese and top with strawberries. Serve with love!

Be Overwhelmed by God's Love and Majesty

February 15

The Word of God to Guide Your Soul
"When I consider Your heavens, the work of Your fingers, the moon and the stars, which You have ordained, what is man that You are mindful of him, and the son of man that You visit him? For you have made him a little lower than the angels, and You have crowned him with glory and honor" (Psalm 8:3-5).

> *Dear Lord, I love You and thank You that even though You created the world and all the beauty of nature, You still care for me more than I can understand. Your love is overwhelming! Send Your Holy Spirit to help me remember today that my problems are in the hands of the Creator of the Universe, and I have nothing to worry about. Help me to comfort others with this assurance as I go through my day. Amen.*

Music to Inspire Your Mind
- Contemporary Christian "Overwhelmed" by Phil Wickham and Mike Weaver, performed by Big Daddy Weave.
- Vocal "How Majestic Is Thy Name" by Darlene Zschech.

- Hymn "O Magnify the Lord"—Text and Music: Melodie and Dick Tunney, performed by Sandi Patty.
- Your music choice: _____

Nutrition to Strengthen Your Body

Cabbage Ramen Slaw

- 3 cups cabbage, chopped
- 2 teaspoons sesame seeds
- 4 green onions, sliced
- 1 package chicken ramen noodles, crumbled dry (reserve seasoning) (air-dried are lower in fat)
- ¼ cup water
- 2 tablespoons olive oil
- 3 tablespoons sugar
- 1 tablespoon vinegar
- 1 package seasoning from ramen noodles
- ⅓ cup slivered almonds, toasted (optional)

Toss together cabbage, sesame seeds, onion, and dry ramen noodles. Mix water, oil, sugar, vinegar, and ramen seasoning to make the dressing. Pour the dressing over cabbage mixture; toss. Sprinkle with almonds, if desired. (If you don't have time to make the dressing, just use your favorite ready-made dressing.)   6 servings

Build Your Life on the Rock

February 16

The Word of God to Guide Your Soul

"Therefore whoever hears these sayings of Mine, and does them, I will liken him to a wise man who built his house on the rock: and the rain descended, the floods came, and the winds blew and beat on that house; and it did not fall, for it was founded on the rock" (Matthew 7:24-25).

> *Dear Lord, I love You and thank You for being my Rock in the storms of life. Send Your Holy Spirit to give me wisdom to always build my life on You and to not let the distractions of the world take my eyes off of You. Give me the strength and boldness today to help others find their way to Your shelter and safety. Amen.*

Music to Inspire Your Mind

- Contemporary Christian "God My Rock" by Paul Baloche.
- Vocal "I Have a Shelter" by Steve Cook, Vicki Cook, and Bob Kauflin, performed by Sovereign Grace.
- Hymn "Rock of Ages"—Text: Augustus M. Toplady, Music: Thomas Hastings, performed by Amy Grant and Vince Gill.

- Your music choice: _____

Nutrition to Strengthen Your Body

Stuffed Green Peppers

- 2 tablespoons olive oil
- ½ cup each shredded carrots, sliced mushrooms, chopped onions, and shredded zucchini
- 1 teaspoon finely chopped fresh garlic (or teaspoon instant minced garlic)
- 1 container (15 ounces) low-fat ricotta cheese, drained (may also use low-fat cottage cheese)
- 1 cup cooked long-grain rice
- 1 egg, slightly beaten, or ¼ cup egg substitute
- 2 tablespoons chopped fresh basil leaves (or 2 teaspoons dried basil)
- ½ teaspoon salt-free seasoning
- 4 medium green peppers, cut in half lengthwise, stems and seeds removed
- 1 can (8 ounces) tomato sauce
- ½ cup (2 ounces) reduced-fat mozzarella cheese, shredded

Preheat oven to 350 degrees. In a 2-quart saucepan, heat oil over medium heat; add carrots, mushrooms, onions, zucchini, and garlic. Cook, stirring occasionally, until vegetables are softened (6 to 8 minutes); set aside. In a large bowl, combine ricotta cheese, rice, egg, basil, and salt-free seasoning; mix well. Stir in vegetable mixture. Place about 1 cup of the vegetable-cheese mixture into each green pepper. In 9-inch square baking pan, spread ½ cup tomato sauce in the bottom of the pan; place green peppers in the pan. Pour remaining tomato sauce over green peppers. Cover; bake for 40 to 45 minutes. Uncover; sprinkle with cheese. Continue baking for 3 to 5 minutes, or until cheese is melted. 4 servings

Rejoice You Are a Citizen of Heaven

February 17

The Word of God to Guide Your Soul
"For our citizenship is in heaven, from which we also eagerly wait for the Savior, the Lord Jesus Christ, who will transform our lowly body that it may be conformed to His glorious body, according to the working by which He is able even to subdue all things to Himself" (Philippians 3:20-21).

> *Dear Lord, I love You and thank You for your reminder that my citizenship is in heaven, and I am merely passing through this short time on earth. Help me to keep that eternal perspective in mind today when I find myself complaining about annoying circumstances or people. Send Your Holy Spirit to help me keep a peaceful mind and heart so I may spread Your peace to all I encounter today. Amen.*

Music to Inspire Your Mind
- Contemporary Christian "Heaven Song" by Phil Wickham.

- Vocal "When I Get Where I'm Goin'" by Rivers Rutherford and George Teren, performed by Brad Paisley, featuring Dolly Parton.
- Hymn "I'm But a Stranger Here"—Text: Thomas R. Taylor, Music: Arthur Sullivan, performed by the Lutheran Quartet (contemporary version by Koine).
- Your music choice: _____

Nutrition to Strengthen Your Body

Vegetable Soup with Pesto Sauce

- 3 cans (14.5 ounces each) vegetable broth
- 1 can (14.5 ounces) stewed tomatoes
- ½ cup sweet onions, chopped
- 1 bag (16 ounces) frozen vegetable combination
- 1 can (15.5 ounces) pinto beans, rinsed, drained
- ½ cup uncooked dried pasta rings (or any pasta you have on hand)
- ½ cup prepared pesto sauce

In a 4-quart saucepan, heat vegetable broth and tomatoes over high heat until the mixture comes to a full boil. Add onions, frozen vegetables, beans, and pasta. Continue cooking, stirring occasionally, until pasta is tender (10 to 12 minutes). Dollop each serving with 1 tablespoon pesto sauce.   8 servings

Love the Lord with All Your Heart

February 18

The Word of God to Guide Your Soul
"You shall love the LORD your God with all your heart, with all your soul, and with all your strength" (Deuteronomy 6:5).

> *Dear Lord, I love You and thank You for opening my heart to Your love. I'm sorry for the times I haven't loved You as I should, and I ask You to send Your Holy Spirit to help me give my heart totally to You. As I go through this day, let Your love shine through me to others so that You may become their all in all. Amen.*

Music to Inspire Your Mind

- Contemporary Christian "Love the Lord" by Lincoln Brewster.
- Vocal "You Are My All in All" by Dennis Jernigan, performed by Nichole Nordeman.
- Hymn "More Love to Thee"—Text: Elizabeth P. Prentiss, Music: William H. Doane, performed by Fernando Ortega.
- Your music choice: _____

Nutrition to Strengthen Your Body

Cheesy Baked Beans

- 1 cup sweet onion, chopped
- ⅔ cup green pepper, chopped
- 1 medium tomato, chopped
- 2 tablespoons olive oil
- 2 cans (16 ounces each) vegetarian baked beans
- 2 cups reduced-fat sharp Cheddar cheese, shredded (divided)

Preheat oven to 350 degrees. In a large skillet, saute onion, green pepper, and tomato in olive oil. Add baked beans and 1½ cups shredded cheese; mix well. Transfer to a 2-quart casserole, and bake for about 30 minutes until bubbly. Garnish with remaining shredded cheese.   8 servings

Trust in Jesus' Mercy and Forgiveness

February 19

The Word of God to Guide Your Soul
"For He made Him who knew no sin to be sin for us, that we might become the righteousness of God in Him" (2 Corinthians 5:21).

> *Dear Lord, I love You and thank You for Your great suffering on the cross and for becoming our sacrificial Lamb. Send Your Holy Spirit to remind me daily of Your great love, mercy, and forgiveness for me and all my loved ones. Give me the faith to believe You will help me "become the righteousness of God" and so lead others to believe You forgive them and yearn for them to come home to You. Amen.*

Music to Inspire Your Mind
- Contemporary Christian "At the Cross" by Reuben Morgan and Darlene Zschech, performed by Hillsong.
- Vocal "Lamb of God" by Twila Paris.

- Hymn "What Wondrous Love Is This"—Text: American Folk Hymn, Music: William Walker's Southern Harmony, 1835, performed by Michelle Tumes.
- Your music choice: _____

Nutrition to Strengthen Your Body

Pasta with Vegetable Sauce

- 3 cups zucchini, thinly sliced
- 1 can (14.5 ounces) stewed tomatoes, undrained
- 1½ cups celery, thinly sliced
- 1½ cups sliced fresh mushrooms (or 8-ounce can sliced mushrooms, drained)
- ½ cup water
- ½ teaspoon thyme
- ½ teaspoon paprika
- ½ teaspoon salt-free seasoning and dash of pepper
- 3 cups (8 ounces) pasta (your choice), uncooked
- Grated Parmesan cheese, as desired
- Nonstick olive oil cooking spray

Combine all ingredients, except pasta, in a large saucepan, sprayed with cooking spray. Cover and cook over medium-high heat, stirring frequently, for 15 minutes or until vegetables are tender. Meanwhile, cook pasta according to package directions and drain. Toss with vegetable sauce; sprinkle with Parmesan cheese and serve.   4 servings

Be Healed by Jesus' Sacrificial Suffering

February 20

The Word of God to Guide Your Soul
"But He was wounded for our transgressions, He was bruised for our iniquities; the chastisement for our peace was upon Him, and by His stripes we are healed" (Isaiah 53:5).

> *Dear Lord, I love You and thank You for bearing the weight of my sins and bringing healing to my life. Send your Holy Spirit to help me truly accept that Your chastisement for my sins makes me whole, and I no longer have to carry guilt and shame for my sins. As You have forgiven me for so much, enable me to forgive others with that same mercy. Amen.*

Music to Inspire Your Mind
- Contemporary Christian "By His Wounds" by Mac Powell, performed by Third Day.
- Vocal "Healer" by Mike Guglielmucci, performed by Kari Jobe.

- Hymn "Rise and Be Healed"—Text and Music: Milton Bourgeois, performed by Ivan Parker.
- Your music choice: _____

Nutrition to Strengthen Your Body

Breakfast for Dinner—Scrambled Eggs with Veggies

- 6 whole large eggs or 1½ cups egg substitute
- ¼ cup low-fat milk
- Salt-free seasoning and pepper to taste
- 1 teaspoon dill weed
- 2 tablespoons olive oil
- ½ cup sweet onions, chopped
- ½ cup cherry tomatoes halved
- 1½ cups baby spinach (or use any favorite or leftover veggies you may have)
- ½ cup reduced-fat Swiss cheese, shredded (or other cheese of choice)

In a medium bowl, whip together the eggs, milk, salt-free seasoning, pepper, and dill weed. In a large skillet, heat olive oil over medium heat. Cook the onions for 5 minutes, then add the tomatoes and spinach (or other veggies of your choice). Stir to begin to soften the spinach, then add the egg mixture. Reduce heat to low; continue to stir until soft curds form. Add the cheese and continue folding the mixture until the eggs are cooked. (As an option, add salsa or pesto to the egg mixture.)

4 servings

Renew Your Joy in Your Salvation

February 21

The Word of God to Guide Your Soul
"Create in me a clean heart, O God, and renew a steadfast spirit within me. Do not cast me away from Your presence, and do not take Your Holy Spirit from me. Restore to me the joy of Your salvation, and uphold me by Your generous Spirit" (Psalm 51:10-12).

> *Dear Lord, I love You and thank You for being a God of second chances and constant renewal. Send Your Holy Spirit to "restore to me the joy of Your salvation" and dispel any depression or despair over difficulties in my life. Help me to remember that I am Your child, and my true home is forever with You in heaven. Let Your encouraging light shine through me to others today and always. Amen.*

Music to Inspire Your Mind
- Contemporary Christian "Nothing's Beyond Broken" by Chris August.
- Vocal "Renew Me" by Bernie Herms and Stephanie Lewis, performed by Avalon.

- Hymn "Change My Heart, O God"—Text and Music: Eddie Espinosa, performed by Maranatha Singers.
- Your music choice: _____

Nutrition to Strengthen Your Body

Cauliflower with Lemon Yogurt Sauce

- 1 bag (10.8 ounces) frozen cauliflower florets
- 2 tablespoons sweet onion, chopped
- 2 tablespoons water
- 1 teaspoon dried parsley or 1 tablespoon snipped fresh parsley
- ¼ teaspoon dried marjoram leaves
- 1 cup sliced fresh mushrooms or 1 can (4 ounces) sliced mushrooms, drained
- Yogurt sauce:
- ½ cup low-fat plain yogurt
- 1 tablespoon fresh lemon juice
- Salt-free seasoning and pepper, as desired

In a 2-quart casserole, combine the first five ingredients. Cover and microwave at high for 4 minutes. Add mushrooms, cover, and microwave for 3 minutes. Drain, and let stand covered. In a small microwavable bowl, blend all sauce ingredients. Microwave at 50 percent for 30 seconds to 1 minute or until heated through. Pour over cauliflower mixture and serve.

4 servings

Forgive and Be Forgiven

February 22

The Word of God to Guide Your Soul
"Judge not, and you shall not be judged. Condemn not, and you shall not be condemned. Forgive, and you will be forgiven" (Luke 6:37).

> *Dear Lord, I love You and thank You for Your Word that imparts so much wisdom. Send Your Holy Spirit to replace my tendency to judge and condemn with overflowing love and forgiveness. Help all those I meet today to experience Your mercy and grace through my words and actions. Amen.*

Music to Inspire Your Mind
- Contemporary Christian "You Know Who I Am" by Matt Maher and Tom Booth, performed by Matt Maher.
- Vocal "In Heaven's Eyes" by Phil McHugh, performed by Sandi Patty.
- Hymn "Prayer of St. Francis"—Text: St. Francis of Assisi, Music: Sebastian Temple, performed by Susan Boyle.
- Your music choice: _____

Nutrition to Strengthen Your Body

Lemony Garden Vegetable Casserole

- 1 package (10.8 ounces) frozen mixed vegetables, microwaved and drained
- 1 cup low-fat cottage cheese
- 2 eggs, beaten, or ½ cup egg substitute
- ¼ cup seasoned bread crumbs
- 1 tablespoon instant minced onion
- 2 teaspoons lemon juice
- ½ teaspoon salt-free seasoning
- ¼ teaspoon marjoram leaves
- Nonstick olive oil cooking spray

Preheat oven to 350 degrees. In a medium bowl, mix all ingredients well, except cooking spray. Spray a 1½-quart casserole dish with cooking spray and place combined ingredients into the dish. Bake for 25 minutes. Let sit for 5 minutes and enjoy!   4 servings

Strive for Holy Meekness

February 23

The Word of God to Guide Your Soul
"Blessed are the meek, for they shall inherit the earth. Blessed are those who hunger and thirst for righteousness, for they shall be filled" (Matthew 5:5-6).

> *Dear Lord, I love You and thank You for becoming one of us and giving us a holy example to follow. Send Your Holy Spirit to bring me back to thoughts of You when I get caught up in the world, which promotes a lifestyle that is the direct opposite of how You would have me live. As I go about my day, let my life remind others of You. Amen.*

Music to Inspire Your Mind
- Contemporary Christian "Who Am I" by Mark Hall, performed by Casting Crowns.
- Vocal "Jesus, Meek and Humble" by Sarah Hart and Ben Walther.
- Hymn "Lead Me, Lord"—Text and Music: John D. Becker, performed by John D. Becker and Spirit and Song Choir.
- Your music choice: _____

Nutrition to Strengthen Your Body

Veggie-Stuffed Baked Potatoes

- 2 large potatoes, microwaved for 5 minutes (turn after 2½ minutes), cool for at least 10 minutes
- ¼ cup low-fat milk
- ½ cup low-fat cottage cheese
- ½ cup green pepper, chopped
- ½ cup carrot, chopped
- ½ cup sweet onion, chopped
- 2 tablespoons sunflower seeds
- ½ cup reduced-fat Cheddar cheese, shredded
- ¼ teaspoon garlic powder
- ¼ teaspoon pepper
- 6 cherry tomatoes, halved

Preheat oven to 400 degrees. Halve and scoop out cooked potatoes, leaving the ¼-inch pulp in shells. Mash potato pulp in a medium bowl. Add all ingredients, except ¼ cup Cheddar cheese and cherry tomatoes. Gently mix to blend thoroughly. Spoon mixture into potato shells, dividing equally. Arrange 3 tomato halves on each, pushing in slightly. Sprinkle with remaining Cheddar cheese. Bake for 10-12 minutes on a baking sheet lined with aluminum foil. 4 servings

Count 100 Percent on the Lord's Enduring Mercy and Faithfulness

February 24

The Word of God to Guide Your Soul
"The LORD will perfect that which concerns me; Your mercy, O LORD, endures forever; do not forsake the works of Your hands" (Psalm 138:8).

> *Dear Lord, I love You and thank You for Your enduring mercy. Send Your Holy Spirit to encourage me with this promise as I go through my day. Even when others reject me, I know I can always count on You to never let go of my hand. Help me to offer my family, friends, and all I encounter that same kind of mercy and faithfulness. Amen.*

Music to Inspire Your Mind
- Contemporary Christian "Here with Me" by Bart Millard and Peter Kipley, performed by MercyMe.
- Vocal "I'll Never Let Go of Your Hand" by Don Francisco.

- Hymn "Jesus, Priceless Treasure"—Text: Johann Franck, Music: Traditional German melody, performed by Coffey Ministries.
- Your music choice: _____

Nutrition to Strengthen Your Body

Corn-Broccoli Casserole

- 1 package (10.8 ounces) frozen, chopped broccoli, microwaved and drained
- 1 can (14-15 ounces) cream-style corn
- 1 package (8.8 ounces) microwaveable long grain and wild rice (microwaved according to package directions)
- 2 tablespoons sweet onions, chopped
- 1 egg, beaten, or ¼ cup egg substitute
- 1 cup reduced-fat sharp Cheddar cheese, shredded (or other cheese of choice)
- Nonstick olive oil cooking spray

Preheat oven to 350 degrees. Spray a 2-quart casserole with cooking spray. In a large mixing bowl, combine all ingredients except cheese. Transfer to a casserole dish. Bake for 35 minutes. Sprinkle with cheese and bake another 15 minutes.   4 servings

Look Forward to Perfect Peace

February 25

The Word of God to Guide Your Soul
"The wolf also shall dwell with the lamb, the leopard shall lie down with the young goat, the calf and the young lion and the fatling together; and a little child shall lead them. They shall not hurt nor destroy in all My holy mountain, for the earth shall be full of the knowledge of the LORD as the waters cover the sea" (Isaiah 11:6, 9).

> *Dear Lord, I love You and thank You for this beautiful reminder of what awaits me when I make the transition to heavenly life. Send Your Holy Spirit to help me envision what perfect peace will be like someday when I dwell on Your holy mountain, especially when I get stressed out with this world today! Enable my peaceful attitude to bring peace to others. Amen.*

Music to Inspire Your Mind
- Contemporary Christian "Well Done" by Matt Fuqua, Josh Havens, and Jason Ingram, performed by The Afters.
- Vocal "On That Holy Mountain" by Joe Mattingly, performed by Joe Mattingly and the Newman Singers.

- Hymn "One Day/When We All Get to Heaven"—Text: Eliza E. Hewitt, Music: Emily D. Wilson, performed by Matt Redman (with additional lyrics of "One Day" by Matt Redman, Beth Redman, and Leonard Jarman).
- Your music choice: _____

Nutrition to Strengthen Your Body

Slow Cooker Lentil and Vegetable Stew

- 1 can lentils (15.5 ounces), rinsed and drained
- 1 package (16 ounces) frozen cut green beans
- 1 package (16 ounces) frozen cauliflower florets
- 1 cup sweet onion, chopped
- 1 cup baby carrots, cut in half crosswise
- 3 cups vegetable broth
- 2 teaspoons paprika
- ¾ teaspoon ground ginger
- 1 can (15 ounces) chunky tomato sauce with garlic and herbs
- ½ cup dry-roasted peanuts (optional)

In order listed, place lentils, green beans, cauliflower, onion, and carrots in a slow cooker. Mix broth, paprika, and ginger in a large bowl; pour over vegetables. Cover and cook on low for 8 to 10 hours. Stir in tomato sauce, cover, and cook on low for 10 minutes. Serve stew in bowls with peanuts, sprinkled evenly over each serving if desired.   *6 servings*

Learn from the Lord's Loving Chastening

February 26

The Word of God to Guide Your Soul
"Do not despise the chastening of the LORD, nor be discouraged when You are rebuked by Him; for whom the LORD loves, He chastens. Now no chastening seems to be joyful for the present, but painful; nevertheless, afterward it yields the peaceable fruit of righteousness to those who have been trained by it" (Hebrews 12:5b-6a, 11).

Dear Lord, I love You and thank You for Your loving chastening, which gets me back on the right track toward a right relationship with You. Send Your Holy Spirit to hold me steadfast in following Your will for my life and help me learn how to be the person You created me to be. Thank you for never giving up on me and never let me give up on others in my life! Amen.

Music to Inspire Your Mind

- Contemporary Christian "Your Love Never Fails" by Anthony Skinner and Chris McClarney, performed by Jesus Culture.
- Vocal "Praise You in This Storm" by Mark Hall and Bernie Herms, performed by Casting Crowns.
- Hymn "God Leads Us Along"—Text and Music: G. A. Young, performed by the Forbes Family.
- Your music choice: _____

Nutrition to Strengthen Your Body

South of the Border Bean Casserole

- 1 cup sweet onion, chopped
- 1 cup celery, chopped
- 2 tablespoons olive oil
- 2 cans (15 ounces each) vegetarian chili with beans
- 1 can (16 ounces) vegetarian refried beans
- 1 can (12 ounces) whole kernel corn, drained
- 2 cans (4 ounces each) taco sauce (mild, medium, or bold, according to preference)
- ¼ teaspoon salt-free seasoning
- 10 corn tortillas, torn up
- 1 cup (4 ounces) reduced-fat sharp Cheddar cheese, shredded

Preheat oven to 350 degrees. In a large saucepan, saute onion and celery in olive oil over medium heat until tender, about

10 minutes. Stir in remaining ingredients, except tortillas and cheese. Arrange half of the tortilla pieces in a 9x13-inch baking dish, sprayed with cooking spray; top with half the chili mixture. Repeat layers. Bake, covered, for 45-50 minutes. Sprinkle cheese on top. Bake, uncovered, 2 to 3 minutes or until cheese is melted.   8 servings

Remain Steadfast and Abide in Jesus' Love

February 27

The Word of God to Guide Your Soul

"And now, little children, abide in Him, that when He appears, we may have confidence and not be ashamed before Him at His coming" (1 John 2:28).

> *Dear Lord, I love You and thank You for the great sacrifice You suffered for love of me. Send Your Holy Spirit to daily keep me steadfast in faith. When I waver, grant me the grace to refocus on abiding in Your amazing love. Enable me, today, to encourage others to remain steadfast in their faith, as we all look forward to Your Second Coming. Amen.*

Music to Inspire Your Mind

- Contemporary Christian "Your Love Defends Me" by Matt Maher and Hannah Kerr, performed by Matt Maher.
- Vocal "I Will Fear No More" by Jason Ingram, Matt Fuqua, Joshua Havens, Dan Ostebo, and Jordan Mohilowski, performed by The Afters.

- Hymn "I Surrender All"—Text: Judson W. VanDeVenter, Music: Winfield S. Weeden, performed by Israel Houghton.
- Your music choice: _____

Nutrition to Strengthen Your Body

Mixed Vegetable Comfort Pie

- 3 tablespoons olive oil
- 1 can (4 ounces) sliced mushrooms, drained
- 1 cup sweet onion, chopped
- 1 large potato, peeled and cut into ½-inch pieces
- ¼ cup all-purpose flour
- 1 can (14 ounces) vegetable broth
- Seasonings: ½ teaspoon salt-free seasoning, ¼ teaspoon pepper, 1 teaspoon dried parsley, 1 teaspoon thyme
- 1 bag (16 ounces) broccoli, cauliflower, and carrots, thawed and well-drained
- ¼ cup low-fat milk
- 3 tablespoons grated Parmesan cheese
- 1 can (8 ounces) refrigerated crescent dinner rolls

Preheat oven to 375 degrees. In a large skillet, saute mushrooms, potato, onions, and seasonings in olive oil, about 10 minutes. Sprinkle flour over skillet mixture, cook and stir for 1 minute. Add broth and heat to boiling. Reduce heat and add vegetables, milk, and cheese. Spray glass pie plate with nonstick cooking spray. Form a crust by pressing crescent rolls into a pie crust, covering the bottom and sides of the pie plate. Pour vegetable mixture over pie crust. Place pie plate on a cookie sheet and bake for 20 to 25 minutes. Optional: top with toasted bread crumbs or sesame seeds.   8 servings

Trust in the Lord's Will for Your Life

February 28

The Word of God to Guide Your Soul

"Cause me to hear Your lovingkindness in the morning, for in You do I trust; cause me to know the way in which I should walk, for I lift up my soul to You. Deliver me, O LORD, from my enemies; in You I take shelter. Teach me to do Your will, for You are my God" (Psalm 143:8-10a).

> *Dear Lord, I love You and thank You for Your faithful guidance. Send Your Holy Spirit to teach me what Your will is for my life and then to keep me on the right path. Thank you for sending special people into my life to give me spiritual direction. Help me to be Your voice to provide help and encouragement to others as I go through this day. Amen.*

Music to Inspire Your Mind
- Contemporary Christian "Day After Day" by Kristian Stanfill, Tim Gibson, and Jason Ingram, performed by Kristian Stanfill.

- Vocal "Peace in Christ" by McKenna Hinson and Nik Day, performed by Claire Ryan Crosby and Dave Crosby.
- Hymn "'Tis So Sweet to Trust in Jesus"—Text: Louisa M.R. Snead, Music: William J. Kirkpatrick, performed by Casting Crowns.
- Your music choice: _____

Nutrition to Strengthen Your Body

Easy and Delicious Stir-Fry Vegetables

- 2 tablespoons olive oil
- 1 package (16 ounces) frozen stir-fry blend vegetables
- 1 tablespoon reduced-sodium soy sauce
- 1 teaspoon garlic powder
- 1 teaspoon ground ginger
- 2 teaspoons sesame seeds, toasted (optional)
- Brown rice, cooked according to directions

Heat oil in a wok or a large skillet over medium-high heat. Add vegetables and stir-fry for 5-7 minutes. Add soy sauce, garlic powder, and ginger and stir until well blended. Serve over rice. Sprinkle with toasted sesame seed if desired.   6 servings

Take a Leap of Faith

February 29

The Word of God to Guide Your Soul
"But let him ask in faith, with no doubting, for he who doubts is like a wave of the sea driven and tossed by the wind" (James 1:6).

> *Dear Lord, I love You and thank You for Your faithfulness throughout my life. Send Your Holy Spirit to increase my faith in You and decrease my doubts. Help me stand strong in every situation and not be "driven and tossed by the wind." May others see my faith in You and be inspired to greater love and faith. Amen.*

Music to Inspire Your Mind
- Contemporary Christian "Give Me Faith" by Matt Brock, Chris Brown, London Gatch, and Wade Joye, performed by Elevation Worship.
- Vocal "Go without Knowing" by Lowell Alexander and Kevin Stokes, performed by Sandi Patty.
- Hymn "Have Faith in God"—Text and Music: Geoff Bullock, performed by Maranatha Praise Band.

- Your music choice: _____

Nutrition to Strengthen Your Body

Banana-Raisin Muffins

- ½ cup sugar
- 1 teaspoon baking soda
- ¼ teaspoon salt
- ¾ cup white flour
- ¾ cup whole wheat flour
- ½ cup margarine, softened
- 2 large, ripe bananas, mashed
- 1 teaspoon vanilla
- ⅓ cup raisins

Preheat oven to 375 degrees. Measure sugar, baking soda, salt, and flour into a bowl. Cut in margarine thoroughly. Add bananas and vanilla; mix just until flour is moistened. Fold in raisins. Fill standard-size greased muffin cups to ⅔ full with batter (or use muffin liners). Bake for 15-20 minutes or until golden brown. Immediately remove from pan.

1 dozen muffins

Find Joy in the Journey with Jesus

March 1

The Word of God to Guide Your Soul
"Until now you have asked nothing in My name. Ask, and you will receive, that your joy may be full" (John 16:24).

> *Dear Lord, I love You and thank You for the joy You bring to my life. Send Your Holy Spirit to guide me in praying for those things that are according to Your will and bring true joy and happiness to me and those I love. I ask that all the people I encounter today will learn to love Your goodness and experience the joy of knowing You. Amen.*

Music to Inspire Your Mind
- Contemporary Christian "King of My Heart" by John Mark McMillan and Sarah McMillan, performed by Kutless.
- Vocal "Joy in the Journey" by Michael Card.
- Hymn "Joy of My Desire"—Text and Music: Jennifer Randolph, performed by Integrity's Hosanna! Music.
- Your music choice: _____

Nutrition to Strengthen Your Body

Mediterranean Vegetable Stew

- 2 tablespoons olive oil
- 1 medium sweet onion, chopped
- 4 cloves garlic, crushed, or ½ teaspoon dried, minced garlic
- 1 small eggplant, peeled and cubed
- 2 medium bell peppers, cut into strips
- 1 cup tomato juice
- ½ cup vegetable broth
- Seasonings: 1 bay leaf, 1 teaspoon each basil and marjoram, ½ teaspoon oregano, 1 teaspoon salt-free seasoning
- 1 medium zucchini, sliced
- 2 medium tomatoes, in chunks
- ½ cup water (as needed)
- 1 cup reduced-fat mozzarella cheese, shredded

In a large pot, heat olive oil over medium-high heat. Saute onion and garlic until tender (about 5 minutes). Add eggplant, peppers, tomato juice, broth, and seasonings; mix well. Cover and simmer until vegetables are tender (about 10-15 minutes). Add zucchini and tomatoes; cover and simmer 10 more minutes or until all vegetables are tender. (Add water as needed.) Garnish with cheese. Serve as a stew or on a bed of brown rice or couscous.   6 servings

Embrace Daily Renewal

March 2

The Word of God to Guide Your Soul
"Do not remember the former things, nor consider the things of old. Behold, I will do a new thing, now it shall spring forth; shall you not know it? I will even make a road in the wilderness and rivers in the desert" (Isaiah 43:18-19).

> *Dear Lord, I love You and thank You for doing something new in my life and in the world every day. Send Your Holy Spirit to help me forget the failures of my past and to embrace the moments of today. Increase my faith so I don't worry about tomorrow. Help me be a positive witness of Your renewal in my life to all I encounter today. Amen.*

Music to Inspire Your Mind
- Contemporary Christian "All Things New" by Ben Fielding and Dean Ussher, performed by Hillsong.
- Vocal "New Again" by Brad Paisley and Sara Evans.
- Hymn "I Will Make All Things New"—Text and Music: Mary McDonald, performed by Lorenz Choir.
- Your music choice: _____

Nutrition to Strengthen Your Body

Crescent Roll Veggie Pizza

- 2 cans (8 ounces each) crescent roll dough
- 1 package (8 ounces) reduced-fat cream cheese, softened in microwave, unwrapped, 15-20 seconds
- ½ cup reduced-fat sour cream
- 1 teaspoon dried dill weed (may also use basil, parsley, rosemary, or thyme, as desired)
- ⅛ teaspoon garlic powder
- ½ cup bite-size broccoli florets
- ½ cup quartered cucumber slices
- ½ cup cherry tomatoes, cut in half
- ¼ cup shredded carrots

Heat oven to 375 degrees. Press dough onto an ungreased cookie sheet, covering the bottom and sides. Bake for 13-17 minutes or until golden brown. Cool for 30 minutes. Mix cream cheese, sour cream, dill, and garlic powder until smooth. Spread over crust. Top with veggies. Serve immediately or cover and refrigerate for 1-2 hours. Cut into 8 rows by 4 rows.   32 pieces

Confess Your Sins

March 3

The Word of God to Guide Your Soul
"If we confess our sins, He is faithful and just to forgive us our sins and to cleanse us from all unrighteousness" (1 John 1:9).

> *Dear Lord, I love You and thank You for Your mercy and forgiveness. Send Your Holy Spirit to open my eyes and confess the sin in my life that keeps me from a more perfect communion with You. Cleanse me "from all unrighteousness." Amen.*

Music to Inspire Your Mind
- Contemporary Christian "At Your Feet" by Mark Hall and Jason Ingram, performed by Casting Crowns.
- Vocal "Please Forgive Me" by Gerald Crabb, performed by Jason Crabb.
- Hymn "Grace Greater than Our Sin"—Text: Julia H. Johnston, Music: Daniel B. Towner, performed by Sovereign Grace Music.
- Your music choice: _____

Nutrition to Strengthen Your Body

Veggie Surprise Mashed Potatoes

- 3 large potatoes, peeled and diced
- 4 medium carrots, peeled and sliced
- ½ cup reduced-fat sour cream
- 1 tablespoon margarine (olive-oil based)
- Salt-free seasoning and pepper to taste
- ¼ teaspoon dried dill weed (or other herbs, as desired)

Combine potatoes and carrots in a large saucepan. Add water to cover. Bring to a boil and cook until tender (about 20 minutes). Drain well. Return potatoes and carrots to the pan. Cover and allow to steam for about 5 minutes. Add sour cream, margarine, and seasonings. Mash with an electric mixer or potato masher until smooth.   4 servings

Dwell with the Spirit of Truth

March 4

The Word of God to Guide Your Soul
"And I will pray the Father, and He will give you another Helper, that He may abide with you forever—the Spirit of truth, whom the world cannot receive, because it neither sees Him nor knows Him; but you know Him, for He dwells with you and will be in you" (John 14:16-17).

> *Dear Lord, I love You and thank You for sending Your Holy Spirit to be with me and lead me through the challenges of my earthly pilgrimage to my heavenly home. Help me to understand that I will always be at odds with the world, and that is okay. Give me grace today to lead others to dwell with Your Spirit of truth. Amen.*

Music to Inspire Your Mind
- Contemporary Christian "Spirit Fall" by Nick Herbert, Chris Lawson Jones, and Susie Woodbridge, performed by New Wine Worship.

- Vocal "Hymn of the Holy Spirit" by Pat Barrett, Christ Tomlin, Jason Ingram, and Brenton Brown, performed by Pat Barrett.
- Hymn "Spirit Song"—Text and Music: John Wimber, arranged by Tom Fettke, performed by Hope Publishing Choir.
- Your music choice: _____

Nutrition to Strengthen Your Body

Italian Baked Beans

- 2 cans (16 ounces each) great northern beans, drained and rinsed
- 1 can (8 ounces) chopped tomatoes, undrained
- 1 medium sweet onion, chopped
- 1 green pepper, seeded and chopped
- 3 tablespoons parsley, minced
- 1 teaspoon dried basil
- 2 tablespoons Romano or Parmesan cheese, grated
- 2 tablespoons Italian-seasoned bread crumbs

Preheat oven to 325 degrees. Combine all ingredients except cheese and bread crumbs in a 2-quart casserole. Cover and bake for 1 hour. Sprinkle with cheese and crumbs and bake uncovered for an additional 10 minutes.   6 servings

Find Healing in Quiet Time Spent with the Lord

March 5

The Word of God to Guide Your Soul
"But to you who fear My name the Sun of Righteousness shall arise with healing in His wings" (Malachi 4:2a).

> *Dear Lord, I love You and thank You for a taste of heaven on earth when I spend time in quiet devotion and prayer. Send Your Holy Spirit to help me be still before You and find healing within the rays of the "Sun of Righteousness." Remind me that time spent with You is necessary and never wasted even though the enemy tries to tell me there are more pressing matters that need my attention. Help me spread your "healing" to my family, friends, and all I meet today. Amen.*

Music to Inspire Your Mind
- Contemporary Christian "Still" by Reuben Morgan, performed by Hillsong United.
- Vocal "Breathe" by Marie Barnett, performed by Michael W. Smith.

- Hymn "O Lord, You're Beautiful"—Text and Music: Keith Green, performed by Jesus Culture.
- Your music choice: _____

Nutrition to Strengthen Your Body

Broccoli Pasta

- 3 cups (8 ounces) rotini or other pasta, uncooked
- 1 clove garlic, minced, or ⅛ teaspoon dried, minced garlic
- ½ teaspoon dried basil
- 2 tablespoons olive oil
- 1 package (16 ounces) frozen broccoli florets, cooked and drained
- ½ cup vegetable broth
- ¼ cup chopped fresh parsley (or 4 teaspoons dried parsley)
- ¼ cup grated Parmesan cheese
- ⅛ teaspoon pepper
- 1 cup reduced-fat cottage cheese

Cook pasta according to package directions and drain. In a large skillet, saute garlic and basil in olive oil over medium heat for about 1 minute. Add cooked broccoli, vegetable broth, parsley, Parmesan cheese, and pepper; cook and stir until heated. Remove from heat; stir in cottage cheese. Toss pasta with broccoli mixture and serve.   6 servings

Thank the Lord for Seeking and Saving You

March 6

The Word of God to Guide Your Soul
"For the Son of Man has come to seek and to save that which was lost" (Luke 19:10).

> *Dear Lord, I love You and thank You for seeking me out, even when I was going astray. Thank you for Your sufferings and death on the cross, all for love of me. Send Your Holy Spirit to keep me by Your side and forever grateful for Your sacrifice. Help me to never give up on my family and friends who still need to accept Your love and salvation. Amen.*

Music to Inspire Your Mind
- Contemporary Christian "The Gospel" by Bryan Fowler, Toby McKeehan, and Ryan Stevenson, performed by Ryan Stevenson.
- Vocal "How He Loves Us" by John Mark McMillian, performed by David Crowder Band.

- Hymn "The Lord Is My Salvation"—Text and Music: Keith Getty, Kristyn Getty, Nathan Nockels, and Jonas Myrin, performed by Keith and Kristyn Getty.
- Your music choice: _____

Nutrition to Strengthen Your Body

Fruit Crisp

- 6 cups peeled, sliced fruit (6 medium apples, peaches, or pears)
- 1 tablespoon lemon juice
- 1 tablespoon water
- ¾ cup firmly packed brown sugar
- ½ cup flour
- ½ cup rolled oats
- 1 teaspoon cinnamon
- ½ cup margarine

Preheat oven to 375 degrees. Place fruit in an 8 or 9-inch square pan. Sprinkle with lemon juice and water. Combine brown sugar, flour, oats, and cinnamon. Cut in margarine until crumbly. Sprinkle over fruit. Bake for 40 to 45 minutes or until fruit is tender.   6 servings

Reflect the Light of God's Kingdom

March 7

The Word of God to Guide Your Soul
"He has delivered us from the power of darkness and conveyed us into the kingdom of the Son of His love, in whom we have redemption through His blood, the forgiveness of sins" (Colossians 1:13-14).

> *Dear Lord, I love You and thank You for delivering me from darkness and bringing me to the kingdom of Your beloved Son. Send Your Holy Spirit to help me reflect the light of that everlasting kingdom in all I do today. Show me how to shine that light into the lives of my family, friends, and all you bring across my path today and always. Amen.*

Music to Inspire Your Mind
- Contemporary Christian "Deliverer" by Matt Maher and Bear Rinehart, performed by Matt Maher.
- Vocal "Our God" by Jonas Myrin, Chris Tomlin, Matt Redman, and Jesse Reeves, performed by Chris Tomlin.
- Hymn "Jesus Paid It All"—Text: Elvina M. Hall, Music: John T. Grape, performed by Kristian Stanfill.

- Your music choice: _____

Nutrition to Strengthen Your Body

Eggplant Parmesan Potatoes

- 4 medium Russet or other white potatoes, pierced with a fork
- 1 large eggplant, peeled and chopped
- 1 can (14.5 ounces) diced tomatoes
- 1 medium green pepper, chopped
- ⅓ cup sweet onion, chopped
- 2 tablespoons tomato paste
- 2 tablespoons olive oil
- ½ teaspoon each dried thyme and oregano
- ¼ teaspoon each dried rosemary, garlic powder, salt-free seasoning, and pepper
- 2 tablespoons grated Parmesan cheese
- 1 cup reduced-fat Swiss cheese, shredded

Arrange potatoes evenly on a paper towel in the microwave. Microwave on high for 10 minutes (turn over after 5 minutes) or until tender. Wrap in a paper towel and set aside. In a large casserole dish, combine remaining ingredients, except for cheeses and potatoes. Cover and microwave on high for 18-24 minutes, or until eggplant is tender, stirring every 5 minutes. Stir in Parmesan cheese. Cut each potato in half lengthwise and place on a serving platter. Top with vegetable mixture and Swiss cheese. Microwave at 70 percent for 2-4 minutes or until cheese melts.   4 servings

Hope in God and Trust in His Timing

March 8

The Word of God to Guide Your Soul
"Why are you downcast, O my soul? And why are you disquieted within me? Hope in God; for I shall yet praise Him, the help of my countenance and my God" (Psalm 42:11).

> *Dear Lord, I love You and thank You for being there for me, even when I am downcast and wondering where You are. Send Your Holy Spirit to grant me hope and faith in Your wisdom and perfect timing. Help me remember that when I feel most disquieted, You will never let go. Make me aware of the trials others are going through today and show me how to comfort them with Your love and peace. Amen.*

Music to Inspire Your Mind
- Contemporary Christian "Before the Morning" by Ben Glover and Josh Wilson, performed by Josh Wilson.
- Vocal "You Never Let Go" by Matt Redman and Beth Redman, performed by Matt Redman.

- Hymn "Lord from Sorrows Deep I Call"—Text and Music: Matt Papa and Matt Boswell, performed by Keith Getty.
- Your music choice: _____

Nutrition to Strengthen Your Body

Warm Celery Salad

- 2 tablespoons olive oil
- 1 medium sweet onion, chopped
- 2 cloves garlic, minced (or ¼ teaspoon dried, minced garlic)
- ½ teaspoon dried thyme
- 1 can (15 ounces) garbanzo beans, drained and rinsed
- 2 tablespoons balsamic vinegar
- 3 large stalks celery, chopped

In a large skillet, saute onion, garlic, and thyme in olive oil over medium heat until onion is soft, about 6 minutes. Reduce heat to medium-low. Stir in vinegar and garbanzo beans until coated; cover and heat until garbanzo beans are warmed. Stir in celery; cover and cook for 5 minutes or until celery is warmed. Serve warm.   4 servings

Keep an Eternal Perspective on Your Earthly Life

March 9

The Word of God to Guide Your Soul

"Do not labor for the food which perishes, but for the food which endures to everlasting life, which the Son of Man will give you, because God the Father has set His seal on Him" (John 6:27).

Dear Lord, I love You and thank You for the promise of an eternity with You. Send Your Holy Spirit to bless me with an eternal perspective and guide me in keeping my earthly priorities in order. I'm sorry for the times I've gotten caught up in conforming to what the world wants me to do versus what You would have me do. Help me inspire everyone I meet today to believe in a deeply personal and eternal relationship with You. Amen.

Music to Inspire Your Mind

- Contemporary Christian "I Can Only Imagine" by Bart Millard, performed by MercyMe.
- Vocal "Eternity" by Misty Edwards.

- Hymn "On Jordan's Stormy Banks"—Text: Samuel Stennett, Music: Traditional American melody, performed by Ken Medema.
- Your music choice: _____

Nutrition to Strengthen Your Body

Glazed Baby Carrots and Brussels Sprouts

- 1 package (16 ounces) baby carrots, microwaved according to directions and drained
- 2 packages (10 ounces each) frozen Brussels sprouts, microwaved according to directions and drained
- ⅓ cup apple juice
- 2 tablespoons cornstarch
- 1 can (10.5 ounces) condensed golden mushroom soup or French onion soup (reduced sodium and fat)
- 1 tablespoon brown sugar
- 2 teaspoons lemon juice
- Dash ground cloves

Preheat oven to 350 degrees. Place cooked and drained vegetables in a large casserole dish. In a medium saucepan, combine soup, brown sugar, lemon juice, and cloves. In a separate cup, dissolve cornstarch in apple juice and add to the soup mixture. Cook until mixture boils, stirring constantly. Pour over vegetables. Bake, covered, about 15 minutes or until heated through.   8 servings

Rejoice in Being Reconciled to God Through His Son

March 10

The Word of God to Guide Your Soul

"Much more then, having now been justified by His blood, we shall be saved from wrath through Him. For if when we were enemies we were reconciled to God through the death of His Son, much more, having been reconciled, we shall be saved by His life" (Romans 5:9-10).

> *Dear Lord, I love You and thank You for Your promise of salvation. Send Your Holy Spirit when I have doubts, and the world closes in with lies and false hopes. Help me be a beautiful example today of what it means to have faith in all that Jesus accomplished by His death and resurrection. Amen.*

Music to Inspire Your Mind

- Contemporary Christian "Amen" by Steven Curtis Chapman.

- Vocal "Washed Away/Nothing but the Blood" by Michael W. Smith and Michael Farran, performed by Michael W. Smith.
- Hymn "There Is Power in the Blood"—Text and Music: Lewis E. Jones, performed by Fernando Ortega.
- Your music choice: _____

Nutrition to Strengthen Your Body

Zesty Brown Rice and Beans

- 1 package (8.8 ounces) whole grain brown rice, ready to microwave
- 1 can (15 ounces) black beans, rinsed and drained (or use other favorite beans)
- ½ cup thick and chunky salsa (mild, medium, or hot—your choice!)
- Lime juice, to taste (optional)

Microwave brown rice, according to package directions. In a 2-quart casserole dish, combine rice, beans, and salsa. Cover and microwave on high for 3 minutes or until heated through. Squeeze a bit of lime juice over each serving, as desired.

4 servings

Boast in the Cross of Christ

March 11

The Word of God to Guide Your Soul
"But God forbid that I should boast except in the cross of our Lord Jesus Christ, by whom the world has been crucified to me, and I to the world" (Galatians 6:14).

Dear Lord, I love You and thank You for Your great sacrifice on the cross. Send Your Holy Spirit to help me keep a spirit of gratitude throughout this day, even when things don't go as I think they should. Give me courage to boast about You and Your amazing love. Amen.

Music to Inspire Your Mind
- Contemporary Christian "Hallelujah for the Cross" by Ross King and Todd Wright, performed by the Newsboys.
- Vocal "I Will Boast" by Chris Tomlin and Jason Ingram, performed by Chris Tomlin.
- Hymn "Near the Cross"—Text: Fanny J. Crosby, Music: William H. Doane, performed by the Heritage Singers.
- Your music choice: _____

Nutrition to Strengthen Your Body

Mom's Scalloped Potatoes

- 8 medium potatoes, peeled and sliced
- ½ cup green pepper, chopped
- ½ cup sweet onion, chopped
- ½ teaspoon garlic powder
- 1 teaspoon salt-free seasoning
- ¼ teaspoon pepper
- 1 can condensed cream of celery or mushroom soup (reduced sodium and fat)
- 1 cup low-fat milk
- Nonstick olive oil cooking spray

Preheat oven to 350 degrees. Spray a 2-quart casserole with nonstick cooking spray. Alternate layers of potatoes, green pepper, and onions in the casserole. In a medium bowl, combine seasonings, mushroom soup, and milk. Pour over the potatoes. Cover and bake for 90 minutes or until tender.

8 servings

Wait for the Lord with Joyful Hope

March 12

The Word of God to Guide Your Soul
"I wait for the LORD, my soul waits, and in His word I do hope. For with the LORD there is mercy, and with Him is abundant redemption" (Psalm 130:5, 7b).

> *Dear Lord, I love You and thank You for Your promise of "abundant redemption." Send Your Holy Spirit to give me patience as I wait to be reunited with You for all eternity. Help others to see the joy I have in looking forward to my heavenly home. Amen.*

Music to Inspire Your Mind
- Contemporary Christian "I Will Wait for You (Psalm 130)" by Stuart Townend, Keith Getty, Jordan Kauflin, and Matthew Merker, performed by Shane & Shane
- Vocal "While I Wait" by Lincoln Brewster and Mitch Wong, performed by Lincoln Brewster
- Hymn "Near to the Heart of God/Sweet Hour of Prayer"— Text: Cleland B. McAfee/William W. Walford, Music:

Cleland B. McAfee/William B. Bradbury, performed by Sandi Patty

- Your music choice: _____

Nutrition to Strengthen Your Body

Greek Vegetable Pasta Salad

- 1½ cups whole grain elbow macaroni or spiral pasta
- ½ medium sweet onion, sliced
- 1 cup tomatoes, chopped
- 1 cup cucumber, chopped
- 1 sweet green pepper, chopped
- 1 sweet red pepper, chopped
- 1 cup black or Kalamata olives, pitted
- ¼ cup reduced-fat Greek dressing (add more or less dressing, as desired)
- ½ cup reduced-fat Feta cheese

Cook macaroni or pasta according to package directions and drain. Meanwhile, combine the rest of the ingredients in a large bowl. Add cooked pasta to vegetable mixture and stir to blend. Season to taste with fresh parsley and other seasonings, as desired. 6 servings

Say Yes to God's Plan

March 13

The Word of God to Guide Your Soul
"Now therefore, if you will indeed obey My voice and keep My covenant, then you shall be a special treasure to Me above all people; for all the earth is Mine" (Exodus 19:5).

> *Dear Lord, I love You and thank You for making a covenant with Your people since the beginning of time. Send Your Holy Spirit to give me excellent hearing so I can obey Your voice and follow Your plan for my life. Let others witness my "yes" to You, Lord, and want to follow You as well. Amen.*

Music to Inspire Your Mind
- Contemporary Christian "Say Yes" by Josh Wilson.
- Vocal "I'll Just Say Yes" by Brian Courtney Wilson and Aaron Lindsey, performed by Brian Courtney Wilson.
- Hymn "Yes, Lord, Yes"—Text and Music: Lynn Keesecker, performed by Studio Musicians.
- Your music choice: _____

Nutrition to Strengthen Your Body

Colorful Italian Cauliflower

- ¼ cup sweet onion, chopped
- 1 small garlic clove, crushed, or ⅛ teaspoon dried, minced garlic
- 2 tablespoons light Italian dressing
- 1 package (16 ounces) frozen cauliflower florets
- ¼ cup water
- 2 tablespoons chopped green pepper
- 1 cup cherry tomatoes, halved
- ½ teaspoon salt-free seasoning
- ⅛ teaspoon dried basil leaves

In a large skillet, saute onion and garlic in salad dressing over medium-high heat. Add cauliflower and ¼ cup water. Cook, covered, over low heat for 10 minutes. Add green pepper; cover and cook another 5 minutes or until tender. Stir in remaining ingredients; heat through.   6 servings

Rejoice in the Reign of Jesus Where All Will Be Made Right

March 14

The Word of God to Guide Your Soul

"Hereafter the Son of Man will sit on the right hand of the power of God. Then they all said, 'Are You then the Son of God?' So He said to them, 'You rightly say that I am'" (Luke 22:69-70).

> *Dear Lord, I love You and thank You that You are in control, and, one day, all evil will be vanquished. Send Your Holy Spirit to give all those who love You the perseverance and vision to see that the Lord is sovereign over us and all the earth. Help me to share that vision of hope with someone who is discouraged today. Amen.*

Music to Inspire Your Mind

- Contemporary Christian "Our God Reigns" by Israel Houghton and BJ Putnam, performed by Israel Houghton.
- Vocal "Sovereign over Us" by Aaron Keyes, Jack Mooring, and Bryan Brown, performed by Michael W. Smith.

- Hymn "Jesus Shall Reign"—Text: Isaac Watts, Music: John Hatton, performed by Keith and Kristyn Getty (Additional lyrics by Keith and Kristyn Getty and Ed Cash).
- Your music choice: _____

Nutrition to Strengthen Your Body

Yummy Banana Pancakes

- 1 cup whole wheat blend pancake mix
- 1 cup reduced-fat milk
- 1 tablespoon vegetable oil
- 1 egg or ¼ cup egg substitute
- 2 medium, ripe bananas, mashed
- 1 tablespoon lemon juice
- 2 tablespoons sugar
- 2 tablespoons margarine
- Maple syrup, as desired

Combine all ingredients except margarine and maple syrup. Stir until large lumps disappear and let stand for 1-2 minutes to thicken. Heat margarine in a large skillet over medium-low heat or 375 degrees for an electric griddle. Pour about ¼ cup batter for each pancake. Turn when pancakes bubble and bottoms are golden brown. Serve with warm maple syrup, as desired.   10-12 pancakes

Grow in Grace and Knowledge

March 15

The Word of God to Guide Your Soul

"But grow in the grace and knowledge of our Lord and Savior Jesus Christ. To Him be the glory both now and forever. Amen" (2 Peter 3:18).

> *Dear Lord, I love You and thank You for blessing me with grace upon grace to daily grow in my love for You and knowledge of Your Word. Send me Your Holy Spirit to keep me focused on You instead of all the distractions of the world. Today, help others see in my life that You are increasing and I am decreasing. Amen.*

Music to Inspire Your Mind
- Contemporary Christian "Grace Got You" by Ben Glover, David Garcia, Bart Millard, John Reuben, and Solomon Olds, performed by MercyMe.
- Vocal "Grace upon Grace" by Josh Wilson.
- Hymn "Be Thou My Vision"—Text and Music: Traditional Irish Hymn, performed by Selah.
- Your music choice: _____

Nutrition to Strengthen Your Body

Corn and Mushroom Medley

- 1 package (10 ounces) frozen whole kernel corn
- ½ cup celery, chopped
- 1 vegetable bouillon cube, crushed
- ⅓ cup water
- ¼ teaspoon garlic powder
- 1 can (4 ounces) sliced mushrooms, drained
- 1 medium tomato, cut in thin wedges
- Black pepper, as desired

In a large saucepan, combine corn, celery, bouillon cube, water, and garlic powder. Bring to boiling; cover and simmer until vegetables are tender, about 5-7 minutes. Stir in mushrooms and tomato wedges and heat through. Season with pepper, as desired. 6 servings

Pray with Purpose and Perseverance

March 16

The Word of God to Guide Your Soul
"Praying always with all prayer and supplication in the Spirit, being watchful to this end with all perseverance and supplication for all the saints" (Ephesians 6:18).

> *Dear Lord, I love You and thank You for the privilege to talk with You and spend precious time in prayer. Send Your Holy Spirit to give me perseverance in taking time for daily prayer and to resist being distracted by so many other people and things calling for my attention. Help me to pray with purpose for others but also to listen for Your gentle voice. Amen.*

Music to Inspire Your Mind
- Contemporary Christian "When We Pray" by Tauren Wells, Ethan Hulse, and Colbey Wedgeworth, performed by Tauren Wells.

- Vocal "A Christian's Daily Prayer"—Text and Music: Matt Merker, Jordan Kauflin, and Dave Fournier, performed by Sovereign Grace Music.
- Hymn "I Must Tell Jesus"—Text and Music: Elisha A. Hoffman, performed by Mary Barrett.
- Your music choice: _____

Nutrition to Strengthen Your Body

Broccoli Brunch Casserole

- 1 package (10 ounces) frozen chopped broccoli
- 4 slices whole grain or oatmeal bread
- 1 cup (4 ounces) reduced-fat sharp Cheddar cheese, shredded
- 1 jar (2 ounces) pimiento, drained and chopped (¼ cup)
- 1 cup (4 ounces) reduced-fat Swiss cheese, shredded
- 4 eggs or 1 cup egg substitute
- 2 cups low-fat milk
- 1 tablespoon sweet onion, chopped
- 1 teaspoon salt-free seasoning and dash of pepper
- ½ teaspoon prepared mustard
- ¼ cup prepared Italian-style bread crumbs
- 2 tablespoons margarine, melted

Preheat oven to 325 degrees. Cook or microwave broccoli according to package directions and drain well. Toast the bread and arrange in an ungreased 9x9-inch baking pan. Top with the Cheddar cheese, then broccoli and pimiento. Sprinkle the

Swiss cheese on top. In a medium bowl, beat eggs and blend in milk, onion, seasonings, and mustard. Pour over casserole. Cover and refrigerate for at least an hour. Melt margarine in a small skillet and add bread crumbs. Sprinkle crumb mixture over top of casserole. Bake, uncovered, for 60 minutes. Let stand 10 minutes before serving.   6 servings

Trust in the Lord with All Your Heart

March 17

The Word of God to Guide Your Soul

"I will give you a new heart and put a new spirit within you;
I will take the heart of stone out of your flesh and give you a
heart of flesh" (Ezekiel 36:26).

> *Dear Lord, I love You and thank You for giving me a new
> heart. Send Your Holy Spirit to give me the grace to always
> trust You with my heart and soul. Thank you for Saint
> Patrick, who persevered in changing hearts with Your love.
> Help me follow his example today. Amen.*

Music to Inspire Your Mind

- Contemporary Christian "Keeper of My Heart" by Kari Jobe,
  Chris Tomlin, and Jason Ingram, performed by Kari Jobe.
- Vocal "Breastplate" (Prayer of St. Patrick) by Liam Lawton.
- Hymn "May the Road Rise to Meet You"—Text and Music:
  traditional Irish blessing, adapted by Lori True, performed
  by Celtic Thunder.
- Your music choice: _____

Nutrition to Strengthen Your Body

Vegetarian Shepherd's Pie

- 6 medium Yukon Gold or Russet (Idaho) potatoes, mashed (see directions)
- 2 tablespoons olive oil
- 1 cup sweet onion, chopped
- 2 cloves garlic, crushed or ¼ teaspoon dried, minced garlic
- ½ teaspoon each dried thyme, oregano and pepper
- 3 large carrots, peeled and diced
- 1 stalk celery, diced
- 16 ounces fresh mushrooms, ½ sliced and ½ chopped or 1 can (8 ounces) sliced and drained
- 2 tablespoons each tomato paste and flour
- 2 cups vegetable broth
- 1 package (16 ounces) frozen peas

Preheat oven to 400 degrees. Make the mashed potatoes. (Peel potatoes, boil for about 20 minutes to fork-tender, drain, mash, and mix in milk or Greek yogurt and margarine, as desired.) In a large pot, heat olive oil over medium-high heat. Saute onions until soft, then add garlic and seasonings. Cook for a few minutes and add carrots, celery, and mushrooms. Saute for about 5 minutes or until vegetables are slightly tender. Add tomato paste, flour, and vegetable broth. Bring to a boil, then reduce heat to low and simmer over low heat to thicken. Stir in the frozen peas. Spoon the filling into a large casserole dish. Top with mashed potatoes and bake for 20-30 minutes.

6 servings

Cling to Hope in God's Promises

March 18

The Word of God to Guide Your Soul

"For we were saved in this hope, but hope that is seen is not hope; for why does one still hope for what he sees? But if we hope for what we do not see, we eagerly wait for it with perseverance" (Romans 8:24-25).

> *Dear Lord, I love You and thank You for giving me hope in Your promise of salvation and eternal life. Send Your Holy Spirit to give me the endurance to have faith, especially when the evil of this world overwhelms me. Remind me that You have already overcome and all will be well. I pray I can help others today learn to cling to Your promises. Amen.*

Music to Inspire Your Mind

- Contemporary Christian "Song of Hope" by Robbie Seay, Taylor Johnson, Ryan Owens, Chase Jenkins, Tedd Tjornhom, and Dan Hamilton, performed by Robbie Seay Band.
- Vocal "Promise of a Lifetime" by Jon Micah Sumrall and Aaron Sprinkle, performed by Kutless.

- Hymn "My Hope"—Text and Music: Anne Barbour, performed by the Tommy Coomes Band.
- Your music choice: _____

Nutrition to Strengthen Your Body

Slow Cooker Peach Treat

- 1 ⅓ cups uncooked old-fashioned oats
- 1 cup granulated sugar
- 1 cup packed light brown sugar
- ⅔ cup buttermilk baking mix
- 2 teaspoons ground cinnamon
- ½ teaspoon ground nutmeg
- 2 packages (16 ounces each) frozen peaches, thawed and drained (or 8 medium fresh peaches, sliced)
- Nonstick cooking spray

In a large bowl, combine all ingredients, except peaches. Fold in peaches and mix until well blended. Pour mixture into a slow cooker, sprayed with cooking spray. Cover and cook on low for 4-6 hours.   10 servings

Find Happiness in Obedience and Service

March 19

The Word of God to Guide Your Soul
"If they obey and serve Him, they shall spend their days in prosperity, and their years in pleasures" (Job 36:11).

> *Dear Lord, I love You and thank You for showing me the way to happiness in Your Word. Send Your Holy Spirit to give me the wisdom and knowledge to understand the best way to obey and serve You and those around me. Help me to always make following Your will the number one priority in my life. Amen.*

Music to Inspire Your Mind
- Contemporary Christian "Whatever" by Steven Curtis Chapman.
- Vocal "Spirit Lead Me" by Whitney Medina, Michael Barkulis, Melody Hernandez, Graham Moore, Michael Ketterer, and Gabriel Wilson, performed by Michael Ketterer and Influence Music.

- Hymn "Trust and Obey"—Text: John H. Sammis, Music: Daniel B. Towner, performed by and additional lyrics by Big Daddy Weave.
- Your music choice: _____

Nutrition to Strengthen Your Body

Salsa and Bean Pita Pockets

- 1 tablespoon olive oil
- ½ cup sweet onion, chopped
- 1 can (16 ounces) vegetarian baked beans
- ½ cup of favorite salsa
- 3 whole wheat pita bread loaves, halved
- 2 cups lettuce, shredded
- 1 cup tomato, chopped
- 1 cup (4 ounces) reduced-fat sharp Cheddar cheese, shredded (or other cheese, as desired)
- Plain low-fat yogurt or sour cream

In a large skillet, saute onion in olive oil over medium-high heat until tender, about 5 minutes. Add beans and salsa. Mix well and heat through. Spoon ½ cup mixture into each pita pocket half. Top with lettuce, tomato, cheese, yogurt or sour cream, and additional salsa, if desired. 6 servings

Take Up Your Cross and Follow Jesus

March 20

The Word of God to Guide Your Soul

"Then Jesus said to His disciples, 'If anyone desires to come after Me, let him deny himself, and take up his cross, and follow Me. For whoever desires to save his life will lose it, but whoever loses his life for My sake will find it'" (Matthew 16:24-25).

> *Dear Lord, I love You and thank You for Your ultimate example of self-denial and for taking up Your cross for the sake of others. Send your Holy Spirit to help me lose my selfish desires for the sake of finding salvation and helping others to do the same. I pray I will always keep my eyes fixed on You and remember the cross You bore to redeem my life. Amen.*

Music to Inspire Your Mind

- Contemporary Christian "Carry the Cross" by James Katina, John L. Katina, Joseph Katina, Jesse Katina, and Samuel Katina, performed by The Katinas.

- Vocal "Take up Your Cross" by Steve Millikan, performed by Ray Boltz.
- Hymn "Wherever He Leads I'll Go"—Text and Music: B.B. McKinney, performed by Alan Jackson.
- Your music choice: _____

Nutrition to Strengthen Your Body

Easy Three-Bean Vegetable Salad

- 1 can (15 ounces) three-bean salad
- 1 can (8.75 ounces) corn, drained
- 1 jar (2 ounces) pimientos, drained and diced
- 2 ribs celery, chopped or sliced
- 1 small red onion, sliced

Combine all ingredients in a salad bowl. Toss lightly before serving.   4 servings

Look to the Lord to Revive Your Spirit

March 21

The Word of God to Guide Your Soul
"For thus says the High and Lofty One who inhabits eternity, whose name is Holy: 'I dwell in the high and holy place, with him who has a contrite and humble spirit, to revive the spirit of the humble, and to revive the heart of the contrite ones'" (Isaiah 57:15).

> *Dear Lord, I love You and thank You for always being there for me when my heart is contrite, and my spirit is humbled. Send Your Holy Spirit to remind me that all will be well and You are in control. Revive my spirit and bring back the joy I have in loving and serving You and those around me. Amen.*

Music to Inspire Your Mind
- Contemporary Christian "Revival" by Jonathan Smith, Parker Welling Nohe, and Zach Williams, performed by Zach Williams.
- Vocal "My Revival" by Lauren Daigle, Paul Mabury, and Jason Ingram, performed by Lauren Daigle.

- Hymn "Revive Us Again"—Text: William P. Mackay, Music: John J. Husband, performed by Selah.
- Your music choice: _____

Nutrition to Strengthen Your Body

Slow Cooker Biscuit Surprise Vegetable Bean Soup

- 3 cans (14 ounces each) vegetable broth
- 2 cups red potatoes, unpeeled and cubed
- 1 medium sweet onion, chopped
- 1 cup celery, sliced
- 1 can (14-15 ounces) diced tomatoes with basil, garlic, and oregano, undrained
- 1 bag (16 ounces) frozen broccoli/carrot mix, slightly thawed
- 1 teaspoon garlic powder
- ¼ teaspoon rosemary
- ½ teaspoon salt-free seasoning
- ¼ teaspoon pepper
- 1 bay leaf
- 1 can (16 ounces) white beans, drained and rinsed
- 1 can (8 biscuits) refrigerated biscuits, cut into 8 pieces each

Mix all ingredients, except beans and biscuits, in a slow cooker. Cook on low for 8-9 hours. Stir in beans and add biscuits to the top of the mixture. Cook for an additional 1-1½ hours, or until biscuits are thoroughly cooked. 10 servings

Honor the Name of Jesus

March 22

The Word of God to Guide Your Soul

"And every creature which is in heaven and on the earth and under the earth and such as are in the sea, and all that are in them, I heard saying: 'Blessing and honor and glory and power be to Him who sits on the throne, and to the Lamb, forever and ever!'" (Revelation 5:13).

> *Dear Lord, I love You and thank You for coming as a Lamb to be crucified for my redemption and as a Lion to defeat evil and reign forever and ever. Send Your Holy Spirit to give me courage to stand up for Your name at every opportunity and the perseverance to honor Your name throughout my life. Amen.*

Music to Inspire Your Mind

- Contemporary Christian "The Cross Has the Final Word" by Cody Carnes, performed by Newsboys (featuring Peter Furler and Michael Tait).
- Vocal "The Lion and the Lamb" by Brenton Brown, Leeland Mooring, and Brian Johnson, performed by Big Daddy Weave.

- Hymn "Blessed Be the Name of the Lord/Celebrate Jesus"—Text and Music: Don Moen/Gary Oliver, performed by Don Moen and the Integrity Singers.
- Your music choice: _____

Nutrition to Strengthen Your Body

Spinach and Pasta Delight

- 1 package (10 ounces) frozen spinach, thawed and drained (or may substitute broccoli)
- ¼ cup sweet onion, chopped
- ½ teaspoon garlic powder
- 2 tablespoons olive oil
- 1 can (10.75 ounces) condensed cream of mushroom soup (reduced sodium and fat)
- 1 cup (4 ounces) reduced-fat Swiss cheese, shredded (or other cheese, as desired)
- 1 cup low-fat milk
- 8 ounces whole wheat pasta (or other pasta, as desired)

Cook pasta according to package directions and drain. Meanwhile, in a large skillet, saute spinach with onion and garlic powder in olive oil over medium heat until tender but not brown. (If using broccoli, cut into ½-inch pieces.) Add soup, cheese, and milk. Heat and stir until cheese melts. Lightly toss cooked pasta with vegetable sauce. (As an alternative, serve over baked potatoes instead of pasta.)   4 servings

Listen to Jesus' Words of Eternal Life

March 23

The Word of God to Guide Your Soul

"Then Jesus said to the twelve, 'Do you also want to go away?' But Simon Peter answered Him, 'Lord, to whom shall we go? You have the words of eternal life. Also we have come to believe and know that You are the Christ, the Son of the living God'" (John 6:67-69).

> *Dear Lord, I love You and thank You for leaving Your heavenly home and bringing Your "words of eternal life" to the earth. Send Your Holy Spirit to provide me with the grace to stay by Your side and never want to leave. Grant me wisdom to live in such a beautiful way that my life helps others "come to believe and know that You are the Christ, the Son of the living God." Amen.*

Music to Inspire Your Mind

- Contemporary Christian "Word of Life" by Jeremy Camp, Ethan Hulse, and Colby Wedgeworth, performed by Jeremy Camp.

- Vocal "Show Us Christ" by Doug Plank and Bob Kauflin, performed by Sovereign Grace.
- Hymn "Wonderful Words of Life"—Text and Music: Philip P. Bliss, performed by Fountainview Academy Choir and Orchestra.
- Your music choice: _____

Nutrition to Strengthen Your Body

Nutty Banana Snack Bites

- 6 bananas
- 12 tablespoons peanut butter (your favorite kind)

Peel bananas and cut in half lengthwise. Spread 6 of the halves with 2 tablespoons peanut butter each and top with remaining halves. Slice each into bite-size sections. 6-12 servings

Cling to God, the Strength of Your Heart

March 24

The Word of God to Guide Your Soul
"My flesh and my heart fail; but God is the strength of my heart and my portion forever" (Psalm 73:26).

> *Dear Lord, I love You and thank You for always being there for me no matter what the situation. Send Your Holy Spirit to help me cling to You, even when "my flesh and my heart fail." Give me the strength to be that rock for others as well when they are going through hard times. Let them see You in all I do and embrace You as their "portion forever." Amen.*

Music to Inspire Your Mind
- Contemporary Christian "God My Rock" by Paul Baloche and Brenton Brown, performed by Paul Baloche.
- Vocal "Rock of My Salvation" by Teresa Muller, performed by Maranatha Singers.
- Hymn "A Shelter in the Time of Storm"—Text: Vernon J. Charlesworth, Music: Ira D. Sankey, performed by A Cappella.
- Your music choice: _____

Nutrition to Strengthen Your Body

Rainbow Vegetable Bake

- 2 potatoes, peeled and thinly sliced
- 1 cup carrots, thinly sliced
- 1 package (10 ounces) frozen French-style green beans, thawed and drained
- 1 cup sweet red pepper, seeded and thinly sliced
- 1 cup sweet onions, thinly sliced
- 2 cups sliced fresh mushrooms or 1 can (8 ounces) sliced mushrooms, drained
- ¼ teaspoon garlic powder
- 1 tablespoon dried parsley flakes
- ¼ teaspoon salt-free seasoning
- ¼ teaspoon pepper
- 1 can (16 ounces) stewed tomatoes, undrained
- Grated Parmesan cheese (optional)
- Nonstick olive oil cooking spray

Preheat oven to 375 degrees. Spray a 2-quart casserole with cooking spray. Layer vegetables in the casserole dish in the order listed. Sprinkle seasonings over vegetables. Spoon stewed tomatoes and liquid evenly over vegetables, breaking up any large pieces of tomato. Cover and bake for one hour. Let sit for 5-10 minutes, sprinkle with Parmesan cheese, if desired, and serve.   8 servings

Magnify the Greatness of the Lord

March 25

The Word of God to Guide Your Soul
"And Mary said: 'My soul magnifies the Lord, and my spirit has rejoiced in God my Savior'" (Luke 1:46-47).

> *Dear Lord, I love You and thank You for being my Savior and Friend. Send Your Holy Spirit to help me be like Mary and magnify Your greatness as I go throughout this day. Let others see how my spirit is rejoicing over all You have done for me and the whole world, for without You, we wouldn't even be able to take our next breath. Amen.*

Music to Inspire Your Mind
- Contemporary Christian "Great Are You Lord" by Jason Ingram, Leslie Jordan, and David Leonard, performed by Casting Crowns.
- Choral "Glorify the Lord" by Liam Lawton, performed by Liam Lawton and choir.

- Hymn "O for a Thousand Tongues to Sing"—Text: Charles Wesley, Music: Carl G. Glazer, performed by David Crowder Band (arranged by David Crowder and Jack Parker).
- Your music choice: _____

Nutrition to Strengthen Your Body

Hot Spinach Artichoke Dip

- 1 package (10 ounces) frozen, chopped spinach, thawed and drained
- 1 can (14 ounces) artichoke hearts, drained and chopped
- ½ cup grated Parmesan cheese
- 1 cup plain yogurt or reduced-fat mayonnaise
- 4 ounces light cream cheese, softened
- 1 clove garlic or ⅛ teaspoon dried, minced garlic
- 1 tablespoon lemon juice
- 1 medium tomato, chopped
- ½ cup red onions, chopped

Preheat oven to 350 degrees. Mix all ingredients, except tomato and onions. Spoon into a 9-inch pie plate. Bake for 20-25 minutes or until lightly browned. Sprinkle with tomato and onions. Serve with fresh vegetables, whole grain crackers, or pita bread.   16 servings

Receive God's Mercy and Grace

March 26

The Word of God to Guide Your Soul

"Seeing then that we have a great High Priest who has passed through the heavens, Jesus the Son of God, let us hold fast our confession. For we do not have a High Priest who cannot sympathize with our weaknesses, but was in all points tempted as we are, yet without sin. Let us therefore come boldly to the throne of grace, that we may obtain mercy and find grace to help in time of need" (Hebrews 4:14-16).

> *Dear Lord, I love You and thank You for understanding what it is like to have weaknesses and temptations. Send Your Holy Spirit to help me "come boldly to the throne of grace" to receive mercy and to "find grace to help in time of need." Open my heart to receive that mercy, but also to give mercy and forgiveness to others as I journey through this day. Amen.*

Music to Inspire Your Mind
- Contemporary Christian "Call It Grace" by Michael Farren, Jonathan Lowry, Chad Mattson, and Seth Mosley, performed by Unspoken.

- Vocal "Mercy Is a Song" by Matthew West, Jordan Feliz, and A. J. Pruis, performed by Matthew West.
- Hymn "Wonderful Grace of Jesus"—Text and Music: Haldor Lillenas, performed by the Browns.
- Your music choice: _____

Nutrition to Strengthen Your Body

Butter Bean Bake

- 2 tablespoons sweet onions, chopped
- 2 tablespoons green pepper, chopped
- 1 tablespoon olive oil
- 1 can (10.75 ounces) condensed tomato soup (reduced sodium and fat)
- ¼ cup water
- 1 tablespoon brown sugar
- 1 tablespoon vinegar
- 1 teaspoon prepared mustard
- 2 cans (16 ounces each) butter beans, drained and rinsed
- Nonstick olive oil cooking spray

Preheat oven to 375 degrees. In a medium skillet, saute onion and green pepper in olive oil over medium-high heat for five minutes or until tender. Add remaining ingredients, except for the beans, and mix well. Heat through over medium heat. Place beans in a 1½-quart casserole sprayed with cooking spray. Pour skillet sauce over beans. Bake for 45 minutes.   6 servings

Find True Contentment

March 27

The Word of God to Guide Your Soul
"Better is a little with the fear of the LORD, than great treasure with trouble" (Proverbs 15:16).

> *Dear Lord, I love You and thank You for providing the way to true happiness and contentment in this life and in the next. Send Your Holy Spirit to keep me focused today on Your love and what truly matters instead of focusing too much on the things of this world. If I start to get anxious for any reason, help me to repeat often as I go through this day, "Jesus, I trust in You." Help others to see my contentment and want that for themselves. Amen.*

Music to Inspire Your Mind
- Contemporary Christian "Your Love" by Brandon Health and Jason Ingram, performed by Brandon Heath.
- Vocal "Sweet Contentment" by Lianna Klassen.
- Hymn "All That I Need"—Text and Music: Twila Paris, performed by Twila Paris.
- Your music choice: _____

Nutrition to Strengthen Your Body

Broiled Italian Salad Muffins

- 3 medium tomatoes, cut into thin wedges
- 1 small red onion, thinly sliced
- 1 roasted red pepper, cut into thin strips
- 10 pitted black olives, sliced
- ½ cup fat-free Italian dressing
- 4 whole grain English muffins, halved
- ¼ cup reduced-fat mozzarella cheese, shredded
- ¼ cup chopped fresh basil or 2 teaspoons dried basil (optional)

Preheat the oven broiler. (For best results, have the ingredients at room temperature.) In a medium bowl, combine tomatoes, onion, red pepper, and olives. Add dressing, and toss well to coat. Let stand for 20 minutes. Spoon tomato mixture evenly onto muffins. Place on a baking sheet lined with aluminum foil. Sprinkle with mozzarella. Broil, 4 inches from heat, until cheese melts and edges of muffins are golden, about 2 minutes. Sprinkle with basil, if desired, and serve immediately.

4 servings

Walk in the Light

March 28

The Word of God to Guide Your Soul

"But if we walk in the light as He is in the light, we have fellowship with one another, and the blood of Jesus Christ His Son cleanses us from all sin" (1 John 1:7).

> *Dear Lord, I love You and thank You for bringing me into the light of Your Son, Jesus. Send Your Holy Spirit to keep me in that radiant light and prevent me from straying into the darkness. Help me to show others today how beautiful life can be in the light of God's love and forgiveness. Amen.*

Music to Inspire Your Mind

- Contemporary Christian "In the Light" by Charlie Peacock, performed by DC Talk.
- Vocal "Walking with the Light" by Mallary Hope.
- Hymn "Shine, Jesus, Shine"—Text and Music: Graham Kendrick, performed by Graham Kendrick and Hosanna Integrity Choir.
- Your music choice: _____

Nutrition to Strengthen Your Body

Easy Potato and Tomato Casserole

- 2 medium potatoes, cubed
- 1 medium tomato, cut into wedges
- 1 medium sweet onion, sliced
- 1 tablespoon olive oil
- ¼ teaspoon garlic powder
- Salt-free seasoning and pepper to taste

Preheat oven to 350 degrees. In a 1½-quart casserole dish, toss vegetables with oil. Season with garlic powder, salt-free seasoning, and pepper. Cover and bake for 30 minutes. Uncover and bake an additional 30 minutes or until potatoes are tender.

4 servings

Wait on the Lord for Help

March 29

The Word of God to Guide Your Soul

"Our soul waits for the LORD; He is our help and our shield. For our heart shall rejoice in Him, because we have trusted in His holy name. Let your mercy, O LORD, be upon us, just as we hope in You" (Psalm 33:20-22).

> *Dear Lord, I love You and thank You for Your help each and every day. Without You, I couldn't even exist. Send Your Holy Spirit to give me patience and faith when life gets difficult, and prayer requests seem to go unanswered. Help me trust that You know what is best for my loved ones and me and to always wait on You with hope. Amen.*

Music to Inspire Your Mind

- Contemporary Christian "Stay and Wait" by Joel Houston, performed by Hillsong United.
- Vocal "Wait on the Lord" by Tommy Walker Ministries, featuring Hector Gabriel.
- Hymn "He Hideth My Soul"—Text: Fanny J. Crosby, Music: William J. Kirkpatrick, performed by Don Moen.
- Your music choice: _____

Nutrition to Strengthen Your Body

Italian Vegetable Stir-fry with Pasta

- 3 cups (8 ounces) fusilli or rotini pasta, uncooked
- 2 tablespoons olive oil
- 3 cups zucchini, thinly sliced
- 1 medium green pepper, cut into strips
- 1 cup sweet onions, thinly sliced
- 1 pound fresh mushrooms, sliced, or 1 can (8 ounces) sliced mushrooms, drained
- 2 cloves garlic, minced, or ¼ teaspoon dried, minced garlic
- 1 tablespoon basil
- 1 teaspoon salt-free seasoning
- ½ teaspoon pepper
- ½ cup dry white wine or water
- ¼ cup grated Parmesan cheese

Cook pasta according to package directions and drain. Meanwhile, heat oil for 1-2 minutes in a large nonstick skillet over medium-high heat. Add all ingredients except wine or water, pasta, and Parmesan cheese; stir-fry vegetables and seasonings for 5 minutes. Stir in wine or water and cover pan for 2 minutes or until vegetables are of desired tenderness. Toss pasta with vegetables and sprinkle Parmesan cheese on top.   6 servings

Let Nothing Trouble You

March 30

The Word of God to Guide Your Soul

"Let not your heart be troubled; you believe in God, believe also in Me. In My Father's house are many mansions; if it were not so, I would have told you. I go to prepare a place for you. And if I go and prepare a place for you, I will come again and receive you to Myself; that where I am, there you may be also" (John 14:1-3).

> *Dear Lord, I love You and thank You for this beautiful promise. Send Your Holy Spirit to increase my faith so my heart is at peace no matter what my circumstances. Help me to take one day at a time and leave the future in Your hands. Let my example of trusting You in all things be an inspiration to someone today. Amen.*

Music to Inspire Your Mind
- Contemporary Christian "Borrow (One Day at a Time)" by Josh Wilson.
- Vocal "Don't Let Your Heart Be Troubled" by Mitch McVicker.

- Hymn "All Your Anxiety"—Text and Music: Edward Henry Joy, performed by the John Marshall Family. (There is also a good Celtic version by Anne McCallum.)
- Your music choice: _____

Nutrition to Strengthen Your Body

Slow Cooker Spinach Spoonbread

- 1 package (10 ounces) frozen chopped spinach, thawed and squeezed dry
- 1 red bell pepper, seeded and diced
- 4 eggs, lightly beaten, or 1 cup egg substitute
- 1 cup reduced-fat cottage cheese
- 1 package (5.5 ounces) cornbread mix
- 6 green onions, sliced
- ½ cup margarine, melted
- 1¼ teaspoons salt-free seasoning
- Nonstick olive oil cooking spray

In a large bowl, mix all the ingredients well, except cooking spray. Spray slow cooker with cooking spray and preheat to low. Pour spinach mixture in and cook covered, but with lid slightly ajar to allow excess moisture to escape. Cook on high for 2 hours or on low for 3-4 hours, until edges are golden and a knife inserted in the center comes out clean. Serve bread spooned from a slow cooker or cut into wedges to serve. (Loosen edges and bottom with a spatula and invert onto a serving plate.) 8 servings

Turn to Jesus for Victory over Sin and Evil

March 31

The Word of God to Guide Your Soul

"Grace to you and peace from God the Father and our Lord Jesus Christ, who gave Himself for our sins, that He might deliver us from this present evil age, according to the will of our God and Father" (Galatians 1:3-4).

> *Dear Lord, I love You and thank You for delivering me from evil and forgiving my sins by Your sacrifice on the cross. Send Your Holy Spirit to keep me forever faithful to You and give me strength to withstand the temptations of this world. Help me be an encouragement to others today to stay true to our commitment to follow Jesus and stand up for Him at all times. Amen.*

Music to Inspire Your Mind

- Contemporary Christian "Greater" by Chris Tomlin, Matt Redman, Ben Fielding, and Ed Cash, performed by Chris Tomlin.

- Vocal "The Power of the Cross" by Keith Getty and Stuart Townend, performed by Kristyn Getty.
- Hymn "Stand Up, Stand Up for Jesus"—Text: George Duffield, Jr., Music: George J. Webb, performed by Elevation Music, featuring Stuart Townend.
- Your music choice: _____

Nutrition to Strengthen Your Body

Snappy Three-Bean Salad

- 1 package (10 ounces) frozen cut green beans, thawed
- 1 package (10 ounces) frozen sugar snap peas, thawed and cut in half
- 1 medium red bell pepper, seeded and thinly sliced
- 1 can (15 ounces) cannellini beans, drained and rinsed
- ½ cup balsamic vinaigrette salad dressing (or other favorite vinaigrette dressing)

Combine green beans, sugar snap peas, and red pepper in a large bowl. Fold in beans. Pour the salad dressing over the bean mixture and gently toss. Cover and refrigerate for 30 minutes before serving. This salad can be stored in the refrigerator for up to 3 days. 8 servings

Be Transformed by the Spirit

April 1

The Word of God to Guide Your Soul
"But we all, with unveiled face, beholding as in a mirror the glory of the Lord, are being transformed into the same image from glory to glory, just as by the Spirit of the Lord" (2 Corinthians 3:18).

> *Dear Lord, I love You and thank You for sending Your Holy Spirit to transform my life more and more into Your image. Remind me throughout this day to invite the Spirit into each moment, as I am weak and unable to follow You without Him. Help me to glorify You with every aspect of my life. Amen.*

Music to Inspire Your Mind
- Contemporary Christian "Hymn of the Holy Spirit" by Pat Barrett, Chris Tomlin, Jason Ingram, and Brenton Brown, performed by Pat Barrett.
- Vocal "Breathe on Us" by Kari Jobe and Ed Cash, performed by Kari Jobe.

- Hymn "Breathe on Me, Breath of God"—Text: Edwin Hatch, Music: Robert Jackson, performed by Steve Green (added chorus by Phil Naish).
- Your music choice: _____

Nutrition to Strengthen Your Body

Orzo and Vegetable April Surprise

- 1 cup (6 ounces) orzo pasta
- 1 package (16 ounces) frozen mixed vegetables (broccoli, carrots, green beans, onion, and red pepper)
- 1 can (15 ounces) black beans (or other favorite bean), rinsed and drained
- 2 tablespoons margarine
- ½ teaspoon dried tarragon leaves
- ½ teaspoon dried thyme leaves
- Black pepper, to taste
- Fresh or dried parsley, as desired

Prepare pasta, according to package directions, in a large saucepan. Drain and return to saucepan. Meanwhile, microwave vegetables and drain. Add vegetables and remaining ingredients to pasta. Stir and heat through over medium heat. Sprinkle with pepper and parsley, as desired, to serve.

6 servings

Make Jesus the Chief Cornerstone of Your Life

April 2

The Word of God to Guide Your Soul

"This is the stone which was rejected by you builders, which has become the chief cornerstone. Nor is there salvation in any other, for there is no other name under heaven given among men by which we must be saved" (Acts 4:11-12).

> *Dear Lord, I love You and thank You for offering Yourself for the salvation of my soul. Send Your Holy Spirit to help me make You the "chief cornerstone" of my life so I can stand firm until I breathe my last breath. I pray for the opportunity today to encourage someone that has rejected You in the past to open their eyes and understand "there is no other name under heaven given among men by which we must be saved." Amen.*

Music to Inspire Your Mind

- Contemporary Christian "Thank You, God, for Saving Me" by Chris Tomlin and Phil Wickham.
- Vocal "New Again" by Brad Paisley and Sara Evans.

- Hymn "Amazing Love"—Text and Music: Graham Kendrick, performed by Graham Kendrick and Integrity Hosanna! Music.
- Your music choice: _____

Nutrition to Strengthen Your Body

Savory Peas and Mushrooms

- 1 package (10 ounces) frozen peas
- 8 ounces fresh mushrooms, washed and sliced, or 1 can (4 ounces) sliced mushrooms, drained
- ½ medium sweet onion, sliced
- 2 tablespoons olive oil
- ¼ teaspoon garlic powder
- ½ teaspoon oregano
- Black pepper, to taste

Prepare peas in microwave, according to directions, and drain. Meanwhile, in a large nonstick skillet, heat oil over medium heat. Add mushrooms, onions, garlic powder, and oregano; saute for about 5 minutes. Reduce heat to low and simmer until mushrooms are tender, 5-8 more minutes. Transfer peas to a serving bowl. Fold in mushroom and onion mixture. Sprinkle with pepper, as desired, before serving.   4 servings

Have Faith in God's Kindness and Mercy

April 3

The Word of God to Guide Your Soul

"'For the mountains shall depart and the hills be removed, but My kindness shall not depart from you, nor shall My covenant of peace be removed,' says the LORD, who has mercy on you" (Isaiah 54:10).

> *Dear Lord, I love You and thank You for this beautiful promise of Your faithful kindness, peace, and mercy. Send Your Holy Spirit to grant me faith in You no matter what may happen today, and help me to stand firm in Your love. Let others see the peace you bring to my life and stir in them a desire to seek Your love and mercy. Amen.*

Music to Inspire Your Mind
- Contemporary Christian "Stand in Your Love" by Josh Baldwin, Mark Harris, Ethan Hulse, and Rita Springer, performed by Josh Baldwin.
- Vocal "How Deep the Father's Love for Us" by Stuart Townend, performed by Selah.

- Hymn "Though the Mountains May Fall"—Text and Music: Dan Schutte, performed by Saint Louis Jesuits and Choir.
- Your music choice: _____

Nutrition to Strengthen Your Body

Baked Potatoes with Veggie Toppers

- 4 large baking potatoes, scrubbed and dried
- Red pepper topper:
- ¾ cup low-fat cottage cheese
- ⅓ cup diced red bell pepper
- 1½ tablespoons grated Parmesan cheese
- 1 teaspoon dried minced onion
- Cheese and vegetable topper:
- ⅔ cup low-fat plain yogurt
- ⅓ cup cooked and diced broccoli (or other desired vegetable—a great way to use leftover vegetables)
- 2 tablespoons reduced-fat Cheddar cheese, shredded
- ¼ teaspoon each salt-free seasoning and pepper

Prick each potato at least 5 times with a fork. Arrange potatoes in the microwave on double thickness paper toweling in spoke style. Microwave on high for 12 minutes, turning and rearranging potatoes after 6 minutes. Potatoes should be tender when pierced with a fork. Wrap each potato in paper toweling and let stand 5-10 minutes. Meanwhile, prepare cheese and vegetable topper by combining ingredients in a medium bowl until well blended. Cut a large X on top of each potato and gently press sides in toward the center to open. Spoon topper over potatoes and serve immediately.

4 servings

Share the Fervent Love of Jesus with All

April 4

The Word of God to Guide Your Soul
"And above all things have fervent love for one another, for 'love will cover a multitude of sins.' Be hospitable to one another without grumbling. As each one has received a gift, minister it to one another, as good stewards of the manifold grace of God" (1 Peter 4:8-10).

> *Dear Lord, I love You and thank You for Your reckless, fervent and perfect love that made You suffer and die for the salvation of the world. Send Your Holy Spirit to help me share that same kind of love with my family, friends, and all I meet today. Show me how I can serve others with the gifts You have so graciously given me. Amen.*

Music to Inspire Your Mind
- Contemporary Christian "Reckless Love" by Cory Asbury, Caleb Culver, and Ran Jackson, performed by Cory Asbury.
- Vocal "Perfect Love (Mary's Song)" by Russell Fragar and Darlene Zschech, performed by Darlene Zschech.

- Hymn "The Servant Song"—Text and Music: Richard Gillard, performed by Maranatha! Promise Band.
- Your music choice: _____

Nutrition to Strengthen Your Body

Kidney Bean Salad

- 1 can (16 ounces) kidney beans, drained and rinsed
- ¼ cup celery, diced
- 3 medium dill or sweet pickles, chopped
- ½ cup red onion, thinly sliced
- 2 hard-cooked eggs, sliced (Use egg whites only, if desired)
- ½ teaspoon salt-free seasoning
- ⅛ teaspoon pepper
- ¼ cup low-fat mayonnaise or sour cream
- Salad greens
- ½ cup (2 ounces) reduced-fat Cheddar cheese, shredded

In a large bowl, mix together beans, celery, pickles, onion, eggs, salt-free seasoning, and pepper. Blend lightly with mayonnaise or sour cream. Chill for at least one hour. (Overnight is best.) Serve on individual plates over salad greens. Garnish with Cheddar cheese.

6 servings

Ask the Holy Spirit for Perseverance and Hope

April 5

The Word of God to Guide Your Soul

"And not only that, but we also glory in tribulations, knowing that tribulation produces perseverance; and perseverance, character; and character, hope. Now hope does not disappoint, because the love of God has been poured out in our hearts by the Holy Spirit who was given to us" (Romans 5:3-5).

> *Dear Lord, I love You and thank You for all the love You pour into my heart through the Holy Spirit. Thank you for all of the challenges and experiences I have gone through in my life, as I know they are making me into the person You envision me to be. Send Your Holy Spirit to give me perseverance and hope and help me to encourage someone else who might be struggling with tribulations today. Amen.*

Music to Inspire Your Mind

- Contemporary Christian "Open Heaven (River Wild)" by Matt Crocker and Marty Sampson, performed by Hillsong Worship.
- Vocal "Holy Spirit" by Bryan Torwalt and Katie Torwalt, performed by Francesca Battistelli.
- Hymn "Where the Spirit of the Lord Is"—Text and Music: Stephen R. Adams, performed by Studio Musicians.
- Your music choice: _____

Nutrition to Strengthen Your Body

Springtime Fun Fruit Kabobs

- 10 medium strawberries
- 2 bananas, peeled and cut into chunks
- 20 seedless grapes
- ½ cantaloupe, cut into cubes or scooped into balls
- 10 skewers

Thread the fruit onto skewers alternately. Be creative and use any fruit available—fresh, frozen, or canned. Serve with reduced-fat cottage cheese and multi-grain toasted English Muffins for breakfast or lunch.   5 servings

Find Peace Through Rejoicing and Thanksgiving

April 6

The Word of God to Guide Your Soul
"Rejoice in the Lord always. Again I will say, rejoice! Be anxious for nothing, but in everything by prayer and supplication, with thanksgiving, let your requests be made known to God; and the peace of God, which surpasses all understanding, will guard your hearts and minds through Christ Jesus" (Philippians 4:4, 6-7).

> *Dear Lord, I love You and thank You for this promise of peace. Send Your Holy Spirit to enable me to rejoice always and "be anxious for nothing." Help me leave all of my burdens and worries at the foot of the cross and in Your loving care. Show me how to live with an attitude of gratitude and spread Your joy and peace to all I interact with today. Amen.*

Music to Inspire Your Mind

- Contemporary Christian "Scars" by Matthew Armstrong, Matthew Hein, Ethan Hulse, and Jon McConnell, performed by I Am They.
- Vocal "Sing" by Josh Wilson and Jeff Pardo, performed by Josh Wilson.
- Hymn "Sunshine in My Soul"—Text: Eliza E. Hewitt, Music: John R. Sweney, performed by Steve Ivey.
- Your music choice: _____

Nutrition to Strengthen Your Body

Colorful Broccoli and Tomato Saute

- 1 package (10.8 ounces) frozen broccoli florets
- 1 tomato, diced
- 1 tablespoon olive oil
- ¼ cup reduced-fat Italian blend shredded cheese (or other favorite cheese)

Microwave the broccoli according to package directions. Meanwhile, heat olive oil in a large skillet over medium heat and saute tomatoes for 2-3 minutes or until hot. Drain broccoli and mix with tomatoes in the skillet. Top with cheese, reduce heat to low, and cover for 1-2 minutes or until cheese is melted.

4 servings

Set the Lord Always Before You

April 7

The Word of God to Guide Your Soul

"I have set the LORD always before me; because He is at my right hand I shall not be moved. Therefore my heart is glad, and my glory rejoices; my flesh also will rest in hope" (Psalm 16:8-9).

> *Dear Lord, I love You and thank You for always being at my side. No one knows or loves me like You do. Send Your Holy Spirit to keep me aware of Your presence and surrender all my moments to You as I go through this day. Help me to spread Your amazing love to others so their hearts may be glad and their souls may rejoice in You. Amen.*

Music to Inspire Your Mind

- Contemporary Christian "With Lifted Hands" by Ryan Stevenson and Chris Stevens, performed by Ryan Stevenson.
- Vocal "You Restore My Soul" by Lauren Harris, Tom Read, and Matt Fury, performed by New Wine Worship, featuring Lauren Harris.

- Hymn "Turn Your Eyes upon Jesus"—Text and Music: Helen H. Lemmel, additional words and music by Lauren Daigle, Dwan Hill, and Paul Mabury, performed by Lauren Daigle.
- Your music choice: _____

Nutrition to Strengthen Your Body

Sesame Zucchini Parmesan Casserole

- 2 tablespoons olive oil
- 2 medium zucchini, sliced about ½-inch thick
- 1 jar (24 ounces) thick and hearty, meatless spaghetti sauce
- ¼ teaspoon garlic powder
- ¼ cup sweet onion, chopped
- ½ green pepper, seeded and chopped
- 1 medium carrot, grated
- ¼ cup Parmesan cheese
- ½ cup toasted sesame seeds
- 2 cups (8 ounces) reduced-fat mozzarella cheese, shredded

Preheat oven to 350 degrees. Heat olive oil in a large skillet over medium-high heat and saute zucchini slices until browned and getting soft, about 10-15 minutes. Set zucchini aside and, in the same skillet, combine the rest of the ingredients, except mozzarella cheese. Cover and simmer over low heat for 15 minutes. Layer eggplant, sauce, and cheese in a 2-quart casserole dish. Bake for 15 minutes. Let rest for 5 minutes before serving. 6 servings

Trust in God's Faithfulness

April 8

The Word of God to Guide Your Soul
"Through the LORD's mercies we are not consumed, because His compassions fail not. They are new every morning; great is Your faithfulness. 'The LORD is my portion,' says my soul, 'therefore I hope in Him!'" (Lamentations 3:22-24).

> *Dear Lord, I love You and thank You that Your "compassions fail not," and Your mercies "are new every morning." Send Your Holy Spirit to help me always trust in Your faithfulness and hope in You. I pray for the grace to know that whatever happens today, You will be by my side, and I can leave all my worries and concerns in Your hands. Let those I encounter today see Your faithfulness and love in all my words and actions. Amen.*

Music to Inspire Your Mind
- Contemporary Christian "You Are Faithful" by Miriam Webster, performed by Hillsong Worship.
- Vocal "Faithful God" by Zach Neese, performed by Zach Neese and Gateway Worship.

- Hymn "Great Is Thy Faithfulness"—Text: Thomas O. Chisholm, Music: William M. Runyan, performed by Chris Rice.
- Your music choice: _____

Nutrition to Strengthen Your Body

Rainbow Egg Salad Sandwiches

- 4 hard-cooked eggs, peeled and chopped
- 3-4 tablespoons light mayonnaise or salad dressing
- Salt-free seasoning and pepper, to taste
- Red pepper or tomato slices
- 2 medium carrots, grated
- Green pepper slices or arugula lettuce
- Purple cabbage leaves or purple grapes halved
- 8 whole grain bread slices (or other favorite bread)
- Prepared yellow mustard, to taste (optional)

In a medium mixing bowl, prepare egg salad by mashing together eggs, mayonnaise, salt-free seasoning, and pepper. Spread 4 slices of bread with mustard, if desired. Assemble sandwiches in order of the colors of the rainbow—red (red pepper or tomato slices), orange (grated carrots), yellow (egg salad), green (green pepper slices or arugula lettuce), and purple (purple cabbage leaves or purple grapes). Top with the second slice of bread and cut diagonally to serve.

4 sandwiches

Do Not Worry About Tomorrow

April 9

The Word of God to Guide Your Soul
"But seek first the kingdom of God and His righteousness, and all these things shall be added to you. Therefore do not worry about tomorrow, for tomorrow will worry about its own things. Sufficient for the day is its own trouble" (Matthew 6:33-34).

> *Dear Lord, I love You and thank You for reminding me not to worry but to seek first Your kingdom. Send Your Holy Spirit to help me cast all my cares upon You and remind me that You hold the world in Your loving hands. Use me today to pass along Your peace and reassurance to someone who is feeling anxious and worried. Amen.*

Music to Inspire Your Mind
- Contemporary Christian "Sparrows" by Mia Fieldes, Jason Gray, and Jonathan Smith, performed by Jason Gray.
- Vocal "Holding My World" by Chris Tomlin, Christy Nockels, and Kristian Stanfill, performed by Kristian Stanfill.
- Hymn "Cares Chorus"—Text and Music: Kelly Willard, performed by Maranatha! Music.

- Your music choice: _____

Nutrition to Strengthen Your Body

Impossible Vegetable Pie

- 1 package (16 ounces) frozen mixed vegetables
- ⅓ cup sweet onion, chopped
- ⅓ cup green bell pepper, chopped
- 1 cup (4 ounces) reduced-fat sharp Cheddar cheese, shredded
- ½ cup biscuit mix (lower in fat)
- 1 cup low-fat milk
- ½ teaspoon salt-free seasoning
- ¼ teaspoon pepper
- 2 eggs or ½ cup egg substitute
- Nonstick olive oil cooking spray

Preheat oven to 400 degrees. Microwave or cook mixed vegetables according to package directions; drain. Spray a 9-inch pie plate with cooking spray. Stir together mixed vegetables, onion, bell pepper, and cheese on a pie plate. In a medium bowl, blend remaining ingredients; pour into pie plate over vegetables. Bake for 35-45 minutes or until golden brown and knife inserted in center comes out clean. Let rest for 5 minutes.   6 servings

Pray for Wisdom

April 10

The Word of God to Guide Your Soul
"When pride comes, then comes shame; but with the humble is wisdom" (Proverbs 11:2).

> *Dear Lord, I love You and thank You for Your Word, which guides me in the way of all wisdom. Send Your Holy Spirit to help me always seek Your wisdom instead of the world's folly. Thank you for gently bringing me back to You when pride has triumphed in the past. Show me how to pass along Your wisdom to someone who is struggling with sin today. Amen.*

Music to Inspire Your Mind
- Contemporary Christian "Different" by Kyle Lee and Micah Tyler, performed by Micah Tyler.
- Vocal "Wisdom Song" by Laura Woodley Osman.
- Hymn "Open My Eyes"—Text and Music: Jesse Manibusan, performed by Jesse Manibusan.
- Your music choice: _____

Nutrition to Strengthen Your Body

Mexican Pasta Salad

- 8 ounces fusilli, macaroni, or other favorite pasta
- 1½ cups chunky salsa (your choice)
- ¾ cup red onion, chopped
- 2 tomatoes, chopped
- 1 red bell pepper, seeded and chopped
- 1 green pepper, seeded and chopped
- 1 can (15 ounces) black beans, rinsed and drained
- 1 package (10 ounces) frozen sweet corn, microwaved or cooked according to directions
- ½ avocado, diced
- Fresh cilantro or parsley (optional)
- ¼ cup sunflower seeds (optional)

Cook pasta according to package directions. Drain and cool to room temperature. In a large bowl, mix with remaining ingredients, except for optional items. Serve with a sprinkle of cilantro or parsley and sunflower seeds, if desired.   6 servings

Be Empowered by the Lord

April 11

The Word of God to Guide Your Soul
"I can do all things through Christ who strengthens me" (Philippians 4:13).

> *Dear Lord, I love You and thank You for empowering me with Your strength. Without You, I wouldn't be able to take my next breath. Send Your Holy Spirit to raise me up and make me strong enough to fulfill Your will for my life. Show me how to pass along Your strength to others who are struggling with suffering and trials. Amen.*

Music to Inspire Your Mind
- Contemporary Christian "Strong Enough" by Matthew West.
- Vocal "You Raise Me Up" by Brendan Graham and Rolf Lovland, performed by Josh Groban.
- Hymn "In the Garden"—Text and Music: C. Austin Miles, performed by Selah.
- Your music choice: _____

Nutrition to Strengthen Your Body

Veggie Chow Mein

- 2 tablespoons olive oil
- 1 cup sliced fresh mushrooms or 1 can (4 ounces) sliced mushrooms, drained
- 1 medium sweet onion, sliced
- 2 stalks celery, sliced
- ½ teaspoon ground ginger
- 3 tablespoons lower-sodium soy sauce
- 1 cube or teaspoon vegetable bouillon
- 1 cup water
- 1 can (16 ounces) chow mein vegetables, drained
- 1 tablespoon cornstarch
- 2 tablespoons water

In large skillet, heat olive oil over medium-high heat. Saute mushrooms and onions until tender. Add celery, ginger, soy sauce, bouillon, and 1 cup water. Cover and simmer for 20 minutes. Add chow mein vegetables. Combine cornstarch with 2 tablespoons of water and stir into vegetable mixture. Bring to boil, stirring constantly. Cover, reduce heat to low and simmer for 10-15 minutes. Serve over brown rice. 4 servings

Share Your Faith

April 12

The Word of God to Guide Your Soul
"That if you confess with your mouth the Lord Jesus and believe in your heart that God has raised Him from the dead, you will be saved. For with the heart one believes unto righteousness, and with the mouth confession is made unto salvation" (Romans 10:9-10).

> *Dear Lord, I love You and thank You for all You suffered for my salvation. Send Your Holy Spirit to give me the courage to share my faith with others and let go of the fear of rejection. Help me not only witness with my words but also with how I live my life. Amen.*

Music to Inspire Your Mind
- Contemporary Christian "We Believe" by Travis Ryan, Matthew Hopper, and Richie Fike, performed by the Newsboys.
- Vocal "People Need the Lord" by Phill McHugh and Greg Nelson, performed by Steve Green.

- Hymn "I Know Whom I Have Believed"—Text: Daniel W. Whittle, Music: James McGranahan, performed by Fountainview Academy Choir.
- Your music choice: _____

Nutrition to Strengthen Your Body

Tuscan-Style Roasted Green Beans

- 1½ pounds fresh green beans, trimmed, or 1 package (16 ounces) frozen green beans, thawed
- 1½ cups grape or cherry tomatoes halved
- 3 tablespoons sliced almonds
- 3 tablespoons olive oil
- 2 garlic cloves, minced, or ¼ teaspoon dried, minced garlic
- 1 teaspoon salt-free seasoning
- ½ teaspoon pepper
- 1 tablespoon lemon juice
- ⅓ cup grated Parmesan cheese
- 1 teaspoon grated lemon zest (use vegetable peeler or grater on outermost rind of lemon)

Preheat oven to 400 degrees. Place green beans, tomatoes, and almonds on a foil-lined 15x10x1-inch baking sheet. Mix 2 tablespoons of olive oil, garlic, salt-free seasoning, and pepper. Add to vegetables and toss to coat. Bake 15-20 minutes. Drizzle with remaining oil and lemon juice. Sprinkle with cheese and lemon zest. Toss to combine.   8 servings

Put Your Hope in Christ Alone

April 13

The Word of God to Guide Your Soul
"Be of good courage, and He shall strengthen your heart, all you who hope in the LORD" (Psalm 31:24).

> *Dear Lord, I love You and thank You for always being by my side. Send Your Holy Spirit to grant me courage, strength, and hope in every situation I encounter today. Help me to keep my heart completely dedicated to You alone and to resist getting distracted by all the things of this world. Let others see how I trust You with my life and, because of my example, be inspired to trust You as well. Amen.*

Music to Inspire Your Mind
- Contemporary Christian "Lead Me to the Cross" by Brooke Fraser, performed by Newsboys.
- Vocal "My Hope" by Paul Baloche, Ed Kerr, Alyssa Mellinger, and Sheila Rabe, performed by Paul Baloche with Kathryn Scott.
- Hymn "In Christ Alone"—Text and Music: Keith Getty and Stuart Townend, performed by Keith and Kristyn Getty.

- Your music choice: _____

Nutrition to Strengthen Your Body

Slow Cooker Red Potato and Veggie Medley

- 1 pound red potatoes, unpeeled and sliced
- 1 green or red bell pepper, thinly sliced
- ¼ cup sweet onion, finely chopped
- 2 tablespoons olive oil
- ½ teaspoon salt-free seasoning
- ½ teaspoon dried thyme
- Black pepper, as desired
- 1 small yellow squash, thinly sliced
- 1 cup (4 ounces) reduced-fat sharp Cheddar cheese, shredded

Place all ingredients, except 1 tablespoon oil, squash, and cheese, in a slow cooker; mix well. Add squash evenly on top and sprinkle with remaining oil. Cover and cook on low for 7 hours or on high for 4 hours. Remove potato mixture to a serving bowl. Sprinkle with cheese and let stand 2 to 3 minutes or until cheese melts.

5 servings

Look Forward to Eternal Life with Jesus

April 14

The Word of God to Guide Your Soul

"I am the living bread which came down from heaven. If anyone eats of this bread, he will live forever; and the bread that I shall give is My flesh, which I shall give for the life of the world" (John 6:51).

> *Dear Lord, I love You and thank You for sacrificing Your flesh "for the life of the world," so You are now the "living bread" I can turn to for saving grace. Because of Your limitless love, I can look forward to spending eternity with You, for my true home is with You in heaven. Send Your Holy Spirit to guide me in living a holy life so others may truly understand heaven is where I belong and where they belong as well. Amen.*

Music to Inspire Your Mind

- Contemporary Christian "Where I Belong" by Jason Ingram and Jason Roy, performed by Building 429.
- Vocal "I Can Only Imagine" by Bart Millard, performed by MercyMe.

- Hymn "The Way of the Cross Leads Home"—Text: Jessie B. Pounds; Music: Charles H. Gabriel, performed by John Chisum.
- Your music choice: _____

Nutrition to Strengthen Your Body

Heavenly Carrot Bread

- 1½ cups all-purpose flour
- 1 teaspoon baking soda
- 2 teaspoons baking powder
- 2 teaspoons cinnamon
- ½ teaspoon salt
- 1 cup vegetable oil
- 1½ cups brown sugar, firmly packed
- 3 eggs or ¾ cup egg substitute
- ½ cup walnuts, chopped
- ½ cup canned crushed pineapple, drained
- ½ cup raisins
- 1 cup carrots, finely shredded

Preheat oven to 350 degrees. Sift the first 5 ingredients into a mixing bowl. In a separate bowl, whisk together the oil, sugar, and eggs. Stir the liquid mixture into the flour and mix well. Add the nuts, pineapple, raisins, and carrots and stir. Grease and flour a 9-inch square pan or 4 mini-loaf pans. Fill the pans ⅔ full of batter. Bake for about 40 minutes (mini loaves about 30 minutes).

Remember You Are a Beautiful Gift to Jesus

April 15

The Word of God to Guide Your Soul

"Father, I desire that they also whom You gave Me may be with Me where I am, that they may behold My glory which You have given Me; for You loved Me before the foundation of the world" (John 17:24).

> *Dear Lord, I love You and thank You for asking the Father to let Your loved ones always be with You. Thank you for Your precious friendship and for wanting me to behold Your glory. Send Your Holy Spirit to lead me in humbly living my life as a special gift to You. Help me to share Your love and friendship with all I meet today. Amen.*

Music to Inspire Your Mind

- Contemporary Christian "Who Am I" by Mark Hall, performed by Casting Crowns.
- Vocal "You Chose to Be My Friend" by Gerald Crabb, performed by Jason Crabb, featuring Gary LeVox.
- Hymn "Jesus Loves Even Me"—Text and Music: Philip Bliss, performed by Cedarmont Kids.

- Your music choice: _____

Nutrition to Strengthen Your Body

Zucchini Pancake Surprise

- 2 medium-sized zucchini (about ¾ pound), grated and squeezed dry
- 1 small potato peeled, grated, and squeezed dry
- 3 green onions, chopped fine
- 2 tablespoons biscuit mix
- 2 eggs, slightly beaten, or ½ cup egg substitute
- 1 clove garlic, crushed, or ⅛ teaspoon dried, minced garlic
- Salt-free seasoning and pepper, to taste
- 2 teaspoons margarine, divided
- 1 tablespoon grated Parmesan cheese

In a medium bowl, combine all ingredients except margarine and Parmesan cheese. Melt 1 teaspoon margarine in a 10-inch nonstick skillet over medium heat. Be sure the bottom and sides of the pan are well coated. Add the zucchini mixture, shaping it with a spatula into one large pancake. Cook, uncovered, over medium heat until golden around the edges (8-10 minutes). Place a large plate over the skillet and invert the pancake onto it. Add the remaining margarine to the skillet; melt over medium heat. Slide the pancake back into the skillet and cook uncovered until firm (about 6-8 minutes). Sprinkle with Parmesan cheese. 4 servings

Trust in the Lord's Mercy

April 16

The Word of God to Guide Your Soul

"So rend your heart, and not your garments; return to the LORD your God, for He is gracious and merciful, slow to anger, and of great kindness; and He relents from doing harm" (Joel 2:13).

> *Dear Lord, I love You and thank You for Your limitless mercy. Show me how to give Your gift of mercy to those who may have hurt me in the past or who wish to do me harm today. Send Your Holy Spirit to open my heart to You every moment of this day and make You my all in all. Lord, I need You to guide me in being "slow to anger and of great kindness." Amen.*

Music to Inspire Your Mind
- Contemporary Christian "Mercy" by Mark Hall, Omega Levine, Sam De Long, and Tauese Tofa, performed by Casting Crowns.
- Vocal "Lord, I Need You" by Christy Nockels, Daniel Carson, Jesse Reeves, Kristian Stanfill, and Matt Maher, performed by Matt Maher.

- Hymn "You Are My All in All"—Text and Music: Dennis L. Jernigan, performed by David Phelps.
- Your music choice: _____

Nutrition to Strengthen Your Body

Chilled Red Beans and Rice

- 1 package (8.8 ounces) long grain and wild rice, microwave-ready
- ½ cup light Italian dressing
- 1 can (15 ounces) red kidney beans, rinsed and drained
- 1 cup celery, sliced
- ¼ cup red onion, chopped
- ¾ cup tomato, chopped

Microwave rice according to package directions and chill. Meanwhile, in a medium bowl, combine the rest of the ingredients and toss well. Mix in rice. Cover and chill for at least one hour. This dish is even more flavorful when chilled for 24 hours before serving.   5 servings

Believe in Resurrection Power

April 17

The Word of God to Guide Your Soul
"Jesus said to her [Martha], 'I am the resurrection and the life. He who believes in Me, though he may die, he shall live. And whoever lives and believes in Me shall never die'" (John 11:25-26a, brackets added for clarity).

> *Dear Lord, I love You and thank You for giving up Your heavenly home and coming to Earth to give me life forever with You. Thank you for Your resurrection and the hope it gives to us all. Send Your Holy Spirit to enable me to live with resurrection power and inspire others to do the same. Amen.*

Music to Inspire Your Mind
- Contemporary Christian "Resurrection Power" by Ed Cash, Ryan Ellis, and Tony Brown, performed by Chris Tomlin.
- Vocal "Alive" by Bernie Herms and Nichole Nordeman, performed by Natalie Grant.
- Hymn "He Lives"—Text and Music: Alfred H. Ackley, performed by Selah.

- Your music choice: _____

Nutrition to Strengthen Your Body

New Potatoes and Sugar Snap Peas

- 4 medium new potatoes
- 1 package (10 ounces) frozen sugar snap peas, thawed
- 1 cup vegetable broth
- 1 small sweet onion, sliced
- 1 teaspoon dried parsley or 1 tablespoon snipped fresh parsley
- ¼ teaspoon each salt-free seasoning and black pepper

Wash and poke new potatoes with a fork tine several times. Place on a paper towel in microwave and space evenly. Microwave for 4 minutes, turn and microwave another 4 minutes. Cool and slice into ½-inch slices. Meanwhile, in a 3-quart saucepan, bring the peas, broth, onion, parsley, and seasonings to a boil over medium heat. Cover and cook the sugar snap peas until they are tender, 3 to 4 minutes. Stir in the potatoes and heat through, about 3 minutes. Serve with a slotted spoon.

4 servings

Thank God for the Gift of His Grace

April 18

The Word of God to Guide Your Soul
"For by grace you have been saved through faith, and that not of yourselves; it is the gift of God, not of works, lest anyone should boast" (Ephesians 2:8-9).

> *Dear Lord, I love You and thank You so much for Your incredibly generous gift of grace. Send Your Holy Spirit to increase my faith so I may completely depend on You today. Let Your love and grace shine through me to others so their hearts may be opened to receiving Your gift of salvation. Amen.*

Music to Inspire Your Mind
- Contemporary Christian "Death Was Arrested" by Brandon Coker, Adam Kersh, Paul Taylor Smith, and Heath Balltzglier, performed by North Point InsideOut.
- Vocal "Your Grace Still Amazes Me" by Shawn Craig and Connie Harrington, performed by Phillips, Craig, and Dean.

- Hymn "By His Grace"—Text and Music: Steve Fry, performed by Maranatha!
- Your music choice: _____

Nutrition to Strengthen Your Body

Vegetable Soup with Cheesy Dill Dumplings

- 2 cans (18.5 ounces each) of your favorite vegetable soup
- 1 cup plus 2 tablespoons biscuit baking mix
- ⅓ cup low-fat milk
- 2 teaspoons chopped fresh dill or ¾ teaspoon dried dill weed
- ½ cup reduced-fat sharp Cheddar cheese, shredded

In a 3-quart saucepan, heat soup over medium heat until hot, reduce heat to medium-low. Meanwhile, in a large bowl, combine the remaining ingredients and mix well. Spoon mixture on top of the soup to make 4 dumplings. Cover and continue cooking until dumplings are cooked through (10-12 minutes). Serve each bowl with a dumpling on top. 4 servings

Abide in Jesus' Love

April 19

The Word of God to Guide Your Soul
"As the Father loved Me, I also have loved you; abide in My love. If you keep My commandments, you will abide in My love, just as I have kept my Father's commandments and abide in His love" (John 15:9-10).

> *Dear Lord, I love You and thank You so much for loving me, as the Father loves You. Send Your Holy Spirit to help me always abide in the shelter of Your love. Grant me the strength and wisdom to keep Your commandments throughout the rest of my days. Show me how to share Your unchanging love with everyone I meet today. Amen.*

Music to Inspire Your Mind
- Contemporary Christian "No Greater Love" by Gannin Arnold, Colton Dixon, and Adam Watts, performed by Colton Dixon.
- Vocal "What Love Is This" by Kari Jobe, Lincoln Brewster, and Mia Fieldes, performed by Kari Jobe.

- Hymn "The Wonder of It All"—Text and Music: George Beverly Shea, performed by The Saints Ministers.
- Your music choice: _____

Nutrition to Strengthen Your Body

Slow Cooker Pineapple and Pears

- 1 can (8 ounces) crushed pineapple in juice, undrained
- ¼ cup pineapple or apple juice
- 3 tablespoons raisins
- 1½ teaspoons quick-cooking tapioca (or 1 tablespoon of cornstarch or flour)
- ¼ teaspoon vanilla
- 2 pears, cored and cut into halves
- ¼ cup granola or other favorite crunchy cereal

In a slow cooker, combine the first five ingredients; mix well. Next, place pears, cut side down, over pineapple mixture. Cover and cook on low for 3½ to 4½ hours. Place pear halves on serving plates. Spoon pineapple mixture over pears. Sprinkle with granola or other cereal.   4 servings

Strive for Holiness with the Holy Spirit's Help

April 20

The Word of God to Guide Your Soul
"And the LORD spoke to Moses, saying, 'Speak to all the congregation of the children of Israel, and say to them: You shall be holy, for I the LORD your God am holy'" (Leviticus 19:1-2).

> *Dear Lord, I love You and thank You for Your Word that gives us so much wisdom to follow. Send Your Holy Spirit to help me be holy, as You are holy. Enlighten my mind so I may know how to be the best version of myself, the person You created me to be. Let me be an example of holiness to others. Amen.*

Music to Inspire Your Mind
- Contemporary Christian "Savior, Please" by Ben Glover and Josh Wilson, performed by Josh Wilson.
- Vocal "Refiner's Fire" by Brian Doerksen, performed by Vineyard Worship.

- Hymn "O to Be Like Thee!"—Text: Thomas O. Chisholm, Music: William J. Kirkpatrick, performed by Herbster Evangelistic Team.
- Your music choice: _____

Nutrition to Strengthen Your Body

Ginger Asian Broccoli

- 1 package (10.8 ounces) frozen broccoli florets
- 3 tablespoons reduced-sodium soy sauce
- 2 teaspoons olive oil (dark sesame oil is good as well and adds a nutty flavor)
- 1 teaspoon honey
- ¼ teaspoon ground ginger
- ¼ teaspoon dry mustard
- 8 small cherry or Roma tomatoes, halved
- ½ cup sliced water chestnuts
- 2 green onions, diagonally sliced

Microwave broccoli, according to package directions. Meanwhile, in a small saucepan, combine soy sauce, oil, honey, ginger, and dry mustard. Mix well and bring to a boil over medium heat. Drain cooked broccoli and transfer to a serving bowl. Pour soy mixture over broccoli. Add remaining ingredients and toss gently to mix. Serve immediately.

4 servings

Let Jesus Be Your Shepherd and Protector

April 21

The Word of God to Guide Your Soul

"For the Lamb who is in the midst of the throne will shepherd them and lead them to living fountains of waters. And God will wipe away every tear from their eyes" (Revelation 7:17).

> *Dear Lord, I love You and thank You for being my Shepherd and Protector. When I am afraid or discouraged, send Your Holy Spirit to remind me that You are always there by my side, and You will lead me to "living fountains of waters." Help me to comfort others with this wonderful promise as well. Amen.*

Music to Inspire Your Mind

- Contemporary Christian "Your Love Defends Me" by Matt Maher and Hannah Kerr, performed by Matt Maher.
- Vocal "Shepherd of My Soul" by Jonathan Ogden, Nathan Stirling, and Kelani Koyejo, performed by Rivers & Robots.

- Hymn "Savior, Like a Shepherd Lead Us"—Text: Attributed to Dorothy A. Thrupp, Music: William B. Bradbury, performed by 4Him.
- Your music choice: _____

Nutrition to Strengthen Your Body

Golden Mashed Potatoes

- 2 medium Russet potatoes, peeled and cut into pieces
- 2 large carrots, peeled and thinly sliced
- 4 green onions, thinly sliced
- ½ cup plain low-fat or nonfat Greek yogurt, plus more as needed
- ¼ cup reduced-fat, extra-sharp Cheddar cheese, finely grated
- ¼ teaspoon garlic powder
- Salt-free seasoning and pepper, as desired

In a 3-quart saucepan, cover the potatoes and carrots with water and bring to a boil. Simmer over medium-low heat until vegetables are tender, for 20 to 25 minutes. Drain the vegetables and return to the pan. Mash coarsely. Add remaining ingredients and mash until combined. If dry, add more yogurt to moisten.   4-6 servings

Nurture God's Creation

April 22

The Word of God to Guide Your Soul

"Then God saw everything that He had made, and indeed it was very good. Then the LORD God took the man and put him in the garden of Eden to tend and keep it" (Genesis 1:31a, Genesis 2:15).

> *Dear Lord, I love You and thank You for the beauty and majesty of Your creation. Send Your Holy Spirit to encourage us all "to tend and keep it." Help me to carefully consider my words and actions today so they are in accord with nurturing all You have made, including myself and others. Amen.*

Music to Inspire Your Mind

- Contemporary Christian "The Maker" by Chris August and Ed Cash, performed by Chris August.
- Vocal "What a Wonderful World" by George David Weiss and Bob Thiele, performed by Susan Boyle.

- Hymn "For the Beauty of the Earth"—Text: Folliott S. Pierpoint, Music: Conrad Kocher, performed by Michelle Swift.
- Your music choice: _____

Nutrition to Strengthen Your Body

Sumptuous Spinach and Mushrooms

- 1 package (10 ounces) frozen, chopped spinach
- 1 can (4 ounces) sliced mushrooms, drained
- 1 teaspoon minced onion
- 1 teaspoon minced garlic
- 1 teaspoon salt-free seasoning
- Dash of pepper
- 1 tablespoon margarine
- ⅓ cup low-fat sour cream
- 2 tablespoons low-fat milk

In a 2-quart casserole, microwave spinach according to package directions; drain well. Combine with remaining ingredients. Microwave for 2 minutes, stir and continue to microwave for 2 more minutes or until heated through. Serve immediately.

4 servings

Slow Down and Enter God's Rest

April 23

The Word of God to Guide Your Soul
"For he who has entered His rest has himself also ceased from his works as God did from His. Let us therefore be diligent to enter that rest, lest anyone fall according to the same example of disobedience" (Hebrews 4:10-11).

> *Dear Lord, I love You and thank You for showing me the importance of slowing down and taking time to rest in Your loving arms. Send Your Holy Spirit to remind me to have a quiet time every day and make Sunday a true day of rest and dedication to You and my family. Provide me the strength and perseverance I need to make the counter-cultural sacrifices that are needed to follow Your example of resting after You created the world and help others to be inspired by my example. Amen.*

Music to Inspire Your Mind
- Contemporary Christian "Rest" by Jason Germain and Marc Martel, performed by Downhere.

- Vocal "I Will Rest in You" by Bryan Brown, Brett Younker, Nathan Nockels and Christy Nockels, performed by Worship Together.
- Hymn "My Faith Has Found a Resting Place"—Text: Lidie H. Edmunds, Music: Norwegian Folk melody, performed by Fountainview Academy.
- Your music choice: _____

Nutrition to Strengthen Your Body

Easy Veggie and Cheese Pita Sandwiches

- 4 (6-inch) pita breads, each cut in half
- 2 cups deli coleslaw
- 1 cup green pepper, chopped
- 1 cup reduced-fat Monterey Jack cheese, shredded
- 8 slices tomato

In a medium bowl, mix coleslaw, green pepper, and cheese. Divide mixture among the pita halves and top with tomato slices. Be creative with whatever veggies and cheese you have on hand!   4 servings

Continue Steadfastly in Prayer

April 24

The Word of God to Guide Your Soul
"Rejoicing in hope, patient in tribulation, continuing steadfastly in prayer" (Romans 12:12).

> *Dear Lord, I love You and thank You for the opportunity to talk with You in prayer. Send Your Holy Spirit to prompt me throughout this day to bring everything to You and persevere in seeking Your will in every situation I may encounter. Thank you also for just being able to sit with You and rest in Your presence. Help others to see how much I focus on You and rely on You for every detail of my life. Amen.*

Music to Inspire Your Mind
- Contemporary Christian "Here in the Presence" by Chris Brown, Mack Brock, and Steven Furtick, performed by Elevation Worship.
- Vocal "Pray" by Chris Rohman, Matt Hammitt, and Chris Stevens, performed by Sanctus Real.

- Hymn "Jesus, the Very Thought of Thee"—Text: Attributed to Bernard of Clairvaux, Music: John B. Dykes, performed by Sally DeFord and James Loynes.
- Your music choice: _____

Nutrition to Strengthen Your Body

Yummy Black Beans and Rice

- 3 cups cooked brown rice (or your favorite rice)
- 2 cloves garlic, minced, or ¼ teaspoon dried, minced garlic
- 1 can (15 ounces) black beans, rinsed and drained
- 1 jar (16 ounces) of your favorite salsa
- 1 cup reduced-fat sharp Cheddar cheese, shredded (optional)

In a large, microwavable casserole dish, mix all ingredients except cheese. Microwave for 3 minutes and stir. Microwave an additional 2 minutes or until heated through. Stir and serve. Top with cheese, if desired.   6 servings

Seek the Lord at All Times

April 25

The Word of God to Guide Your Soul
"Glory in His holy name; let the hearts of those rejoice who seek the Lord! Seek the LORD and His strength; seek His face evermore!" (Psalm 105:3-4).

> *Dear Lord, I love You and thank You for seeking a close, personal relationship with me. Send Your Holy Spirit to help me seek a close, personal relationship with You as well. Help me to rely on You and constantly seek Your will for me every moment of every day. Guide me in all my decisions, great or small. Let me be a witness today of how seeking You, Jesus, leads to joy no matter what the circumstances. Amen.*

Music to Inspire Your Mind
- Contemporary Christian "O Lord, We Seek Your Face" by Andy Campbell, Chris Cope, and Isaac Williams, performed by Worship Central.
- Vocal "The More I Seek You" by Zach Neese, performed by Kari Jobe.

- Hymn "Seekers of Your Heart"—Text and Music: Melodie Tunney, Dick Tunney, and Beverly Darnall, performed by Sandi Patty, Larnelle Harris, and Steve Green.
- Your music choice: _____

Nutrition to Strengthen Your Body

Make-Ahead Layered Veggie Potato Salad

- 4-5 medium Red or Yukon Gold potatoes
- 1 cup light Italian dressing (or other favorite dressing)
- ½ cup sweet onions, chopped
- 2 tablespoons chopped parsley (or 1 teaspoon dried parsley)
- Salt-free seasoning and pepper, to taste
- 2 tomatoes, sliced
- 1½ cups zucchini, shredded

Wash and poke potatoes with a fork tine several times. Place on a paper towel in microwave and space evenly. Microwave for 4 minutes, turn, and microwave another 4 minutes or until tender. Cool and slice potatoes ¼-inch thick (leave skin on). Whisk together dressing, onions, parsley, salt-free seasoning, and pepper. In a serving bowl, layer half the potatoes, tomatoes, and zucchini. Stir dressing again and pour half over the vegetables. Top with remaining potatoes, tomatoes, zucchini, and stirred dressing. Cover and chill for at least 5 hours or overnight. (Get creative and use whatever veggies you have, instead of tomatoes and zucchini!) 6 servings

Rejoice in Your Salvation

April 26

The Word of God to Guide Your Soul
"For this is good and acceptable in the sight of God our Savior, who desires all men to be saved and to come to the knowledge of the truth" (1 Timothy 2:3-4).

> *Dear Lord, I love You and thank You so much for saving me and giving me the grace "to come to the knowledge of the truth." Send Your Holy Spirit to remind me to rejoice in this, even when trials come, and I become discouraged. Inspire me to always have a heavenly perspective to my earthly existence. Provide me with the opportunity and the courage today to help someone else "to be saved and to come to the knowledge of the truth." Amen.*

Music to Inspire Your Mind
- Contemporary Christian "Mighty to Save" by Ben Fielding and Reuben Morgan, performed by Maranatha! Music.
- Vocal "Thank You, God, for Saving Me" by Chris Tomlin and Phil Wickham, performed by Chris Tomlin.

- Hymn "O Happy Day!"—Text: Philip Doddridge, Music: Attributed to Edward F. Rimbault, performed by Voices of Hope Children's Choir.
- Your music choice: _____

Nutrition to Strengthen Your Body

Sesame Corn Saute

- 3 tablespoons olive oil
- ½ cup sweet onion, chopped
- ½ cup red bell pepper, diced
- 2 cloves garlic, finely chopped, or ¼ teaspoon dried, minced garlic
- 2-4 tablespoons sesame seeds
- 1 package (10 ounces) frozen corn, thawed
- ¼ teaspoon basil
- ½ teaspoon salt-free seasoning
- ¼ teaspoon black pepper
- ¼ cup chopped parsley (optional)
- ¼ cup grated Parmesan cheese (optional)

In a large skillet, heat olive oil over medium-high heat. Saute onion, bell pepper, garlic, and sesame seeds until lightly browned (about 3 minutes). Blend in remaining ingredients, except for parsley and Parmesan cheese. Saute until corn is thoroughly warmed. To serve, sprinkle cheese on top and garnish with parsley, if desired.   4 servings

Praise the Lord's Glorious Name

April 27

The Word of God to Guide Your Soul

"In Your hand is power and might; in Your hand it is to make great and to give strength to all. Now therefore, our God, we thank You and praise Your glorious name" (1 Chronicles 29:12b-13).

> *Dear Lord, I love You and thank You for giving me glimpses of Your majesty, splendor, and glory. Send Your Holy Spirit to make me aware of those glimpses as I go through my day, perhaps in the warmth of the sunshine or the beauty of someone's smile. Help me to keep an attitude of gratitude and often think of how You are supporting me with Your love and strength. Show me ways to help others appreciate "Your glorious name" today. Amen.*

Music to Inspire Your Mind

- Contemporary Christian "How Majestic" by Kari Jobe, Chris Tomlin, Matt Redman, and Jason Ingram, performed by Kari Jobe.

- Vocal "How Majestic Is Your Name" by Michael W. Smith, performed by Sandi Patty.
- Hymn "Glorious Is Thy Name"—Text and Music: B. B. McKinney, performed by Mike Hohnholz.
- Your music choice: _____

Nutrition to Strengthen Your Body

Mediterranean Tomato-Bean Skillet Dish

- 2 tablespoons olive oil
- 1 clove garlic, chopped, or ⅛ teaspoon minced garlic
- 1 can (15 ounces) cannellini beans or other beans, drained and rinsed
- 2 cans (3.8 ounces each) black olives, sliced and drained
- 1 pint grape tomatoes, halved
- ¼ cup parsley, diced, or 2 teaspoons dried parsley
- Salt-free seasoning and pepper, as desired

In a large skillet, over medium heat, cook garlic in olive oil for 1 minute. Add beans and olives and cook for 5 minutes. Add the tomatoes and cook for 5 minutes more. Stir in parsley, salt-free seasoning, and pepper. (Make it a meal by serving over couscous, brown rice, or other favorite rice. This is also a good topping for baked potatoes.)   4 servings

Diligently Guard Your Heart

April 28

The Word of God to Guide Your Soul
"Keep your heart with all diligence, for out of it spring the issues of life" (Proverbs 4:23).

> *Dear Lord, I love You and thank You for how much You love me and want to protect me. Send Your Holy Spirit to guide me in discerning what leads me to grow and become all You want me to be. Help me also to avoid whatever would lead me down the wrong path, away from You. Show me how to diligently guard my heart and keep it pure and full of life. Grant me courage to share my heart's love for You with those I meet today and encourage them to give their hearts to You for safekeeping. Amen.*

Music to Inspire Your Mind
- Contemporary Christian "Guard Your Heart" by Dave Wyatt, Lauren Taylor Bach, and Molly Reed, performed by 1 Girl Nation.
- Vocal "Here's My Heart" by Chris Tomlin, Jason Ingram, and Louie Giglio, performed by Casting Crowns.

- Hymn "O for a Heart to Praise My God"—Text: Charles Wesley, Music: Brian Buda, additional lyrics by Stephanielynn Buda, performed by Lorenz Corporation Choir.
- Your music choice: _____

Nutrition to Strengthen Your Body

Easy Veggie Pizza

- 1 package reduced-fat crescent rolls
- 2 tablespoons olive oil
- 1 cup fresh mushrooms, sliced or 1 can (8 ounces) mushrooms, sliced and drained
- 1 cup zucchini, sliced
- ⅓ cup green pepper, chopped
- ⅓ cup green onion, sliced
- 1 cup pizza or marinara sauce
- 1 cup reduced-fat mozzarella cheese, shredded
- Nonstick olive oil cooking spray

Preheat oven to 350 degrees. Spread crescent roll dough into a 12-inch circle on a baking sheet sprayed with olive oil nonstick cooking spray. Pinch seams together to seal. Bake 10-12 minutes or until lightly browned. While crust is baking, slice and chop vegetables. Saute in olive oil over medium-high heat until tender. Reduce heat to medium and add pizza or marinara sauce to vegetable mixture and heat through. Spread pizza sauce over crust and sprinkle with cheese. Bake a few more minutes until cheese is melted. (Vary cheese and vegetables, as desired.)   6 servings

Live Soberly, Righteously, and Godly

April 29

The Word of God to Guide Your Soul
"For the grace of God that brings salvation has appeared to all men, teaching us that, denying ungodliness and worldly lusts, we should live soberly, righteously, and godly in the present age" (Titus 2:11-12).

> *Dear Lord, I love You and thank You for Your saving grace. Send Your Holy Spirit to bless me with the strength and discernment to reject godless ways and worldly desires. Show me how the world is creeping into my life and causing me to live apart from Your love. Pour Your grace into my heart and help me to "live soberly, righteously, and godly," becoming a reflection to others of Your unconditional love. Amen.*

Music to Inspire Your Mind
- Contemporary Christian "No More" by Benji Cowart, Jeff Pardo, and Josh Wilson, performed by Josh Wilson.

- Vocal "Kindness" by Chris Tomlin, Louie Giglio, and Jesse Reeves, performed by Chris Tomlin.
- Hymn "Living for Jesus"—Text: Thomas O. Chisholm, Music: C. Harold Lowden, performed by Steven Anderson and Choir.
- Your music choice: _____

Nutrition to Strengthen Your Body

Tasty Steamed Cauliflower

- ½ cup vegetable broth
- ½ teaspoon dried thyme leaves
- ¼ teaspoon dried marjoram leaves
- 1 bay leaf
- 1 medium head cauliflower, about 1½ pounds, trimmed
- 1 cup reduced-fat sharp Cheddar cheese, shredded

In a large casserole, combine broth and herbs. Place cauliflower upside down in casserole and cover. Microwave on high for 15 to 20 minutes until the base is tender. Turn cauliflower over after half the time. Let stand for five minutes, covered. Remove bay leaf. Sprinkle with cheese and cover again to let cheese melt.

4 servings

Listen to the Holy Spirit

April 30

The Word of God to Guide Your Soul
"Now we have received, not the spirit of the world, but the Spirit who is from God, that we might know the things that have been freely given to us by God" (1 Corinthians 2:12).

> *Dear Lord, I love You and thank You for blessing me with Your Holy Spirit. I pray that I will always listen to Your Spirit and understand all You have so freely given to me. I also pray for protection from "the spirit of the world" so I will never be led astray. Grant me the courage to generously share "the Spirit who is from God" with others as I go through my day. Amen.*

Music to Inspire Your Mind
- Contemporary Christian "Spirit Lead Me" by Graham Moore, Melody Hernandez, and Michael Barkulis, performed by Michael Ketterer and Influence Music.
- Vocal "Fill Me Now" by Christina Peppin and Michael Hansen, performed by Cameron Hammon and Vineyard Worship.

- Hymn "Come, Holy Spirit"—Text: Gloria Gaither and William J. Gaither, Music: William J. Gaither, performed by Bryan Duncan.
- Your music choice: _____

Nutrition to Strengthen Your Body

Make-Ahead Tomato and Vegetable Strata

- Mushroom mixture: 1 tablespoon olive oil, 1½ cups mushrooms, sliced, 1 cup onion, chopped
- Cottage cheese mixture: 1 container (16 ounces) low-fat cottage cheese and 1 package (10 ounces) frozen, chopped spinach, thawed and well-drained, ¼ teaspoon ground nutmeg, and ¼ teaspoon coarsely ground pepper
- Strata: 1 can (16 ounces) herb and garlic chunky tomato sauce, ½ loaf (8 ounces) Italian or French bread, cut into ¼-inch slices, and 1 cup reduced-fat mozzarella cheese, shredded
- 1 cup low-fat milk
- 4 eggs or 1 cup egg substitute
- Nonstick olive oil cooking spray

Preheat oven to 375 degrees. In a medium skillet, heat olive oil on medium-high heat. Add mushrooms and onions and saute until tender, about 6-8 minutes; set aside. In a large bowl, combine cottage cheese mixture ingredients; mix well. Spray a 13x9-inch baking dish with cooking spray. Spread ¼ cup tomato sauce in the bottom of the pan. Place half of the bread slices on tomato sauce, top with cottage cheese mixture, remaining bread slices, mushroom mixture, mozzarella cheese, and remaining tomato sauce. In a small bowl, combine milk and eggs, mixing well. Slowly pour egg mixture over strata until all mixture has been absorbed. Cover and refrigerate overnight. Bake, uncovered, for 45 to 50 minutes or until knife inserted in center comes out clean and strata is puffed and golden brown. Let stand 10 minutes before serving.   8 servings

Be a Blessing to Someone Today

May 1

The Word of God to Guide Your Soul
"Rejoice with those who rejoice, and weep with those who weep. If it is possible, as much as depends on you, live peaceably with all men" (Romans 12:15, 18).

> *Dear Lord, I love You and thank You for working through me to be a blessing to others. Send Your Holy Spirit to help me decrease so You may increase when I am involved with ministry at church, work, or home. Grant me a discerning spirit so I will know when You need to minister to others through my words, actions, and prayers. Amen.*

Music to Inspire Your Mind
- Contemporary Christian "Blessed to Be a Blessing" by Lara Martin, performed by Hillsong, featuring Mark Stevens.
- Vocal "Make Me a Servant" by Kelly Willard, performed by Maranatha! Singers featuring Kelly Willard.
- Hymn "Make Me a Blessing"—Text: Ira B. Wilson, Music: George S. Schuler, performed by Luther Barnes and the Red Budd Gospel Choir.

- Your music choice: _____

Nutrition to Strengthen Your Body

Cucumber and Tomato Cottage Cheese Salad

- 2 cups reduced-fat cottage cheese
- 1 tablespoon lemon juice
- 2 tablespoons chopped, fresh parsley or 2 teaspoons dried parsley
- ¼ teaspoon paprika
- ¼ teaspoon black pepper
- 1 cup cucumber, chopped
- 2 medium tomatoes, seeded and chopped
- ¼ cup sweet onion, chopped
- 4 large lettuce leaves
- Multigrain or whole wheat pita chips (optional)

In a medium bowl, combine the first five ingredients. Stir in the cucumbers, tomatoes, and onion. To serve, place a lettuce leaf on each plate and spoon the cottage cheese mixture onto the lettuce. Add several pita chips to each plate, if desired.

4 servings

Take Time Just to Be with Jesus

May 2

The Word of God to Guide Your Soul
"Then you will call upon Me and go and pray to Me, and I will listen to you. And you will seek Me and find Me, when you search for Me with all your heart" (Jeremiah 29:12-13).

> *Dear Lord, I love You and thank You for always being with me, even when I lose my focus on You. Send Your Holy Spirit to keep me focused on You throughout this day and to remind me about the importance of taking some time just to rest in Your presence and soak up Your love. Let others see how I call upon You and search for You with all my heart. Amen.*

Music to Inspire Your Mind
- Contemporary Christian "With You" by Chris Brown, Steven Furtick, and Tiffany Hammer, performed by Elevation Worship.
- Vocal "Still" by Justin Ebach and Molly E. Reed, performed by Hillary Scott and the Scott Family.

- Hymn "In His Presence"—Text and Music: Dick and Melodie Tunney, performed by Sandi Patty.
- Your music choice: _____

Nutrition to Strengthen Your Body

Shell Pasta with Vegetable Sauce

- ½ cup sweet onion, chopped
- ½ cup fresh parsley, chopped, or 1 tablespoon dried parsley
- 2 cloves garlic, minced, or ¼ teaspoon dried, minced garlic
- 1 tablespoon olive oil
- 2 cups chopped, peeled tomatoes or 1 can (15 ounces) diced tomatoes, drained
- 1 package (10 ounces) angel hair coleslaw (finely shredded green cabbage)
- ½ cup carrots, thinly sliced
- ½ cup vegetable broth
- ¼ cup tomato paste
- Seasonings: ½ teaspoon basil, ½ teaspoon salt-free seasoning, ¼ teaspoon oregano, and ⅛ teaspoon pepper
- 3 cups (8 ounces) medium shell pasta, uncooked (substitute your favorite pasta, if desired)
- Grated Parmesan cheese (optional)

In a large skillet, saute onions, parsley, and garlic in olive oil over medium heat until tender. Add the rest of the ingredients, except pasta and Parmesan cheese. Cover and simmer for 10-12 minutes or until vegetables are desired tenderness. Meanwhile, cook pasta according to package directions and drain. Spoon vegetable sauce over pasta. Sprinkle with Parmesan cheese, if desired.   6 servings

Receive the Abundant Peace That Jesus Offers

May 3

The Word of God to Guide Your Soul
"Then, the same day at evening, being the first day of the week, when the doors were shut where the disciples were assembled, for fear of the Jews, Jesus came and stood in the midst, and said to them, 'Peace be with you.' When He had said this, He showed them His hands and His side. Then the disciples were glad when they saw the Lord" (John 20:19-20).

> *Dear Lord, I love You and thank You for offering me the same peace that You gave to Your disciples following Your crucifixion and resurrection. Send Your Holy Spirit to open my heart and mind to receive that abundant peace, even in the midst of the noise and turmoil of this crazy world. Help me lead others to experience the supernatural peace only You can give. Amen.*

Music to Inspire Your Mind

- Contemporary Christian "Peace Be Still" by Hope Darst, Mia Fieldes, and Andrew Holt, performed by The Belonging Co, featuring Lauren Daigle.
- Vocal "Perfect Peace" by Laura Story.
- Hymn "My Peace"—Text and Music: Keith Routledge, performed by Maranatha Singers.
- Your music choice: _____

Nutrition to Strengthen Your Body

Ranch Vegetable Medley

- 2 tablespoons olive oil
- 2 packages (16 ounces each) frozen mixed vegetables (e.g. cauliflower, carrots, and snow pea pods)
- 1 envelope (1.2 ounces) Ranch salad dressing mix (may also use Caesar or other flavors)

In a large nonstick skillet, heat olive oil over medium heat. Add vegetables and dressing mix to skillet. Cover and cook for 5 to 7 minutes, stirring frequently to desired tenderness. 6 servings

Look to the Lord for Guidance

May 4

The Word of God to Guide Your Soul
"I will instruct you and teach you in the way you should go; I will guide you with My eye" (Psalm 32:8).

> *Dear Lord, I love You and thank You for Your instruction, counsel, and protection. Send Your Holy Spirit to give me eyes to see and ears to hear the guidance You so long to give me. Don't let the voices and worries of this world drown out Your ever-present voice of wisdom. Show me today where You can work through me to give counsel to someone struggling with indecision and "the way" they should go. Amen.*

Music to Inspire Your Mind
- Contemporary Christian "Walk by Faith" by Jeremy Camp.
- Vocal "The Perfect Wisdom of Our God" by Stuart Townend and Keith Getty, performed by Keith and Kristyn Getty.
- Hymn "Here I Am, Lord"—Text and Music: Daniel L. Schutte, performed by Chris Bray.
- Your music choice: _____

Nutrition to Strengthen Your Body

Fruity Sheet Pan Pancakes

- 3½ cups whole wheat pancake mix (may also use buttermilk, if preferred)
- 2 cups water
- 1 teaspoon vanilla extract
- ½ teaspoon cinnamon
- ½ medium banana
- ½ cup strawberries
- ½ cup blueberries
- Nonstick cooking spray

Preheat oven to 425 degrees. In a large bowl, stir pancake mix, water, vanilla extract, and cinnamon. Let stand for 10 minutes. Spray an 11x17-inch baking pan with nonstick cooking spray. Pour batter in the pan, spreading to the corner. Scatter fruit on top. Bake for about 13-14 minutes, until slightly risen and cooked through. Cool 2 minutes and slice with a pizza cutter or cookie cutters.   4 servings

Follow Your Shepherd to Eternal Life

May 5

The Word of God to Guide Your Soul

"My sheep hear My voice, and I know them, and they follow Me. And I give them eternal life, and they shall never perish; neither shall anyone snatch them out of My hand" (John 10:27-28).

> *Dear Lord, I love You and thank You for leading me to eternal life with You. When I get discouraged due to earthly problems and pressures, help me take a moment to remember my true home is in heaven. Send Your Holy Spirit to fill me with joy and peace in knowing no one can snatch me out of Your hand. Help me to spread that joy and peace to others today. Amen.*

Music to Inspire Your Mind

- Contemporary Christian "Heaven Song" by Phil Wickham.
- Choral "Going Home" Text: Williams Arms Fisher, Music: Antonin Dvorak, performed by Libera.
- Hymn "Sweet By and By"—Text: Sanford F. Bennett, Music: Joseph P. Webster, performed by Dolly Parton.

- Your music choice: _____

Nutrition to Strengthen Your Body

Salsa Scramble

- 2 tablespoons olive oil
- 1 medium green pepper, chopped
- 1 medium sweet onion, chopped
- 1 medium tomato, chopped
- ½ cup frozen whole kernel corn
- 1 can (15 ounces) pinto beans, drained, rinsed, and coarsely chopped
- 4 eggs, beaten or 1 cup egg substitute
- ½ cup reduced-fat sharp Cheddar cheese, shredded
- ¼ cup of your favorite salsa sauce
- Salt-free seasoning and pepper to taste (optional)

In a large nonstick skillet, saute green pepper and onion in olive oil over medium heat until tender. Stir in tomato, corn, and beans. Add eggs and cheese; fold and stir to make scrambled eggs. Season with salt-free seasoning and pepper, if desired. Serve with warmed salsa.   4-6 servings

Sing to the Lord in Your Heart

May 6

The Word of God to Guide Your Soul

"But be filled with the Spirit, speaking to one another in psalms and hymns and spiritual songs, singing and making melody in your heart to the Lord, giving thanks always for all things to God the Father in the name of our Lord Jesus Christ" (Ephesians 5:18b-20).

> *Dear Lord, I love You and thank You for all the blessings You give me each and every day. Send Your Holy Spirit to help me give thanks "always for all things" and to understand how You are working in every situation I encounter. Let my heart be filled with the music of the angels and the saints, and show me how to spread that joy to others throughout the day. Amen.*

Music to Inspire Your Mind

- Contemporary Christian "10,000 Reasons (Bless the Lord)" by Jonas Myrin and Matt Redman, performed by Matt Redman.
- Vocal "Sing to Jesus" by Fernando Ortega.

- Hymn "I Love You, Lord"—Text and Music: Laurie Klein, performed by Laurie Klein.
- Your music choice: _____

Nutrition to Strengthen Your Body

Apple Orange Crunch

- 3 medium apples, sliced
- ¾ cup orange juice
- 1 teaspoon cinnamon
- 1 teaspoon lemon juice
- ¾ cup graham cracker crumbs
- 1 tablespoon margarine, melted

Preheat oven to 400 degrees. In a 1½-quart casserole, toss together apples, orange juice, cinnamon, and lemon juice. Combine graham cracker crumbs with margarine and sprinkle over apples. Cover and bake for 30 minutes. Uncover and bake for an additional 10 minutes.   6 servings

Treasure God's Word

May 7

The Word of God to Guide Your Soul
"I have not departed from the commandment of His lips; I have treasured the words of His mouth more than my necessary food" (Job 23:12).

> *Dear Lord, I love You and thank You for preserving Your words in Holy Scripture. Send Your Holy Spirit to never let me take Your words for granted, but to always study and treasure them. Thank You also for sending people into my life to help me understand and follow Your words and commands. Let me share Your words and promises with someone today who needs to know Your story and how much You love them. Amen.*

Music to Inspire Your Mind
- Contemporary Christian "Living Word" by Ian Eskelin, performed by Jeremy Camp.
- Vocal "Every Promise of Your Word" by Keith Getty and Stuart Townend, performed by Keith and Kristyn Getty.

- Hymn "Ancient Words"—Text and Music: Lynn Deshazo, performed by Michael W. Smith and choir.
- Your music choice: _____

Nutrition to Strengthen Your Body

Eggplant Parmigiana

- 2 eggplants (about 1 pound each), pared and sliced ½-inch thick
- 2 tablespoons olive oil
- 2 medium sweet onions, sliced
- 1 can (28 ounces) whole, peeled tomatoes
- 1 teaspoon oregano
- ½ teaspoon basil
- ½ teaspoon salt-free seasoning
- ½ teaspoon pepper
- 2 cups (8 ounces) reduced-fat mozzarella cheese, shredded
- ¼ cup Parmesan cheese, grated
- Nonstick olive oil cooking spray

Preheat oven to 350 degrees. In a large nonstick skillet, saute eggplant slices in olive oil over medium heat until browned. Arrange slices in a 9x9-inch baking dish, sprayed with cooking spray. Top with onions. Combine tomatoes and seasonings and pour over eggplant. Bake for 30 minutes. Top with mozzarella cheese, then sprinkle with Parmesan cheese. Bake another 15 minutes. Serve with your favorite pasta.   4 servings

Praise Your Heavenly Father for His Saving Love and Goodness

May 8

The Word of God to Guide Your Soul

"Jesus therefore answered and said to them, 'Do not murmur among yourselves. No one can come to Me unless the Father who sent me draws him; and I will raise him up at the last day'" (John 6:43-44).

> *Dear Lord, I love You and thank You for Your love and goodness, which draws me to You. Send Your Holy Spirit to calm me and show me how to serenely rest in Your heavenly love. Thank you for the promise of raising me on the last day to live with You forever. Help me spread Your saving love and goodness around to all I meet today. Amen.*

Music to Inspire Your Mind

- Contemporary Christian "Goodness of God" by Brian and Jenn Johnson, Jason Ingram, Ed Cash, and Ben Fielding, performed by Bethel Music.
- Vocal "Good Good Father" by Pat Barrett and Anthony Brown, performed by Chris Tomlin.

- Hymn "Father God"—Text and Music: Jack W. Hayford, additional lyrics by Lauren Reilly, performed by Lauren Reilly and Believers Sanctuary.
- Your music choice: _____

Nutrition to Strengthen Your Body

Slow Cooker Carrots, Onions, and Peas

- 1 pound carrots, peeled and sliced
- 1 large sweet onion, sliced
- ¼ cup water
- ¼ cup margarine, melted
- 4 garlic cloves, minced, or ½ teaspoon dried, minced garlic
- ½ teaspoon basil
- ½ teaspoon oregano
- ½ teaspoon salt-free seasoning
- ½ teaspoon pepper
- 1 package (16 ounces) frozen peas

Combine all the ingredients in a slow cooker, except peas. Cover and cook on low for 5 hours. Stir in peas. Cover and cook on high for 15-25 minutes or until vegetables are desired tenderness.   8 servings

Walk in the Lord's Truth

May 9

The Word of God to Guide Your Soul

"Teach me Your way, O LORD; I will walk in Your truth; unite my heart to fear Your name. I will praise You, O Lord my God, with all my heart, and I will glorify Your name forevermore" (Psalm 86:11-12).

> *Dear Lord, I love You and thank You for opening my eyes, ears, and heart to Your truth. Send Your Holy Spirit to give me the strength and wisdom to always walk in Your truth. Let those I interact with today see You in all of my actions and words and join me in glorifying Your name forevermore. Amen.*

Music to Inspire Your Mind

- Contemporary Christian "Jesus" by Chris Tomlin and Ed Cash, performed by Chris Tomlin.
- Vocal "The Voice of Truth" by Mark Hall and Stephen Curtis Chapman, performed by Casting Crowns.
- Hymn "Open My Eyes That I May See"—Text and Music: Clara H. Scott, performed by Fountainview Academy Choir.

- Your music choice: _____

Nutrition to Strengthen Your Body

Tex-Mex Macaroni Salad

- 8 ounces whole grain macaroni pasta
- ¾ cup red onion, chopped
- 2 tomatoes, diced, or 1 can (14.5 ounces) diced tomatoes, drained
- 1 green pepper, cored and chopped
- 1 cup black beans, rinsed and drained
- 1 cup frozen corn, cooked and drained
- ½ avocado, diced
- 1 ½ cups salsa, divided
- ¼ cup sunflower seeds (optional)

Cook pasta according to package directions. Drain and cool to room temperature. Mix pasta with all ingredients, except salsa and sunflower seeds. Toss with half of the salsa and garnish with sunflower seeds, if desired. Serve with remaining salsa on the side.

6 servings

Cast Aside All Your Fears

May 10

The Word of God to Guide Your Soul
"Fear not, for I have redeemed you; I have called you by your name; you are mine" (Isaiah 43:1b).

> *Dear Lord, I love You and thank You for redeeming me and assuring me that all will be well. Send Your Holy Spirit to help me replace all of my fears with thoughts of You and my heavenly home. It is such a blessing to know I am Yours, and You have called me by name. Grant me the courage to share that extraordinary news with someone today. Amen.*

Music to Inspire Your Mind
- Contemporary Christian "Fear Is a Liar" by Jason Ingram, Jonathan Smith, and Zach Williams, performed by Zach Williams.
- Vocal "I Will Fear No More" by Matthew Fuqua, Joshua Havens, Jason Ingram, Jordan Mohilowski, and Dan Ostebo, performed by The Afters.

- Hymn "Be Not Afraid"—Text based on Isaiah 43:2-3, Luke 6:20, Text and Music: Robert J. Dufford, SJ, performed by Kitty Cleveland.
- Your music choice: _____

Nutrition to Strengthen Your Body

Vegetable-Cheese Layered Casserole

- 4 slices whole grain bread, quartered
- 1 package (20-ounce) frozen broccoli florets (or 4 cups fresh)
- 1 medium sweet onion, chopped
- 4 ounces mushrooms, sliced, or 1 can (4 ounce) sliced mushrooms, drained
- ¾ cup low-fat cottage cheese
- 4 ounces reduced-fat Colby-Jack cheese, sliced
- 2 eggs or ½ cup egg substitute
- 2 cups low-fat milk
- ½ teaspoon dry mustard
- Nonstick olive oil cooking spray

Preheat oven to 350 degrees. Spray a 1½-quart casserole dish or an 8-inch square pan with cooking spray. Place half of bread pieces in a layer on the bottom. Add vegetables on top of bread. Spread cottage cheese over vegetables, then top with cheese slices (overlapping if necessary). Mix eggs, milk, and mustard in a medium bowl. Dip remaining bread pieces into the egg mixture and add as a top layer of the casserole. Pour the remaining egg mixture over the casserole. With the back of a spoon, lightly press bread pieces into casserole. Bake for 35-40 minutes, or until a knife inserted in the center comes out clean. Cover, if necessary, to avoid excessive browning. Let stand five minutes before cutting to serve. (Pairs well with a salad or soup.)   4 servings

Give Glory to God

May 11

The Word of God to Guide Your Soul
"Blessed are the people who know the joyful sound! They walk, O LORD, in the light of Your countenance. In Your name they rejoice all day long" (Psalm 89:15-16a).

> *Dear Lord, I love You and thank You for bringing Your "joyful sound" into my life. Send Your Holy Spirit to help me give You all the glory and praise, even in the midst of challenging times. May my life be inspiring to everyone I interact with today so they will yearn to walk "in the light of Your countenance" and know the joy You bring to all who love You. Amen.*

Music to Inspire Your Mind
- Contemporary Christian "Glorious" by Paul Baloche and Brenton Brown, performed by Paul Baloche.
- Orchestral "Glory Overture" by Michael W. Smith, arranged by David Hamilton, performed by the London Symphonica.
- Hymn "To God Be the Glory"—Text: Fanny J. Crosby, Music: William H. Doane, performed by Royal Albert Hall (London) Audience and Stage Choirs.

- Your music choice: _____

Nutrition to Strengthen Your Body

Peach-Blueberry Crumble

- 1 can (16 ounces) peach slices in light syrup, or 6 ripe peaches, peeled and sliced
- 3 cups fresh blueberries or 3 cups frozen whole blueberries
- Crumble topping: ¾ cup whole wheat or white flour, 1 teaspoon baking powder, ¼ teaspoon salt, ½ cup firmly packed brown sugar, 1 tablespoon cold margarine, and 1 egg or ¼ cup egg substitute
- ½ teaspoon ground cinnamon
- 1 tablespoon brown sugar
- 1 tablespoon wheat germ (optional)

Preheat oven to 375 degrees. Arrange peach slices in an even layer in an 8x13-inch baking dish. Scatter the blueberries over the peach slices. In a medium bowl, mix the flour, baking powder, salt, and brown sugar. Cut the margarine in by using a pastry blender or 2 knives. Add the egg and blend it in for 5-10 seconds. (The size of the crumbs should be large.) Sprinkle the crumble topping over the blueberries. In a small bowl, stir together the cinnamon, the remaining tablespoon of brown sugar, and the wheat germ (if desired). Sprinkle mixture over the topping. Bake until the topping is brown and the juices bubble up around the edges for 45-55 minutes.   8 servings

Stand Fast in the Faith with Love

May 12

The Word of God to Guide Your Soul
"Watch, stand fast in the faith, be brave, be strong. Let all that you do be done with love" (1 Corinthians 16:13-14).

> *Dear Lord, I love You and thank You for Your words of wisdom and encouragement. Send Your Holy Spirit to help me stand fast in the faith with courage, strength, and love. Show me the best way to handle situations where my faith is challenged. Let me always look to You for the right words to say and remind me to pray for all those who persecute You through me. Amen.*

Music to Inspire Your Mind
- Contemporary Christian "Stand Firm in the Faith" by Tito Cayamanda, Edwin Cruz, and Mimmon Vicente, performed by Ablaze Music.
- Vocal "Find Us Faithful" by Jon Mohr, performed by Steve Green.

- Hymn "My Faith Still Holds"—Text: Gloria Gaither and William J. Gaither, Music: William J. Gaither, performed by Gaither Vocal Band.
- Your music choice: _____

Nutrition to Strengthen Your Body

Ranch Potato Salad

- 6 medium potatoes (about 2 pounds), peeled and cubed
- 1 cup celery, sliced
- ¾ cup green or red sweet pepper, chopped
- ¼ cup red onion, finely chopped
- 1 cup low-fat ranch dressing
- ½ teaspoon dried dill weed
- 1 to 2 tablespoons of low-fat milk (if needed)

In a large saucepan, cook potatoes, covered, in a small amount of lightly salted boiling water until just tender, for about 20-25 minutes. Drain potatoes well. In a large mixing bowl, combine celery, green or red sweet pepper, and onion. Add cooked potatoes and toss to mix. Toss with ranch dressing and dill weed. Cover and chill for at least 5 hours. If the salad seems dry after refrigerating, stir in 1 to 2 tablespoons of milk to moisten.

8 servings

Be Rich in Mercy

May 13

The Word of God to Guide Your Soul
"Therefore be merciful, just as your Father also is merciful"
(Luke 6:36).

> *Dear Lord, I love You and thank You for Your abundant*
> *mercy, beyond my comprehension. Send Your Holy Spirit*
> *to remind me Your mercy is so much greater than all my*
> *sins. Grant me the grace and love to be merciful to all*
> *who have wronged me or disappointed me, as You are so*
> *forgiving and merciful to me. Amen.*

Music to Inspire Your Mind
- Contemporary Christian "Mercy" by Matt Redman and Jonas Myrin, performed by Matt Redman.
- Vocal "Mercy" by Mark Hall, Omega Levine, Sam De Long, and Tauese Tofa, performed by Casting Crowns.
- Hymn "There's a Wideness in God's Mercy"—Text: Frederick W. Faber, Additional Refrain and Music: Ed Bolduc, performed by Ed Bolduc.
- Your music choice: _____

Nutrition to Strengthen Your Body

Spring Vegetable-Rice Medley

- 1 package (16 ounces) mixed spring vegetables with asparagus
- 2 tablespoons olive oil
- 1 medium red bell pepper, cut into ¼-inch strips
- 1 medium sweet onion, chopped
- 4 cups cooked long grain and wild rice (or use 2 packages of ready rice, microwaved according to directions)
- 2 tomatoes, coarsely chopped and seeded
- ¾ teaspoon salt-free seasoning
- ½ teaspoon pepper (ground, if available)
- 1 can (15-16 ounces) garbanzo beans, rinsed and drained
- 1 package (10 ounces) frozen green peas, thawed

Microwave mixed vegetables according to package directions and drain. Meanwhile, in a large saucepan or Dutch oven, heat olive oil over medium-high heat. Saute bell pepper and onion for about 5 minutes, stirring occasionally, until onion is crisp-tender. Add vegetables to pepper and onions, along with remaining ingredients. Cook for 5-10 minutes, stirring frequently, until hot.   8 servings

Dwell Abundantly with the Spirit

May 14

The Word of God to Guide Your Soul
"But if the Spirit of Him who raised Jesus from the dead dwells in you, He who raised Christ from the dead will also give life to your mortal bodies through His Spirit who dwells in you" (Romans 8:11).

> *Dear Lord, I love You and thank You for sending Your Spirit to dwell within me and guide me. Help me be more open to Your Spirit and the abundant life You so want to give me out of Your unconditional love. Don't let me become so caught up in this life that I lose sight of my true destiny, an eternity with You. Let others see today in me the beauty of a Spirit-filled life. Amen.*

Music to Inspire Your Mind
- Contemporary Christian "Spirit of the Living God" by Mia Fieldes and Jacob Sooter, performed by Meredith Andrews.
- Vocal "Holy Spirit, Come Fill This Place" by CeCe Winans.
- Hymn "Spirit of the Living God"—Text and Music: Daniel Iverson, performed by Invitation Music.

- Your music choice: _____

Nutrition to Strengthen Your Body

Cheesy and Nutty Baked Potato Splits

- 2 large potatoes, microwaved (scrub and prick several times, cook on high for 5 minutes, turn and cook for 5 more minutes, let sit for at least 5 minutes)
- ¼ cup low-fat milk
- ½ cup low-fat cottage cheese
- ½ cup each chopped green pepper, chopped carrot, and sliced green onions (or whatever veggies you have on hand)
- 2 tablespoons sunflower seeds
- ½ cup reduced-fat Cheddar cheese, shredded
- ¼ teaspoon garlic powder
- ¼ teaspoon pepper
- 6 cherry tomatoes, halved

Preheat oven to 450 degrees. Halve and scoop out potatoes, leaving the ¼-inch pulp in shells. Mash potato pulp in a medium bowl. Add the remaining ingredients, except half of Cheddar cheese and cherry tomato halves. Gently mix to blend thoroughly. Mound into potato shells, dividing equally. Arrange 3 tomato halves on each, pushing slightly in. Sprinkle with remaining Cheddar cheese. Bake for 10-12 minutes until cheese is melted and potatoes are heated through.   4 servings

Give Thanks for Jesus' Victory Over Death

May 15

The Word of God to Guide Your Soul
"Death is swallowed up in victory. O Death, where is your sting? O Hades, where is your victory? The sting of death is sin, and the strength of sin is the law. But thanks be to God, who gives us the victory through our Lord Jesus Christ" (1 Corinthians 15:54b-57).

> *Dear Lord, I love You and thank You for Your sacrifice that makes victory over death possible. Help me to comfort myself and others with these words of hope as we wait for the day when we will be reunited with loved ones that have already passed on to new life in You. Send Your Holy Spirit to all who are grieving on this day and give them comfort and peace in knowing You have destroyed the power and sting of death and replaced it with the glory and joy of heaven. Amen.*

Music to Inspire Your Mind
- Contemporary Christian "Christ Is Risen" by Matt Maher and Mia Fieldes, performed by Matt Maher.

- Choral "Rise Up with Him" by Janet Vogt, performed by "Behold the Lamb" Choir.
- Hymn "The Strife Is O'er"—Text: Latin, 12th century, translated by Francis Pott, Music: Giovanni da Palestrina, adapted by Willam H. Monk, performed by Journeysongs Choir.
- Your music choice: _____

Nutrition to Strengthen Your Body

Fabulous Vegetable Stir-Fry

- 2 tablespoons olive oil
- 1 package (16 ounces) frozen stir-fry vegetables
- 1 clove garlic, minced, or ⅛ teaspoon dried, minced garlic
- 1 medium red bell pepper, cut into ¼-inch strips
- ¼ cup sweet onion, chopped
- ¼ teaspoon salt-free seasoning
- ¼ teaspoon basil
- Dash pepper to taste
- Light balsamic vinaigrette dressing, to taste

In a large nonstick skillet, heat olive oil over medium-high heat. Add stir-fry vegetable mix and cook according to directions. Mix in garlic, bell pepper, onion, salt-free seasoning, basil, and pepper. Stir-fry for about 2 minutes or until vegetables are crisp-tender. Serve over brown rice with balsamic dressing.

4 servings

Let God's Grace Abound in Your Life

May 16

The Word of God to Guide Your Soul
"But where sin abounded, grace abounded more, so that as sin reigned in death, even so grace might reign through righteousness to eternal life through Jesus Christ our Lord" (Romans 5:20b-21).

> *Dear Lord, I love You and thank You for Your beautiful gift of grace. Send Your Holy Spirit to let Your grace abound in my life now and forever in eternity. I am overwhelmed by Your love for me and Your never-ending forgiveness of my sins. Let others see today how thankful I am for Your overflowing and amazing grace. Amen.*

Music to Inspire Your Mind
- Contemporary Christian "Call It Grace" by Michael Farren, Jonathan Lowry, Chad Mattson, and Seth Mosley, performed by Unspoken.
- Vocal "Overflow" by Matt Maher.

- Hymn "Amazing Grace"—Text: John Newton and John P. Rees, Music: Traditional American melody, arranged by Edwin Othello Excell, arrangement and additional refrain by Chris Tomlin and Louie Giglio, performed by Chris Tomlin.
- Your music choice: _____

Nutrition to Strengthen Your Body

Italian Salad Blend—Mangia!

- ¼ cup canned artichoke hearts
- ¼ cup roasted red peppers
- 4 plum tomatoes
- 1 bag romaine salad blend (8-10 ounces)
- ¼ cup green olives, sliced
- ½ cup seasoned croutons
- ¼ cup light Italian salad dressing

Dice artichokes and red peppers into small, bite-size pieces. Quarter tomatoes lengthwise. In a large salad bowl, combine salad blend, artichokes, peppers, tomatoes, and olives. Chill until ready to serve. Add croutons and salad dressing; toss and serve.   6-8 servings

Dwell in the Beauty of God's Goodness and Mercy

May 17

The Word of God to Guide Your Soul
"Surely goodness and mercy shall follow me all the days of my life; and I will dwell in the house of the LORD forever" (Psalm 23:6).

> *Dear Lord, I love You and thank You for all of the beautiful things You have created, but mostly I thank You for Your beautiful goodness and mercy. Thank you for pursuing me, even when I was lost and following my own path. Send Your Holy Spirit to keep me close to Your unconditional love so that "I will dwell in the house of the LORD forever." Let me also have a part in leading others to Your forever home. Amen.*

Music to Inspire Your Mind
- Contemporary Christian "Beautiful One" by Tim Hughes, performed by Jeremy Camp.
- Vocal "Psalm 23" by Steve Merkel, performed by Don Moen.
- Hymn "The King of Love My Shepherd Is"—Text: Henry Baker, Music: Traditional Irish Melody, arranged by Tony Alonso, performed by Tony Alonso.

- Your music choice: _____

Nutrition to Strengthen Your Body

Breakfast for Dinner

- 2 baked potatoes
- ½ cup green peppers, chopped
- ½ cup sweet onion, chopped
- ½ teaspoon garlic powder
- ½ teaspoon basil
- Pepper to taste
- 2 teaspoons margarine
- 4 eggs or 1 cup egg substitute
- ¼ cup low-fat milk
- ½ cup reduced-fat mozzarella or other cheese, shredded
- 1-2 tomatoes, sliced

Clean and pierce potatoes with a fork. Cook on high in a microwave for 3 minutes; turn and cook for another 3 minutes. Let potatoes sit for 5 minutes and cut into bite-sized pieces. Add green pepper, onion, garlic powder, basil, and pepper to potatoes in a medium mixing bowl. Melt margarine over medium-high heat in a large non-stick skillet. Saute potato mixture for 2-3 minutes until tender. Reduce heat to medium. In a small bowl, beat eggs with milk and fold gently into the potato mixture. Cook until firm. Sprinkle with cheese and cover briefly until cheese is melted. Serve with sliced tomatoes.

4 servings

Rest in the Deep Peace of Christ

May 18

The Word of God to Guide Your Soul
"Peace I leave with you, My peace I give to you; not as the world gives do I give it to you. Let not let your heart be troubled, neither let it be afraid" (John 14:27).

> *Dear Lord, I love You and thank You for imparting Your peace to me and to a troubled world. Send Your Holy Spirit to grant me the grace to embrace Your peace and let go of worries and fears. Let my words and actions today impart Your peace to others. May they see how the world cannot give them peace but only faith and trust in You, dear Jesus. Amen.*

Music to Inspire Your Mind
- Contemporary Christian "Perfect Peace" by Laura Story.
- Choral "Deep Peace" by John Rutter, performed by Libera
- Hymn "Wonderful Peace"—Text: W. D. Cornell, Music: W. G. Cooper, performed by The Heritage Singers.
- Your music choice: _____

Nutrition to Strengthen Your Body

Greek Deep-Dish Pizza—Opa!

- 1 package crescent rolls
- ¼ cup olive oil
- ½ pound sliced, fresh mushrooms or 1 can (8 ounces) sliced mushrooms, drained
- ½ cup sweet onion, chopped
- 2 garlic cloves, minced, or ¼ teaspoon dried, minced garlic
- 1 package (10 ounces) frozen, chopped spinach, thawed
- ½ cup pitted Kalamata olives, quartered
- ½ cup chopped marinated artichoke hearts, drained and patted dry
- 1 tablespoon lemon juice
- 1 teaspoon each basil and oregano
- 1 cup reduced-fat mozzarella cheese, shredded
- 1 cup reduced-fat Feta cheese, crumbled
- 2 medium ripe tomatoes, sliced
- ½ cup seasoned bread crumbs

Preheat oven to 375 degrees. Separate dough into 8 triangles. Place in an ungreased 9-inch square pan or a 10-inch pie plate. Press in bottom and up sides to form crust. In a large skillet, heat olive oil over medium-high heat and saute mushrooms, onion, and garlic until tender. Add the remaining ingredients, except cheese, tomatoes, and bread crumbs. Heat through and spoon mixture into a crust-lined pan. Sprinkle with cheeses.

Coat both sides of tomato slices with bread crumbs and arrange over the top. Bake for 14-17 minutes or until crust is deep golden brown and cheese is melted.　　　6 servings

Presevere in Prayer and Gratitude

May 19

The Word of God to Guide Your Soul

"Rejoice always, pray without ceasing, in everything give thanks; for this is the will of God in Christ Jesus for you" (1 Thessalonians 5:16-18).

> *Dear Lord, I love You and thank You for every circumstance that has happened in my life. Send Your Holy Spirit to help me offer every situation up to You in prayer with gratitude. Even though I may not understand at the time, thank You for Your promise that all of my past, present, and future is guided by Your love and is Your will for me in Christ Jesus. Remind me to "pray without ceasing" for my family, friends, and all I meet today. Amen.*

Music to Inspire Your Mind

- Contemporary Christian "When We Pray" by Tauren Wells, Ethan Hulse, and Colby Wedgeworth, performed by Tauren Wells.

- Vocal "God Who Listens" by Chris Tomlin, David Garcia, Thomas Rhett, and Ashley Gorley, performed by Chris Tomlin, featuring Thomas Rhett.
- Hymn "The Lord's Prayer"—Text: Matthew 6:9-13, Music: Albert Hay Malotte, performed by Andrea Bocelli.
- Your music choice: _____

Nutrition to Strengthen Your Body

Slow Cooker Corn Pudding with Black Bean Salsa

Corn Pudding:
- 1 can (15 ounces) cream style corn
- 2 cans (15 ounces each) sweet corn, drained
- ½ cup margarine, melted
- ½ cup low-fat sour cream
- ½ package (4 ounces) light cream cheese, cubed
- 1 cup (8 ounces) reduced-fat sharp Cheddar cheese, shredded
- ½ cup low-fat milk
- 2 large eggs, slightly beaten, or ½ cup egg substitute
- 1 box (8.5 ounces) cornbread mix
- ¼ cup granulated sugar
- ½ teaspoon salt-free seasoning
- ½ teaspoon pepper
- Black Bean Salsa Topping: 1 can (15 ounces) black beans, rinsed, drained and 1 cup thick and chunky salsa, drained.

Spray slow cooker with nonstick cooking spray. Place all ingredients for corn pudding into slow cooker and stir to combine. Cover and cook on high for 5 hours or until mixture is set. In a small casserole, combine black beans and salsa. Microwave for 2-3 minutes. Serve as a topping for corn pudding.   12 servings

Focus Your Thoughts on Praiseworthy Things

May 20

The Word of God to Guide Your Soul
"Finally, brethren, whatever things are true, whatever things are noble, whatever things are just, whatever things are pure, whatever things are lovely, whatever things are of good report, if there is any virtue and if there is anything praiseworthy—meditate on these things" (Philippians 4:8).

> *Dear Lord, I love You and thank You for Your encouraging words to focus my thoughts on the positive and beautiful things in this world rather than dwelling on the negative. I can only do that with the help of the Holy Spirit, so please send Your Spirit in extra measure whenever my mind gets discouraged due to the evil we all have to constantly battle. Grant me the grace to help others be positive and focus on all that is good as I go about my day. Amen.*

Music to Inspire Your Mind
- Contemporary Christian Rock "Think on These Things" by Robert Hartman, performed by Petra.

- Vocal "Phil 4:8" by Christie Chong.
- Hymn "Beautiful Savior"—Text: Psalm 45:3, Music: Traditional Silesian melody, performed by Beyond 5.
- Your music choice: _____

Nutrition to Strengthen Your Body

Easy Italian Cauliflower

- 1 package (10.5 ounces) frozen cauliflower
- 1 tablespoon margarine
- ¼ cup seasoned Italian breadcrumbs

Prepare cauliflower according to package directions and drain. In a large nonstick skillet, melt margarine over medium heat. Add breadcrumbs. Cook and stir for about 5 minutes. Add cauliflower to the pan with breadcrumbs. Toss until well coated. Serve immediately. 4 servings

Delight in Knowing You Are an Heir to God's Eternal Kingdom

May 21

The Word of God to Guide Your Soul
"Then the King will say to those on His right hand, 'Come, you blessed of my Father, inherit the kingdom prepared for you from the foundation of the world'" (Matthew 25:34).

> *Dear Lord, I love You and thank You for this beautiful promise that You have prepared a place for me in Your kingdom, both now and forevermore. It is beyond my comprehension that You have thought of me since "the foundation of the world." Send Your Holy Spirit to help me live each day as Your obedient and grateful child. Grant me the courage today to share this amazing promise with someone who needs to understand what a good and loving Father You are. Amen.*

Music to Inspire Your Mind
- Contemporary Christian "Soon" by Brooke Ligertwood, performed by Hillsong United.

- Vocal "I Can Only Imagine" by Bart Millard, performed by MercyMe with London Symphony Orchestra.
- Hymn "Soon and Very Soon"—Text and Music: Andrae Crouch, performed by Faith Celebration Choir.
- Your music choice: _____

Nutrition to Strengthen Your Body

Butterfly Salad

- 4 large lettuce leaves
- 4 pineapple slices (canned or fresh)
- 1 can jellied cranberry sauce
- 1 cup low-fat cottage cheese
- 8 whole cloves

For each serving, place a lettuce leaf on a luncheon-size plate. Cut the pineapple slices in half and place back to back, butterfly fashion. Cut 4 slices of jellied cranberry sauce and then cut each in half. Place on the top of pineapple slices, layering so pineapple shows about ½ inch at the top. Place ¼ cup of cottage cheese along the center and 2 whole cloves at the top of cottage cheese as antennae. (Let your kids have fun helping you make these!)   4 servings

Cast All Your Cares Upon the Lord

May 22

The Word of God to Guide Your Soul
"Therefore humble yourselves under the mighty hand of God, that He may exalt you in due time, casting all your care upon Him, for He cares for you" (1 Peter 5:6-7).

Dear Lord, I love You and thank You for Your loving care. Send Your Holy Spirit to increase my faith in Your providence so my worries and anxious thoughts are dispelled. Remind me of all the times in the past You have seen me through difficult times and trials. Let me share with someone today why I never have to worry because the One who created heaven and earth is taking care of me. Amen.

Music to Inspire Your Mind
- Contemporary Christian "Run to the Father" by Ran Jackson, Matt Maher, and Cody Carnes, performed by Cody Carnes.
- Vocal "Holding My World" by Chris Tomlin, Christy Nockels, and Kristian Stanfill, performed by Kristian Stanfill.

- Hymn "Jehovah Jireh"—Text and Music: Merla Watson, performed by Don Moen and Integrity's Hosanna! Music.
- Your music choice: _____

Nutrition to Strengthen Your Body

Bean and Rice Bowl

- 1 package (8.5 ounces) whole grain medley rice (microwaveable ready rice)
- 1 can (15 ounces) black beans (or other favorite beans), rinsed and drained
- 1 cup salsa
- 4 ounces reduced-fat Cheddar or Mexican-blend cheese, shredded
- ½ cup prepared guacamole
- Hot sauce (optional)
- Multigrain tortilla chips, as desired

Prepare rice according to package directions. In a medium casserole dish, combine beans and salsa. Partially cover and microwave on high power until warmed through, for about 2-3 minutes. Stir in rice, partially cover, and cook until hot, for about 2-3 minutes longer. Divide into bowls and top with cheese and guacamole. Add hot sauce, if desired. Serve with tortilla chips.   3-4 servings

Remember Jesus is Always by Your Side

May 23

The Word of God to Guide Your Soul

"I will bring the blind by a way they did not know; I will lead them in paths they have not known. I will make darkness light before them, and crooked places straight. These things I will do for them, and not forsake them" (Isaiah 42:16).

> *Dear Lord, I love You and thank You for never forsaking me. Even when I turn away, You are always there to lead, guide, and make my "crooked places straight." Send Your Holy Spirit to keep me focused on the fact that You are always by my side, and I can always depend on You. Help me today to bring Your light into the darkness of this world. Amen.*

Music to Inspire Your Mind

- Contemporary Christian "By Your Side" by Jason Ingram, Michael Donehey, and Phillip LaRue, performed by Tenth Avenue North.

- Vocal "Imagine Me without You" by Rudy Perez and Mark Portmann, performed by Jaci Velasquez.
- Hymn "Under His Wings"—Text: William O. Cushing, Music: Ira D. Sankey, performed by the King's Heralds.
- Your music choice: _____

Nutrition to Strengthen Your Body

Mediterranean Chopped Salad

- 1 can (15 ounces) garbanzo beans, rinsed and drained
- 1 large cucumber, peeled and chopped
- 2 cups small cherry or grape tomatoes, cut in half
- 1 cup red, yellow, or orange bell peppers, chopped
- ½ cup Kalamata olives, pitted and chopped
- ½ cup red onion, chopped
- 6 ounces (about 1 cup) reduced-fat Feta cheese, crumbled
- Balsamic vinaigrette salad dressing (or other favorite vinaigrette dressing)

In a large salad or mixing bowl, mix all ingredients, except cheese and dressing. Add the Feta cheese and pour the salad dressing on top. Mix well to combine ingredients. (This can be made ahead and stored in a well-sealed container for up to 3 days.)   6 servings

Never Give Up on God's Love

May 24

The Word of God to Guide Your Soul

"For God so loved the world that He gave His only begotten Son, that whoever believes in Him should not perish but have everlasting life" (John 3:16).

> *Dear Lord, I love You and thank You for Your unfailing love and the promise of eternal life. Even when I don't love You as I should, You still love me. You don't see what I've been in the past, only what I can be in the future. Send Your Holy Spirit to grant me perseverance and faith so I never lose sight of Your love for me. Help me to pass Your love along to others today. Amen.*

Music to Inspire Your Mind

- Contemporary Christian "Your Love Never Fails" by Anthony Skinner and Chris McClarney, performed by Newsboys.
- Vocal "Oh What Love" by Elias Dummer, Eric Fusilier, Josh Vanderlaan, and Aaron Powell, performed by The City Harmonic.

- Hymn "Think about His Love"—Text and Music: Walter Harrah, performed by Kelly Willard and Rick Riso.
- Your music choice: _____

Nutrition to Strengthen Your Body

Pan Roasted Veggies

- ⅓ cup margarine
- ½ teaspoon thyme
- ½ teaspoon oregano
- ¼ teaspoon salt-free seasoning
- ¼ teaspoon pepper
- 3 cups cauliflower florets (about 1 medium head or 2 pounds)
- 2 cups broccoli florets (about 5 ounces)
- 2 cups (4 medium) carrots, julienne strips
- 2 small sweet onions, quartered

Preheat oven to 400 degrees. In a 13x9-inch pan, melt margarine over medium heat on the stovetop. Stir in thyme, oregano, salt-free seasoning, and pepper. Add vegetables and toss to coat. Cover with aluminum foil and bake for 25-27 minutes. (Get creative and change the vegetables as you like.)   6 servings

Turn to the Lord in Times of Temptation

May 25

The Word of God to Guide Your Soul
"No temptation has overtaken you except such as is common to man; but God is faithful, who will not allow you to be tempted beyond what you are able, but with the temptation will also make the way of escape, that you may be able to bear it" (1 Corinthians 10:13).

> *Dear Lord, I love You and thank You for giving me strength in times of temptation. Send Your Holy Spirit to help me remember You are always faithful and will provide "a way of escape" with any trial I may be going through. Remind me that all things are passing, and only Your love remains forever. Show me how I can be a comfort to a family member or friend today who is going through a time of trial or temptation. Amen.*

Music to Inspire Your Mind
- Contemporary Christian "Strong Enough" by Matthew West.

- Choral "A Prayer in Trial" by Heather Schopf and Hannah Schopf, performed by Forever Be Sure.
- Hymn "Through It All"—Text and Music: Andrae Crouch, performed by Lynda Randle.
- Your music choice: _____

Nutrition to Strengthen Your Body

Edamame Succotash

- 1 tablespoon olive oil
- 1 small sweet onion, chopped
- 2 cloves garlic, chopped, or ¼ teaspoon dried, minced garlic
- ½ cup red bell pepper, chopped
- ½ cup corn kernels (thawed, if frozen)
- 1 cup shelled edamame (thawed, if frozen)
- Salt-free seasoning and pepper, to taste

In a large skillet, heat olive oil over medium heat. Saute onion and garlic until softened for about 4 minutes. Add remaining vegetables and saute for another 3-4 minutes or until tender. Season to taste with salt-free seasoning and pepper. 6 servings

Depend on Jesus to Never Change

May 26

The Word of God to Guide Your Soul
"I am the Alpha and the Omega, the Beginning and the End, the First and the Last" (Revelation 22:13).

> *Dear Lord, I love You and thank You for being unchanging throughout all of time and space. Send your Holy Spirit to help me understand how You are always there for me and have loved me from the beginning of the universe. Thank you that even though I change daily and get distracted by so many worldly things, you never change. Help others see my faith today in Your unchanging love. Amen.*

Music to Inspire Your Mind
- Contemporary Christian "You Never Change" by Marcus Dawes, Aaron Ivey, and Jesse Reeves, performed by Austin Stone Worship.
- Vocal "I Am" by Mark Schultz.

- Hymn "Yesterday, Today, Forever"—Text: Albert B. Simpson, Music: James H. Burke, performed by Haven a cappella.
- Your music choice: _____

Nutrition to Strengthen Your Body

Egg Salad Stuffed Tomatoes

- 6 hard-cooked eggs, chopped (may only use egg whites, if desired)
- ⅓ cup pimiento-stuffed green olives, chopped
- ¼ cup celery, chopped
- 2 tablespoons red onion, chopped
- ¼ teaspoon dry mustard
- Dash pepper
- ½ cup plain low-fat yogurt or cottage cheese
- 2 large tomatoes, pulp removed and cut in half

In a medium bowl, combine ingredients; mash and stir until blended. (Makes about 2 cups.) Chill. Divide filling into tomato shells.   4 servings

Ponder the Infinite Mercies of God's Love

May 27

The Word of God to Guide Your Soul
"But God, who is rich in mercy, because of His great love with which He loved us, even when we were dead in trespasses, made us alive together with Christ (by grace you have been saved), and raised us up together, and made us sit together in the heavenly places in Christ Jesus, that in the ages to come He might show the exceeding riches of His grace in His kindness toward us in Christ Jesus" (Ephesians 2:4-7).

> *Dear Lord, I love You and thank You for Your matchless mercy and love. When I think how You loved me, even when I was still "dead in trespasses," I can't even begin to know how to thank You. Send Your Holy Spirit to keep me safe in the infinite mercy of Your love and never let me be separated from You again. Let Your love flow from me to all those I interact with today. Amen.*

Music to Inspire Your Mind

- Contemporary Christian "Because of Your Love" by Paul Baloche and Brenton Brown, performed by Paul Baloche.
- Vocal "Magnificent, Marvelous, Matchless Love" by Keith and Kristyn Getty, Matt Papa, Aaron Keyes, and Luke Brown, performed by Kristyn Getty.
- Hymn "And Can It Be?"—Text: Charles Wesley, Music: Thomas Campbell, performed by Stuart Townend.
- Your music choice: _____

Nutrition to Strengthen Your Body

Fast and Easy Berry Cobbler

- 2 bags (12 ounces each) frozen mixed berries (or berries of your choice)
- 1 box lemon cake mix (or cake mix of your choice)
- 1 can (12 ounces) clear soda (diet or regular)

Preheat oven to 350 degrees. In a 9x13-inch baking pan, spread out the 2 bags of frozen berries. Sprinkle the entire box of cake mix over berries. Break up any large lumps. Pour the can of soda evenly over the mixture. Do not stir. Let the mixture sit for 3-5 minutes. Bake for 45-50 minutes.   12 servings

Remember the Marvelous Works of the Lord

May 28

The Word of God to Guide Your Soul
"Seek the LORD and His strength; seek His face evermore! Remember His marvelous works which He has done, His wonders, and the judgments of His mouth" (Psalm 105:4-5).

> *Dear Lord, I love You and thank You for Your marvelous works and the beauty of all You have created. Send Your Holy Spirit to urge me to constantly seek Your face. Help me often remember how the Creator of the universe cares about me and will help me in any problem I may be facing. As I go through this day, dear Jesus, let me be a witness to Your most marvelous work of all—Your loving sacrifice on the cross, which lifted me from darkness to light. Amen.*

Music to Inspire Your Mind
- Contemporary Christian "Indescribable" by Laura Story and Jesse Reeves, performed by Chris Tomlin.
- Vocal "God, You're so Good" by Brooke and Scott Ligertwood, Kristian Stanfill, and Brett Younker, performed by Passion featuring Kristian Stanfill and Melodie Malone.

- Hymn "He Lifted Me"—Text and Music: Charles H. Gabriel, arranged by Jim Spencer, performed by Ryan Baird.
- Your music choice: _____

Nutrition to Strengthen Your Body

Cheesy Spanish Casserole

- 1 small sweet onion, chopped
- 1 medium green pepper, chopped
- 2 tablespoons olive oil
- 1 can (14.5 ounces) diced tomatoes
- 1 teaspoon Worcestershire sauce
- ¼ teaspoon pepper
- 1 can (16 ounces) pinto or butter beans, rinsed and drained
- 1 can (16 ounces) kidney beans, rinsed and drained
- 2 cups (8 ounces) reduced-fat mozzarella cheese, shredded

Preheat oven to 350 degrees. In a large skillet, sauté the onion and green pepper in olive oil over medium-high heat until tender. Reduce heat to medium. Add tomatoes and simmer for 10 minutes. Stir in the rest of the ingredients, except cheese. In a two-quart casserole, alternate layers of the bean mixture and mozzarella cheese. Bake for 30 minutes. Serve with brown rice, if desired.   6 servings

Set Your Mind on Heavenly Things

May 29

The Word of God to Guide Your Soul
"Set your mind on things above, not on things on the earth. For you died, and your life is hidden with Christ in God. When Christ who is our life appears, then you also will appear with Him in glory" (Colossians 3:2-4).

> *Dear Lord, I love You and thank You for Your great sacrifice on the cross, which allows me to become so close to You that my life is now "hidden" with Yours. Send Your Holy Spirit to help me focus "on things above, not on things on the earth," remembering all things are passing, and only Your love remains. Grant me the opportunity and courage today to share my hopes and dreams of being with You in glory someday with a family member, friend, or co-worker. Amen.*

Music to Inspire Your Mind
- Contemporary Christian "Better" by Pat Barrett, Ed Cash and Chris Tomlin, performed by Pat Barrett.

- Vocal "One Day" by Michael Cochren, Bryan Fowler and Matt Armstrong, performed by Cochren and Company.
- Hymn "I Am Resolved"—Text: Palmer Hartsough, Music: James H. Fillmore, performed by The Shotgun Rubies.
- Your music choice: _____

Nutrition to Strengthen Your Body

Tasty Sugar Snap Peas

- 1 package (16 ounces) frozen sugar snap peas
- 1 tablespoon margarine
- 1 garlic clove, minced, or ⅛ teaspoon dried, minced garlic
- ¾ teaspoon lemon-pepper seasoning
- ¼ teaspoon salt-free seasoning

Cook sugar snap peas according to package directions and drain. In a large skillet, melt margarine over medium heat and add seasonings. Add sugar snap peas. Cook and stir until well coated, 2-3 minutes. 4 servings

Put on the Whole Armor of God

May 30

The Word of God to Guide Your Soul
"Finally, my brethren, be strong in the Lord and in the power of His might. Put on the whole armor of God, that you may be able to stand against the wiles of the devil" (Ephesians 6:10-11).

> *Dear Lord, I love You and thank You for promising Your mighty power to those who call upon Your name. Thank you for all of the brave men and women who have given their lives in defending our freedoms, including our right to freely worship You. Send Your Holy Spirit to help me "put on the whole armor of God" and have the courage to always stand up for You and for what is right. Let me be an example to others of what it means to "stand against the wiles of the devil." Amen.*

Music to Inspire Your Mind
- Contemporary Christian "Stand in Your Love" by Josh Baldwin, Mark Harris, Ethan Hulse, and Rita Springer, performed by Josh Baldwin.

- Vocal "Christ Our Hope in Life and Death" by Keith Getty, Matt Papa, Jordan Kauflin, Matt Boswell, and Matthew Marker, performed by Matt Papa and Kristyn Getty.
- Hymn "Eternal Father, Strong to Save"—Text: William Whiting and Robert Nelson Spencer, Music: John Bacchus Dykes, performed by the United States Naval Academy Glee Club.
- Your music choice: _____

Nutrition to Strengthen Your Body

Veggie Burgers with Cucumber Sauce

- ½ cup low-fat sour cream
- ¼ cup cucumber, finely chopped
- ¼ teaspoon ground cumin
- ¼ teaspoon salt-free seasoning
- 1 tablespoon olive oil
- 1 package (12.8 ounces) vegetable burgers
- 4 lettuce leaves
- 4 slices ripe tomato
- 2 (8-inch) pita breads, cut in half, warmed

In a small bowl, combine sour cream, cucumber, cumin, and salt-free seasoning. Set aside. In a 10-inch skillet, heat oil over medium heat and add vegetable burgers. Cook until lightly browned (5-8 minutes), turning halfway through. To assemble burgers, place 1 lettuce leaf and 1 tomato slice inside each pita bread. Add 1 burger and about 2 tablespoons of cucumber sauce. 4 servings

Dwell Secure in God's Love

May 31

The Word of God to Guide Your Soul
"Lord, You have been our dwelling place in all generations. Before the mountains were brought forth, or ever You had formed the earth and the world, even from everlasting to everlasting, You are God" (Psalm 90:1-2).

> *Dear Lord, I love You and thank You for always being there for me. Even when I wasn't aware of it, You were thinking of me and loving me. Send Your Holy Spirit to give me a greater awareness of You in every moment of this day. Don't let me lose sight of Your constant presence and help. Let Your presence shine through me, so others can see how beautiful it is to dwell securely in Your love. Amen.*

Music to Inspire Your Mind
- Contemporary Christian "Always" by Jason Ingram and Kristian Stanfill, performed by Kristian Stanfill.
- Vocal "Glorious Christ" by Bob Kauflin, performed by Sovereign Grace.

- Hymn "O God, Our Help in Ages Past/To Every Generation"—
  Text: Isaac Watts, Music: William Croft, additional chorus
  by Bill Batstone, performed by Maranatha! Vocal Band.
- Your music choice: _____

Nutrition to Strengthen Your Body

Zucchini and Tomato Pasta Salad

- 1¼ cups (8 ounces) orzo, cooked, drained and cooled
  (may use other pasta of choice)
- 2 cups zucchini, thinly sliced
- ¾ cup green pepper, chopped
- ¼ cup green onions, thinly sliced
- 1 cup (8-ounce container) plain low-fat yogurt
- 1 teaspoon dill weed
- ¾ teaspoon salt-free seasoning
- ¼ teaspoon pepper
- 2 tomatoes, cut into wedges

In a large bowl, combine cooked, drained, and cooled orzo,
zucchini, green pepper, and onions. In a small bowl, combine
the yogurt, dill weed, salt-free seasoning, and pepper and
blend well. Pour yogurt mixture over the orzo mixture and toss
lightly. Chill. Add tomato wedges just before serving and toss
lightly. (Another variation is to use tzatziki sauce in place of
this yogurt mixture.)   4 servings

Seek Jesus Above All

June 1

The Word of God to Guide Your Soul
"He [Jesus] must increase, but I must decrease. He who comes
from above is above all; he who is of the earth is earthly and
speaks of the earth. He who comes from heaven is above all"
(John 3:30-31) (brackets added for clarity).

> *Dear Lord, I love You and thank You for giving up your*
> *beautiful heavenly home to come to earth to suffer and die*
> *for the love of me. When I start feeling that things aren't*
> *going my way today, send Your Holy Spirit to remind me*
> *that You must increase, and I must decrease. Remind me*
> *also that the way to true happiness is to seek You above all*
> *else and focus on loving You and others. Amen.*

Music to Inspire Your Min
- Contemporary Christian "Jesus Messiah" by Daniel Carson,
  Chris Tomlin, Ed Cash, and Jesse Reeves, performed by
  Chris Tomlin.
- Vocal "Above All" by Paul Baloche and Lenny LeBlanc,
  performed by Michael W. Smith.

- Hymn "More Precious than Silver"—Text and Music: Lynn De Shazo, performed by Lynn De Shazo.
- Your music choice: _____

Nutrition to Strengthen Your Body

Cheesy Broccoli Quiche

- 3 cups fresh broccoli florets, boiled for 4 minutes in 2 cups water and drained well, or 1 package (10 ounces) frozen broccoli florets, microwaved or cooked according to directions
- 2 cups (16 ounces) reduced-fat cottage cheese
- ¾ cup reduced-fat Cheddar cheese, shredded
- 1 cup sweet onion, chopped
- 3 eggs, beaten, or ¾ cup egg substitute
- 3 tablespoons grated Parmesan cheese
- Herbs, as desired (Suggestion: 1 teaspoon each dill weed, basil, and oregano)
- Nonstick olive oil cooking spray

Preheat oven to 375 degrees. Coat a 9-inch pie pan with cooking spray. In a medium-sized mixing bowl, combine the cottage cheese, cheddar cheese, onion, eggs, Parmesan cheese, and herbs. Stir the broccoli into the cheese mixture. Pour the mixture into the pie pan and bake for 35-45 minutes until the center of the quiche is set. Cool for about 10 minutes before serving. 6 servings

Rejoice and Be Glad

June 2

The Word of God to Guide Your Soul
"This is the day the LORD has made; we will rejoice and be glad in it" (Psalm 118:24).

> *Dear Lord, I love You and thank You for another day to love You and praise you. Help me to rejoice in all the circumstances that come my way so others may see the joy You bring to my life. Send your Holy Spirit to radiate through me and bring the gifts of Your joy and love to all I encounter today. Amen.*

Music to Inspire Your Mind
- Contemporary Christian "Hosanna (Praise Is Rising)" by Paul Baloche and Brenton Brown, performed by Paul Baloche.
- Vocal "Sing for Joy" by Lamont Hiebert, performed by Don Moen.
- Hymn "Rejoice, Ye Pure in Heart"—Text: Edward H. Plumptre, Music: Arthur H. Messiter, arranged by Jay Rouse, performed by the Lorenz Corporation Choir.

- Your music choice: _____

Nutrition to Strengthen Your Body

Bean Medley Salad

- 1 can (15 ounces) great northern beans, drained and rinsed
- 1 can (15 ounces) kidney beans, drained and rinsed
- 1 can (15 ounces) garbanzo beans, drained and rinsed
- 1 cup sweet onion, coarsely diced
- 1 cup light Italian, balsamic, or vinaigrette dressing (your choice!)
- Ground pepper to taste
- Lettuce leaves, tomato wedges

In a large mixing bowl, combine beans and onions together; mix lightly with dressing. Serve over lettuce leaves and garnish with pepper and tomato wedges. (Hint: make ahead and marinate in the refrigerator for several hours or up to 3 days. The longer the beans marinate, the better they taste!)

12 servings

Thank Your Guardian Angel for Watching Over You

June 3

The Word of God to Guide Your Soul
"For He shall give His angels charge over you, to keep you in all your ways" (Psalm 91:11).

> *Dear Lord, I love You and thank You for my guardian angel. Thank you for all the times I've been protected from danger and evil and didn't even know it! Send your Holy Spirit to help me be aware of my angel today and rest in the knowledge I have a defender and friend. I pray for protection from evil for all my family, friends, and those I interact with today. Keep them safe in Your loving arms and one day bring them home to love you and praise You with the angels and saints forevermore. Amen.*

Music to Inspire Your Mind
- Contemporary Christian "Whom Shall I Fear (God of Angel Armies)" by Chris Tomlin, Ed Cash, and Scott Cash, performed by Chris Tomlin.
- Choral "Angel" by Robert Prizeman, performed by Libera.

- Hymn "My Guardian Angel" by Elan Catrin Parry, Jon Cohen, Enzo De Rosa, and Phil Da Costa, performed by Elan Catrin Parry.
- Your music choice: _____

Nutrition to Strengthen Your Body

Chocolate and Berry Angelic Dessert

- 1½ cups small angel food cake cubes
- 1 cup raspberries, strawberries, or blueberries (or mixture)
- 1½ cups cold low-fat milk
- ¼ teaspoon vanilla
- 1 package (4-serving size) chocolate flavor instant pudding and pie filling (sugar free, if desired)
- 1 cup thawed light whipped topping

Divide cake cubes and berries evenly among seven dessert dishes or layer in an 8-inch square pan. Pour milk and vanilla into a medium bowl. Add pudding mix. Beat with wire whisk for 1 to 2 minutes or until well blended. Let stand 5 minutes. Gently stir in whipped topping. Spoon into dessert dishes or pan. Refrigerate for at least 2 hours or until ready to serve.

7 servings

Take Time to Reflect on Jesus' Love

June 4

The Word of God to Guide Your Soul
"But Mary kept all these things and pondered them in her heart" (Luke 2:19).

> *Dear Lord, I love You and thank You for the beautiful example of your mother, Mary. Help me to take moments during the day when I just pause and reflect on You and Your love. Send Your Holy Spirit to help me appreciate all the blessings You send my way, and show me how I can spread Your love and blessings to others. Amen.*

Music to Inspire Your Mind
- Contemporary Christian "Because of Your Love" by Phil Wickham.
- Vocal "Magnificat" by Keith and Kristyn Getty and Stuart Townend, performed by Kristyn Getty.
- Hymn "No One Ever Cared for Me like Jesus"—Text and Music: Charles F. Weigle, performed by Sandi Patty.
- Your music choice: _____

Nutrition to Strengthen Your Body

Mediterranean Sandwiches

- 10-ounce carton hummus in flavor of choice (Suggestion: olive tapenade)
- 8 slices of whole wheat bread (toasted, if preferred)
- 4 green lettuce leaves
- 2 cups alfalfa sprouts
- 1 medium cucumber, thinly sliced
- 1 medium tomato, sliced and halved
- ½ cup Greek yogurt or tzatziki sauce

Spread hummus mixture evenly on top of 4 slices of bread. Place 1 lettuce leaf on each slice. Divide alfalfa sprouts, tomatoes, and cucumber evenly among bread. Drizzle 1 tablespoon yogurt or tzatziki sauce over each sandwich. Top each with an additional slice of bread. Cut into fourths, diagonally.   4 servings

Count Your Blessings

June 5

The Word of God to Guide Your Soul
"Do not sorrow, for the joy of the LORD is your strength" (Nehemiah 8:10b).

> *Dear Lord, I love You and thank You for the many blessings you have given me that bring so much joy to my life. Thank You for Your tremendous sacrifice that opened the pathway to live with You forever in heaven. Thank You for a foretaste of heaven on earth through my family, my church, and the beauty of nature. Thank You also for the difficult times, as they help me learn to trust and depend on You. Send Your Holy Spirit to help me count my blessings throughout the coming day and to bless others with Your love, joy, and peace. Amen.*

Music to Inspire Your Mind
- Contemporary Christian "Counting Every Blessing" by Gareth Gilkeson and Chris Llewellyn, performed by Rend Collective.
- Vocal "Blessings" by Laura Story.

- Hymn "Count Your Blessings"—Text: Johnson Oatman, Jr., Music: Edwin O. Excell, performed by Guy Penrod.
- Your music choice: _____

Nutrition to Strengthen Your Body

Yellow Squash Casserole

- 3 medium yellow squash (about 1¾ pounds), sliced
- 1 cup sweet onion, chopped
- ½ cup cream of celery or mushroom soup, undiluted (lower in sodium and fat)
- ½ cup Italian bread crumbs
- ½ cup low-fat sour cream
- 1 jar (4 ounces) diced pimiento, drained
- ¼ teaspoon pepper
- ¼ teaspoon garlic powder
- ¼ teaspoon dried basil
- Nonstick olive oil cooking spray

Preheat oven to 350 degrees. In a large saucepan, cook squash and onion in a small amount of boiling water for 10 to 12 minutes or until tender. Drain well. Mash squash mixture with a potato masher. Add soup and the next 7 ingredients to squash mixture and mix well. Spoon into a 1½-quart casserole coated with cooking spray. Bake, uncovered, for 25 to 30 minutes or until thoroughly heated. 8 servings

Awaken to the Abundant Life

June 6

The Word of God to Guide Your Soul
"I have come that they may have life, and that they may have it more abundantly" (John 10:10b).

> *Dear Lord, I love You and thank You for blessing me with such an abundant life. Even if all is taken away, I still have You and the promise of eternal life. Help me to remain focused on You because when I take my eyes off of You, the world can be a dark and dreary place. Send Your Holy Spirit to awaken me to hope and the courage to live my life with passion. Bless all those that cross my path today with an abundant life in You. Amen.*

Music to Inspire Your Mind
- Contemporary Christian "Thrive" by Mark Hall and Matthew West, performed by Casting Crowns.
- Vocal "Awakening" by Chris Tomlin and Reuben Morgan, performed by Chris Tomlin.
- Hymn "How Can I Keep from Singing"—Text and Music: Robert Lowry, arranged and performed by Audrey Assad.

- Your music choice: _____

Nutrition to Strengthen Your Body

Nutty Pear and Raisin Salad

- 4 large pears, unpeeled and chopped into chunks
- 1 cup golden raisins
- ½ cup walnuts, coarsely chopped
- 1 teaspoon fresh grated lemon rind
- 1 cup low-fat cottage cheese
- ¼ cup plain Greek yogurt
- 1 tablespoon lemon juice
- 1 tablespoon honey

In a large bowl, toss together the pears, raisins, walnuts, and lemon rind. Place cottage cheese, yogurt, lemon juice, and honey into a blender and process for about 2 minutes until smooth and creamy. Pour cottage cheese dressing over pear mixture and stir to combine well. Chill until serving time.

4 servings

Reflect on All the Ways God Takes Care of You

June 7

The Word of God to Guide Your Soul

"I will love You, O LORD, my strength. The LORD is my rock and my fortress and my deliverer; my God, my strength, in whom I will trust; my shield, and the horn of my salvation, my stronghold" (Psalm 18:1-2).

> *Dear Lord, I love You and thank You for being my strength in times of trouble, my friend in times of need, and my deliverer every moment of the day. I'm sorry for the times I have not loved and trusted You as I should. Send Your Holy Spirit to keep my mind on Your love for me and my love for You. As I go through my day, show me how to pass Your loving care along to others. Amen.*

Music to Inspire Your Mind

- Contemporary Christian "Lord, I Need You" by Christy Nockels, Daniel Carson, Jesse Reeves, Kristian Stanfill, and Matt Maher, performed by Matt Maher.
- Vocal "I Lift My Hands" by Chris Tomlin, Louie Giglio, and Matt Maher, performed by Chris Tomlin.

- Hymn "A Mighty Fortress Is Our God"—Text and Music: Martin Luther, additional words and music by Matt Boswell, performed by Matt Boswell.
- Your music choice: _____

Nutrition to Strengthen Your Body

Spaghetti with Veggie Sauce

- 12 ounces thin whole wheat spaghetti (or other pasta, as desired)
- 1 medium green pepper, finely chopped
- 1 medium sweet onion, finely chopped
- 2 tablespoons olive oil
- 1 jar (24 ounces) spaghetti sauce
- 1 package (10 ounces) frozen chopped spinach, thawed
- 2 medium carrots, finely chopped or shredded
- ½ teaspoon garlic powder
- 1¼ teaspoons dill weed
- Grated Parmesan cheese (optional)

Cook spaghetti according to package directions and drain. Meanwhile, in a large nonstick skillet, saute green pepper and onions in olive oil over medium heat until tender. Add spinach, carrots, garlic powder, and dill weed; cover and cook 5 minutes longer. Add spaghetti sauce and heat through. Serve veggie sauce over spaghetti. Garnish with grated Parmesan cheese, if desired.   6 servings

Let God Transform You

June 8

The Word of God to Guide Your Soul
"But now, O LORD, You are our Father; we are the clay, and You our potter; and all we are the work of Your hand" (Isaiah 64:8).

Dear Lord, I love You and thank You for creating me in a special and wonderful way. Transform and mold me into Your instrument so my life will be perfectly in tune with Your will for me. Send Your Holy Spirit to lead me and guide me today so I may help lead others to Your love and mercy. Amen.

Music to Inspire Your Mind
- Contemporary Christian "The Potter's Hand" by Darlene Zschech, performed by Hillsong.
- Vocal "Change My Heart, O God" by Eddie Espinosa, performed by Maranatha! Music.
- Hymn "We Are an Offering"—Text and Music: Dwight Liles, performed by Chris Christian.
- Your music choice: _____

Nutrition to Strengthen Your Body

Fun Fruit Cobbler

- 2 packages (16 ounces each) frozen blueberries, thawed
- 1 can (8 ounces) crushed pineapple in juice, undrained
- ½ cup sugar
- 2½ tablespoons cornstarch
- ¼ teaspoon almond extract
- Nonstick cooking spray
- 1 package reduced-fat crescent roll dough
- 1½ teaspoons sugar
- ¼ teaspoon cinnamon

Preheat oven to 400 degrees. In a large saucepan, combine the first five ingredients. Bring to a boil over medium heat, stirring constantly. Cook for 1 minute or until thickened. Remove from heat and let cool slightly. Pour blueberry mixture into a 9-inch square baking dish coated with cooking spray. Set aside. Spread out crescent roll dough and cut into hearts or other shapes with 2-inch cookie cutters. (Get creative!) Place over fruit mixture and spray with cooking spray. Combine sugar and cinnamon; sprinkle evenly over the cobbler. Bake for 30 to 35 minutes or until crescent roll cut-outs are golden and filling is bubbly.   8 servings

Pursue Purity

June 9

The Word of God to Guide Your Soul
"Beloved, now we are children of God; and it has not yet been revealed what we shall be, but we know that when He is revealed, we shall be like Him, for we shall see Him as He is. And everyone who has this hope in Him purifies himself, just as He is pure" (1 John 3:2-3).

> *Dear Lord, I love You and thank You for making me Your child. Help me remember that I am a child of the One True King, especially when others are putting me down and making me question my worth. Send Your Holy Spirit to give me a purity of intention in everything I do and think. Grant me the grace to love others, even when they are unlovable. Amen.*

Music to Inspire Your Mind
- Contemporary Christian "Hello, My Name Is" by Matthew West.
- Vocal "To Be Like Jesus" by Dick and Melodie Tunney.

- Hymn "Whiter than Snow"—Text: James Nicholson, Music: William G. Fischer, performed by Neville Peter.
- Your music choice: _____

Nutrition to Strengthen Your Body

Mixed Vegetable Stir-Fry with an Orange Twist

- ½ cup orange juice
- 1 tablespoon reduced-sodium soy sauce
- ¼ teaspoon ground ginger
- ¼ teaspoon garlic powder
- 2 teaspoons honey
- 1 tablespoon cornstarch
- 1 tablespoon olive oil
- 1 package (10.8 ounces) frozen mixture of broccoli, cauliflower, and carrots (or other mixture, as desired)

Microwave vegetables for 3 minutes and set aside. In a small bowl, combine the first six ingredients. Mix until cornstarch is dissolved. In a large nonstick skillet, heat olive oil over medium heat. Add vegetables and cook, stirring frequently, for about 2 minutes. Stir orange juice mixture and pour over vegetables. Cook, stirring constantly, for a few minutes, until vegetables are evenly coated and sauce is thick and clear. Serve over brown rice or couscous.   4 servings

Have an Attitude of Gratitude

June 10

The Word of God to Guide Your Soul
"Now may He who supplies seed to the sower, and bread for food, supply and multiply the seed you have sown and increase the fruits of your righteousness, while you are enriched in everything for all liberality, which causes thanksgiving through us to God. Thanks be to God for His indescribable gift!" (2 Corinthians 9:10-11, 15).

> *Dear Lord, I love You and thank You so much for supplying my needs and working through me to further Your unshakable kingdom of love and mercy for all. Send Your Holy Spirit to grant me an attitude of gratitude all day, no matter what may come. "Increase the fruits" of all I do to serve You and let others see how thankful I am for the "indescribable gift" You are to me. Amen.*

Music to Inspire Your Mind
- Contemporary Christian "Thank You" by Ben Fielding and Reuben Morgan, performed by Hillsong.

- Vocal "My Heart Is Filled with Thankfulness" by Stuart Townend and Keith Getty, performed by Keith and Kristyn Getty.
- Hymn "I Just Want to Thank You Lord"—Text and Music: Judy Marshall, performed by Daywind.
- Your music choice: _____

Nutrition to Strengthen Your Body

Watermelon Star Salad

- Lettuce leaf
- ½ slice medium watermelon (1-inch thick)
- ½ cup reduced-fat cottage cheese
- 1 tablespoon blueberries

Wash lettuce leaf, pat dry with a paper towel, and place on a salad plate. Cut the watermelon slice into 5 wedges. Trim away the white part and green rind. Arrange melon wedges on the lettuce leaf in a circle with the points outward to make a star. Spoon ½ cup cottage cheese into the center of the watermelon star. Sprinkle the cottage cheese with the blueberries. 1 serving

Remember God's Promise of Mercy

June 11

The Word of God to Guide Your Soul

"Blessed are the merciful, for they shall obtain mercy. Blessed are the pure in heart, for they shall see God" (Matthew 5:7-8).

> *Dear Lord, I love You and thank You for Your unending mercy and faithfulness. Even when I strayed in the past, You never gave up on me. Help me, likewise, to be merciful to those in my life that have hurt me. Send Your Holy Spirit to enable me to see those people through Your eyes of love and forgive them. Amen.*

Music to Inspire Your Mind

- Contemporary Christian "From the Inside Out" by Joel Houston, performed by Hillsong.
- Vocal "Lord Have Mercy" by Steve Merkel, performed by Michael W. Smith and Amy Grant.
- Hymn "Wonderful, Merciful Savior"—by Dawn Rodgers and Eric Wyse, performed by Philips, Craig, and Dean.
- Your music choice: _____

Nutrition to Strengthen Your Body

Avocado Veggie Soft Tacos

- Bean mixture: ½ large sweet onion, diced, ¼ teaspoon garlic powder (or ½ teaspoon chili powder), ¼ teaspoon salt-free seasoning, ¼ cup water, 1 can (15 ounces) black beans, drained and rinsed (To save time, you can substitute a 16-ounce can of fat-free refried beans, warmed, for bean mixture.)
- 1 tablespoon olive oil
- 8 (6-inch) flour or corn tortillas
- Lettuce, spinach leaves, or shredded cabbage
- 1 medium avocado, sliced
- Salsa to taste
- Lime wedges (optional)

In a large skillet, heat 1 tablespoon of olive oil over medium-high heat. Add the onion and saute until softened, for about 2 minutes. Stir in seasonings. Add beans and water. Cover and simmer for 5 minutes. Partially mash beans. Taste and adjust seasonings, as desired. Stack tortillas on a microwave-safe plate and cover with a damp paper towel. Microwave in 30-second intervals until warm. Fill tortillas with black bean mixture (or refried beans), add lettuce, spinach, or cabbage, and then add avocado slices and salsa. Serve with lime wedges, if desired.   8 servings

Rest Assured God is with You

June 12

The Word of God to Guide Your Soul
"Behold, I am with you and will keep you wherever you go, and will bring you back to this land; for I will not leave you until I have done what I have spoken to you" (Genesis 28:15).

Dear Lord, I love You and thank You for Your promise that You will never leave me. Thank You for leading and protecting me through this life until I can come home to You. Send Your Holy Spirit to remind me throughout the day that You are protecting me, and I am never alone. Help me to comfort someone today that might be feeling lonely and depressed and fill that person with Your joy and peace. Amen.

Music to Inspire Your Mind
- Contemporary Christian "Your Grace Is Enough" by Matt Maher.
- Vocal "Unfailing Love" by Chris Tomlin, Cary Pierce and Ed Cash, performed by Chris Tomlin and Steven Curtis Chapman.

- Hymn "Just a Closer Walk with Thee"—Unknown composer, performed by Alabama.
- Your music choice: _____

Nutrition to Strengthen Your Bod

Strawberry Lemon-Lime Slushy

- 1 can (12 ounces) lemon-lime flavored soda (sugar-free, if desired)
- 1 package (10 ounces) frozen strawberries (or 1 cup fresh strawberries, sliced)
- 1 teaspoon lemon juice
- 3½ cups crushed ice

Combine all ingredients in a blender. Start the blender on low and increase speed until the mixture is smooth. Don't blend for too long. Pour into tall glasses.   3 servings

Shine Your Light

June 13

The Word of God to Guide Your Soul

"Let your light so shine before men, that they may see your good works and glorify your Father in heaven" (Matthew 5:16).

> *Dear Lord, I love You and thank You for another day to sing Your praises. Help me be a light to others, showing them the way to You. Send Your Holy Spirit to give me wisdom and joy so I may only show kindness and love to all I meet. Amen.*

Music to Inspire Your Mind

- Contemporary Christian "Shine a Light" by Chris Brown, Jane Williams, Matthew Ntlele, Steven Furtick, performed by Elevation Worship.
- Vocal "Go Light Your World" by Chris Rice.
- Hymn "We Are the Light of the World"—Text: based on the Beatitudes, adapted by Jean Anthony Greif, Music: Jean Anthony Greif, performed by the Spirit and Song Choir.
- Your music choice: _____

Nutrition to Strengthen Your Body

Light Potato Salad

- 7-8 (1 pound) small red potatoes
- 2 celery ribs, chopped
- 2 boiled eggs, peeled and chopped (may use only egg whites, if desired)
- ½ cup red onion, chopped
- ½ red or green bell pepper, chopped
- ¼ teaspoon each black pepper, garlic powder and dill weed
- ½ cup light ranch dressing or other favorite light dressing

Pierce potatoes with a fork and place on a paper towel in the microwave. Cook for 4 minutes and turn. Cook for another 4 minutes or until fork-tender. Cool and cut into cubes. In a large mixing bowl, combine potatoes, celery, onions, eggs, bell pepper, seasonings, and dressing. Cover and refrigerate for at least 2 hours before serving.   4 servings

Learn and Follow the Lord's Way

June 14

The Word of God to Guide Your Soul

"Show me Your ways, O LORD; teach me Your paths. Lead me in Your truth and teach me, for You are the God of my salvation; on You I wait all the day" (Psalm 25:4-5).

> *Dear Lord, I love You and thank You for Your goodness and patience in teaching me Your ways. Help me to study hard and learn all You long to teach me. Send Your Holy Spirit to open my heart and mind to the path You would like me to follow on this day. Bless me with the courage to lead others on the path to find Your love and goodness. Amen.*

Music to Inspire Your Mind

- Contemporary Christian "I Will Follow You" by Kristene DiMarco.
- Vocal "Follow Me" by Beth Farris, performed by Casting Crowns.
- Hymn "All the Way My Savior Leads Me"—Text: Fanny J. Crosby, Music: Robert Lowry, arrangement and additional

lyrics by Chris Tomlin and Matt Redman, performed by Chris Tomlin.

- Your music choice: _____

Nutrition to Strengthen Your Body

Summer Vegetable Saute

- 1 tablespoon olive oil
- 1 clove garlic, finely chopped, or teaspoon dried minced garlic
- ½ cup chopped sweet onion
- 1½ cups yellow summer squash, coarsely chopped or sliced
- 1 cup zucchini, coarsely chopped or sliced
- 1 tablespoon balsamic vinegar or vinaigrette dressing
- 1½ cups coarsely chopped tomatoes (about 2 medium)
- 1 teaspoon basil
- 1 teaspoon oregano
- ¼ teaspoon salt-free seasoning
- Dash of pepper

In a large skillet, heat olive oil over medium heat. Saute onion and garlic in oil for about 2-3 minutes, until onion is tender. Add vegetables and balsamic vinegar or dressing and saute for 3-4 minutes more, until vegetables are crisp-tender. Stir in tomatoes and seasonings, stirring frequently, until tomatoes are heated through.   4 servings

Hope in the Lord with All Your Heart

June 15

The Word of God to Guide Your Soul
"But sanctify the Lord God in your hearts, and always be ready to give a defense to everyone who asks you a reason for the hope that is in you" (1 Peter 3:15).

> *Dear Lord, I love You and thank You for blessing my heart with hope. I'm sorry for the times I have let worry cloud the beauty of my life with You. Send Your Holy Spirit to increase my faith, hope, and love so I can lead by example and inspire others to ask me to explain the reason for my great hope in You as my Lord and Savior. Amen.*

Music to Inspire Your Mind
- Contemporary Christian "Even If" by Bart Millard, David Garcia, Ben Glover, Tim Timmons, and Crystal Lewis, performed by MercyMe.
- Vocal "Hope in Front of Me" by Bernie Herms, Danny Gokey, and Brett James Cornelius, performed by Danny Gokey.

- Hymn "My Hope Is in the Lord"—Text and Music: Norman J. Clayton, performed by Matt Hoffland.
- Your music choice: _____

Nutrition to Strengthen Your Body

Scrumptious Spinach and Cheese Squares

- 3 eggs or ¾ cup egg substitute
- 6 tablespoons whole wheat flour (may also use white flour)
- 2 packages (10 ounces each) frozen, chopped spinach
- 16 ounces reduced-fat cottage cheese
- 8 ounces (2 cups) reduced-fat sharp Cheddar cheese, shredded (or other cheese, as desired)
- ½ teaspoon salt-free seasoning
- Nonstick olive oil cooking spray

Preheat oven to 350 degrees. Microwave spinach according to directions, drain well, and set aside. Meanwhile, in a large bowl, beat eggs and flour until smooth. Add cottage cheese, cheddar cheese, and salt-free seasoning to eggs and flour; mix well. Finally, stir in cooked spinach. Spray an 8x12-inch baking pan with cooking spray, and pour in the mixture. Spread evenly throughout the pan. Bake, uncovered, for 45 minutes. Let rest for at least 5 minutes before cutting into squares.   6-8 servings

Forgive and Forget

June 16

The Word of God to Guide Your Soul
"And be kind to one another, tenderhearted, forgiving one another, even as God in Christ forgave you" (Ephesians 4:32).

> *Dear Lord, I love You and thank You for dying on the cross and rising to new life so I may be forgiven of my sins. Send Your Holy Spirit to give me a forgiving heart toward all I meet today, even those who cut me off in traffic! Help me to truly forgive and forget all of my past hurts and disappointments with family, friends, and co-workers. Amen.*

Music to Inspire Your Mind
- Contemporary Christian "Forgiveness" by Matthew West.
- Vocal "A Heart That Forgives" by Kevin LeVar.
- Hymn "Freely, Freely"—Text and Music: Carol Owens, performed by Divine Hymns.
- Your music choice: _____

Nutrition to Strengthen Your Body

Lemon Parmesan Brussels Sprouts

- 1 package (10 ounces) frozen Brussels sprouts
- 2 teaspoons olive oil-based margarine
- 1 tablespoon lemon juice
- 1 tablespoon grated Parmesan cheese
- ½ teaspoon dried dill weed
- ⅛ teaspoon garlic powder
- Black pepper, to taste

Microwave Brussels sprouts according to package directions, drain, and set aside. Melt margarine in a small skillet or pan and add lemon juice, Parmesan cheese, dill weed, and garlic powder. Place Brussels sprouts in the serving dish and pour warm margarine mixture over sprouts. Toss to combine. Sprinkle on pepper, as desired.   4 servings

Trust that All Things Work for Good

June 17

The Word of God to Guide Your Soul
"And we know that all things work together for good to those who love God, to those who are called according to His purpose" (Romans 8:28).

> *Dear Lord, I love You and thank You for Your promise that all things work for good for those who love You. Send Your Holy Spirit to help me place all my trust in You, even when things look bleak and frightening. Help others to see my faith in You throughout this day so they will seek Your love and find Your purpose for their lives. Amen.*

Music to Inspire Your Mind
- Contemporary Christian "Your Love Never Fails" by Anthony Skinner and Chris McClarney, performed by Chris Quilala and Jesus Culture.
- Vocal "Grace upon Grace" by Josh Wilson and Jeff Pardo, performed by Josh Wilson.

- Hymn "All Things"—Text and Music: Don Moen, performed by Integrity's Hosanna! Music.
- Your music choice: _____

Nutrition to Strengthen Your Body

Yogurt Fruit Salad

- 1 cup strawberries, cut in chunks
- 1 cup grapes, sliced in halves
- 1 cup blueberries
- ¼ teaspoon cinnamon
- ½ teaspoon vanilla extract
- ½ cup plain low-fat yogurt
- 2-4 teaspoons sugar (or 1-2 packets of sugar substitute)

In a medium bowl, combine fruits. In a small bowl, mix the remaining ingredients and blend well. Mix yogurt mixture with fruit and refrigerate for at least 1 hour.   6 servings

Follow Your Loving Shepherd

June 18

The Word of God to Guide Your Soul
"He will feed His flock like a shepherd; He will gather the lambs with His arm, and carry them in His bosom, and gently lead those who are with young" (Isaiah 40:11).

Dear Lord, I love You and thank You for being my Shepherd and watching over me. Send me Your Holy Spirit to help me hear Your voice and follow where You lead. Remind me to rest in Your most sacred heart when I get weary and discouraged. Carry my family, friends, and all those I meet today in Your strong and loving arms. Amen.

Music to Inspire Your Mind
- Contemporary Christian "Shepherd" by Amanda Cook (Bethel Music).
- Vocal "Shepherd of My Heart" by Dick Tunney and David Mark Baldwin, performed by Sandi Patty.
- Hymn "Good Shepherd of My Soul" by Fionan de Barra, Keith Getty, Kristyn Getty, and Stuart Townend, performed by Keith and Kristyn Getty.

- Your music choice: _____

Nutrition to Strengthen Your Body

Southwestern Veggies

- 1 package (10.8 ounces) frozen lightly seasoned southwestern corn (microwave in bag)
- 1 tablespoon olive oil
- ½ medium sweet onion, chopped
- 1 medium green or red pepper, chopped
- 1 medium tomato, cut in thin wedges
- ¼ teaspoon celery seed (optional)
- Dash black pepper

Microwave corn according to package directions. In a large skillet, heat olive oil over medium heat and saute onion and green or red pepper until tender, for about 8 to 10 minutes, stirring occasionally. Stir in tomato wedges, corn, and seasonings until heated through.   6 servings

Appreciate God's Glory in Nature

June 19

The Word of God to Guide Your Soul
"The heavens declare the glory of God; and the firmament shows His handiwork. Day unto day utters speech, and night unto night reveals knowledge" (Psalm 19:1-2).

> *Dear Lord, I love You and thank You for the beautiful nature You have created for everyone to enjoy. Send Your Holy Spirit to open my eyes to the wonder of the clouds in the sky, the incredible melodies the birds sing, and the majestic trees and flowers. Help me to sing Your praises throughout this day and spread that joy to all I see. Amen.*

Music to Inspire Your Mind
- Contemporary Christian "God of Wonders" by Steve Hindalong and Marc Byrd, performed by Third Day.
- Vocal "Creation Song" by Fernando Ortega.
- Hymn "This Is My Father's World"—Text: Maltbie D. Babcock; Music: Traditional English melody, performed by Amy Grant.

- Your music choice: _____

Nutrition to Strengthen Your Body

Grilled Vegetable Kabobs

- ½ cup light Italian dressing
- 1 tablespoon minced fresh parsley or 1 teaspoon dried parsley flakes
- 1 teaspoon dried basil
- 1 medium-size yellow squash, cut into 1-inch slices
- 1 medium-size zucchini, cut into 1-inch slices
- 1 large sweet onion, cut in chunks
- 8 cherry tomatoes
- 8 medium-size fresh mushrooms
- Nonstick olive oil cooking spray

Combine dressing, parsley, and basil in a small bowl; cover and chill. Alternate vegetables on 8 skewers. Coat grill rack with cooking spray; place on grill over medium heat. Place kabobs on a rack and cook 15 minutes or until vegetables are tender, turning and basting frequently with dressing mixture. Serving suggestion: place ½ cup rice on plate and top with 2 vegetable kabobs. (If you don't have a grill, you can roast the vegetable kabobs in the oven at 400 degrees for about 10-12 minutes in a shallow sheet pan in a single layer. Drizzle the dressing mixture over the vegetables and let sit for 10 minutes before baking. Serve immediately.)   4 servings

Do Not Fear

June 20

The Word of God to Guide Your Soul
"Are not two sparrows sold for a copper coin? And not one of them falls to the ground apart from your Father's will. But the very hairs of your head are all numbered. Do not fear therefore; you are of more value than many sparrows" (Matthew 10:29-31).

> *Dear Lord, I love You and thank You for how much You protect me, know me, and love me. Send Your Holy Spirit to calm me, especially when fear tries to overtake my thoughts. Remind me that You are in control, and nothing happens apart from Your will. Help me to comfort others as well when they experience fearful trials and tribulations. Amen.*

Music to Inspire Your Mind
- Contemporary Christian "Fear Not" by Kristene DeMarco, Seth Mosley, and Robby Busick, performed by Kristene DeMarco and Bethel Music.
- Vocal "Bridge over Troubled Water" by Paul Simon, performed by Josh Groban and Brian McKnight.

- Hymn "Love Divine, All Loves Excelling"—Text: Charles Wesley, Music: John Zundel, performed by National Lutheran Choir.
- Your music choice: _____

Nutrition to Strengthen Your Body

Frozen Watermelon Balls

- 1 whole watermelon, seedless
- 10-12 Popsicle sticks

Cut the watermelon in half, lengthwise. Using an ice cream scooper, scoop out balls of watermelon and place in loaf pans or deep baking pans. Push a Popsicle stick into the middle of each watermelon ball and freeze overnight.   10-12 servings

Have Courage and Be Kind

June 21

The Word of God to Guide Your Soul
"But love your enemies, do good, and lend, hoping for nothing in return; and your reward will be great, and you will be sons of the Most High. For He is kind to the unthankful and evil. Therefore, be merciful, just as your Father also is merciful" (Luke 6:35-36).

> *Dear Lord, I love You and thank You for Your kindness and mercy. Send Your Holy Spirit to give me the courage to be kind to those who are less than kind to me today. Grant me the grace to live unselfishly, "hoping for nothing in return." Help me to pray for those who persecute me and don't understand my love for You. Amen.*

Music to Inspire Your Mind
- Contemporary Christian "Kindness" by Chris Tomlin, Louie Giglio and Jesse Reeves, performed by Chris Tomlin and Passion.
- Vocal "Humble and Kind" by Lori McKenna, performed by Tim McGraw.

- Hymn "St. Theresa's Prayer" by John Michael Talbot.
- Your music choice: _____

Nutrition to Strengthen Your Body

Greek Sugar Snap Peas

- 1 package (10 ounces) frozen sugar snap peas
- 3-4 tablespoons light Greek salad dressing
- 2-3 tablespoons low-fat Feta cheese, crumbled

Microwave sugar snap peas according to package directions and drain. Toss with salad dressing and Feta cheese.   4 servings

Live for the One Who Loves You

June 22

The Word of God to Guide Your Soul
"I have been crucified with Christ; it is no longer I who live, but Christ lives in me; and the life which I now live in the flesh I live by faith in the Son of God, who loved me and gave Himself for me" (Galatians 2:20).

> *Dear Lord, I love You and thank You for Your amazing love and sacrifice! Send Your Holy Spirit to show me how to "live by faith" in all circumstances. Remind me that this world is temporary and passing, but my life with You is eternal. Help me to keep things in the right priority today and to pass Your love around to all I meet. Amen.*

Music to Inspire Your Mind
- Contemporary Christian "Amazing Love (You Are My King)" by Billy James Foote, performed by Hillsong.
- Vocal "The Love that You've Been Looking For" by Nick Lachey, performed by 98 Degrees.
- Hymn "My Savior's Love"—Text and Music: Charles H. Gabriel, performed by Don Moen.

- Your music choice: _____

Nutrition to Strengthen Your Body

Mushroom, Lettuce, and Tomato (MLT) Sandwich

- 1 Portobello mushroom, thinly sliced
- 1 tablespoon olive oil
- 3 teaspoons reduced-sodium soy sauce
- ⅛ teaspoon chili powder (optional)
- ⅛ teaspoon garlic powder
- Reduced-fat mayonnaise (if desired, add 1 teaspoon dry mustard powder to 3 tablespoons of mayo)
- 1 tomato, thinly sliced
- 2-4 romaine lettuce leaves (may also use spinach leaves)
- 2 slices of favorite bread, toasted

In a large skillet, heat olive oil over medium heat. Add soy sauce, chili powder, and garlic powder. Stir to mix well. Add mushroom slices and cook on each side for about 3-5 minutes, until the mushrooms have cooked down to about half their original size. Toast bread and spread with mayo on each slice. Layer the tomato slices and lettuce leaves on the bread. Then top with the mushroom "bacon."   1 sandwich

Take Up the Cause of Christ

June 23

The Word of God to Guide Your Soul
"For if we live, we live to the Lord; and if we die, we die to the
Lord. Therefore, whether we live or die, we are the Lord's"
(Romans 14:8).

> *Dear Lord, I love You and thank You for making me Your
> child. Send Your Holy Spirit to help me live only for You,
> and when You call me to my heavenly home, help me to die
> in Your grace. Grant me the courage to take up Your cause
> and be ever faithful. As I go through this day, let others see
> I truly live to do Your will. Amen.*

Music to Inspire Your Mind
- Contemporary Christian "None but Jesus" by Brooke
  Fraser, performed by Hillsong.
- Vocal "The Cause of Christ" by Kari Jobe, Benjamin
  Hastings, and Bryan Fowler, performed by Kari Jobe.
- Hymn "We Are God's People"—Text: Bryan Jeffery Leach,
  Music: Johannes Brahms, performed by Shawnee Press
  Church Chorale.

- Your music choice: _____

Nutrition to Strengthen Your Body

Mixed Vegetable Frittata

- 1 package (10.8 ounces) frozen broccoli, carrots, and cauliflower (or other mixture, as desired)
- 6 eggs, beaten or 1½ cups egg substitute
- ½ cup low-fat milk
- 1 tablespoon minced, dried onions
- 2 tablespoons prepared mustard
- ¼ teaspoon garlic powder
- ½ teaspoon dill weed
- ¼ teaspoon salt-free seasoning
- ⅛ teaspoon pepper
- ½ cup reduced-fat sharp Cheddar cheese, shredded (or other favorite cheese)
- Salsa (your favorite variety)
- Nonstick olive oil cooking spray

Microwave vegetables according to package directions. Drain and chop into smaller pieces. In a medium bowl, beat together eggs, milk, onions, and seasonings; stir in cooked vegetables. Coat medium skillet with cooking spray. Heat over medium-high heat. Pour in egg/vegetable mixture; reduce heat to medium-low and cook until eggs are set, for about 20-25 minutes. Top frittata with cheese, cover, and heat on low until cheese is melted. Serve with salsa warmed in a microwave.

6 servings

Be Filled with Peace and Gratitude

June 24

The Word of God to Guide Your Soul
"And let the peace of God rule in your hearts, to which also you were called in one body; and be thankful" (Colossians 3:15).

> *Dear Lord, I love You and thank You for sending me Your peace—the blessed peace the world cannot understand and provide. Send Your Holy Spirit to fill me with gratitude for all You have sacrificed for me to be with You for eternity. Help me to keep a calm and thankful heart throughout this day and let Your perfect peace shine through me to others. Amen.*

Music to Inspire Your Mind
- Contemporary Christian "Eye of the Storm" by Ryan Stevenson.
- Vocal "Perfect Peace" by Laura Story.
- Hymn "He Keeps Me Singing"—Text and Music: Luther B. Bridgers, performed by Babbie Mason.
- Your music choice: _____

Nutrition to Strengthen Your Body

Seashell Pasta Garden Salad

- 2 cups (8 ounces) seashell macaroni
- 1 cup low-fat cottage cheese
- 1 cucumber, peeled and thinly sliced
- 12 radishes, thinly sliced
- ½ cup celery, diced
- 1 tablespoon red onion, chopped
- 1 teaspoon salt-free seasoning
- ½ teaspoon dry mustard
- 3 tablespoons light Italian dressing (or other favorite dressing)
- Romaine lettuce leaves (optional)

Cook seashell macaroni according to package directions; drain and cool. (Rinse with cold water to cool quickly; drain well.) In a large bowl, combine remaining ingredients, except lettuce; toss with macaroni. Chill for at least 2 hours. Serve salad over lettuce leaves, if desired.   4 servings

Sing Praise to the Lord

June 25

The Word of God to Guide Your Soul
"Let the word of Christ dwell in you richly in all wisdom, teaching and admonishing one another in psalms and hymns and spiritual songs, singing with grace in your hearts to the Lord" (Colossians 3:16).

> *Dear Lord, I love You and thank You for the gift of music. Send Your Holy Spirit to grant me the grace to praise You throughout this day in my heart and in my actions. Help me to always lift You up in worship in a way that is pleasing and consoling to You and inspirational to others. Amen.*

Music to Inspire Your Mind
- Contemporary Christian "Ever Be" by Kalley Heiligenthal, Gabriel Wilson, Chris Greely, and Bobby Strand, performed by Aaron Shust.
- Vocal "Sing Your Praise to the Lord" by Rich Mullins, performed by Amy Grant.
- Hymn "Holy God, We Praise Thy Name"—Text: Ignace Franz, Music: from Te Deum (4th Century), arranged by

Michael Card and Craig Duncan, performed by Michael Card.

- Your music choice: _____

Nutrition to Strengthen Your Body

Easy Chili Baked Potatoes

- 4 Russet or Yukon Gold potatoes
- 1 can (15 ounces) vegetarian chili
- ½ cup reduced-fat sour cream
- 1 cup reduced-fat sharp Cheddar cheese, shredded (or other favorite cheese)
- Fresh parsley for garnish (optional)

Scrub potatoes and prick several times with a fork. Place on a paper towel in the microwave. Cook on full power for 5 minutes. Turn over and continue to cook for 5 more minutes. Poke with a fork to check if done. In the meantime, warm chili, according to directions. To serve, split open potatoes with a knife and squeeze the potato from both ends to open. Ladle chili into the center of the potato. Top with sour cream, cheese, and parsley, if desired. 4 servings

Keep an Eternal Point of View

June 26

The Word of God to Guide Your Soul
"And the Spirit and the bride say, 'Come!' And let him who hears say, 'Come!' And let him who thirsts come. Whoever desires, let him take the water of life freely" (Revelation 22:17).

> *Dear Lord, I love You and thank You for the gift of life-giving water and the promise of eternal life. Send Your Holy Spirit to grant me an eternal perspective on life, rather than getting so caught up in earthly problems and trials. Help me, today, to invite others to freely "take the water of life." Amen.*

Music to Inspire Your Mind
- Contemporary Christian "The Spirit and the Bride" by Leeland Mooring, Matt Maher, and Robbie Seay, performed by Matt Maher.
- Choral "Going Home"—Text: William Arms Fisher, Music: Antonin Dvorak (Largo theme from New World, Symphony No. 9), performed by Libera Choir.

- Hymn "My Savior First of All"—Text: Fanny J. Crosby, Music: John R. Sweney, performed by Joshua Cehulik.
- Your music choice: _____

Nutrition to Strengthen Your Body

Heavenly Banana Splits

- 2 small bananas
- 1 container (8 ounces) frozen strawberry yogurt
- 1 container (8 ounces) frozen vanilla yogurt
- 1 can (8 ounces) crushed pineapple in juice, drained
- ½ cup fresh or frozen blueberries
- ½ cup granola cereal

Peel and cut bananas in half lengthwise and place ½ banana in each of 4 bowls. Place 1 small scoop of strawberry frozen yogurt and 1 small scoop of vanilla frozen yogurt in each bowl on top of the banana slice. Top the strawberry yogurt with crushed pineapple and the vanilla yogurt with blueberries. Sprinkle each banana split with 2 tablespoons granola cereal.   4 servings

Welcome the Holy Spirit

June 27

The Word of God to Guide Your Soul
"For the kingdom of God is not eating and drinking, but righteousness and peace and joy in the Holy Spirit" (Romans 14:17).

> *Dear Lord, I love You and thank You for sending the Holy Spirit to be my comforter and companion. Help me to welcome and be aware of the Holy Spirit's guidance today. Enable me to bear the fruit of the Holy Spirit: love, joy, peace, patience, kindness, goodness, faithfulness, gentleness, and self-control. Amen.*

Music to Inspire Your Mind
- Contemporary Christian "Holy Spirit" by Bryan and Katie Torwalt, performed by Francesca Battistelli.
- Vocal "Spirit of the Living God" by Mia Fieldes and Jacob Sooter, performed by Meredith Andrews.
- Hymn "Holy Spirit, Breathe on Me" Text: Edwin Hatch, Music: B. B. McKinney, performed by Anne Jernigan.
- Your music choice: _____

Nutrition to Strengthen Your Body

Mediterranean Salad

- 2 cans (15 ounces each) sliced beets, drained
- ½ red onion, chopped
- ½ cup balsamic vinaigrette dressing
- ½ cup chopped walnuts or slivered almonds
- ½ cup reduced-fat Feta cheese, crumbled
- 3 tablespoons fresh parsley, chopped, or 1 tablespoon dried parsley
- ¼ teaspoon pepper

Mix beets, red onion, and balsamic dressing together and marinate 1 or more hours. (The longer you marinate, the better the flavor.) Toss the beet mixture with the remaining ingredients before serving.   8 servings

Praise God for His Lovingkindness

June 28

The Word of God to Guide Your Soul
"So I have looked for You in the sanctuary, to see Your power and Your glory. Because your lovingkindness is better than life, my lips shall praise You" (Psalm 63:2-3).

> *Dear Lord, I love You and thank You for Your lovingkindness. Send Your Holy Spirit to remind me, throughout this day, that You are the God of the universe and You created everything, yet You still love and care for me. Help me to worship and praise You in a way that is pleasing to You and shows others how much You mean to me. Amen.*

Music to Inspire Your Mind
- Contemporary Christian "God of All My Days" by Mark Hall and Jason Ingram, performed by Casting Crowns.
- Vocal "Behold Our God" by Jonathan Baird, Meghan Baird, Ryan Baird, Stephen Altrogge, performed by Sovereign Grace Ministries.

- Hymn "Come, Thou Fount of Every Blessing"—Text: Robert Robinson, Music: Traditional American melody, performed by Chris Rice.
- Your music choice: _____

Nutrition to Strengthen Your Body

Scrumptious Green Beans

- 1 pound fresh green beans
- 2 tablespoons olive oil
- ¼ cup vegetable broth
- 1 tablespoon chopped, fresh oregano or 1 teaspoon dried and crumbled
- Black pepper, to taste
- 1 cup frozen pearl onions
- ¼ cup seasoned bread crumbs
- ¼ cup slivered almonds

Trim green beans and slice into 2-inch sections. In a large nonstick skillet, heat olive oil over medium-high heat. Add green beans and saute for 1 to 2 minutes, stirring constantly, so beans cook evenly. Add broth, oregano, pepper, and onions. Blend well and cook, covered, over medium-low heat for 6-8 minutes, or until beans are tender-crisp. Transfer to a serving dish and sprinkle with bread crumbs and almonds.   6 servings

Fall Into Your Father's Arms

June 29

The Word of God to Guide Your Soul
"And the son said to him, 'Father, I have sinned against heaven and in your sight, and am no longer worthy to be called your son.' But the father said to his servants, 'Bring out the best robe and put it on him, and put a ring on his hand and sandals on his feet. For this my son was dead and is alive again; he was lost and is found'" (Luke 15:21-22, 24a).

> *Dear Lord, I love You and thank You for Your unconditional, merciful love. There have been so many times I've wandered away, and, like a loving Father, You're always there to welcome me back. Send Your Holy Spirit to prevent me from ever wandering away from You again. Show me how I can help to bring other wandering souls back to You, today and always. Amen.*

Music to Inspire Your Mind
- Contemporary Christian "Prodigal" by Mark Hall, performed by Casting Crowns.

- Vocal "When God Ran" by Benny Hester and John Parenti, performed by Phillips, Craig, and Dean.
- Hymn "Softly and Tenderly"—Text and Music: Will L. Thompson, performed by Carrie Underwood.
- Your music choice: _____

Nutrition to Strengthen Your Body

Melon Surprise

- 1 medium honeydew or cantaloupe melon
- 1 package (4-serving size) watermelon gelatin (use other flavors or sugar-free, as desired)

Cut melon in half lengthwise; remove seeds. Scoop out melon balls and divide between 4 parfait or 8-ounce glasses. Make gelatin according to package directions and pour over melon balls in glasses. Refrigerate 3 hours or until firm.   4 servings

Find Strength in the Way of the Lord

June 30

The Word of God to Guide Your Soul
"The way of the Lord is strength for the upright, but destruction will come to the workers of iniquity" (Proverbs 10:29).

> *Dear Lord, I love You and thank You for being my source of strength throughout this coming day. Send Your Holy Spirit to remind me that with You, all things are possible, even when I don't see a way out of a difficult situation. Help me always trust in You, so others may see the confidence I have in You and Your faithfulness. Amen.*

Music to Inspire Your Mind
- Contemporary Christian "Our God" by Chris Tomlin, Jonas Myrin, and Ed Cash, performed by Chris Tomlin.
- Vocal "Find Us Faithful" by Jon Mohr, performed by Steve Green.
- Hymn "O Beauty Ever Ancient"—Text (based on a prayer from St. Augustine) and Music: Robert F. O'Connor, SJ, performed by Journeysongs Choir.

- Your music choice: _____

Nutrition to Strengthen Your Body

Marinated Vegetable Snacks

- 2 cups fresh broccoli florets
- 2 cups fresh cauliflower, broken into flowerets
- 1 medium cucumber, halved and thinly sliced
- 1 cup fresh mushrooms, sliced
- 1 cup cherry tomatoes, halved
- 1 can (6 ounces) black pitted olives, drained
- ¾ cup light Italian salad dressing (or other favorite dressing)

In a large bowl, combine the vegetables. Add dressing and toss to coat. Cover and refrigerate for 24 hours to give time to marinate. Drain, if needed, and serve. (This can also be used as an appetizer and served with toothpicks.)   6 servings

Discover the Power of Christ in Your Weaknesses

July 1

The Word of God to Guide Your Soul

"And He said to me, 'My grace is sufficient for you, for My strength is made perfect in weakness.' Therefore most gladly I will rather boast in my infirmities, that the power of Christ may rest upon me. Therefore I take pleasure in infirmities, in reproaches, in needs, in persecutions, in distresses, for Christ's sake. For when I am weak, then I am strong" (2 Corinthians 12:9-10).

> *Dear Lord, I love You and thank You for my weaknesses, as they help me learn to depend on You rather than on myself. Send Your Holy Spirit to fill me with Your grace and power so I may step out in faith to follow Your will, even when I feel inadequate for the assignment You give me. Grant me the courage to leave my comfort zone today and reach out to someone who needs to hear about Your love. Amen.*

Music to Inspire Your Mind

- Contemporary Christian "Always" by Jason Ingram, performed by Kristian Stanfill.
- Vocal "You Raise Me Up" by Brendan Graham and Rolf Lovland, performed by Josh Groban.
- Hymn "God Will Make a Way"—Text and Music: Don Moen, performed by Don Moen.
- Your music choice: _____

Nutrition to Strengthen Your Body

Grilled Cheese and Tomato Sandwiches

- 1 large or 2 medium tomatoes
- 8 slices multigrain bread
- 8 slices reduced-fat sharp Cheddar or mozzarella cheese (or 4 slices of each)
- Olive-oil based margarine, as needed

Thinly slice the tomatoes and lay them on a paper towel. Let sit to release any water for about 15 minutes; pat dry. Lay out 4 slices of bread. Layer each with 1 slice of cheese, 2 slices of tomato, and 1 more slice of cheese. Top with remaining bread slices. Thinly and evenly spread margarine on top and bottom slices of bread. Place two sandwiches into a large, nonstick skillet over medium heat. Cover the skillet with a lid and cook until the bread is evenly golden brown, for about 2 minutes. Flip, cover again and cook until the bread is golden brown and the cheese is visibly melted, for about 2 minutes more. Repeat with the remaining sandwiches. 4 servings

Pray for Wisdom

July 2

The Word of God to Guide Your Soul
"How much better to get wisdom than gold! And to get understanding is to be chosen rather than silver" (Proverbs 16:16).

> *Dear Lord, I love You and thank You for another day to do Your will. Send Your Holy Spirit to grant me wisdom in every situation and to always look to You for guidance. There are so many distractions that tempt me to take my eyes off of You and cause me to start sinking in the ocean of the world's ways. Help me to ignore the world and always seek Your wisdom, love, and peace. Amen.*

Music to Inspire Your Mind
- Contemporary Christian "None but Jesus" by Brooke Fraser, performed by Hillsong.
- Vocal "Wisdom Song" by Laura Woodley Osman.
- Hymn "The Perfect Wisdom of Our God" by Keith Getty and Stuart Townend, performed by Keith and Kristyn Getty.
- Your music choice: _____

Nutrition to Strengthen Your Body

Homemade Sweet Potato Chips

- 2-3 medium sweet potatoes, peeled and thinly sliced
- 1-2 tablespoons olive oil
- Seasonings, as desired (some suggestions: salt-free seasoning, cinnamon, rosemary, lemon pepper, or garlic powder)

Line a large microwave-safe plate with two layers of paper towels or parchment paper. Put sweet potato slices in a bowl, then add the oil and seasonings. Toss to coat. Arrange as many potato slices on the paper towels in one layer without touching. Microwave at medium power for 1½ minutes. Flip over and microwave another 1½ minutes. If chips aren't crisp after 3 minutes, continue to microwave in 30-second increments until done. Chips should be dry and crispy. Monitor to be sure the chips don't burn. A little browning is okay. Serve with hummus, salsa, or yogurt-based dips.   6 servings

Believe and Be Blessed

July 3

The Word of God to Guide Your Soul
"Jesus said to him, 'Thomas, because you have seen Me, you have believed. Blessed are those who have not seen and yet have believed'" (John 20:29).

> *Dear Lord, I love You and thank You for blessing me with faith. Send Your Holy Spirit to increase my faith in times of doubt, especially when I question Your plan for my life. Thank you for Your example of mercy when You helped Thomas with his doubt. Help me to encourage someone today who may be dealing with doubts and despair. Amen.*

Music to Inspire Your Mind
- Contemporary Christian "They Just Believe" by Josh Wilson and Phillip LaRue, performed by Josh Wilson.
- Vocal "Hands That Are Holding Me" by Meredith Andrews, Tyler Miller, and Hank Bentley, performed by Meredith Andrews.
- Hymn "We Walk by Faith"—Text: Henry Alford, Music: Marty Haugen, performed by Marty Haugen and Choir.

- Your music choice: _____

Nutrition to Strengthen Your Body

Italian Cucumber Tomato Salad

- 2 cucumbers, sliced
- 6 Roma tomatoes, sliced
- ½ medium red onion, sliced
- 1 cup small mozzarella cheese balls or reduced-fat mozzarella, shredded
- 2 tablespoons olive oil
- 2 tablespoons lemon juice
- 1 tablespoon Italian seasoning
- Black pepper, to taste

In a large bowl, combine cucumber, tomatoes, onion, and mozzarella cheese balls. Gently toss. In a small bowl, whisk the olive oil, lemon juice, and Italian seasoning. Add to the veggies and cheese and toss. Sprinkle with pepper.   4 servings

Pray for All Government Leaders

July 4

The Word of God to Guide Your Soul
"Therefore I exhort first of all that supplications, prayers, intercessions, and giving of thanks be offered for all men, for kings and all who are in authority, that we may lead a quiet and peaceable life in all godliness and reverence" (1 Timothy 2:1-2).

Dear Lord, I love You and thank You for the blessing of our great country and those in authority that work so hard to preserve our freedoms and keep us safe. Send Your Holy Spirit to guide all of our government leaders and those in the service of our country, both home and abroad, that they would lead us with wisdom and justice. Help us all to show kindness and friendship to each other, no matter what our political affiliation. Amen.

Music to Inspire Your Mind
- Contemporary Christian "God Bless the USA" by Lee Greenwood.

- Orchestral "Liberty Fanfare" by John Williams, performed by Boston Pops Orchestra.
- Hymn "America the Beautiful"—Text: Katherine L. Bates, Music: Samuel A. Ward, performed by the US Navy Band Sea Chanters Chorus. (Nashville Children's Choir is beautiful as well.)
- Your music choice: _____

Nutrition to Strengthen Your Body

Patriotic Parfaits

- 2 packages (10 ounces each) frozen strawberries, halved and thawed
- 3 cups fresh blueberries, washed
- 2 containers (8 ounces each) of low-fat lemon yogurt
- 1 cup light whipped topping
- 1 cup granola

In six parfait glasses or other 8-ounce glasses, layer yogurt, strawberries, more yogurt, and then the blueberries. Finish with a dollop of light whipped topping and sprinkle granola on top for a tasty crunch. 6 servings

Slow Down and Be Amazed

July 5

The Word of God to Guide Your Soul
"All Your works shall praise You, O LORD, and Your saints shall bless you. They shall speak of the glory of Your kingdom, and talk of Your power" (Psalm 145:10-11).

> *Dear Lord, I love You and thank You for the wonder of Your beautiful creation all around me. Send Your Holy Spirit to open my eyes to see heaven breaking through to illuminate my earthly existence. Help me to keep the passion and excitement of childhood when I look at miracles surrounding me each and every day and help me to share that childlike awe and faith with others. Amen.*

Music to Inspire Your Mind
- Contemporary Christian "Blown Away" by Josh Wilson and Jeff Pardo, performed by Josh Wilson.
- Vocal "Across the Lands" by Keith Getty and Stuart Townend, performed by Kristyn Getty.

- Hymn "How Excellent Is Thy Name"—Text: Paul Smith and Melodie Tunney, Music: Dick Tunney, performed by Larnelle Harris.
- Your music choice: _____

Nutrition to Strengthen Your Body

Perfect Pea and Celery Salad

- 1 package (10.8 ounces) frozen peas, partially thawed
- 2 hard cooked eggs, chopped (may use only egg whites, if preferred)
- 1 cup (4 ounces) reduced-fat sharp Cheddar cheese, cubed or shredded (or other favorite cheese)
- 1 cup celery, diced
- ½ cup light ranch dressing or other favorite light dressing (enough to moisten)

In a medium mixing bowl, gently stir ingredients together, chill and serve. Can also be eaten immediately.   4 servings

Believe All Things Are Possible with God

July 6

The Word of God to Guide Your Soul
"But Jesus looked at them and said to them, 'With men this is impossible, but with God all things are possible'" (Matthew 19:26).

> *Dear Lord, I love You and thank You for Your promise that You are a God of miracles and unlimited possibilities. Send Your Holy Spirit to encourage me when others think negatively about my dreams and Your plans for my life. Help me to seek Your will and follow where You lead, even though there may be obstacles in my way. Amen.*

Music to Inspire Your Mind
- Contemporary Christian "Impossible Things" by Chris Tomlin, Brenton Brown, Chris McClarney, and Ed Cash, performed by Chris Tomlin and Danny Gokey.
- Vocal "Great Expectations" by Steven Curtis Chapman.
- Hymn "Only Believe"—Text and Music: Paul Rader, performed by Elvis Presley.

- Your music choice: _____

Nutrition to Strengthen Your Body

Parmesan and Veggie Couscous

- 1 package (5.8 ounces) roasted garlic and olive oil couscous
- 2 tablespoons olive oil
- ½ cup green bell pepper, chopped
- ½ cup sweet onion, chopped
- ⅛ teaspoon dried, minced garlic or 1 clove garlic, minced
- 1 medium tomato, chopped
- ¼ teaspoon basil
- Dash of pepper
- ¼ cup grated Parmesan cheese

Preheat oven to 350 degrees. Prepare couscous according to package directions. Meanwhile, in a large nonstick skillet, heat oil over medium heat. Saute green pepper, onion, and garlic for 3-4 minutes. Add tomatoes, basil, cooked and fluffed couscous, and pepper. Mix together and transfer to a 1½-quart casserole dish. Bake for 20 minutes and sprinkle with Parmesan cheese while still warm.   4 servings

Abound in Thanksgiving

July 7

The Word of God to Guide Your Soul

"As you therefore have received Christ Jesus the Lord, so walk in Him, rooted and built up in Him and established in the faith as you have been taught, abounding in it with thanksgiving" (Colossians 2:6-7).

> *Dear Lord, I love You and thank You for walking with me through life and into eternity. Send Your Holy Spirit to give me a thankful heart for all You have done for me. Let me never complain about my circumstances or what I don't have. I am Your child and, therefore, have everything I could possibly need or want. Let others see my thankfulness today, no matter what the day may bring. Amen.*

Music to Inspire Your Mind

- Contemporary Christian "For These Reasons" by Lincoln Brewster.
- Vocal "Grateful Heart" by Don Chapman and Adam Fisher, performed by Don Chapman.

- Hymn "Give Thanks"—Text and Music: Henry Smith, performed by Don Moen.
- Your music choice: _____

Nutrition to Strengthen Your Body

Peachy Cottage Cheese Salad

- 2 cups salad greens
- 2 medium peaches, sliced (or use 1 can sliced peaches, drained)
- 1½ cups low-fat cottage cheese
- Light raspberry vinaigrette (or other favorite flavors)

Layer the salad greens and peaches in two salad bowls. Top with the cottage cheese and drizzle with the vinaigrette.

2 servings

Spread God's Love Around

July 8

The Word of God to Guide Your Soul
"[Love] bears all things, believes all things, hopes all things, endures all things. And now abide faith, hope, love, these three; but the greatest of these is love" (1 Corinthians 13:7, 13, brackets added for clarity).

> *Dear Lord, I love You and thank You for reminding me about the importance of doing everything with love. Send Your Holy Spirit to increase in me the virtues of faith, hope, and love but, most of all, love. Help me remember that You are Love and show me how to spread You around to others today. Amen.*

Music to Inspire Your Mind
- Contemporary Christian "Greatest of These" by Joel Houston, performed by Hillsong United.
- Vocal "Love in Any Language" by Jon Mohr and John Mays, performed by Sandi Patty.

- Hymn "Faith, Hope, and Love"—Text and Music: David Haas, performed by David Haas, Kate Cuddy, and Rob Glover.
- Your music choice: _____

Nutrition to Strengthen Your Body

Spanish Veggie Lasagna

- 3 cans (8 ounces each) tomato sauce
- ¼ cup sweet onions, chopped
- ½ cup green peppers, chopped
- ¼ cup black olives, sliced
- 1 can (16 ounces) pinto beans or black beans, rinsed and drained
- ¼ teaspoon garlic powder
- ½ teaspoon dried oregano
- ½ teaspoon dried dill weed
- 6 (6-inch) corn or flour tortillas, cut into quarters
- 1 cup reduced-fat sharp Cheddar cheese, shredded (or other favorite cheese)
- Nonstick olive oil cooking spray

Preheat oven to 375 degrees. Spray a 9x13-inch baking pan with cooking spray. Spread ¼ cup of tomato sauce in the bottom of the pan. In a large bowl, combine remaining ingredients, except tortillas and cheese. Mix well. Arrange ⅓ of the tortilla sections over sauce in a pan. Spread ⅓ of sauce mixture over tortillas. Sprinkle with ⅓ of the cheese. Repeat layers two more times. Cover and bake for 20 minutes. Uncover and continue baking for 15 more minutes. Let stand for 5 minutes before serving. Serve with Spanish rice. 6 servings

Have Courageous Faith

July 9

The Word of God to Guide Your Sou

"She said to herself, 'If only I can touch his cloak, I shall be cured.' Jesus turned around and saw her, and said, 'Courage, daughter! Your faith has saved you.' And from that hour the woman was cured" (Matthew 9:21-22).

> *Dear Lord, I love You and thank You for Your unfailing love and encouragement. Send Your Holy Spirit to increase my faith in You, so I may know that with only one touch and glance Your way, You will impart healing power and grace. Help me to touch others with Your love today. Amen.*

Music to Inspire Your Mind

- Contemporary Christian "Walk by Faith" by Jeremy Camp.
- Vocal "Just One Touch" by Jordan Frye, Kim Walker-Smith, and Skyler Smith, performed by Kim Walker-Smith.
- Hymn "By Faith" by Keith and Kristyn Getty, and Stuart Townend, performed by Kristyn Getty.
- Your music choice: _____

Nutrition to Strengthen Your Body

Scrambled Eggs with an Asian Twist

- 6 eggs, beaten, or 1½ cups egg substitute
- 2 tablespoons olive oil
- 1 can (16 ounces) bean sprouts, drained
- 1 small sweet onion, chopped
- ¼ cup green pepper, chopped
- 2 tablespoons reduced-sodium soy sauce

In a large nonstick skillet, saute onion and green pepper in oil over medium heat until tender. Add eggs, bean sprouts, and soy sauce. Reduce heat, cook slowly, and fold eggs to scramble, occasionally stirring from outside edge of pan to center to allow uncooked egg to flow to the bottom of the pan. Cook until set but still moist.

4 servings

Remember the Hope You Have in Jesus

July 10

The Word of God to Guide Your Soul
"That the God of our Lord Jesus Christ, the Father of glory, may give to you the spirit of wisdom and revelation in the knowledge of Him, the eyes of your understanding being enlightened; that you may know what is the hope of His calling" (Ephesians 1:17-18a).

> *Dear Lord, I love You and thank You for giving me hope in spite of what may be happening around me. Send Your Holy Spirit to grant me a "spirit of wisdom and revelation" in knowing You more deeply. Help me guide others to an "enlightened" understanding of the hope that can be found in a personal relationship with their Savior and King. Amen.*

Music to Inspire Your Mind
- Contemporary Christian "Hope in Front of Me" by Bernie Herms, Danny Gokey, and Brett James Cornelius, performed by Danny Gokey.

- Vocal "Hope of the Broken World" by Carl Cartee and Jennie Lee Riddle, performed by Selah.
- Hymn "My Hope Is Jesus"—Text: Edward Mote and Ron Hamilton, Music: Ron Hamilton, performed by The Hamilton Family.
- Your music choice: _____

Nutrition to Strengthen Your Body

Veggie Pockets

- 1 package (10 ounces) roasted red pepper hummus (or other favorite flavor)
- 3 whole wheat pita breads, cut in half
- 2 cucumbers, peeled and sliced
- 1 cup carrots, shredded

Open the pita pockets and line them with cucumber slices. Next, fill each pita half with 3-4 tablespoons of the hummus; sprinkle shredded carrot on top. Get creative and use whatever leftover veggies you might have on hand!   6 servings

Trust in Jesus to Perfect and Strengthen You

July 11

The Word of God to Guide Your Soul

"But may the God of all grace, who called us to His eternal glory by Christ Jesus, after you have suffered a while, perfect, establish, strengthen, and settle you" (1 Peter 5:10).

> *Dear Lord, I love You and thank You for your promise to "perfect, establish, strengthen and settle" me. Send Your Holy Spirit to renew the joy of my salvation, giving me the strength and encouragement I need to follow You. Help me to show that same encouragement and love to all I meet today. Amen.*

Music to Inspire Your Mind

- Contemporary Christian "You Lead" by Jamie Grace, Toby McKeehan, Dave Wyatt, Gabe Patillo, and Tim Rosenau, performed by Jamie Grace.
- Vocal "Lord of My Life" by Matt Maher, Ran Jackson, and Jonathan Smith, performed by Matt Maher.

- Hymn "Trusting Jesus"—Text: Edgar P. Stites, Music: Ira D. Sankey, performed by the Hyles-Anderson College Choir.
- Your music choice: _____

Nutrition to Strengthen Your Body

Make-Ahead Three Bean Salad

- 1 can (15 ounces) green and wax bean blend, drained
- 1 can (8 ounces) kidney beans (may also use red or white beans), drained and rinsed
- ½ red bell pepper, cut into strips
- ½ medium red onion, sliced into thin rings
- 2 tablespoons olive oil
- ¼ cup apple cider or white vinegar
- 2 teaspoons white sugar
- ½ teaspoon garlic powder
- ½ teaspoon celery seed
- Salt-free seasoning and black pepper, to taste

In a large bowl, combine beans, bell pepper, and onion. In a small bowl, mix together the rest of the ingredients and pour over the bean mixture. Toss to coat with dressing. Cover and refrigerate for at least 12 hours. Toss again before serving.

6 servings

Appreciate You Are God's Handiwork

July 12

The Word of God to Guide Your Soul

"For You formed my inward parts; You covered me in my mother's womb. I will praise You, for I am fearfully and wonderfully made; marvelous are Your works, and that my soul knows very well" (Psalm 139:13-14).

> *Dear Lord, I love You and thank You for loving me into existence and creating me as a unique person with a special purpose in life only I can fulfill. Send Your Holy Spirit to make me the best version of myself and to always follow Your plan for my life. Help me to show others today how wonderful and unique they all are to God, their Father and Creator. Amen.*

Music to Inspire Your Mind

- Contemporary Christian "Symphony" by Josh Wilson and Wes Pickering, performed by Josh Wilson.
- Vocal "Fingerprints of God" by Steven Curtis Chapman.

- Hymn "O God, You Search Me"—Text (based on Psalm 139) and Music: Bernadette Farrell, performed by Journeysongs Choir.
- Your music choice: _____

Nutrition to Strengthen Your Body

Parmesan Brussels Sprouts

- 1 package (10.8 ounces) frozen Brussels sprouts
- ¼ cup Italian-style seasoned bread crumbs
- 2 tablespoons margarine
- ½ cup low-fat milk
- 1 can (10.75 ounces) condensed cream of celery or mushroom soup (lower in sodium and fat)
- ¼ cup grated Parmesan cheese

Microwave Brussels sprouts according to package directions, drain, and set aside. Meanwhile, in a small skillet, brown bread crumbs in margarine over medium heat. In a small saucepan, combine milk and soup. Heat through over medium-high heat. Place the microwaved Brussels sprouts in the serving dish. Pour on soup, sprinkle with Parmesan cheese, and top with the browned bread crumbs. Serve with a slotted spoon.   4 servings

Remember the Lord is Always with You

July 13

The Word of God to Guide Your Soul
"Though I walk in the midst of trouble, You will revive me; You will stretch out Your hand against the wrath of my enemies, and Your right hand will save me. The LORD will perfect that which concerns me; Your mercy, O LORD, endures forever; do not forsake the works of Your hands" (Psalm 138:7-8).

> *Dear Lord, I love You and thank You for promising to stay by my side every minute of every day. Send Your Holy Spirit to remind me of Your promise, even when I'm feeling alone and unsure of where my circumstances are leading. Help me to support all those I love with the same type of loyalty and faithfulness. Amen.*

Music to Inspire Your Mind
- Contemporary Christian "Jesus Loves Me" by Reuben Morgan, Chris Tomlin, and Ben Glover, performed by Chris Tomlin.
- Vocal "Faithful God" by Laura Story.

- Hymn "He Leadeth Me"—Text: Joseph Gilmore, Music: William B. Bradbury, performed by Candi Pearson.
- Your music choice: _____

Nutrition to Strengthen Your Body

Veggie-filled Potato Salad

- 2 pounds red potatoes, peeled, cooked, and chilled
- 1 tablespoon apple cider or rice wine vinegar
- ½ cup reduced-fat sour cream
- ¼ cup reduced-fat mayonnaise with olive oil
- 1 tablespoon yellow mustard
- 3 hardboiled eggs (2 eggs peeled and chopped, and 1 egg peeled and sliced for garnish)
- 1 cup cooked, mixed vegetables (use leftovers, if available)
- ½ medium red onion, finely chopped
- 3 celery stalks, finely chopped
- 1 medium dill pickle, finely chopped
- 3 teaspoons dried parsley (or ¼ cup fresh)
- Pinch of salt-free seasoning and pepper
- Paprika

Chop potatoes into bite-size chunks, then add to a large bowl. Sprinkle the vinegar and salt-free seasoning over potatoes. In a small bowl, combine sour cream, mayonnaise, and mustard. Add sour cream mixture and the rest of the ingredients to the potatoes, except one sliced hard-boiled egg and paprika. Gently stir to combine. Garnish with slices of egg and sprinkle with paprika. Refrigerate for at least 60 minutes before serving.

6 servings

Rest in the Arms of Jesus

July 14

The Word of God to Guide Your Soul

"Come to Me, all you who labor and are heavy laden, and I will give you rest. Take My yoke upon you and learn from Me, for I am gentle and lowly in heart, and you will find rest for your souls. For My yoke is easy and My burden is light" (Matthew 11:28-30).

> *Dear Lord, I love You and thank You for promising me rest and peace in the midst of this crazy world. Send Your Holy Spirit to remind me when I get busy and stressed today, I just need to come to You and rest in Your arms, for Your "yoke is easy" and Your "burden is light." Amen.*

Music to Inspire Your Mind
- Contemporary Christian "Rest in the Arms" by Matthew West, Doug Mckelvey, Jason Ingram, and Aaron Shust, performed by Aaron Shust.
- Vocal "I Will Rest in You" by Brent Bourgeois and Michelle Tumes, performed by Jaci Velasquez.

- Hymn "Like a River Glorious"—Text: Frances R. Havergal, Music: James Mountain, performed by Oasis Chorale.
- Your music choice: _____

Nutrition to Strengthen Your Body

Baked Oatmeal with Bananas and Berries

- 2 medium ripe bananas, sliced into ½-inch pieces
- 1 cup blueberries (divided)
- 1 cup strawberries, chopped into blueberry-size pieces (divided)
- ¼ teaspoon cinnamon
- 1 tablespoon honey
- Oat mixture: 1 cup uncooked quick oats, ½ teaspoon baking powder, ½ teaspoon cinnamon, and pinch of salt
- Milk mixture: 1 cup low-fat milk, 1 egg or ¼ cup egg substitute, 1 teaspoon vanilla extract, and 3 tablespoons of honey
- Nonstick olive oil cooking spray

Preheat oven to 375 degrees. Lightly spray an 8x8-inch (or a 9x9-inch) ceramic baking dish with cooking spray. Arrange the banana slices in a single layer on the bottom. Sprinkle half of the blueberries and strawberries over the bananas, ¼ teaspoon of the cinnamon, 1 tablespoon of the honey, and cover with foil. Bake for 15 minutes. In a medium bowl, combine the oats, baking powder, cinnamon, and salt; stir together. In a separate bowl, whisk together the milk, egg, vanilla extract, and honey.

Remove the fruit mixture from the oven, then pour the oat mixture over the fruit. Pour the milk mixture over the oats, distributing evenly. Sprinkle the remaining berries over the top. Bake the oatmeal for about 30 minutes, or until the top is golden brown and the oatmeal has set. Serve warm from the oven. 6 servings

Lean on the Lord for Strength and Courage

July 15

The Word of God to Guide Your Soul
"The LORD is my strength and song, and He has become my salvation; He is my God, and I will praise Him; my father's God, and I will exalt Him" (Exodus 15:2).

> *Dear Lord, I love You and thank You for being the source of my strength and courage on this day. Send Your Holy Spirit to comfort me and remind me that I can depend on You, no matter what happens. Show me how to be a source of strength and comfort to those who are going through trials and difficulties. Help me be Your shoulder for them to lean on. Amen.*

Music to Inspire Your Mind
- Contemporary Christian "Shoulders (On Your Shoulders)" by Ben Glover, Joel Smallbone, Luke Smallbone, and Tedd Tjornhom, performed by For King and Country.
- Vocal "Take Courage" by Kristene DiMarco, Jeremy Riddle, and Joel Taylor, performed by Kristene DiMarco.

- Hymn "It Is Well with My Soul"—Text: Horatio G. Spafford, Music: Philip P. Bliss, performed by Audrey Assad.
- Your music choice: _____

Nutrition to Strengthen Your Body

Lentil and Artichoke Salad

- 2 cans (15 ounces each) lentils, drained and rinsed
- 1 cup broccoli, chopped
- 1 cup cauliflower, chopped
- ½ small (½ cup) red pepper, chopped
- ½ cup Kalamata or ripe olives, pitted and chopped
- ¼ cup red onions, chopped
- 1 jar (6.5 ounces) marinated artichoke hearts, undrained
- ½ cup lime vinaigrette dressing, light Greek dressing, or other dressing, as desired

In a large bowl, combine all salad ingredients and mix well. Add dressing and toss to coat.   6 servings

Depend on God's Promises

July 16

The Word of God to Guide Your Soul
"For You are my hope, O Lord GOD; You are my trust from my youth. By You I have been upheld from birth; You are He who took me out of my mother's womb. My praise shall be continually of You" (Psalm 71:5-6).

> *Dear Lord, I love You and thank You for Your promise to take care of me and guide me. Send Your Holy Spirit to help me relax and enjoy life today, knowing You are my Father and Lord of my life. I let so many things take away the peace You long to give me in spite of what troubles may surround me or those that are dear to me. Allow all those I encounter today to see Your hope and joy in my life. Amen.*

Music to Inspire Your Mind
- Contemporary Christian "Build My Life" by Pat Barrett, Matt Redman, Brett Younker, Kirby Kaple, and Karl Martin, performed by Pat Barrett, featuring Chris Tomlin.
- Vocal "The Glorious Unfolding" by Steven Curtis Chapman.

- Hymn "Standing on the Promises"—Text and Music: R. Kelso Carter, performed by Alan Jackson.
- Your music choice: _____

Nutrition to Strengthen Your Body

Macaroni and Cheese with Veggies

- 1 box (6 ounces) whole grain macaroni and cheese
- 1 package (10.8 ounces) frozen mixed vegetables
- 1 tablespoon Dijon mustard
- ⅛ teaspoon Worcestershire sauce
- ⅛ teaspoon garlic powder
- ⅛ teaspoon pepper
- Parmesan cheese, grated (optional)

In a large saucepan, prepare macaroni and cheese, according to light prep directions. Prepare mixed vegetables according to package directions and drain. Add vegetables and the remaining ingredients to prepared macaroni and cheese. Sprinkle with Parmesan cheese, if desired.   4 servings

Trust in Your Good Shepherd

July 17

The Word of God to Guide Your Soul
"I am the good shepherd; and I know My sheep, and am known by my own. As the Father knows Me, even so I know the Father; and I lay down My life for the sheep" (John 10:14-15).

> *Dear Lord, I love You and thank You for being my good shepherd and watching over me. Send Your Holy Spirit to help me trust that You will always take care of me and those I love. Remind me that sheep are not load-bearing animals so I am meant to cast all my cares upon You. Grant me courage to share with others today how You are the Lord and Shepherd of my life. Amen.*

Music to Inspire Your Mind
- Contemporary Christian "Good Shepherd" by Jon Azzarello, performed by Mercy Hill Worship.
- Vocal "The Good Shepherd" by Mac Powell and Fernando Ortega, performed by Fernando Ortega.
- Hymn "Shepherd Me, O God"—Text and Music: Marty Haugen, performed by Marty Haugen.

- Your music choice: _____

Nutrition to Strengthen Your Body

Tasty Rice and Beans

- 1 medium green pepper, chopped
- 1 small sweet onion, chopped
- 1 medium tomato, chopped
- 2 ground garlic cloves or ¼ teaspoon dried, minced garlic
- 2 tablespoons olive oil
- 1 teaspoon salt-free seasoning
- 1 package (8.8 ounces) brown rice, microwave-ready
- 1 can (15 ounces) black or pinto beans, rinsed and drained
- Favorite salsa (optional)

In a large skillet, saute green pepper, onion, tomato, and garlic in olive oil over medium heat until tender. Reduce heat to low. Add microwaved brown rice, beans, and salt-free seasoning. Stir well, cover, and heat through for 10-15 minutes. Serve with favorite salsa on the side or put a dollop on top of each serving, as desired. 6 servings

Love Mercy and Walk Humbly

July 18

The Word of God to Guide Your Soul

"He has shown you, O man, what is good; and what does the Lord require of you but to do justly, to love mercy, and to walk humbly with your God?" (Micah 6:8).

> *Dear Lord, I love You and thank You for Your guidance in living a holy life. Send Your Holy Spirit to always inspire me to do what is just, love mercy, and walk in humility, putting others before myself. Thank you, Jesus, for Your example of being meek and humble of heart and help me to follow in Your footsteps today. Amen.*

Music to Inspire Your Mind

- Contemporary Christian "This Is the Way (Walk in It)" by Dave and Jess Ray (Doorpost Songs).
- Vocal "Litany of Humility" by Danielle Rose.
- Hymn "Micah 6:8" by Bob Sklar, performed by the Maranatha Singers.
- Your music choice: _____

Nutrition to Strengthen Your Body

Watermelon and Tomato Salad

- 2 cups watermelon, cut into bite-sized pieces
- 2 medium tomatoes, cut into bite-sized pieces
- 3 cups fresh salad greens (or more, if desired)
- ½ cup reduced-fat Feta cheese, crumbled
- ½ cup champagne vinaigrette (or other favorite salad dressing)

In a medium bowl, combine watermelon and tomatoes. Place salad greens in a serving bowl; top with watermelon and tomato. Sprinkle on crumbled Feta cheese and drizzle with dressing. Toss and serve. 6 servings

Look to the Lord for Help

July 19

The Word of God to Guide Your Soul
"I will lift up my eyes to the hills—from whence comes my help?
My help comes from the LORD, who made heaven and earth"
(Psalm 121:1-2).

Dear Lord, I love You and thank You for Your unfailing help. Send Your Holy Spirit to keep my eyes on You and not get caught up in the world with all its empty distractions. When I look at Your beautiful works in nature, keep me aware that You are the Creator of all that exists, and You can surely help me with anything that comes my way. Let others see that You are the source of all my help. Amen.

Music to Inspire Your Mind
- Contemporary Christian "I Will Lift My Eyes" by Bebo Norman and Jason Ingram, performed by Bebo Norman.
- Choral "My Help (Cometh from the Lord)" by Jackie Gouche Farris, performed by the Brooklyn Tabernacle Choir.
- Hymn "He Will Not Let You Fall" by Bill Batstone, performed by the Maranatha Singers.

- Your music choice: _____

Nutrition to Strengthen Your Body

Slow Cooker Veggie Spaghetti

- 2 tablespoons olive oil
- 1 medium sweet onion, chopped
- 1 cup carrots, chopped
- 2 cups fresh mushrooms, sliced, or 1 can (8 ounces) mushrooms, sliced and drained
- 1 medium green bell pepper, chopped
- 2 jars (24 ounces each) of your favorite meatless spaghetti sauce
- 12 ounces uncooked spaghetti (whole wheat or vegetable-based)
- Parmesan cheese, grated (optional)

In a medium skillet, heat oil over medium-high heat. Saute onions and carrots for 3 to 4 minutes, stirring frequently, until crisp-tender. Add in mushrooms and bell peppers; saute for an additional 2 to 3 minutes. Spoon vegetables into a slow cooker. Add spaghetti sauce to vegetables and mix well. Cover and cook on low heat setting for 8 hours or until vegetables are tender. Cook and drain spaghetti as directed on the package. Serve sauce over spaghetti. Sprinkle with Parmesan cheese, as desired. 6 servings

Look Forward to Heaven and Eternal Life

July 20

The Word of God to Guide Your Soul
"But you, beloved, building yourselves up on your most holy faith, praying in the Holy Spirit, keep yourselves in the love of God, looking for the mercy of our Lord Jesus Christ unto eternal life" (Jude 20-21).

> *Dear Lord, I love You and thank You for the hope of eternal life. Send Your Holy Spirit to fill me with the realization that heaven is my true home, and I am but a pilgrim on this earth. When I get tied up with the frustrations and trials of this life, remind me that all things are passing, and God alone never changes. Help me today to pass this hope along to others. Amen.*

Music to Inspire Your Mind
- Contemporary Christian "There Will Be a Day" by Jeremy Camp.
- Vocal "Another Time, Another Place" by Gary Driskell, performed by Sandi Patty and Wayne Watson.

- Hymn "Beyond the Sunset"—Text: Virgil P. Brock, Music: Blanche Kerr Brock, performed by B. J. Thomas.
- Your music choice: _____

Nutrition to Strengthen Your Body

Heavenly Strawberry Angel Food Cake

- 1 prepared angel food cake
- 2 cups frozen nonfat strawberry yogurt, slightly softened
- 1 tablespoon sugar
- 1 tablespoon cornstarch
- 1 cup orange juice
- ¼ teaspoon vanilla or almond extract
- 1½ cups sliced fresh strawberries (about 1 pint)

Slice cake horizontally into 3 layers. Place one layer on a serving plate; spread with 1 cup yogurt. Repeat with the second cake layer and remaining 1 cup yogurt; top with the remaining cake layer. Cover; freeze 1 to 2 hours or until firm. Meanwhile, combine sugar and cornstarch in a small saucepan. Stir in orange juice. Cook over medium heat, stirring constantly, until mixture comes to a boil and thickens. Remove from heat and stir in extract. Let cool. Combine orange juice mixture and strawberries in a bowl and stir gently. Cover and chill for 30 minutes. Serve over angel food cake.   8 servings

Receive Forgiveness

July 21

The Word of God to Guide Your Soul
"To Him all the prophets witness that, through His name, whoever believes in Him will receive remission of sins" (Acts 10:43).

> *Dear Lord, I love You and thank You for Your sacrificial death that made it possible for me to receive forgiveness of all my sins. Send Your Holy Spirit to help me forgive others, as You have forgiven me. Help me to forgive myself as well for all the times I have let You down. Thank You so much for Your amazing love and grace. You are truly my Lord and King! Amen.*

Music to Inspire Your Mind
- Contemporary Christian "Forgiven" by Chris Rohman, Dan Gartley, Mark Graalman, Matt Hammitt, and Peter Prevost, performed by Sanctus Real.
- Vocal "Amazing Love (You Are My King)" by Billy James Foote, performed by Hillsong.

- Hymn "O How He Loves You and Me"—Text and Music: Kurt Kaiser, performed by On Pointe.
- Your music choice: _____

Nutrition to Strengthen Your Body

Greek Scrambled Eggs

- 4 eggs or 1 cup egg substitute
- 1 tablespoon dried parsley
- ¼ teaspoon dried oregano leaves
- 2 tablespoons olive oil
- ½ cup sweet onions, chopped
- 4 ounces (¾ cup) garbanzo beans, drained and rinsed
- ⅓ cup reduced-fat Feta cheese, crumbled
- Salt-free seasoning, to taste
- Black pepper, to taste

In a medium bowl, beat together eggs, parsley, and oregano. In a large skillet, heat oil over medium heat. Add onions and saute for 2-3 minutes. Stir in garbanzo beans. Add egg mixture and stir occasionally to scramble. Stir in cheese until blended. Season with salt-free seasoning and pepper, as desired.

4 servings

Remember God is with You Now and for Eternity

July 22

The Word of God to Guide Your Soul

"Then I, John, saw the holy city, New Jerusalem, coming down out of heaven from God, prepared as a bride adorned for her husband. And I heard a loud voice from heaven saying, 'Behold, the tabernacle of God is with men, and He will dwell with them, and they shall be His people. God Himself will be with them and be their God'" (Revelation 21:2-3).

Dear Lord, I love You and thank You for Your promise to dwell with all Your people and me forever. Send Your Holy Spirit to comfort me with this promise when I get discouraged by the problems and evils of this world. Remind me that all will be made right someday, and justice and love will prevail. Help me to show others the joy I have in You even as I wait for You, as a bride waits for her groom. Amen.

Music to Inspire Your Mind

- Contemporary Christian "Come, Lord Jesus (Even So, Come)" by Chris Tomlin, Jess Cates, and Jason Ingram, performed by Kristian Stanfill.
- Vocal "The New Jerusalem" by Michael Card and Scott Brasher, performed by Michael Card.
- Hymn "Until Then"—Text and Music: Stuart Hamblen, performed by Linda McCrary-Fisher (at Billy Graham's funeral).
- Your music choice: _____

Nutrition to Strengthen Your Body

Colorful Bell Pepper Saute

- 2 tablespoons olive oil
- 1 large green bell pepper (seeded and cut into ½-inch strips)
- 1 large red bell pepper (seeded and cut into ½-inch strips)
- ½ medium sweet onion, sliced
- 2 cloves garlic, finely minced, or ¼ teaspoon dried, minced garlic
- 1 tablespoon basil
- 1 tablespoon parsley
- Salt-free seasoning, to taste

In a large skillet, heat oil over medium-high heat. Add the pepper strips and onions; saute for 5-7 minutes or until vegetables are desired tenderness. Turn the heat down to low and add the remaining ingredients. (Be creative with the seasonings!) Heat through and serve.   6 servings

Listen for the Holy Spirit's Guidance

July 23

The Word of God to Guide Your Soul
"Do you not know that you are the temple of God and that the Spirit of God dwells in you?" (1 Corinthians 3:16).

> *Dear Lord, I love You and thank You for the promise that Your Holy Spirit dwells in me. Open my eyes, ears, and heart to listen to Your guidance, and thereby become the person You created me to be, holy and consecrated to You. Come, Holy Spirit, and fill me with Your love and wisdom. Don't let me miss one word You speak! Amen.*

Music to Inspire Your Mind
- Contemporary Christian "I'm Listening" by Chris McClarney, Benji Cowart, and Josh Bronleewe, performed by Chris McClarney, featuring Hollyn.
- Vocal "Spirit Speaks" by David Leonard, Leslie Jordan, and Drew Cline, performed by All Sons and Daughters.
- Contemporary Worship Hymn "Spirit of the Living God" by Mia Fieldes and Jacob Sooter, performed by Meredith Andrews and the Vertical Church Band.

- Your music choice: _____

Nutrition to Strengthen Your Body

Sweet Potato and Pineapple Pie

- Crust: 2 tablespoons margarine, 2 tablespoons firmly packed brown sugar, 1 tablespoon maple syrup, ground cinnamon, as desired
- 1 can (8 ounces) pineapple chunks, drained
- Filling: 1 can (15 ounces) sweet potatoes, 1½ teaspoons vanilla extract, ¾ teaspoon ground cinnamon, and 1 tablespoon firmly packed brown sugar
- Nonstick cooking spray

Preheat oven to 350 degrees. Spray a 9-inch pie pan with nonstick cooking spray. In a small skillet, melt margarine over medium heat. Stir in brown sugar and maple syrup. Mix well and spread evenly over the bottom of the pie pan. Sprinkle with cinnamon, as desired. Arrange pineapple chunks in a single layer over crust mixture. In a large bowl, combine all sweet potato filling ingredients. Blend well with a fork or potato masher until smooth. Spread sweet potato mixture evenly over pineapple chunks. Cover with aluminum foil and bake for 45 minutes. Let sit for 5 minutes, then remove foil and serve. (You may also run a knife around the edge of the pan and invert onto a serving plate for an upside-down pie!)　　6 servings

Count Your Blessings and Give Thanks

July 24

The Word of God to Guide Your Soul

"Enter into His gates with thanksgiving, and into His courts with praise. Be thankful to Him, and bless His name. For the LORD is good; His mercy is everlasting, and His truth endures to all generations" (Psalm 100:4-5).

> *Dear Lord, I love You and thank You for all of my blessings. Thank you for salvation; thank you for my life, family, and friends; but, most of all, thank You for Your faithfulness in loving me, even when I don't return love for You as I should. Send Your Holy Spirit to help me love You and others with unconditional and faithful love like Yours. Amen.*

Music to Inspire Your Mind

- Contemporary Christian "10,000 Reasons (Bless the Lord)" by Matt Redman and Jonas Myrin, performed by Matt Redman.
- Vocal "The Beautiful Things We Miss" by Matthew West and AJ Pruis, performed by Matthew West.

- Hymn "What a Faithful God"—Text and Music: Robert and Dawn Critchley, performed by Islington Baptist Church Music Ministry.
- Your music choice: _____

Nutrition to Strengthen Your Body

Broccoli and Rice Stir-Fry

- 1 package (10 ounces) frozen chopped broccoli
- 1 tablespoon olive oil
- ½ cup sweet onion, chopped
- 1 clove garlic, minced, or ⅛ teaspoon dried, minced garlic
- 2 cups cooked brown rice
- 1 tablespoon reduced-sodium soy sauce
- Chow mein noodles (optional)

Microwave broccoli according to package directions. Drain well, and set aside. Prepare brown rice according to package directions to make 2 cups. Meanwhile, in a large skillet, heat oil over medium-high heat. Add onion and garlic; saute until tender, for about 3-4 minutes. Stir in broccoli, rice, and soy sauce. Reduce heat to medium-low and cook until mixture is thoroughly heated, stirring frequently. Garnish each serving with chow mein noodles if desired.   6 servings

Turn to the Lord for Comfort and Hope

July 25

The Word of God to Guide Your Soul
"May our Lord Jesus Christ Himself, and our God and Father, who has loved us and given us everlasting consolation and good hope by grace, comfort your hearts and establish you in every good word and work" (2 Thessalonians 2:16-17).

> *Dear Lord, I love You and thank You for comforting my heart as I travel through this amazing life You've given me with all its ups and downs. Send Your Holy Spirit when I forget to look to You for consolation, for only by looking to You will I find true hope. Help me to encourage others today with a "good word and work" that will inspire them to discover the hope found only in a personal relationship with You. Amen.*

Music to Inspire Your Mind
- Contemporary Christian "He Will Not Let Go" by Laura Story.
- Choral "Inscription of Hope" by Z. Randall Stroope, performed by the New Jersey Honor Choir. (Lyrics are

based on words found scrawled on a cellar wall by Jews hiding from the Nazis in Cologne, Germany, during World War II.)

- Hymn "Lord of All Hopefulness"—Text: Jan Struther, Music: Traditional Irish Melody, performed by choir and congregation at the Royal Wedding of Prince Harry and Megan Markle
- Your music choice: _____

Nutrition to Strengthen Your Body

Shell Pasta and Barbecue Bean Salad

- 8 ounces medium shell pasta (or other favorite pasta shape)
- 1 bag (16 ounces) frozen broccoli, corn and red peppers (or other favorite vegetable blend)
- 1 can (15 ounces) barbecue-style beans, undrained
- ½ cup light Italian dressing (or other favorite dressing)
- 1 tablespoon fresh parsley, chopped or 1 teaspoon dried parsley

In a large saucepan, cook pasta according to package directions; drain and return to the pan. Meanwhile, microwave vegetables, drain, and set aside. Add cooked vegetables, beans, dressing, and parsley to pasta. Stir so ingredients are thoroughly mixed. Serve warm or refrigerate to serve cold later.   8 servings

Share the Joy of the Lord

July 26

The Word of God to Guide Your Soul
"A man has joy by the answer of his mouth, and a word spoken in due season, how good it is! The light of the eyes rejoices the heart, and a good report makes the bones healthy" (Proverbs 15:23, 30).

> *Dear Lord, I love You and thank You for all You have sacrificed to bring me salvation and joy. Send Your Holy Spirit to renew that joy in me daily, especially during difficult days. Show me how to look beyond earthly circumstances and let my heart rejoice when I think about my heavenly home. Help me to bring joy to others today through my smiles, encouraging words, and positive attitude. Amen.*

Music to Inspire Your Mind
- Contemporary Christian "Shout for Joy" by Lincoln Brewster, Paul Baloche, and Jason Ingram, performed by Lincoln Brewster.
- Vocal "The Joy of the Lord" by Twila Paris.

- Hymn "Joy Unspeakable"—Text and Music: Barney Elliott Warren and Todd Agnew, performed by Todd Agnew.
- Your music choice: _____

Nutrition to Strengthen Your Body

Saucy Lima Beans

- 1 can (14.5 ounces) stewed tomatoes, seasoned with basil, garlic, and oregano
- 1 package (10 ounces) frozen lima beans
- ¾ cup celery, chopped
- Salt-free seasoning and pepper, as desired

In a large saucepan, heat tomatoes to boiling. Stir in the remaining ingredients. Heat to boiling again. Separate beans with a fork; reduce heat to medium-low. Cover and simmer until lima beans are tender, for about 5 minutes.   4 servings

Trust in God's Will for Your Life

July 27

The Word of God to Guide Your Soul
"And do not be conformed to this world, but be transformed by the renewing of your mind, that you may prove what is that good and acceptable and perfect will of God" (Romans 12:2).

> *Dear Lord, I love You and thank You for guiding me and keeping me on the right path of what is "good and acceptable and perfect." Send Your Holy Spirit to grant me discernment and trust in Your will for my life and those who I love. Enable me to surrender all into Your hands today and help me show others how beautiful it is to be transformed in Your love. Amen.*

Music to Inspire Your Mind
- Contemporary Christian "Trust in You" by Lauren Daigle, Michael Farren, and Paul Mabury, performed by Lauren Daigle.
- Vocal "Thy Will" by Bernie Herms, Emily Weisband, and Hillary Scott, performed by Hillary Scott.

- Hymn "Footsteps of Jesus"—Text: Mary B. C. Slade, Music: Asa B. Everett, performed by Steve Ivey—Celtic Hymns.
- Your music choice: _____

Nutrition to Strengthen Your Body

Seasoned Potatoes and Green Beans

- 1 tablespoon olive oil
- ½ cup sweet onion, chopped
- 1 cup water
- 1 teaspoon instant vegetable broth granules
- ¼ teaspoon thyme, crumbled
- Lemon pepper seasoning, to taste
- 6 small red potatoes, quartered
- 1 package (10 ounces) frozen cut green beans

In a large saucepan, heat olive oil over moderate heat. Add onion and saute for 3-4 minutes, until tender. Add water, vegetable broth granules, thyme, and lemon pepper seasoning; stir well. Next, mix in the potatoes and green beans. Bring mixture to a boil. Reduce the heat to medium-low, cover, and simmer for 15-20 minutes or until potatoes are tender. Drain liquid and serve. 4 servings

Rejoice in the Lord!

July 28

The Word of God to Guide Your Soul
"Glory in His holy name; let the hearts of those rejoice who seek the LORD! Seek the LORD and His strength; seek His face evermore!" (1 Chronicles 16:10-11).

> *Dear Lord, I love You and thank You for showing me Your glory and majesty all around me. Send Your Holy Spirit to constantly remind me to look up to You and rejoice in Your holy name, especially when the world tries to turn me away from You. Let my life this day be a testimony of Your love and mercy, and let me be Your hands and feet. Amen.*

Music to Inspire Your Mind
- Contemporary Christian "Lifesong" by Mark Hall, performed by Casting Crowns.
- Vocal "Come, People of the Risen King" by Keith and Kristyn Getty and Stuart Townend, performed by Kristyn Getty.
- Hymn "Jesus, Draw Me Ever Nearer (May This Journey)"—Music: Keith Getty, Text: Margaret Becker, performed by Margaret Becker, Maire Brennan, and Joanne Hogg.

- Your music choice: _____

Nutrition to Strengthen Your Body

Spinach and Artichoke Egg Squares

- 2 packages (10 ounces each) frozen, chopped spinach
- 2 tablespoons olive oil
- 1 pound fresh mushrooms, sliced or 1 can (8 ounces) sliced mushrooms, drained
- 1 medium sweet onion, chopped
- 1 clove garlic, crushed or teaspoon dried, minced garlic
- 2 jars (6 ounces each) marinated artichoke hearts (one drained and one with liquid)
- 6 eggs or 1½ cups egg substitute
- ¾ cup Parmesan cheese, grated
- 1 cup (4 ounces) reduced-fat sharp Cheddar cheese, shredded
- Dash of basil and salt-free seasoning
- Nonstick olive oil cooking spray

Preheat oven to 350 degrees. Microwave spinach according to package directions and drain, squeezing out excess moisture. Meanwhile, in a medium skillet, saute mushrooms, onions, and garlic in olive oil over medium-high heat for 4-5 minutes or until tender. In a large mixing bowl, slightly beat eggs and mix in the remaining ingredients. Pour into a 9x13-inch baking dish, sprayed with nonstick cooking spray. Bake covered for 40 minutes. Let sit for at least 5 minutes before cutting into squares to serve.   6 servings

Be Strong and of Good Courage

July 29

The Word of God to Guide Your Soul
"Have I not commanded you? Be strong and of good courage; do not be afraid, nor be dismayed, for the LORD your God is with you wherever you go" (Joshua 1:9).

> *Dear Lord, I love You and thank You for being with me wherever I go. Send Your Holy Spirit to grant me the courage to stay strong and steadfast no matter what may come my way today. Help others to see the confidence I have in You and Your plan for my life and for the world. Amen.*

Music to Inspire Your Mind
- Contemporary Christian "Take Courage" by Jeremy Riddle, Joel Taylor, and Kristene DiMarco, performed by Kristene DiMarco.
- Vocal "I Believe" by Eric Levi, performed by Katherine Jenkins and Andrea Bocelli.
- Hymn "I Am His, and He Is Mine"—Text: George W. Robinson, Music: James Mountain, performed by Amy Shreve.

- Your music choice: _____

Nutrition to Strengthen Your Body

Spaghetti Veggie Salad

- 8 ounces thin whole wheat spaghetti, broken into 1-inch pieces
- 1 pint cherry tomatoes, cut in half
- 1 large cucumber, peeled and diced
- 1 green or red bell pepper, seeded and diced
- ½ medium red onion, chopped
- 1 can (2.25 ounces) sliced black olives, drained
- 1 cup light Italian salad dressing (or other favorite dressing)
- ¼ cup Parmesan cheese, grated

Cook the pasta according to package directions; drain and rinse in cold water. In a large bowl, combine vegetables, olives, and pasta. Pour salad dressing over mixture, add Parmesan cheese, and toss until coated. Cover and refrigerate for at least 3 hours or overnight. (Be creative with this recipe. You can vary the vegetables to whatever you like. Maybe add some broccoli and cauliflower as well, or use up leftover vegetables.)

6 servings

Have a Childlike Faith and Wonder

July 30

The Word of God to Guide Your Soul
"Then Jesus called a little child to Him, set him in the midst of them, and said, 'Assuredly, I say to you, unless you are converted and become as little children, you will by no means enter the kingdom of heaven. Therefore whoever humbles himself as this little child is the greatest in the kingdom of heaven'" (Matthew 18:2-4).

> *Dear Lord, I love You and thank You for reminding me to have childlike faith. Send Your Holy Spirit to help me keep the wonder of You and all that You are to me. As I go through this day, remind me that I am Your child, a child of the King, and to show others I depend on You for everything. Amen.*

Music to Inspire Your Mind
- Contemporary Christian "I Wanna Go Back" by David Dunn, Benji Cowart, and Hank Bentley, performed by David Dunn.

- Vocal "Your Grace Still Amazes Me" by Shawn Craig and Connie Harrington, performed by Phillips, Craig, and Dean.
- Hymn "A Child of the King"—Text: Harriet E. Buell, Music: John B. Sumner, performed by Fountainview Academy Choir and Orchestra.
- Your music choice: _____

Nutrition to Strengthen Your Body

Asian Oats Pilaf

- 1½ cups oats (quick or old fashioned, uncooked)
- 1 egg, beaten, or ¼ cup egg substitute
- 1 cup fresh mushrooms, sliced or 1 can (4 ounces) sliced mushrooms, drained
- ½ cup green onions, sliced
- ½ cup celery, sliced
- 2 tablespoons olive oil
- ½ cup vegetable broth
- 2 tablespoons reduced-sodium soy sauce
- 2 teaspoons sugar
- 1 package (6 ounces) frozen snow pea pods, thawed

In a medium bowl, combine oats and egg, mixing until oats are thoroughly coated. In a large skillet, heat oil over medium heat and saute mushrooms, green onions, and celery for 3 to 4 minutes or until tender. Add oats mixture; cook, stirring constantly, for about 8 minutes or until oats are dry, separated, and lightly browned. In a small bowl, combine vegetable broth, soy sauce, and sugar. Add to the skillet and continue cooking for 3 to 5 minutes, or until liquid is absorbed, stirring occasionally. Reduce heat to low, add pea pods, cover, and heat through.

6 servings

Delight in Daydreaming About Your Eternal Home

July 31

The Word of God to Guide Your Soul

"For we know that if our earthly house, this tent, is destroyed, we have a building from God, a house not made with hands, eternal in the heavens. For in this we groan, earnestly desiring to be clothed with our habitation which is from heaven" (2 Corinthians 5:1-2).

Dear Lord, I love You and thank You for the reminder that my life on earth is temporary, and my real, forever life is in heaven with You. Send Your Holy Spirit to help me keep this perspective when trials and tribulations try to overwhelm me. Show me how to inspire others to look forward to their eternal home and to maintain hope and joy in a personal relationship with You in spite of the challenging circumstances that life here on earth can bring. Amen.

Music to Inspire Your Mind

- Contemporary Christian "Home" by Chris Tomlin, Ed Cash, and Scott Cash, performed by Chris Tomlin.
- Vocal "Eternity" by Brian Doerksen, performed by Vineyard Worship.
- Hymn "Goin' Home"—Text: William Arms Fisher, Music: Antonin Dvorak, performed by Libera.
- Your music choice: _____

Nutrition to Strengthen Your Body

Easy Pesto Vegetables

- 1 package (16 ounces) frozen broccoli, cauliflower, and carrots
- ⅓ cup prepared pesto (your choice)
- 2 tablespoons Parmesan cheese, grated

Prepare vegetables according to package directions and drain. In a medium bowl, toss vegetables and pesto. Serve warm and sprinkle with Parmesan cheese. 5 servings

Be Confident That Nothing Can Separate You from the Love of God

August 1

The Word of God to Guide Your Soul

"For I am persuaded that neither death nor life, nor angels nor principalities nor powers, nor things present nor things to come, nor height nor depth, nor any other created thing, shall be able to separate us from the love of God which is in Christ Jesus our Lord" (Romans 8:38-39).

> *Dear Lord, I love You and thank You for the promise that nothing in this universe can separate me from Your love. Send Your Holy Spirit to help me love and trust You with all my heart and show me how I can share Your wondrous, ever-present love to all those I meet along life's path today. Amen.*

Music to Inspire Your Mind
- Contemporary Christian "Nothing Ever (Could Separate Us)" by Ben Calhoun, Jason Ingram, and Seth Mosley, performed by Citizen Way.

- Vocal "The Power of Your Love" by Geoff Bullock, performed by Hillsong.
- Hymn "The Steadfast Love of the Lord"—Text and Music: Edith McNeill, performed by Dave Hunt.
- Your music choice: _____

Nutrition to Strengthen Your Body

Watermelon Star Fruit Salad

- 1 (1-inch thick) slice of whole watermelon or 2 (1-inch thick) slices of a half watermelon
- ¾ pound seedless green grapes, washed and separated into smaller clusters
- 1 pint blueberries, washed

Cut watermelon slice(s) into 5 wedges. On a large serving platter, arrange watermelon wedges with points facing outward to form a large star. Place clusters of grapes in the center of the star and put blueberries to fill in space between each wedge.   5 servings

Ask Jesus for an Abundant Life

August 2

The Word of God to Guide Your Soul

"I have come that they may have life, and that they may have it more abundantly" (John 10:10b).

> *Dear Lord, I love You and thank You for Your promise of an abundant life. Send Your Holy Spirit to help me fully realize what it means to live life "more abundantly," even when difficulties and trials come. Grant me the wisdom to be an encouragement to others today and help make their lives more abundant in peace and joy. Amen.*

Music to Inspire Your Mind

- Contemporary Christian "He Is With Us" by Chris Rademaker, Jodi King, and Seth Mosley, performed by Love and the Outcome.
- Vocal "My Wish" by Steve Robson and Jeffrey Steele, performed by Rascal Flatts.
- Hymn "I Then Shall Live"—Text: Gloria Gaither, Music: Jean Sibelius, performed by Gaither Vocal Band.
- Your music choice: _____

Nutrition to Strengthen Your Body

Garden Vegetables with Cheesy Rice

- 2 small cloves garlic, minced, or ¼ teaspoon dried, minced garlic
- 2 tablespoons olive oil
- Vegetables: 1 medium sweet onion, chopped, 1 large green or red pepper, chopped, 2 small summer squash, sliced, 1 package (10 ounces) frozen spinach, microwaved and drained, 1 can (4 ounces) sliced mushrooms, drained, or 6 large fresh mushrooms, sliced, and 2 large tomatoes, chopped
- 2 tablespoons Worcestershire sauce
- 2 tablespoons reduced-sodium soy sauce
- 1 can (6 ounces) tomato paste
- 2 tablespoons reduced-fat sour cream
- 1 ⅓ cups quick-cooking brown rice
- Salt-free seasoning and black pepper, to taste
- 2 cups (8 ounces) reduced-fat Cheddar cheese, shredded

In a large skillet, saute garlic, onion, and green or red pepper over medium heat in olive oil until onions are translucent. Stir in squash and spinach. Cook, stirring frequently, for 5 minutes. Add mushrooms and tomatoes; cook for another 5 minutes, continuing to stir frequently. Stir in the rest of the ingredients, except cheese, until well mixed. Cover and cook for 10 minutes, or until rice is done. Sprinkle cheese evenly over the top. Cover the skillet and heat for 3 minutes more, or until cheese is melted. Cut into wedges and serve.   6 servings

Let Nothing Make You Afraid

August 3

The Word of God to Guide Your Soul
"The LORD is my light and my salvation; whom shall I fear? The LORD is the strength of my life; of whom shall I be afraid?" (Psalm 27:1).

> *Dear Lord, I love You and thank You for being my light, my salvation, and my strength. Send Your Holy Spirit to give me courage and keep me focused on Your presence when I let fears creep into my life and my thoughts. Help me to comfort others when they are afraid and to remind them of Your unfailing love and help. Amen.*

Music to Inspire Your Mind
- Contemporary Christian "By Your Side" by Jason Ingram, Michael Donehey, and Phillip LaRue, performed by Tenth Avenue North.
- Vocal "Faith above Fear" by Issa Rodriguez, performed by Feast Worship, featuring Vanya Castor.
- Hymn "Hiding in Thee"—Text: William O. Cushing, Music: Ira D. Sankey, performed by Nashville String Machine.

- Your music choice: _____

Nutrition to Strengthen Your Body

California Tortilla Wrap

- ¼ cup light mayonnaise
- 1 tablespoon fresh lime juice
- 1 teaspoon grated lime peel
- 4 (8-inch round) whole wheat flour tortillas
- 1 package (5 ounces) fresh baby spinach leaves
- 1 package (8 ounces) chunky guacamole
- 1 medium red bell pepper, seeded and cut into strips
- 1 cup reduced-fat sharp Cheddar cheese, shredded

In a small bowl, combine mayonnaise, lime juice, and lime peel. Spread each tortilla evenly with the mayonnaise mixture. Arrange spinach leaves on top of the mayonnaise, then the guacamole, bell pepper strips, and ¼ cup cheese. Roll the tortillas up tightly. Place seam sides down on serving plates.

4 servings

Enrich Your Life with Heavenly Music

August 4

The Word of God to Guide Your Soul

"Let the word of Christ dwell in you richly in all wisdom, teaching and admonishing one another in psalms and hymns and spiritual songs, singing with grace in your hearts to the Lord" (Colossians 3:16).

> *Dear Lord, I love You and thank You for the heavenly music You provide to comfort and encourage me on my earthly journey. Send Your Holy Spirit to help me appreciate the beauty of so many wonderful "psalms and hymns and spiritual songs" You have inspired people to write. Let others see how my heart sings with Your grace as I go about my day. Amen.*

Music to Inspire Your Mind

- Contemporary Christian "Sing to the Lord" by Matt Crocker and Mike Guglielmucci, performed by Hillsong Worship.
- Vocal "Listen to Our Hearts" by Steven Curtis Chapman and Geoff Moore, performed by Casting Crowns.

- Hymn "Come, Christians, Join to Sing"—Text: Christian H. Bateman, Music: Traditional Spanish Melody, performed by Amen Choir.
- Your music choice: _____

Nutrition to Strengthen Your Body

Italian-style Frittata

- 2 medium potatoes, peeled and sliced
- 2 tablespoons olive oil
- ½ cup sweet onion, chopped
- ¼ cup green pepper, finely chopped
- 2 cloves garlic, minced, or ¼ teaspoon dried, minced garlic
- 2 cups fresh or 1 package (10 ounces) frozen chopped broccoli, thawed
- 6 eggs or 1½ cups egg substitute
- ¼ cup Parmesan cheese, grated
- ¼ cup water
- ½ teaspoon dried basil
- ⅛ teaspoon pepper
- ½ cup reduced-fat Monterey Jack cheese, shredded (or other favorite cheese)

In a large skillet, cook potatoes in olive oil over medium heat for 10 minutes, turning occasionally. Add onion, green pepper, and garlic. Saute until onion is tender. Add broccoli; reduce heat to medium-low. Cook, covered, for 5 minutes. In a medium bowl, beat together the remaining ingredients (except cheese). Pour over vegetables in the skillet. Cook, covered, over low heat for 10 to 15 minutes or until eggs are set. Sprinkle with cheese. Remove from heat. Cover and let stand for 5 minutes before serving.   6 servings

Follow in Jesus' Footsteps on Your Great Adventure

August 5

The Word of God to Guide Your Soul

"If you keep My commandments, you will abide in My love, just as I have kept my Father's commandments and abide in His love" (John 15:10).

> *Dear Lord, I love You and thank You for Your example of how to live the Christian life and follow Your Father's commandments. Send Your Holy Spirit to help me follow in Your footsteps and keep Your commandments so my life may be consecrated to You. Let my life help others to see what a great adventure it is to follow You. Amen.*

Music to Inspire Your Mind

- Contemporary Christian "The Great Adventure" by Steven Curtis Chapman and Geoff Moore, performed by Steven Curtis Chapman.
- Vocal "Living Prayer" by Ron Block, performed by Alison Krauss and Union Station.

- Hymn "We Have Been Told"—Text and Music: David Haas, performed by the Georgetown University Chapel Choir.
- Your music choice: _____

Nutrition to Strengthen Your Body

Black Bean and Artichoke Salad

- 2 jars (6½ ounces each) marinated artichoke hearts, drained
- 1 can (15 ounces) black beans, rinsed and drained
- 1 cup bell peppers, chopped (red, green, yellow, orange, or mixed, as desired)
- ⅓ cup chopped, fresh chives or 1 tablespoon dried chives
- 1 bag (10 ounces) or 6 cups mixed salad greens
- Reduced-fat Feta cheese, crumbled, or other favorite cheese (optional)
- Favorite salad dressing (optional)

In a large bowl, combine artichoke hearts, black beans, bell peppers, and chives. Arrange salad greens on 4 salad plates; spoon bean mixture over greens. Sprinkle with Feta cheese and favorite dressing, as desired.   4 servings

Call Upon the Name of the Great I Am

August 6

The Word of God to Guide Your Soul
"And God said to Moses, 'I AM WHO I AM.' And He said, 'Thus you shall say to the children of Israel, "I AM has sent me to you."' Moreover God said to Moses, 'Thus you shall say to the children of Israel: "The LORD God of your fathers, the God of Abraham, the God of Isaac, and the God of Jacob, has sent me to you. This is My name forever, and this is My memorial to all generations"'" (Exodus 3:14-15).

> *Dear Lord, I love You and thank You that I can call on Your name and share all my joys and sorrows. Send Your Holy Spirit to remind me that You are the same yesterday, today, and forever. As you sent Moses to rescue the Israelites in Egypt, send me today to help bring Your freedom to those caught in the slavery of sin and the attractions of the world. Amen.*

Music to Inspire Your Mind
- Contemporary Christian "The Only Name (Yours Will Be)" by Benji Cowart, performed by Big Daddy Weave.
- Vocal "I Am" by Mark Schultz.

- Hymn "Jesus, Name Above All Names"—Text and Music: Naida Hearn, performed by Brad Parsley and New Life Worship.
- Your music choice: _____

Nutrition to Strengthen Your Body

Broccoli and Orzo Summer Surprise

- 6 ounces uncooked orzo
- 3 tablespoons olive oil
- 1 teaspoon minced garlic or ¼ teaspoon dried, minced garlic
- 2 packages (10 ounces each) frozen, chopped broccoli, thawed
- ½ cup Italian-style bread crumbs
- 1 teaspoon salt-free seasoning
- 2 cups tomatoes, coarsely chopped
- 2 tablespoons balsamic vinegar or vinaigrette dressing

Cook orzo as directed on package. Drain and cover to keep warm. Meanwhile, heat oil in a large skillet over medium heat. Add garlic and broccoli; saute for 3 minutes. Stir in bread crumbs and salt-free seasoning; cook 1 minute. Stir in tomatoes and vinegar; cook 1 to 2 minutes or until tomatoes are warm, stirring occasionally. Stir in pasta and heat through; serve warm.   6 servings

Remember You Are Part of the Family of God and Never Alone

August 7

The Word of God to Guide Your Soul
"Now, therefore, you are no longer strangers and foreigners, but fellow citizens with the saints and members of the household of God" (Ephesians 2:19).

> *Dear Lord, I love You and thank You for making me a part of Your forever family. Send Your Holy Spirit to show me how I can encourage my brothers and sisters in Christ on this day. When I'm feeling alone, remind me to reach out to my earthly and heavenly family. Words cannot express how thankful I am for Your great sacrifice, which makes me a fellow citizen with the saints and a member of Your household. Amen.*

Music to Inspire Your Mind
- Contemporary Christian "Family of God" by Mark Stuart and Seth Mosley, performed by Newsboys.
- Vocal "Friends" by Michael W. Smith and Deborah D. Smith, performed by Michael W. Smith and Amy Grant.

- Hymn "People of God"—Text and Music: Wayne Watson, performed by Wayne Watson.
- Your music choice: _____

Nutrition to Strengthen Your Body

Refreshing Spinach Mediterranean Salad

- 4 large plum tomatoes, chopped
- 1 large cucumber, peeled and diced
- 1 can (15 ounces) garbanzo beans, rinsed and drained
- 2 cups (8 ounces) reduced-fat sharp Cheddar cheese, shredded
- ¾ cup reduced-fat sour cream
- 2 tablespoons fresh lime juice
- ½ teaspoon salt-free seasoning
- ¼ teaspoon black pepper
- 3 cups (5 ounces) baby spinach leaves
- ¼ cup chopped fresh cilantro (optional)

In a large bowl, combine tomatoes, cucumber, garbanzo beans, and cheese. In a small bowl, combine sour cream, lime juice, salt-free seasoning, and pepper. Add to bean mixture and toss well. Spoon over spinach leaves and sprinkle with cilantro, if desired.   6 servings

Find Purpose in Serving Others

August 8

The Word of God to Guide Your Soul

"For even the Son of Man did not come to be served, but to serve, and to give His life a ransom for many" (Mark 10:45).

> *Dear Lord, I love You and thank You for giving Your life as a ransom for my soul. Send Your Holy Spirit to help me follow Your example to serve others rather than being served. Show me how, when, and where I can help others, and grant me the perseverance to follow through. Let others find You and come to understand Your sacrifice in that service I offer. Amen.*

Music to Inspire Your Mind
- Contemporary Christian "Do Something" by Matthew West.
- Vocal "Helping Hand" by Tommy Sims, Amy Grant, and Beverly Darnall, performed by Amy Grant.
- Hymn "Serve Others"—Text and Music: Kenn Mann, arranged by Kyle Hill, performed by Discover Worship.
- Your music choice: _____

Nutrition to Strengthen Your Body

Asparagus Pilaf

- 1 package (8 ounces) frozen, steam-in-bag asparagus spears
- 1 tablespoon olive oil
- ½ cup sweet onion, chopped
- 1 cup long-grain wild rice or brown rice
- 2 cups vegetable broth
- Grated zest of one lemon
- 1 tablespoon lemon juice
- ½ teaspoon dried thyme
- Black pepper, to taste

Microwave asparagus according to package directions. Let cool and cut into 1-inch pieces. Meanwhile, in a large skillet, saute onion in oil over medium-high heat until tender. Add rice and saute until rice is opaque. Add vegetable broth, lemon zest, thyme, and pepper. Bring to a boil, reduce heat to low, cover, and cook for 10 minutes. Add asparagus pieces and heat through for about 5 minutes. Remove from heat and stir in 1 tablespoon lemon juice. 6 servings

Know that You Have Eternal Life

August 9

The Word of God to Guide Your Soul
"These things I have written to you who believe in the name of the Son of God, that you may know that you have eternal life, and that you may continue to believe in the name of the Son of God" (1 John 5:13).

> *Dear Lord, I love You and thank You for Your promise of eternal life for those who believe. Send Your Holy Spirit to keep reminding me that my true home is in heaven and my earthly trials are temporary and passing. As I go about my day, let others see a reflection of that eternal life even now, in the midst of a dark and fallen world. Help me to overcome that darkness with Your radiant love! Amen.*

Music to Inspire Your Mind
- Contemporary Christian "Almost Home" by Bart Millard, Barry Graul, Robby Shaffer, Nathan Cochran, Ben Glover, and Mike Scheuchzer, performed by MercyMe.
- Vocal "When You Believe" by Stephen Schwartz, performed by One Voice Children's Choir.

- Hymn "We'll Understand It Better By and By"—Text and Music: Charles A. Tindley, performed by Guy Penrod.
- Your music choice: _____

Nutrition to Strengthen Your Body

Northern Italian Cauliflower

- 1 package (16 ounces) frozen cauliflower florets, thawed
- 2 tablespoons olive oil
- 4 cloves garlic, finely minced, or ½ teaspoon dried, minced garlic
- ¼ teaspoon black pepper
- 2 tablespoons red wine vinegar
- 2 tablespoons water

In a large skillet, heat oil over medium heat and saute garlic, stirring constantly, until just starting to brown. Add cauliflower and stir for 2-3 minutes. Add pepper, vinegar, and water. Cook over low heat, covered, for about 5 minutes or until cauliflower is tender. (You can also prepare delicious broccoli in this way.)

4 servings

Be Encouraged—the Lord is Watching Over You

August 10

The Word of God to Guide Your Soul
"For the eyes of the LORD run to and fro throughout the whole earth, to show Himself strong on behalf of those whose heart is loyal to Him" (2 Chronicles 16:9a).

> *Dear Lord, I love You and thank You for always watching over me and encouraging me to carry on with Your plan for my life. Send Your Holy Spirit to keep me completely devoted to You with my whole heart, mind, body, and soul. When I get discouraged, help me focus on Your sacrificial love and remember that You are always by my side. As I go through this day, grant me the grace to be an encourager to all those You place in my path. Amen.*

Music to Inspire Your Mind
- Contemporary Christian "You're Gonna Be Okay" by Jenn Johnson, Seth Mosley, and Jeremy Riddle, performed by Brian and Jenn Johnson.
- Vocal "I Will Be Here" by Steven Curtis Chapman.

- Hymn "Sun of My Soul"—Text: John Keble, Music: Traditional, additional lyrics by Suzanna Pautz, performed by Suzanna Pautz.
- Your music choice: _____

Nutrition to Strengthen Your Body

Slow Cooker Bean and Vegetable Medley

- 1 can (10.75 ounces) tomato soup, condensed (lower sodium and fat)
- ½ cup packed brown sugar
- ¼ cup water
- 1 medium sweet onion, chopped
- 2 celery ribs, chopped
- 1 medium green pepper, chopped
- 1 teaspoon ground mustard
- 1 bay leaf
- ⅛ teaspoon pepper
- 2 cans (16 ounces each) vegetarian baked beans
- 1 can (15 ounces) kidney beans, rinsed and drained
- 1 can (15 ounces) pinto beans, rinsed and drained

Combine the first 9 ingredients in a slow cooker and mix well. Stir in the beans. Cover and cook on low for 5-6 hours or until onion and green pepper are tender. Discard bay leaf. Serve over brown rice.   8 servings

Ask the Lord to Increase Your Faith

August 11

The Word of God to Guide Your Soul
"But without faith it is impossible to please Him, for he who comes to God must believe that He is, and that He is a rewarder of those who diligently seek Him" (Hebrews 11:6).

> *Dear Lord, I love You and thank You for the gift of faith. Send Your Holy Spirit to increase my faith, for I cannot increase it on my own; it is a grace only You can bestow. Open my eyes today to see how You are always faithful and exist in all You have created. Help me to persevere in seeking You and leading others to do the same. Amen.*

Music to Inspire Your Mind
- Contemporary Christian "Give Me Faith" by Matt Brock, Chris Brown, London Gatch, and Wade Joye, performed by Elevation Worship.
- Vocal "Faithful One" by Brian Doerksen, performed by Selah.

- Hymn "My Faith Looks Up to Thee/Holy, Holy, Holy! Lord God Almighty"—Text: Ray Palmer/Reginald Heber, Music: Lowell Mason/John B. Dykes, performed by Sheila Walsh.
- Your music choice: _____

Nutrition to Strengthen Your Body

Pineapple and Asian Veggie Stir Fry

- 1 can (8 ounces) pineapple chunks
- 2 tablespoons, plus 1 teaspoon cornstarch
- ¼ teaspoon ground ginger
- 1½ cups vegetable broth
- 3 tablespoons brown sugar
- 2 tablespoons reduced-sodium soy sauce
- 2 tablespoons olive oil
- 2 cups celery, chopped
- 1 small sweet onion, chopped
- 1 medium green pepper, cut in strips
- ½ cup (4 ounces) water chestnuts, finely chopped
- 1 can (4 ounces) sliced mushrooms, drained, or 8 ounces raw mushrooms, sliced
- 1 can (14 ounces) chop suey vegetables
- 1 can (10 ounces) chow mein noodles

Drain pineapple, reserving juice; set pineapple aside. In a medium bowl, mix pineapple juice, cornstarch, and ginger until smooth. Stir in broth, brown sugar, and soy sauce. Heat the olive oil over medium heat in a large nonstick pan. Stir fry vegetables until crisp-tender. Stir cornstarch mixture and add to the pan. Bring to a boil; cook and stir for 1-2 minutes or until sauce is thickened. Add reserved pineapple and heat through. Serve over chow mein noodles.   4 servings

Let Hope Enlighten Your Calling

August 12

The Word of God to Guide Your Soul

"That the God of our Lord Jesus Christ, the Father of glory, may give to you the spirit of wisdom and revelation in the knowledge of Him, the eyes of your understanding be enlightened; that you may know what is the hope of His calling, what are the riches of the glory of His inheritance in the saints" (Ephesians 1:17-18).

> *Dear Lord, I love You and thank You for "a spirit of wisdom and revelation" as I pursue Your calling upon my life. Send Your Holy Spirit to enlighten my heart today with hope as I think about the glorious riches You have waiting for me not just in heaven but even now, here on earth. Help me discern how to spread Your wisdom and hope to someone who is doubting Your calling upon their life today. Amen.*

Music to Inspire Your Mind

- Contemporary Christian "Promise of a Lifetime" by Jon Micah Sumrall and Aaron Sprinkle, performed by Kutless.
- Vocal "Hope of the World" by Reuben Morgan, Jason Ingram, and Matthew Bronleewe, performed by Hillsong.

- Hymn "On Christ the Solid Rock"—Text: Edward Mote, Music: William B. Bradbury, performed by Phillips, Craig, and Dean.
- Your music choice: _____

Nutrition to Strengthen Your Body

Tortilla Stacks

- 1 cup salsa
- 6 whole wheat tortillas
- 1 package (10 ounces) frozen mixed vegetables (corn, peas, carrots, and green beans), thawed
- 1 can (16 ounces) red kidney beans, rinsed and drained
- 1½ cups reduced-fat Monterey Jack cheese or other favorite cheese, shredded
- Nonstick olive oil cooking spray

Preheat oven to 350 degrees. Coat a 1½-quart round casserole with cooking spray. Spread ¼ cup of salsa in the bottom of the casserole. Layer 2 tortillas on top of the salsa, overlapping them to cover the bottom of the casserole dish. Spread with another ¼ cup of salsa and sprinkle with ¾ cup of vegetables, ½ cup of beans, and ½ cup of cheese. Repeat the layers twice more. (You can use up all ingredients in the last layer.) Cover the casserole with foil and bake for 15 minutes. Uncover and bake until the cheese is bubbly, for 5-7 minutes. Let stand for 10 minutes. Cut into wedges to serve.   4 servings

Trust in the Love, Mercy, and Faithfulness of Jesus

August 13

The Word of God to Guide Your Soul

"For Your mercy reaches unto the heavens, and Your truth unto the clouds. Be exalted, O God, above the heavens; let Your glory be above all the earth" (Psalm 57:10-11).

Dear Lord, I love You and thank You for Your unconditional love, mercy, and faithfulness. Send Your Holy Spirit to grant me the grace to trust You in every situation and whatever circumstance I may find myself in today. Wipe out any worry and help me spread Your peace and joy to those who may be anxious about what the future holds. Amen.

Music to Inspire Your Mind
- Contemporary Christian "Mountain" by Brian Torwalt, Katie Torwalt, and Phil Wickham, performed by Brian and Katie Torwalt.
- Vocal "Trust His Heart" by Eddie Carswell and Babbie Mason, performed by Babbie Mason.

- Hymn "Be Exalted, O God"—Text and Music: Brent Chambers, performed by Maranatha Music.
- Your music choice: _____

Nutrition to Strengthen Your Body

Refreshing Pasta and Vegetable Summer Salad

- 8 ounces seashell pasta
- 2 cups cucumbers, peeled and cubed
- 2 cups tomatoes, chopped
- 2 cups broccoli flowerets
- 2 cups green peppers, chopped
- 1 cup of light Italian dressing or your favorite dressing of choice

Cook seashell pasta according to package directions. Drain and set aside to cool. Prepare vegetables and combine all the ingredients in a large salad bowl. Refrigerate overnight.

8 servings

Rely on God Who Richly Provides

August 14

The Word of God to Guide Your Soul

"Command those who are rich in this present age not to be haughty, nor to trust in uncertain riches but in the living God, who gives us richly all things to enjoy" (1 Timothy 6:17).

> *Dear Lord, I love You and thank You for showering me with Your limitless resources to provide for all my needs. Send Your Holy Spirit to infuse me with faith, so I can always have the assurance You will take care of me and my family, both physically and spiritually. Thank you for providing me with talents and abilities that allow You to work through me. Let my life show others that I completely rely on You to richly provide for everything I need and enjoy. Amen.*

Music to Inspire Your Mind
- Contemporary Christian "Miracle" by Chad Mattson, Jonathan Lowry, Jason Walker, and Tedd Tjornhom, performed by Unspoken.

- Vocal "God Who Moves the Mountains" by David Leonard, Richie Fike, and Dustin Smith, performed by Corey Voss.
- Hymn "He Giveth More Grace"—Music: Annie Johnson Flint, Text: Hubert Mitchell, performed by Don Moen.
- Your music choice: _____

Nutrition to Strengthen Your Body

Strawberry-Lemon Trifle

- 1 package (3.5 ounces) instant vanilla pudding
- 1¾ cup low-fat milk
- 12 ounces lemon yogurt
- 1 angel food cake
- 1 quart fresh strawberries, washed and sliced
- ⅓ cup sliced almonds, toasted (optional)

Prepare vanilla pudding according to package directions, except for using 1¾ cup low-fat milk. After the pudding has thickened, add yogurt and stir until blended. Meanwhile, cut angel food cake into 1-inch cubes. In a deep glass serving bowl, place ⅓ of cake cubes on the bottom; spread ⅓ of pudding mixture over cubes; then top with ⅓ of sliced strawberries. Repeat layers of cake, pudding, and strawberries two more times. Top with sliced toasted almonds, if desired. (Be creative and substitute strawberries for other fruit in season, such as peaches, blueberries, or raspberries, or use a different fruit for each layer.)   8 servings

Keep the Faith and Receive a Crown of Righteousness

August 15

The Word of God to Guide Your Soul

"I have fought the good fight, I have finished the race, I have kept the faith. Finally, there is laid up for me the crown of righteousness, which the Lord, the righteous Judge, will give to me on that Day, and not to me only but also to all who have loved His appearing" (2 Timothy 4:7-8).

> *Dear Lord, I love You and thank You for Your promise of a crown of righteousness in Your heavenly kingdom. Send Your Holy Spirit to grant me the grace to fight the good fight, finish the race, and keep the faith. Help me to strengthen and encourage the faith of all my family members, friends, and those I encounter along the path of life so they will all be with me in heaven on "that Day." Amen.*

Music to Inspire Your Mind

- Contemporary Christian "Good Fight" by Jonathan Lowry, Chad Mattson, and Tyrus Morgan, performed by Unspoken.

- Vocal "Heaven Is Where You Are" by Paul Baloche, Chris Brown, and Steven Furtick, performed by Paul Baloche and Chris Brown.
- Hymn "Before the Throne of God Above"—Text and Music: Vikki Cook and Charitie Bancroft, performed by Selah.
- Your music choice: _____

Nutrition to Strengthen Your Body

Tomato and Artichoke Bake

- 2 tablespoons olive oil
- 1 package (9 ounces) frozen artichoke hearts, thawed and drained
- 2 ripe tomatoes, each cut into 8 wedges
- ½ cup Italian-style seasoned bread crumbs
- ¼ cup Parmesan cheese, grated
- 2 tablespoons margarine
- ¼ teaspoon salt-free seasoning

Preheat oven to 350 degrees. In a large skillet, heat olive oil over medium heat and saute artichokes and tomato wedges until heated through for about 3-4 minutes. Transfer to a 9-inch square baking pan or a 2-quart casserole. In a small bowl, mix together the remaining ingredients to make a crumb topping. Sprinkle topping over vegetables. Bake for 25 to 30 minutes or until heated through.   6 servings

Listen Closely to the Holy Spirit

August 16

The Word of God to Guide Your Soul
"These things I have spoken to you while being present with you. But the Helper, the Holy Spirit, whom the Father will send in My name, He will teach you all things, and bring to your remembrance all things that I said to you" (John 14:25-26).

> *Dear Lord, I love You and thank You for sending the Holy Spirit to be my Helper and Teacher. Grant me the grace to always follow where the Spirit leads and listen closely to His teachings and reminders. Enable my mind to discern the Holy Spirit's voice from the voices that would lead me away from You and Your plan for my life. As I go through this day, let me be a shining example to others of an abundant, Spirit-filled life. Amen.*

Music to Inspire Your Mind
- Contemporary Christian "Holy Spirit" by Sam Evans and Mike Guglielmucci, performed by Planetshakers.
- Choral "By the Waking of Our Hearts" by Ricky Manalo, performed by Journeysongs Choir.

- Hymn "The Comforter Has Come"—Text: Frank Bottome, Music: William J. Kirkpatrick, performed by Chase Wagner.
- Your music choice: _____

Nutrition to Strengthen Your Body

Black Bean and Brown Rice Salad

- 2 cups cooked brown rice, cooled
- 1 can (16 ounces) black beans, rinsed and drained
- ½ cup light Italian dressing
- ¼ cup green pepper, finely chopped
- ⅛ teaspoon salt-free seasoning
- ⅛ teaspoon black pepper
- 1 medium tomato, seeded and chopped
- 8 pitted black olives
- 2 tablespoons fresh cilantro or 1 tablespoon dried cilantro (optional)

In a large bowl, combine all ingredients, except cilantro. Stir to combine. Stir in cilantro, if desired. Cover with plastic wrap and chill for at least 5 hours or overnight. Stir before serving.

8 servings

Keep Your Heart's Treasure in Heaven

August 17

The Word of God to Guide Your Soul

"Do not fear, little flock, for it is your Father's good pleasure to give you the kingdom. Sell what you have and give alms; provide yourselves money bags which do not grow old, a treasure in the heavens that does not fail, where no thief approaches nor moth destroys. For where your treasure is, there your heart will be also" (Luke 12:32-34).

> *Dear Lord, I love You and thank You for giving me Your kingdom and "a treasure in the heavens that does not fail." Send Your Holy Spirit to keep my heart focused on that true treasure rather than the false treasure of earthly things. Help me have a part today in leading others to receive all the treasures of grace You provide. Amen.*

Music to Inspire Your Mind

- Contemporary Christian "Jesus, My Treasure" by Koby Orr, Michael Monroe, Chelsea Mason, Elisha Yeley, and Carson Heffner, performed by Canyon Hills Worship.

- Vocal "Yet Not I but through Christ in Me" by Michael Farren, Rich Thompson, and Jonny Robinson, performed by CityAlight.
- Hymn "Something for Thee"—Text: Sylvanus D. Phelps, Music: Robert Lowry, performed by Kai McQueen.
- Your music choice: _____

Nutrition to Strengthen Your Body

Mediterranean Egg Casserole

- 8 large eggs or 2 cups egg substitute
- 1½ cups low-fat milk
- ½ teaspoon baking powder
- Seasonings: 1 teaspoon dried oregano, 1 teaspoon paprika, ¼ teaspoon nutmeg, pepper, to taste
- 3 slices whole grain bread, toasted and cut into ½-inch pieces
- ½ cup sweet onion, diced
- 1 medium tomato, diced
- 1 package (10 ounces) frozen spinach, microwaved and drained
- ½ cup black or Kalamata olives, sliced
- ½ cup reduced-fat Feta cheese, crumbled
- 1 cup chopped, fresh parsley or ¼ cup dried parsley
- 1 bell pepper (any color), seeded and sliced into rounds

Preheat oven to 375 degrees. In a large mixing bowl, whisk together the eggs, milk, baking powder, and seasonings. Add the remaining ingredients, except the bell pepper. Spray a 9x13-inch baking pan with nonstick olive oil spray. Transfer the egg and vegetable mixture into the pan and spread evenly. Arrange the bell pepper slices on top. Bake for 45 minutes or until the center looks firm. Let rest for 5 minutes before cutting into squares.   6 servings

Cast All Your Burdens on the Lord

August 18

The Word of God to Guide Your Soul
"Cast your burden on the LORD, and He shall sustain you; He shall never permit the righteous to be moved" (Psalm 55:22).

> *Dear Lord, I love You and thank You for Your support in all the trials and problems of life. Send Your Holy Spirit to remind me that instead of worrying, I should pray and cast all of my burdens on You. Grant me the grace to keep my eyes on You and show others how to find peace and hope in any situation, no matter how challenging or troubling. Amen.*

Music to Inspire Your Mind
- Contemporary Christian "Broken Hallelujah" by Dan Ostebo, Jordan Mohilowski, Josh Havens, and Matt Fuqua, performed by The Afters.
- Vocal "Keep Your Eyes on Me" by Faith Hill, Shane McAnally, Tim McGraw, and Lori McKenna, performed by Tim McGraw and Faith Hill.

- Hymn "He Is Our Peace"—Text and Music: Kandela Groves, performed by Heritage Singers.
- Your music choice: _____

Nutrition to Strengthen Your Body

Pasta Primavera

- 1 package (10.5 ounces) frozen mixed vegetables (broccoli, cauliflower and carrots)
- 8 ounces linguine or other pasta
- 1 container (15 ounces) reduced-fat ricotta or cottage cheese
- ½ cup light sour cream
- 1 cup low-fat milk
- ½ cup Parmesan cheese, grated
- ½ teaspoon basil
- ½ teaspoon oregano
- ¼ teaspoon garlic powder
- Black pepper, to taste

Prepare frozen vegetables according to package directions and drain. Prepare pasta as directed and drain. In a large serving dish, combine vegetables and linguine. Meanwhile, in a medium saucepan, combine the remaining ingredients. Heat thoroughly, but do not boil. Add to vegetables and linguine, mix lightly, and serve at once.   4 servings

Hold on to God's Promises

August 19

The Word of God to Guide Your Soul
"If My people who are called by My name will humble themselves, and pray and seek My face, and turn from their wicked ways, then I will hear from heaven, and will forgive their sin and heal their land" (2 Chronicles 7:14).

> *Dear Lord, I love You and thank You for Your promise to hear my prayers and forgive my sins. Send Your Holy Spirit to grant me the grace and power to humble myself and pray, seek Your face, and turn away from sin. Let my life be an inspiring example to others of what it means to hold on to Your promises and receive healing and forgiveness. Amen.*

Music to Inspire Your Mind
- Contemporary Christian "You Promised" by Jennie Lee Riddle, performed by Corey Voss.
- Vocal "Your Promises" by Steven Furtick, Mack Brock, Chris Brown, and Wade Joye, performed by Elevation Worship.

- Hymn "Every Promise of Your Word"—Text and Music: Keith Getty and Stuart Townend, performed by Keith and Kristyn Getty.
- Your music choice: _____

Nutrition to Strengthen Your Body

Savory Oven Fries

- 2 teaspoons Parmesan cheese, grated
- ½ teaspoon garlic powder
- ½ teaspoon paprika
- ¼ teaspoon onion powder
- ¼ teaspoon chili powder
- ¼ teaspoon lemon pepper
- 4 large potatoes
- ¼ cup olive oil

Preheat oven to 350 degrees. Mix seasonings together. Cut each potato into 8 wedges; brush with oil and place on a baking sheet lined with foil or sprayed with nonstick olive oil cooking spray. Sprinkle with seasoning mixture. Bake until soft when pricked with a fork, for about 45 minutes. For crisp fries, bake 1 hour. Get creative with the seasonings and come up with your own favorite mixture! 8 servings

Bring Comfort and Hope to Those in Need

August 20

The Word of God to Guide Your Soul
"Blessed be the God and Father of our Lord Jesus Christ, the Father of mercies and God of all comfort, who comforts us in all our tribulation, that we may be able to comfort those who are in any trouble, with the comfort with which we ourselves are comforted by God" (2 Corinthians 1:3-4).

> *Dear Lord, I love You and thank You for comforting me in the difficult moments of life. Send Your Holy Spirit to empower me to bring comfort and hope to all those in need. Help me share Your love in both material and spiritual ways wherever I can. Let me be Your smiling face to someone who is hurting and needs to be comforted by You. Amen.*

Music to Inspire Your Mind
- Contemporary Christian "God of All Comfort" by Tim Hughes, performed by Iron Bell Ministries.

- Vocal "Not for a Moment (After All)" by Mia Fieldes, Jacob Sooter, and Meredith Andrews, performed by Meredith Andrews.
- Hymn "He Who Began a Good Work in You"—Text and Music: Jon Mohr, performed by Steve Green.
- Your music choice: _____

Nutrition to Strengthen Your Body

Cherry Tomato and Cucumber Salad

- 2 cups (½ pint) cherry tomatoes, halved
- 2 small (2 cups) cucumbers, cut into ¼-inch slices
- 4 ounces (1 cup) reduced-fat Monterey Jack cheese, cut into ½-inch cubes or shredded
- ½ cup light Italian salad dressing (or other favorite dressing)
- 2 tablespoons chopped fresh basil or 2 teaspoons dried basil leaves

In a large bowl, combine tomatoes, cucumbers, and cheese. In a glass measuring cup, combine salad dressing and basil. Mix well and pour dressing over salad ingredients. Stir gently to combine.   4 servings

Take Time to Appreciate God's Numerous, Wonderful Works

August 21

The Word of God to Guide Your Soul

"Many, O LORD my God, are Your wonderful works which You have done; and Your thoughts toward us cannot be recounted to You in order; if I would declare and speak of them, they are more than can be numbered" (Psalm 40:5).

> *Dear Lord, I love You and thank You for this wonderful world You have created. Send Your Holy Spirit to help me appreciate Your "wonderful works" and glimpses of heaven as I go through this day. From the rising of the sun to the starry night sky, let me think of You and how special it is to be part of Your creation. Help me to "declare" and share how much You love each and every one of us and all of Your creation. Amen.*

Music to Inspire Your Mind

- Contemporary Christian "Every Good Thing" by Matt Fuqua, David Garcia, Ben Glover, and Josh Havens, performed by The Afters.

- Vocal "What a Wonderful World" by George David Weiss and Bob Thiele, performed by Katie Melua and Eva Cassidy.
- Hymn "Let Us Give Thanks to the Lord" Text: Roger Thornhill, Music: Brad Nix, performed by Hal Leonard and Shawnee Press Choir.
- Your music choice: _____

Nutrition to Strengthen Your Body

Mixed Veggies with Wild Rice

- 1 can (14.5 ounces) vegetable broth
- 2 tablespoons margarine
- 1 package (16 ounces) frozen cauliflower, carrots and asparagus (or your choice of vegetable medley)
- 1 package (6.2 ounces) long grain and wild rice mix
- 1 cup reduced-fat Cheddar cheese, shredded (or other favorite cheese), optional

In a large saucepan, heat broth and margarine to boiling. Stir in vegetables, rice, and contents of seasoning packet. Heat to boiling; reduce heat to low. Cover and simmer for 5-6 minutes or until vegetables and rice are tender. Sprinkle servings with shredded cheese, if desired.   4 servings

Follow Jesus' Plan for Your Life

August 22

The Word of God to Guide Your Soul
"His [Jesus'] mother said to the servants, 'Whatever He says to you, do it'" (John 2:5, brackets added for clarity).

Dear Lord, I love You and thank You for sharing the amazing wisdom and faith of Your mother, Mary. Send Your Holy Spirit to help me follow her advice, to do whatever You tell me. Grant me the grace to be able to distinguish Your voice from the many other voices calling and distracting me from focusing on You. Let me be an example today of following only Your plan for my life. Amen.

Music to Inspire Your Mind
- Contemporary Christian "Build My Life" by Pat Barrett, Matt Redman, Brett Younker, Kirby Kaple, and Karl Martin, performed by Pat Barrett, featuring Cory Asbury.
- Vocal "I Will Follow" by Chris Tomlin, Jason Ingram, and Reuben Morgan, performed by Chris Tomlin.
- Hymn "Lead Me Lord"—Text and Music: Gary Valenciano, performed by Gary Valenciano.

- Your music choice: _____

Nutrition to Strengthen Your Body

Banana-Raisin Oatmeal Cookies

- 1½ cups all-purpose flour
- 1 cup sugar
- ¾ teaspoon cinnamon
- ½ teaspoon baking soda
- ½ teaspoon salt
- ¼ teaspoon nutmeg
- ¾ cup margarine
- 1¾ cups quick-cooking oats
- 1 cup ripe banana (2-3), mashed
- 1 egg, beaten, or ¼ cup egg substitute
- ½ cup nuts, chopped
- 1 cup raisins

Preheat oven to 400 degrees. In a large bowl, mix together all dry ingredients. Cut in margarine. Add oats, mashed bananas, an egg, nuts, and raisins. Mix thoroughly until well blended. Drop by teaspoonfuls onto a nonstick cookie sheet or cookie sheet sprayed with nonstick cooking spray. Bake for 10-12 minutes.   4 dozen

Remember Jesus Wants to Spend Eternity with You

August 23

The Word of God to Guide Your Soul

"But when the kindness and the love of God our Savior toward man appeared, not by works of righteousness which we have done, but according to His mercy He saved us, through the washing of regeneration and renewing of the Holy Spirit, whom He poured out on us abundantly through Jesus Christ our Savior, that having been justified by His grace we should become heirs according to the hope of eternal life" (Titus 3:4-7).

> *Dear Lord, I love You and thank You for always being there for me, even when I'm not aware of Your presence. Thank you for loving me so much You want to spend eternity with me. Send Your Holy Spirit to renew my faith and give me eyes to see the abundant spiritual riches You give to me every moment of every day. Help me to pass those riches along to others so they can also be justified by Your grace and "become heirs according to the hope of eternal life." Amen.*

Music to Inspire Your Mind

- Contemporary Christian "Abide with Me" by Matt Maher, Matt Redman, Jason Ingram, and David Crowder, performed by Matt Maher.
- Vocal "There Was Jesus" by Zach Williams, Jonathan Smith, and Casey Michael Beathard, performed by Zach Williams and Dolly Parton.
- Hymn "Jesus Never Fails"—Text and Music: Gary Driskell, performed by Cana's Voice.
- Your music choice: _____

Nutrition to Strengthen Your Body

Seasoned Baby Carrots and Sugar Snap Peas

- 8 ounces fresh baby-cut carrots, peeled, washed, and ready to eat
- 2 tablespoons water
- 8 ounces fresh sugar snap peas, washed and ready to eat
- 1 tablespoon margarine
- ¼ teaspoon garlic powder
- ½ teaspoon salt-free seasoning

Place carrots and water in a microwave-safe 2-quart casserole. Cover and microwave on high for 5 minutes. Add remaining ingredients. Cover and microwave on high for 3-4 minutes or until tender. Stir and serve.   4 servings

Let the Lord, Your Good Shepherd, Restore Your Soul

August 24

The Word of God to Guide Your Soul

"The LORD is my shepherd; I shall not want. He makes me to lie down in green pastures; He leads me beside the still waters. He restores my soul; He leads me in the paths of righteousness for His name's sake" (Psalm 23:1-3).

Dear Lord, I love You and thank You for being my Good Shepherd and restoring my soul when I get worried or discouraged. Send Your Holy Spirit to help me trust that You will lead me "in the paths of righteousness" until I'm safely home and in Your loving arms forever. Let me be a positive example today of how beautiful it is to be under Your watchful care and guidance. Amen.

Music to Inspire Your Mind

- Contemporary Christian "Carry Me" by Josh Wilson and Ben Glover, performed by Josh Wilson.

- Vocal "You Restore My Soul" by Lauren Harris, Tom Read, and Matt Fury, performed by New Wine Worship, featuring Lauren Harris.
- Hymn "The Lord's My Shepherd"—Text and Music: Stuart Townend, performed by Stuart Townend.
- Your music choice: _____

Nutrition to Strengthen Your Body

Chilled Veggie and Bean Balsamic Salad

- 1 cup balsamic vinaigrette dressing
- 1 cup small cauliflower florets
- 1 cup small broccoli florets
- 2 medium carrots, peeled and thinly sliced
- 1 can (16 ounces) red kidney beans, drained and rinsed
- 2 cups (8 ounces) reduced-fat mozzarella cheese, finely shredded

In a large salad bowl, toss together all ingredients except cheese. Blend well. Add cheese and toss lightly. Cover and chill for at least 3 hours, stirring occasionally. 8 servings

Be Confident that Nothing Can Separate You From God's Love

August 25

The Word of God to Guide Your Soul
"For I am persuaded that neither death nor life, nor angels nor principalities, nor powers, nor things present nor things to come, nor height nor depth, nor any other created thing, shall be able to separate us from the love of God which is in Christ Jesus our Lord" (Romans 8:38-39).

> *Dear Lord, I love You and thank You for Your blessed assurance that nothing can separate me from Your love. Send Your Holy Spirit to convince me that no matter what happens today, You will still love me. Let nothing disturb or worry me because Your love is all I need in this life and in the next. Grant me the courage to share Your steadfast love with my family, friends, and all I meet on the path of life. Amen.*

Music to Inspire Your Mind
- Contemporary Christian "Nothing Ever Could Separate Us" by Ben Calhoun, Jason Ingram, and Seth Mosley, performed by Citizen Way.

- Vocal "What Can Separate You?" by Babbie Mason and Donna Douglas, performed by Babbie Mason.
- Hymn "Blessed Assurance"—Text: Fanny J. Crosby, Music: Phoebe P. Knapp, additional text and music by Jeremy Riddle, performed by Jeremy Riddle and the Worship Circle.
- Your music choice: _____

Nutrition to Strengthen Your Body

Mixed Vegetables with Couscous

- 2 tablespoons olive oil
- 1 cup (4 ounces) fresh mushrooms, sliced, or 1 can (4 ounces) sliced mushrooms, drained
- 1 can (14.5 ounces) vegetable broth
- 1 teaspoon dried dill weed, basil or tarragon (your choice)
- 1 package (14 ounces) frozen pepper stir fry mix
- 1 cup uncooked couscous
- 1 cup frozen peas

In a 2-quart saucepan, heat oil over medium-high heat and stir in mushrooms. Saute until mushrooms are softened (for 4-5 minutes). Add vegetable broth and chosen seasoning. Increase heat to high and cook until mixture comes to a full boil. Add all remaining ingredients and stir well. Cover; reduce heat to low and cook until all broth is absorbed (for 5-7 minutes).

6 servings

Relax and Know Jesus is with You in Every Moment

August 26

The Word of God to Guide Your Soul

"I will not leave you orphans; I will come to you. A little while longer and the world will see Me no more, but you will see Me. Because I live, you will live also" (John 14:18-19).

> *Dear Lord, I love You and thank You for promising You will never leave me, whether I am in this temporal world or in eternity. Send Your Holy Spirit to help me discern Your presence each and every moment so I keep focused on my life with You rather than on my earthly life with its many troubles. As I go through this day, show me how to lead others to "see" You and "live." Amen.*

Music to Inspire Your Mind

- Contemporary Christian "He Will Carry Me" by Mark Schultz.
- Vocal "I Will Never Leave You Alone" by Janet Paschal.

- Hymn "Moment by Moment"—Text: Daniel W. Whittle, Music: May Whittle Moody, performed by the Fountainview Academy Choir.
- Your music choice: _____

Nutrition to Strengthen Your Body

Snow Peas Teriyaki

- 2 tablespoons sesame, peanut or olive oil
- 1 cup sliced fresh carrots
- 8 ounces fresh snow peas, washed and ready to eat
- 1 can (8 ounces) sliced water chestnuts, rinsed and drained
- ¼ cup teriyaki sauce

Preheat large, nonstick skillet or wok on medium-high heat for 2-3 minutes. Place oil and carrots in the pan; cook and stir 1 minute. Add snow peas; cook and stir for 1 minute. Stir in remaining ingredients; cook and stir 2-3 more minutes or until tender.   4 servings

Have Faith God is Always in Control

August 27

The Word of God to Guide Your Soul
"Who among all these does not know that the hand of the LORD has done this, in whose hand is the life of every living thing, and the breath of all mankind?" (Job 12:9-10).

> *Dear Lord, I love You and thank You for keeping every breath of my life in Your loving hands. Send Your Holy Spirit to remind me of that when I feel like the world is out of control and worry starts to permeate my thoughts. As I go through this day, help me to reflect Your peace and unconditional love to "every living thing" and "all mankind." Amen.*

Music to Inspire Your Mind
- Contemporary Christian "Always" by Kristian Stanfill and Jason Ingram, performed by Kristian Stanfill
- Vocal "God Is in Control" by Twila Paris
- Hymn "He's Got the Whole World in His Hands"—Text and Music: Traditional Spiritual, performed by Pat Boone
- Your music choice: _____

Nutrition to Strengthen Your Body

Vegetarian Tater Tot Casserole

- 2 tablespoons olive oil
- 1 cup sweet onion, diced
- ½ cup celery, finely diced
- ½ cup carrot, finely diced
- 3 cloves garlic, finely chopped, or ½ teaspoon dried, minced garlic
- Salt-free seasoning and pepper, to taste
- 1 package (10 ounces) frozen sweet corn
- 1 package (10 ounces) frozen baby or sweet peas
- ¼ cup fresh parsley, chopped, or 1 tablespoon dried parsley
- 1 can condensed cream of celery or mushroom soup (lower in sodium and fat)
- 1 cup (4 ounces) reduced-fat sharp Cheddar cheese or Monterey Jack cheese, shredded
- 1 bag (16 ounces) frozen tater tots
- Nonstick olive oil cooking spray

Preheat oven to 375 degrees. In a large skillet, heat olive oil over medium heat. Add onion, celery, and carrots, and saute for 2-3 minutes. Add garlic, salt-free seasoning, and pepper. Stir and saute for another 3 minutes or until tender. Add frozen corn and peas; stir for 1-2 minutes. Add parsley and soup. Stir until well blended. Transfer to a 9x13-inch baking dish sprayed with cooking spray and spread evenly. Sprinkle cheese on top and then place tater tots evenly across the top of the cheese. Bake for 30 minutes until bubbly and tater tots are golden brown. Let sit for 5 minutes before serving.   6-8 servings

Strive to Be Humble

August 28

The Word of God to Guide Your Soul
"For whoever exalts himself will be humbled, but he who humbles himself will be exalted" (Luke 14:11).

> *Dear Lord, I love You and thank You for showing me what it means to be truly humble and put the needs of others before my own. You gave up Your perfect home in heaven to be born in a stable and die on a cross to redeem me from my sins. Thank you for that amazing example of the virtue of humility! Send Your Holy Spirit to help me grow in that virtue and be an example of humility that others can imitate. Amen.*

Music to Inspire Your Mind
- Contemporary Christian "Lay It Down" by Amber Sky records, featuring Mark "Moxie" Gibson.
- Vocal "To Be Like You" by Brooke Ligertwood and Matt Crocker, performed by Hillsong.
- Hymn "Humble Thyself in the Sight of the Lord"—Text and Music: Bob Hudson, performed by Maranatha! Singers.

- Your music choice: _____

Nutrition to Strengthen Your Body

Seven-Layer Southwestern Salad

- 1 can (15.5 ounces) vegetarian barbecue baked beans
- ½ bag (14 ounces) salad greens (about 5 cups)
- 1 large tomato, diced
- 1 cup reduced-fat Monterey Jack cheese, shredded (or other favorite cheese)
- 1 can (2.25 ounces) sliced black ripe olives, drained
- 2 green onions, sliced
- 1 avocado
- 1 bottle (8 ounces) light cucumber ranch dressing (or other favorite ranch dressing)

Spoon beans into a large salad bowl (preferably glass so you can see the layers). Top with lettuce. Reserve about ⅓ cup tomato for garnish and spoon remaining tomato over lettuce. Layer cheese, olives, and onions over tomato. In a small bowl, mash avocado and gradually stir in dressing until almost smooth. Spoon mixture over salad, sealing to edges of the bowl. Top with reserved tomato. Refrigerate at least for 5 hours before serving. 8 servings

Trust in the Lord's Plans for Your Future

August 29

The Word of God to Guide Your Soul

"For I know the thoughts that I think toward you, says the LORD, thoughts of peace and not of evil, to give you a future and a hope" (Jeremiah 29:11).

> *Dear Lord, I love You and thank You for a future that is full of peace and hope. Send Your Holy Spirit to help me trust in You at all times, even when things don't make sense. Grant me the grace to see my life from Your perspective rather than my own. Let me be a calming influence today so others can see how beautiful it is to be Your child and follow Your will. Amen.*

Music to Inspire Your Mind

- Contemporary Christian "Trust in You" by Lauren Daigle, Michael Farren, and Paul Mabury, performed by Lauren Daigle.
- Vocal "When God Has Another Plan" by Amy Keffer-Shellem and Daryl Williams, performed by The Greenes.

- Hymn "I'll Go Where You Want Me to Go"—Text: Mary Brown and Charles E. Prior, Music: Carrie E. Rounsefell, performed by Christian Berdahl.
- Your music choice: _____

Nutrition to Strengthen Your Body

Baked Spinach Ziti

- 1 small sweet onion, chopped
- 1 clove garlic, minced, or ⅛ teaspoon dried, minced garlic
- 1 tablespoon olive oil
- 2 cups reduced-fat cottage cheese
- 2 packages (10 ounces each) frozen, chopped spinach, microwaved and drained well
- 2 eggs, beaten, or ½ cup egg substitute
- 1 teaspoon Italian seasoning
- 1 box (16 ounces) ziti, prepared according to package directions and drained
- 1 jar (24 ounces) meatless spaghetti sauce
- 1 cup (4 ounces) reduced-fat mozzarella cheese, shredded
- 2 tablespoons Parmesan cheese, grated
- Nonstick olive oil cooking spray

Preheat oven to 375 degrees. In a medium skillet, heat olive oil over medium heat and saute onion and garlic until tender. In a large bowl, combine cottage cheese, spinach, eggs, Italian seasoning, ziti, 1 cup spaghetti sauce, ½ cup mozzarella cheese, onion, and garlic. Spray bottom and sides of a 13x9-inch baking dish with cooking spray and spread ¼ cup spaghetti sauce to coat bottom. Top with ziti mixture, remaining mozzarella cheese, and spaghetti sauce. Sprinkle with Parmesan cheese. Cover and bake for 20 minutes. Uncover and bake for 25 more minutes or until bubbly. Let stand 10 minutes before serving.

8 servings

Live in the Light of Christ

August 30

The Word of God to Guide Your Soul
"Then Jesus spoke to them again, saying, 'I am the light of the world. He who follows Me shall not walk in darkness, but have the light of life'" (John 8:12).

> *Dear Lord, I love You and thank You for being "the light of the world" and illuminating my way as I follow You. Send Your Holy Spirit to give me discernment so I may never "walk in darkness." Shine Your light on this troubled earth so many will have their eyes opened and discover You, "the light of life." I pray this especially for all of my family, friends, and those I encounter as I go about my day. Amen.*

Music to Inspire Your Mind
- Contemporary Christian "My Lighthouse" by Rend Collective.
- Vocal "Shine on Us" by Michael W. Smith and Debbie Smith, performed by Phillips, Craig and Dean.

- Hymn "Morning Has Broken"—Text: Eleanor Farjeon, Music: Traditional Gaelic melody, performed by Orla Fallon.
- Your music choice: _____

Nutrition to Strengthen Your Body

Fresh Fruit Yogurt Parfait

- 1 cup plain, low-fat yogurt
- 2 tablespoons maple syrup
- 1 teaspoon vanilla
- ½ teaspoon cinnamon
- 2 medium bananas, sliced
- 2 cups strawberries, sliced

In a small bowl, blend together yogurt, syrup, vanilla, and cinnamon. Layer bananas and strawberries in four parfait or other glasses with a yogurt mixture between each layer. (Substitute other fruits, as desired.) 4 servings

Build Your Life's Foundation on Loving the Lord

August 31

The Word of God to Guide Your Soul
"Blessed be the LORD, for He has shown me His marvelous kindness in a strong city! Oh, love the LORD, all you His saints! For the LORD preserves the faithful, and fully repays the proud person. Be of good courage, and He shall strengthen your heart, all you who hope in the LORD" (Psalm 31:21, 23-24).

Dear Lord, I love You and thank You for showing me Your "marvelous kindness." Send Your Holy Spirit to provide the spiritual gifts I need to build and preserve a firm foundation on You and the selfless sacrifice You made for my salvation. As I go through this day, help me to love You completely, in each moment, so I can lead others to love You with their whole hearts. Amen.

Music to Inspire Your Mind
- Contemporary Christian "Love God Love People" by Danny Gokey, Colby Wedgeworth, and Ben Glover, performed by Danny Gokey.

- Vocal "The Words I Would Say" by Ben McDonald, David Frey, and Sam Mizell, performed by Sidewalk Prophets.
- Hymn "How Firm a Foundation"—Text: Rippon's Selection of Hymns, 1787, Music: Traditional American Melody, performed by Fernando Ortega.
- Your music choice: _____

Nutrition to Strengthen Your Body

Pan-Fried Potato Slices

- 4 microwaved or baked potatoes, cooled and sliced ¼-inch thick (Yukon Gold is a good choice.)
- 2-3 tablespoons olive oil
- 1 small sweet onion, thinly sliced
- ½ teaspoon rosemary
- ¼ teaspoon garlic powder
- Black pepper, to taste
- ½ cup light ranch dressing (optional)

In a large skillet, heat olive oil over medium heat. Add potatoes and onions, turning often, until tender and golden brown. Add seasonings and toss to blend. Add dressing, if desired, and heat through. 4 servings

Let the Peace of God Rule in Your Heart

September 1

The Word of God to Guide Your Soul
"And let the peace of God rule in your hearts, to which also you were called in one body; and be thankful" (Colossians 3:15).

> *Dear Lord, I love You and thank You for bringing the possibility of peace into my life and into the world. Send Your Holy Spirit to grant me the grace to let the peace of God always rule in my heart, no matter what is happening around me. Don't let worry and fear overcome the peace from You that passes all understanding. Let Your peace and love shine through me to all who are dear to me and to all I encounter today. Amen.*

Music to Inspire Your Mind
- Contemporary Christian "Peace Be Still" by Hope Darst, Mia Fieldes, and Andrew Holt, performed by The Belonging Company, featuring Lauren Daigle.

- Vocal "Peace" by Ed Cash, performed by We The Kingdom (Bethel Music).
- Hymn "Peace like a River"—Text and Music: Traditional, performed by Carman.
- Your music choice: _____

Nutrition to Strengthen Your Body

Spaghetti Squash with Tomatoes and Olives

- 1 (2-3 pound) spaghetti squash
- 2 medium tomatoes, chopped
- ⅓ cup red onions, chopped
- 2 tablespoons olive oil
- ⅓ cup sliced green olives, drained
- ⅓ cup sliced Kalamata olives, drained
- ¼ teaspoon salt-free seasoning
- ¼ teaspoon pepper
- Nonstick olive oil cooking spray

Preheat oven to 375 degrees. Lightly coat a shallow baking pan with cooking spray. Halve squash lengthwise and discard seeds. Arrange squash, cut sides down in a pan. Bake squash for 30 minutes or until tender when pierced with a fork. Set aside. Meanwhile, chop tomatoes and onions. In a medium bowl, mix tomatoes and onions with remaining oil and olives. Season with salt-free seasoning and pepper. When squash has cooled down enough to handle, use a large fork to shred the stringy pulp from the squash and place in a medium serving bowl. Top with tomato and olive mixture to serve.   4 servings

Find Your Delight in the Lord

September 2

The Word of God to Guide Your Soul
"Trust in the LORD, and do good; dwell in the land, and feed on His faithfulness. Delight yourself also in the LORD, and He shall give you the desires of your heart" (Psalm 37:3-4).

> *Dear Lord, I love You and thank You for blessing me with the grace to securely dwell with You. Send Your Holy Spirit to guide me moment by moment so I may find my delight only in You. Fulfill my heart's desire to have You be my constant companion throughout this life and into eternity. Today, let others see how much I love You and what a difference You make in my life. Amen.*

Music to Inspire Your Mind
- Contemporary Christian "My Delight Is in You" by Christy Nockels, Jesse Reeves, and Chris Tomlin, performed by Passion Worship, featuring Christy Nockels.
- Vocal "There Is None Like You" by Lenny LeBlanc, performed by Lenny LeBlanc.

- Hymn "The Greatest Thing"—Text and Music: Mark Pendergrass, performed by Divine Hymns Worship.
- Your music choice: _____

Nutrition to Strengthen Your Body

Italian Sliced Tomato Salad

- 2 large tomatoes, each cut in 6 slices
- ¾ cup low-fat cottage cheese
- ¼ teaspoon black pepper
- 2 tablespoons chopped, fresh basil or 2 teaspoons dried basil
- 2 teaspoons oregano
- 2 teaspoons balsamic vinegar dressing
- 2 teaspoons olive oil (extra virgin preferred)

Arrange tomatoes in a single layer on 4 serving plates. Spoon cottage cheese evenly over tomatoes. Sprinkle with pepper, basil, and oregano. Drizzle balsamic vinegar dressing and olive oil. (Vary herbs and spices, as desired.) 4 servings

Overcome Trouble with Trust

September 3

The Word of God to Guide Your Soul

"For the Father Himself loves you, because you have loved Me, and have believed that I came forth from God. These things I have spoken to you, that in Me you may have peace. In the world you will have tribulation; but be of good cheer, I have overcome the world" (John 16:27, 33).

> *Dear Lord, I love You and thank You for Your encouraging words that give me comfort and hope. Send Your Holy Spirit to strengthen my belief that You have "overcome the world." Grant me peace in knowing this troubled world is quickly passing, and my true home is in heaven with you. Let nothing disturb me so others can see the trust I have in You. Amen.*

Music to Inspire Your Mind

- Contemporary Christian "Overcomer" by Ben Glover, Chris Stevens, and David Garcia, performed by Mandisa.
- Vocal "Healer" by Mike Guglielmucci, performed by Kari Jobe.

- Hymn "Only Trust Him"—Text and Music: John H. Stockton, performed by David Phelps.
- Your music choice: _____

Nutrition to Strengthen Your Body

Oven-Baked Vegetable-Bean Soft Tacos

- 8 whole wheat tortillas (fajita size)
- 1 small sweet onion, chopped
- 2 cloves garlic, minced, or ¼ teaspoon dried, minced garlic
- 1 tablespoon olive oil
- ½ cup each red and green bell pepper, diced
- 2 cans (16 ounces each) black beans, rinsed and drained
- ¾ cup salsa
- 1 teaspoon taco seasoning
- 2 cups (8 ounces) reduced-fat Monterey Jack cheese, shredded (or other favorite cheese)
- ½ cup chopped fresh cilantro (optional)
- Topping suggestions: lettuce, tomatoes, light sour cream, extra salsa, or guacamole

Preheat oven to 375 degrees. In a large skillet, saute onion and garlic in olive oil for 5 minutes or until softened, stirring occasionally. Add bell peppers and cook for 2 minutes. Partially mash one can of beans with a potato masher. Add mashed beans, remaining can of beans, salsa, and seasoning to skillet. Cook over low heat for 10 minutes, stirring occasionally. Meanwhile, fold flour tortillas in a taco shape and place upright, side by side, in a 9x13-inch baking pan sprayed with nonstick olive oil cooking spray. Sprinkle ½ cup of cheese down the center of each tortilla and spoon bean mixture over cheese. Bake for 5-10 minutes, or until shells are heated through. Carefully remove from the pan and top tacos with favorite toppings.   4 servings

Serve Jesus by Serving Others

September 4

The Word of God to Guide Your Soul

"And the King will answer and say to them, 'Assuredly, I say to you, inasmuch as you did it to one of the least of these My brethren, you did it to Me'" (Matthew 25:40).

Dear Lord, I love You and thank You for opening my eyes to Your presence in every person. Send Your Holy Spirit to grant me a servant soul so I may serve Jesus and others in all I do. Help me follow the example of Mother Teresa, as she prayed, "Let every action of mine be something beautiful for God." Show me today how I might make this world a better place for all I meet. Amen.

Music to Inspire Your Mind

- Contemporary Christian "Take a Little Time" by Jeremy Camp.
- Choral "Prayer of Mother Teresa" by Craig Courtney, performed by Beckenhorst Press Choir.
- Hymn "Whatsoever You Do"—Text and Music: Willard F. Jabusch, performed by Robert Kochis.

- Your music choice: _____

Nutrition to Strengthen Your Body

Greek-Style Green Beans

- 2 tablespoons olive oil
- ½ medium red pepper, thinly sliced
- 1 clove garlic, minced, or teaspoon dried, minced garlic
- 1 bag (16 ounces) frozen whole green beans
- ½ cup vegetable broth
- ½ teaspoon dried oregano
- ½ cup reduced-fat Feta cheese, crumbled

In a large skillet, heat oil over medium heat. Saute pepper and garlic for 5 minutes. Add green beans, broth, and oregano. Cook, stirring occasionally, for 7-8 minutes, or until beans are tender. Sprinkle with cheese and serve.   4 servings

Devote Your Work to the Lord

September 5

The Word of God to Guide Your Soul
"Therefore, my beloved brethren, be steadfast, immovable, always abounding in the work of the Lord, knowing that your labor is not in vain in the Lord" (1 Corinthians 15:58).

> *Dear Lord, I love You and thank You for giving me work to do in sharing Your love with the world and being of service to my neighbor. Send Your Holy Spirit to help me "be steadfast, immovable, always abounding" in this labor of love. Show me how to offer up all I do, whether it be small tasks or large, to Your glory and honor. Let my work be an example to others of how beautiful and purposeful a life lived for You can be. Amen.*

Music to Inspire Your Mind
- Contemporary Christian "Lifesong" by Mark Hall, performed by Casting Crowns.
- Vocal "Set the World on Fire" by Britt Nicole, Jason Ingram, and Cindy Morgan, performed by Britt Nicole.

- Hymn "I Give All to You"—Text and Music: Larnelle Harris, performed by Larnelle Harris.
- Your music choice: _____

Nutrition to Strengthen Your Body

Chili-Topped Potatoes

- 1 can (15 ounces) vegetarian chili with beans
- 4 medium potatoes
- ½ cup reduced-fat Cheddar cheese, shredded (or other favorite cheese)
- ½ cup light sour cream

In a 2-quart saucepan, heat chili over medium-low heat, stirring occasionally. Meanwhile, microwave potatoes. Scrub and pierce several times with a fork. Place on a paper towel in the microwave, spacing evenly. Cook on full power for 5 minutes. Turn over and cook for 5 minutes more or until the potatoes are easily pierced with a fork all the way to the center. Let rest for 2 minutes. Slice lengthwise at the top of the potato and fluff with a fork before adding toppings. Spoon chili over each potato. Sprinkle with cheese and then top with a dollop of sour cream.   4 servings

Presevere in Running the Race of Faith

September 6

The Word of God to Guide Your Soul
"Therefore we also, since we are surrounded by so great a cloud of witnesses, let us lay aside every weight, and the sin which so easily ensnares us, and let us run with endurance the race that is set before us, looking unto Jesus, the author and finisher of our faith" (Hebrews 12:1-2a).

> *Dear Lord, I love You and thank You for surrounding me with Your love and "so great a cloud of witnesses." Send Your Holy Spirit to help me persevere, rid myself of sin, and keep my eyes on You. Grant me the grace to consistently live a life that reflects Your love and compassion for all. Let me be a beautiful witness to others today of how amazing life can be when following You, Jesus, "the author and finisher of our faith." Amen.*

Music to Inspire Your Mind
- Contemporary Christian "Never Been a Moment" by Jeff Pardo and Micah Tyler, performed by Micah Tyler.

- Vocal "Turn Your Eyes" by Kevin Winebarger, Nic Trout, George Romanacce, and Nathan Stiff, performed by Sovereign Grace Music.
- Hymn "I Want to Walk as a Child of the Light"—Text and Music: Kathleen Thomerson, arranged by Mark Hayes, performed by Hope Publishing Choir.
- Your music choice: _____

Nutrition to Strengthen Your Body

Sauteed Brussels Sprouts and Carrots

- 1 package (16 ounces) frozen Brussels sprouts, thawed (or 1 pound, fresh, stems trimmed)
- 3 tablespoons margarine
- 1 package (5 ounces) matchstick carrots
- ¼ teaspoon garlic powder
- ¼ teaspoon salt-free seasoning
- ¼ teaspoon pepper

Cut thawed or fresh Brussels sprouts into quarters. In a large skillet, melt margarine on medium-high heat. Place sprouts and carrots in pan; saute and stir for 2-3 minutes. Reduce heat to medium, cover, and cook for 6-7 more minutes, or until desired tenderness. Season with garlic powder, salt-free seasoning, and pepper. Toss to blend with margarine and seasonings.   4 servings

Believe Anything is Possible

September 7

The Word of God to Guide Your Soul
"Jesus said to him, 'If you can believe, all things are possible to him who believes.' Immediately the father of the child cried out and said with tears, 'Lord, I believe; help my unbelief!'" (Mark 9:23-24)

> *Dear Lord, I love You and thank You for Your promise that "all things are possible to him who believes." Send Your Holy Spirit to increase my faith and decrease my doubt and worries. I know I can't even take my next breath without You, so never let me forget that You are the source of all I am and all I accomplish. Let me always turn to You with confidence and show others that I believe anything is possible with You by my side. Amen.*

Music to Inspire Your Mind
- Contemporary Christian "What Faith Can Do" by Scott Davis and Scott Krippayne, performed by Kutless.
- Vocal "Jesus I Believe" by Jason Ingram and Michael Weaver, performed by Big Daddy Weave.

- Hymn "Help My Unbelief"—Text: John Newton, Music: Clint Wells, performed by Red Mountain Music.
- Your music choice: _____

Nutrition to Strengthen Your Body

Macaroni and Cheese Veggie Salad

- 1 package (6 ounces) whole grain macaroni and cheese dinner
- ½ cup frozen peas, thawed
- ½ cup light ranch dressing (may also use low-fat plain yogurt or tzatziki sauce)
- ½ cup celery slices
- ½ cup carrot slices
- ¼ teaspoon garlic powder
- ¼ teaspoon pepper

Prepare macaroni and cheese dinner as directed on package. Add remaining ingredients and mix lightly. Transfer to a serving bowl, cover, and chill. Add additional dressing before serving if salad needs moistening.   6-8 servings

Rejoice in the Lord's Saving Love

September 8

The Word of God to Guide Your Soul
"I will greatly rejoice in the LORD, my soul shall be joyful in my God; for He has clothed me with the garments of salvation, He has covered me with the robe of righteousness, as a bridegroom decks himself with ornaments, and as a bride adorns herself with her jewels" (Isaiah 61:10).

> *Dear Lord, I love You and thank You for clothing me with "the garments of salvation" and covering me in a "robe of righteousness." Send Your Holy Spirit to fill my soul with joy at the beauty of Your love for me and inspire me to look beyond this world into the happiness You have, waiting for me. To consider that I will be with You forever is a true joy, for You are my soul's glory, joy, and crown. Help my family, friends, and those I meet today understand that all of the joy and happiness in my life comes from being loved by You. Amen.*

Music to Inspire Your Mind

- Contemporary Christian "Alive and Breathing" by Matt Maher and Elle Limebear.
- Vocal "Beautiful" by Israel Houghton, Nicole Binion, David Binion, and Joshua Dufrene, performed by Covenant Worship.
- Hymn "Fairest Lord Jesus (My Soul's Glory)"—Text and Music: Anonymous German Hymn, additional music by Paul Baloche, performed by Paul Baloche and Worship Circle Hymns.
- Your music choice: _____

Nutrition to Strengthen Your Body

Vegetable Oat Pilaf

- ½ cup fresh mushrooms, chopped or 1 can (4 ounces) mushrooms, drained and chopped
- ½ cup green pepper, chopped
- ½ cup sweet onions, chopped
- 2 tablespoons olive oil
- 1¾ cups oats (quick or old fashioned, uncooked)
- 1 egg or ½ cup egg substitute
- ¾ cup vegetable broth

In a large skillet, saute mushrooms, green pepper, and onions in olive oil on medium heat for 2-3 minutes. In a small mixing bowl, combine oats and egg until oats are evenly coated. Add oats to vegetable mixture in the skillet; cook over medium heat until oats are dry and separated, for about 5-6 minutes. Add broth; continue cooking for 2-3 minutes until liquid is absorbed.   8 servings

Run the Race to Win an Imperishable Crown

September 9

The Word of God to Guide Your Soul

"Do you not know that those who run in a race all run, but one receives the prize? Run in such a way that you may obtain it. And everyone who competes for the prize is temperate in all things. Now they do it to obtain a perishable crown, but we for an imperishable crown" (1 Corinthians 9:24-25).

> *Dear Lord, I love You and thank You for Your great sacrifice that makes it possible for me to one day have an imperishable crown. Send Your Holy Spirit to fill me with self-control and discipline so I may run the race of life in a way that is pleasing to You and inspiring to others. Amen.*

Music to Inspire Your Mind

- Contemporary Christian "I Will Run" by Jeff Lucas, performed by Exalt Worship.
- Vocal "Run the Race" by Holly Starr and Bryan Fowler, performed by Holly Starr.

- Hymn "May the Mind of Christ, My Savior"—Text: Kate B. Wilkinson, Music: A. Cyril Barham-Gould, performed by The Worship Team.
- Your music choice: _____

Nutrition to Strengthen Your Body

Make-Ahead Baked Berry French Toast

- 1 small (8-9 ounces) day-old loaf of multigrain or oatmeal bread
- 3 eggs or ¾ cup egg substitute
- 3 tablespoons sugar
- 1 teaspoon vanilla extract
- 2¼ cups low-fat milk
- ½ cup all-purpose flour
- 6 tablespoons brown sugar
- ½ teaspoon ground cinnamon
- ¼ cup margarine
- 1 cup fresh or frozen blueberries
- 1 cup sliced strawberries

Spray a 9x13-inch baking dish with nonstick cooking spray. Diagonally cut bread and place in the baking dish. In a medium bowl, lightly beat eggs, sugar, and vanilla. Stir in milk until well blended. Pour mixture over bread in the baking dish, turning slices to coat well. Cover and refrigerate overnight. The next day, preheat the oven to 375 degrees. In a small bowl, combine flour, brown sugar, and cinnamon. Cut in margarine until mixture resembles coarse crumbs. Turn bread slices over in the baking dish. Scatter blueberries over bread; sprinkle evenly with crumb mixture. Bake for about 40 minutes or until golden brown. Let rest for 10 minutes, cut into squares, and top with strawberries.   8 servings

Abide in Jesus to Bear Much Fruit

September 10

The Word of God to Guide Your Soul
"I am the vine, you are the branches. He who abides in Me, and I in him, bears much fruit; for without Me you can do nothing" (John 15:5).

> *Dear Lord, I love You and thank You for always being there for me. Send Your Holy Spirit to increase my dependence on You and decrease my dependence on myself. May I be a branch that "bears much fruit" as I abide in Your love and peace. Work through me to help any struggling soul that is searching for You in this troubled world. Amen.*

Music to Inspire Your Mind
- Contemporary Christian "My Prayer for You" by Michael Farren and Jessica Campbell, performed by Alisa Turner.
- Vocal "I'll Never Let Go of Your Hand" by Don Francisco.
- Hymn "I Am the Vine"—Text and Music: John Michael Talbot, performed by John Michael Talbot.
- Your music choice: _____

Nutrition to Strengthen Your Body

Easy Cheesy Bean and Tomato Squares

- 1 can (16 ounces) Great Northern or pinto beans, rinsed and drained
- 1 egg, beaten, or ¼ cup egg substitute
- 1 cup low-fat milk
- 1 teaspoon Worcestershire sauce
- ½ teaspoon dry mustard
- ¼ cup minced onion or 1 tablespoon dried, minced onion
- 1 package (8.8 ounces) brown and wild rice (ready to microwave)
- 1½ cups reduced-fat Cheddar cheese, shredded
- 1 medium tomato, sliced
- Nonstick olive oil cooking spray

Preheat oven to 325 degrees. Spray an 8-inch square baking pan with nonstick cooking spray. Microwave rice according to package directions. In a large mixing bowl, combine all ingredients except tomato slices and ½ cup cheese for topping. Pour into the baking pan. Bake for 45-60 minutes or until set. Top with sliced tomatoes, sprinkle with reserved cheese and bake for another 10 minutes. Allow to set for 10 minutes. Cut into squares.   6 servings

Return a Blessing for an Insult

September 11

The Word of God to Guide Your Soul
"Finally, all of you be of one mind, having compassion for one another; love as brothers, be tenderhearted, be courteous, not returning evil for evil or reviling for reviling, but on the contrary blessing, knowing that you were called to this, that you may inherit a blessing" (1 Peter 3:8-9).

> *Dear Lord, I love You and thank You for teaching me to bless and forgive my enemies. Send Your Holy Spirit to grant me the grace of unconditional love, as You have unconditionally loved me. I'm sorry for the times I haven't forgiven others; after all, You suffered for my forgiveness and salvation. As I go through this day, help me to look at others through Your eyes of love and treat all with kindness, compassion, and goodness. Amen.*

Music to Inspire Your Mind
- Contemporary Christian "Forgiveness" by Matthew West.
- Vocal "Where Were You (When the World Stopped Turning)" by Alan Jackson.

- Hymn "Blessed Redeemer"—Text: Avis B. Christiansen, Music: Mark Hall and Bernie Herms, performed by Casting Crowns.
- Your music choice: _____

Nutrition to Strengthen Your Body

Mini Veggie Pizzas

- 4 English muffins
- 1 jar (24 ounces) marinara sauce of choice
- 2 cups veggies of choice—onions, mushrooms, spinach, tomatoes, green peppers, etc. (or use any leftover veggies)
- 2 cups reduced-fat mozzarella or Italian-blend cheese, shredded

Preheat oven to 400 degrees. Split the English muffins in half and toast until crispy. Place on a baking sheet lined with aluminum foil. Spoon marinara sauce over each half. Top with preferred veggie toppings. Sprinkle with cheese. Bake for 10 minutes. Serve warm.   4 servings

Hold Fast to the Word of God

September 12

The Word of God to Guide Your Soul
"Above all, taking the shield of faith with which you will be able to quench all the fiery darts of the wicked one. And take the helmet of salvation, and the sword of the Spirit, which is the word of God" (Ephesians 6:16-17).

> *Dear Lord, I love You and thank You for Your Word, which is my sword and shield against the wicked one. Send Your Holy Spirit to help me be diligent in studying, memorizing, and reflecting on Your Word so I am always prepared to stand firm in my faith and "quench all the fiery darts" that Satan may try to throw at me. Grant me the grace to share Your Word with others today, Lord, so they may also hold fast to You and live with You forever. Amen.*

Music to Inspire Your Mind
- Contemporary Christian "Word of God Speak" by Bart Millard and Pete Kipley, performed by MercyMe.
- Vocal "Your Word" by Chris Davenport, performed by Hillsong Worship.

- Hymn "Hidden in My Heart"—Text and Music: Jay Stocker, performed by Michael Rossback of Scripture Lullabies.
- Your music choice: _____

Nutrition to Strengthen Your Body

Slow-Cooker Mixed Vegetables

- 4 celery ribs, cut into 1-inch pieces
- 4 small carrots, cut into 1-inch pieces
- 2 medium tomatoes, cut into chunks
- 2 medium sweet onions, thinly sliced
- 2 cups fresh green beans, cut into 1-inch pieces or 1 package (10 ounces) frozen cut green beans
- 1 medium green pepper, seeded, and cut into 1-inch pieces
- ¼ cup margarine, melted
- 3 tablespoons quick-cooking tapioca
- 1 tablespoon sugar
- 1 teaspoon salt-free seasoning
- ⅛ teaspoon pepper

Spray a slow cooker with nonstick olive oil cooking spray. Add all vegetables in the order listed. In a small bowl, combine the remaining ingredients and stir well. Pour over vegetables. Cover and cook on low for 7-8 hours or until vegetables are tender. Serve with a slotted spoon.   8 servings

Follow Jesus to Eternal Life with the Father

September 13

The Word of God to Guide Your Soul
"Thomas said to Him, 'Lord, we do not know where You are going, and how can we know the way?' Jesus said to him, 'I am the way, the truth, and the life. No one comes to the Father except through Me'" (John 14:5-6).

> *Dear Lord, I love You and thank You for being my way, my truth, and my life. Send Your Holy Spirit to grant me the grace and fortitude to follow You all the way to eternal life with the Father. Show me how to best live this day so all will know that I am Your follower by both my words and actions. Amen.*

Music to Inspire Your Mind
- Contemporary Christian "The Way (New Horizon)" by Daniel Bashta, Ben Smith, and Pat Barrett, performed by Pat Barrett.
- Vocal "Lord of Eternity" by Fernando Ortega and John Andrew Schreiner, performed by Fernando Ortega.

- Hymn "I Have Decided to Follow Jesus"—Text: Source Unknown, Music: Folk melody from India, performed by Marisa Frantz and Caleb Rexius.
- Your music choice: _____

Nutrition to Strengthen Your Body

Peas with Pizazz

- 1 cup celery, sliced diagonally
- ⅓ cup sweet onion, thinly sliced
- 2 packages (10 ounces each) frozen peas
- Dash of garlic powder
- Salt-free seasoning and pepper, to taste

In a large saucepan, boil ½ cup of water and cook celery for 3 minutes. Add onion and peas; return to a rapid boil. Cook for 5 minutes, or until peas are tender. Remove from heat. Drain and add garlic powder, salt-free seasoning, and pepper, as desired. Toss gently and serve.   6 servings

Let Go of All Your Fear and Ask God for Strength and Peace

September 14

The Word of God to Guide Your Soul

"Fear not, for I am with you; be not dismayed, for I am your God. I will strengthen you, yes, I will help you, I will uphold you with My righteous right hand" (Isaiah 41:10).

> *Dear Lord, I love You and thank You for Your beautiful promise of always being with me and upholding me. Send Your Holy Spirit to help me give all my fears and anxieties to You and lay them at the foot of the cross. I pray for the grace of strength and peace in the midst of any circumstance or trial. Let others see how You are always there to hold me fast to Your steady, unchanging love. Amen.*

Music to Inspire Your Mind

- Contemporary Christian "Savior, Please" by Ben Glover and Josh Wilson, performed by Josh Wilson.
- Vocal "Everyone Needs a Little" by Kari Jobe, Ed Cash, and Chris Tomlin, performed by Kari Jobe.

- Hymn "He Will Hold Me Fast"—Text and Music: Matthew Merker, Ada R. Habershon, and Jean Sibelius, performed by Keith and Kristyn Getty.
- Your music choice: _____

Nutrition to Strengthen Your Body

Delicious Baked Stuffed Apples

- 4 large apples
- ⅓ cup raisins
- ¼ cup brown sugar
- ⅓ cup graham cracker crumbs
- 2 tablespoons margarine, softened
- 1 teaspoon cinnamon
- 1 cup water

Preheat oven to 350 degrees. Remove core from apples. In a medium bowl, mix remaining ingredients, except water. Stuff ¼ of the mixture into each apple. Pour water into an 8-inch square baking pan and place apples in the pan. Bake for one hour.   4 servings

Have Faith in God's Perfect Timing

September 15

The Word of God to Guide Your Soul

"To everything there is a season, a time for every purpose under heaven. I know that whatever God does, it shall be forever. Nothing can be added to it, and nothing taken from it" (Ecclesiastes 3:1, 14a).

> *Dear Lord, I love You and thank You for Your perfect timing in my life. Send Your Holy Spirit to grant me patience in waiting for answers to prayers and questions I have about Your will for my life. Increase my faith to always trust You, even when things don't make sense to me and don't happen the way I think would be best. As I go through this day, help others to see how much faith I have in You so they will also trust in Your love and perfect timing. Amen.*

Music to Inspire Your Mind

- Contemporary Christian "Yes I Will" by Mia Fieldes, Eddie Hoagland, and Jonathan Smith, performed by Vertical Worship.

- Vocal "The Waiting" by Jamie Grace Harper, Morgan Harper Nichols, and Natalie Grant, performed by Jamie Grace.
- Hymn "In God's Perfect Time"—Text and Music: Dan Schutte, performed by OCP Choir.
- Your music choice: _____

Nutrition to Strengthen Your Body

Penne Pasta with Veggie Sauce

- 3½ cups (12 ounces) uncooked penne pasta
- 3½ cups fresh broccoli florets or 1 package (12 ounces) frozen broccoli florets
- 1 tablespoon olive oil
- 2 to 4 garlic cloves, minced, or ¼ to ½ teaspoon dried, minced garlic
- 1 can (28 ounces) crushed tomatoes, undrained
- ¼ cup red wine vinegar
- 1 tablespoon chopped fresh basil or 1 teaspoon dried basil leaves
- 1 teaspoon sugar
- ½ teaspoon salt-free seasoning

Cook pasta to desired doneness as directed on package, adding broccoli during last 4 minutes of cooking time. (If using frozen broccoli, cook or microwave separately and drain. Drain pasta when done and mix pasta and broccoli together.) Meanwhile, in a large skillet, heat oil over medium heat until hot. Add garlic;

cook and stir 2 to 3 minutes or until tender. Stir in tomatoes and remaining ingredients; simmer for 15 to 20 minutes or until thickened, stirring occasionally. To serve, drain penne and broccoli; arrange on serving platter. Spoon sauce over the top. If desired, sprinkle with grated Parmesan cheese.

6 servings

Pour Out Your Heart to the Lord

September 16

The Word of God to Guide Your Soul
"In God is my salvation and my glory; the rock of my strength, and my refuge, is in God. Trust in Him at all times, you people; pour out your heart before Him; God is a refuge for us" (Psalm 62:7-8).

> *Dear Lord, I love You and thank You for being "the rock of my strength" at all times, both easy and difficult. Send Your Holy Spirit to give my heart the words to pour out all my feelings, hopes, and dreams to You. Help me also to pour out my heart in perfect praise and thanksgiving for all the graces You have given me. During this day, let me share with those I meet the joy it is to know and love You! Amen.*

Music to Inspire Your Mind
- Contemporary Christian "Pour Out My Heart" by Craig Musseau, performed by Sun Garden.
- Vocal "I Lift My Hands" by Chris Tomlin, Louie Giglio, and Matt Maher, performed by Chris Tomlin.

- Hymn "Precious Lord, Take My Hand"—Text: Thomas A. Dorsey, Music: George N. Allen, performed by Krissa Somero.
- Your music choice: _____

Nutrition to Strengthen Your Body

Saucy Asparagus

- 1 can (10.75 ounces) cream of asparagus soup (lower sodium and fat version)
- 2 tablespoons low-fat milk
- 2 packages (10 ounces each) frozen asparagus cuts or 1½ pounds fresh asparagus spears (about 24-30), trimmed and cut into 1-inch pieces
- 1 cup (4 ounces) reduced-fat mozzarella or Cheddar cheese, shredded (optional)

In a 2-quart saucepan over medium heat, combine soup and milk. Heat to boiling, stirring often. Add asparagus. Cover; cook over low heat for 10 minutes or until asparagus is tender, stirring occasionally. Sprinkle with mozzarella or Cheddar cheese, if desired, before serving.　　　　8 servings

Pray for an Increase in the Virtue of Mercy

September 17

The Word of God to Guide Your Soul
"Blessed are the merciful, for they shall obtain mercy" (Matthew 5:7).

> *Dear Lord, I love You and thank You for offering salvation and mercy to me, a sinner, through Your suffering, death, and resurrection. Send Your Holy Spirit to increase in me the virtue of mercy so I may forgive others, as You have forgiven me. Help me today to reach out to someone who needs my mercy and forgiveness. Amen.*

Music to Inspire Your Mind
- Contemporary Christian "Mercy Is a Song" by Matthew West, Jordan Feliz, and A. J. Pruis, performed by Matthew West, featuring Jordan Feliz.
- Vocal "Over and Over" by Jason Ingram, Ben Fielding, Chris McClarney, and Amanda Cook, performed by Chris McClarney.

- Hymn "Redeemed"—Text: Fanny J. Crosby, Music: William J. Kirkpatrick, performed by the Gaither Vocal Band.
- Your music choice: _____

Nutrition to Strengthen Your Body

Black-eyed Peas and Rice

- 4 cups hot, cooked brown rice
- 1 medium sweet onion, finely chopped
- 2 tablespoons olive oil
- 2 cans (15 ounces each) black-eyed peas, drained and rinsed
- 2 cloves garlic, chopped, or ¼ teaspoon dried, minced garlic
- 1 teaspoon oregano
- 1 cup vegetable broth

Prepare rice according to package directions. Meanwhile, in a large skillet, saute onion in olive oil over medium heat until transparent. Add remaining ingredients to the skillet and heat, stirring often, until warmed through. Serve over rice.

6 servings

Give Generously of Your Time, Talent, and Treasure to Those in Need

September 18

The Word of God to Guide Your Soul
"If you extend your soul to the hungry and satisfy the afflicted soul, then your light shall dawn in the darkness, and your darkness shall be as the noonday. The LORD will guide you continually, and satisfy your soul in drought, and strengthen your bones; you shall be like a watered garden, and like a spring of water, whose waters do not fail" (Isaiah 58:10-11).

> *Dear Lord, I love You and thank You for richly blessing me with so many good things—not just material, but, most importantly, spiritual riches beyond measure. Send Your Holy Spirit to grant me a generous heart that is willing to share these blessings with all those you bring into my life. Help me offer my time, talent, and treasure to bring others material and spiritual comfort. Amen.*

Music to Inspire Your Mind

- Contemporary Christian "Generosity" by Jerome JC Collins.
- Vocal "Let It Start with Me" by Sam Allen and Laura Allen, performed by No Other Name.
- Hymn "Little Is Much When God Is in It"—Text and Music: Kittie L. Suffield, performed by The Great Hope Ministers.
- Your music choice: _____

Nutrition to Strengthen Your Body

Mixed Vegetable Caesar Surprise

- 2 tablespoons olive oil
- 2 packages (16 ounces each) frozen cauliflower, carrots, and snow pea pods
- 1 envelope (1.2 ounces) Caesar salad dressing mix

In a large skillet, heat oil over medium heat. Add frozen vegetables and salad dressing mix; blend well. Cover and cook for 5-7 minutes, stirring frequently, until vegetables are desired tenderness.   6 servings

Discern and Follow God's Will

September 19

The Word of God to Guide Your Soul
"And the world is passing away, and the lust of it; but he who does the will of God abides forever" (1 John 2:17).

> *Dear Lord, I love You and thank You for revealing the truth about the world and its passing pleasures. Send Your Holy Spirit to guide me in discerning what Your will is for my life. When I get caught up in this world and what it offers, please help me back on the right path to eternity with You. As I go about my day, let me be an example to others of total and complete surrender to Your plan for my life. Amen.*

Music to Inspire Your Mind
- Contemporary Christian "My Will" by Michael Tait, Toby McKeehan, Daniel Pitts, and Joey Elwood, performed by DC Talk.
- Vocal "Breakthrough" by Lindsey Sweat, Jeff Pardo, and Chris McClarney, performed by Chris McClarney.
- Hymn "Have Thine Own Way"—Text: Adelaide A. Pollard, Music: George C. Stebbins, arrangement by Jon Goode and

Ian Yates, Refrain by Stephen Gibson, performed by Elim
Sound, featuring Fiona Crow.

- Your music choice: _____

Nutrition to Strengthen Your Body

Tomato, Mozzarella, and Cucumber Salad

- 2 large tomatoes, sliced
- 4 mozzarella cheese slices (fresh from deli is best)
- 2 cucumbers, peeled and sliced
- ½ cup balsamic vinaigrette dressing
- 6 leaves fresh basil, chopped, or ½ teaspoon dried basil

On salad plates, layer slices of tomato, cheese, and cucumber.
Drizzle with the dressing. Sprinkle with basil.   4 servings

Abound in Hope by the Power of the Holy Spirit

September 20

The Word of God to Guide Your Soul
"Now may the God of hope fill you with all joy and peace in believing, that you may abound in hope by the power of the Holy Spirit" (Romans 15:13).

> *Dear Lord, I love You and thank You for sending Your Holy Spirit to bring abundant hope and joy to my life. Help me to always be aware of the power and guidance of the Spirit in every circumstance, especially when I start depending on myself to figure things out. Today, let others see how the Holy Spirit is filling me with "all joy and peace in believing." Amen.*

Music to Inspire Your Mind
- Contemporary Christian "Holy Spirit Come" by Josh Gilbert, Dana Potvin, and Jones Beene, performed by Josh Gilbert Band.

- Vocal "Holy Spirit, Living Breath of God" by Keith Getty and Stuart Townend, performed by Kristyn Getty, incorporating "Gabriel's Oboe" by Ennio Morricone.
- Hymn "Come, Holy Ghost"—Text: Veni, Creator Spiritus; attributed to Rabanus Maurus, Music: Louis Lambillotte, performed by Sarah Hart, arranged by Sarah Hart and Kevin B. Hipp.
- Your music choice: _____

Nutrition to Strengthen Your Body

Cheesy Brown Rice with Red Peppers and Peas

- 1 tablespoon olive oil
- ½ cup red pepper, diced
- 1 cup water
- 1 cup frozen peas
- 4 ounces (1 cup) reduced-fat Sharp Cheddar cheese, shredded (or other favorite cheese)
- 1 can (4 ounces) sliced mushrooms, drained
- 1½ cups instant brown rice

In a large saucepan, heat olive oil over medium heat. Add red pepper and saute for 3 minutes. Add water and peas. Bring to a boil. Add cheese and mushrooms. Return to a gentle boil, stirring constantly. Add rice. Stir well, cover, remove from heat, and let stand 10 minutes. Stir and serve.   6 servings

Offer a Sacrifice of Praise

September 21

The Word of God to Guide Your Soul

"For here we have no continuing city, but we seek the one to come. Therefore by Him let us continually offer the sacrifice of praise to God, that is, the fruit of our lips, giving thanks to His name" (Hebrews 13:14-15).

> *Dear Lord, I love You and thank You so much for loving me and granting me the grace to love You back with my whole heart. Send Your Holy Spirit to help me offer You a sacrifice of praise in every situation and moment of my life. Grant me boldness and courage to confess Your name, Jesus, and to tell the story of Your great sacrifice to all who will listen. Amen.*

Music to Inspire Your Mind

- Contemporary Christian "Blessed Be Your Name" by Matt and Beth Redman, performed by Matt Redman.
- Vocal "Better Than a Hallelujah" by Chapin Hartford and Sarah Hart, performed by Amy Grant.

- Hymn "We Declare Your Majesty"—Text and Music: Malcolm du Plessis, performed by Maranatha! Promise Band.
- Your music choice: _____

Nutrition to Strengthen Your Body

Mixed Fruit Cobbler

- 4 cups (1 cup of each) sliced fresh or canned fruit, drained (pears, peaches, apples, berries, etc.)
- ½ teaspoon cinnamon
- 2 tablespoons sugar, divided
- 1 cup baking mix (healthy version)
- ⅓ cup low-fat milk
- 1 tablespoon brown sugar
- 8 ounces low-fat strawberry or lemon yogurt (optional)

Preheat oven to 425 degrees. Place fruit in a microwave-safe bowl. Sprinkle with cinnamon and 1 tablespoon sugar. Microwave on high for 4 minutes. In a medium bowl, combine the remaining 1 tablespoon sugar, baking mix, and milk. Stir until ingredients are moistened. Using a teaspoon, drop small mounds of dough over fruit. Thinly spread out dough. Sprinkle top with brown sugar. Bake for 12 to 15 minutes. Top with yogurt, if desired.   6 servings

Take Comfort in the Sure Promise of Eternal Life

September 22

The Word of God to Guide Your Soul
"In hope of eternal life which God, who cannot lie, promised before time began" (Titus 1:2).

> *Dear Lord, I love You and thank You so much for Your promise of eternal life. Send Your Holy Spirit to increase my faith and hope in the day I will live with You forever in perfect love, beauty, and joy. Grant me the grace today to see glimpses of my heavenly home, perhaps in an amazing sunset or lyrical bird song. Help me to share Your promise with someone who may be losing hope or grieving the death of a loved one. Amen.*

Music to Inspire Your Mind
- Contemporary Christian "Love Has Come" by Mark Schultz, Brown Bannister, Sam Mizell, and Matthew West, performed by Mark Schultz.
- Choral "There Are Many Rooms" by Liam Lawton, performed by Liam Lawton and Choir.

- Hymn "Eye Has Not Seen"—Text and Music: Marty Haugen, performed by Marty Haugen and Choir.
- Your music choice: _____

Nutrition to Strengthen Your Body

Minestrone Casserole

- 1 package (7 ounces) whole grain elbow macaroni
- 2 cups (8 ounces) reduced-fat Cheddar cheese, shredded (or other favorite cheese)
- 1 can (16 ounces) vegetarian baked beans
- 1 can (8 ounces) stewed tomatoes
- 1 green bell pepper, diced
- 1 red bell pepper, diced
- ½ cup Parmesan cheese, grated
- Nonstick olive oil cooking spray

Preheat oven to 375 degrees. Prepare elbow macaroni according to package directions and drain. Spray a 2-quart casserole dish with cooking spray. In a large bowl, combine cooked macaroni, 1½ cups Cheddar cheese, beans, tomatoes, and bell peppers; mix well. Transfer mixture to a casserole dish. Sprinkle with remaining Cheddar cheese and Parmesan cheese. Bake for 25 to 30 minutes or until heated through. Let stand for 10 minutes before serving. (Can be mixed ahead, covered, and refrigerated. Increase baking time to 35-40 minutes.)   8 servings

Take Time Each Day to Seek God's Face

September 23

The Word of God to Guide Your Soul

"Hear, O LORD, when I cry with my voice! Have mercy also upon me, and answer me. When You said, 'Seek My face,' my heart said to You, 'Your face, LORD, I will seek'" (Psalm 27:7-8).

> *Dear Lord, I love You and thank You for always being there for me. Send Your Holy Spirit to encourage me to take some quiet time with You every day and seek Your face. Only then will I be able to start experiencing the ocean of mercy and love You want to share with me. Help me to just be in Your presence and love You. Then show me how to share Your love with all those I meet today. Amen.*

Music to Inspire Your Mind

- Contemporary Christian "Came to My Rescue" by Marty Sampson, Dylan Thomas, and Joel Davies, performed by Hillsong United.

- Vocal "Just Be" by Mia Fieldes, Kim Walker-Smith, and Jonathan Lindley Smith, performed by Jesus Culture, featuring Kim Walker-Smith.
- Hymn "Lord, You Have My Heart"—Text and Music: Lenny LeBlanc, Rachel Wilson, and Martin Smith, performed by Lenny LeBlanc and Integrity's Hosanna! Music.
- Your music choice: _____

Nutrition to Strengthen Your Body

Savory Sweet Potatoes and Onions

- 2 tablespoons olive oil
- 1 cup sweet onions, chopped
- 2 medium sweet potatoes, peeled, cut into ½-inch cubes
- ½ teaspoon ground cinnamon
- ¼ teaspoon dried thyme
- ½ cup water

In a large skillet, heat oil over medium heat. Add onions, sweet potatoes, cinnamon, and thyme; cook for 10 minutes, or until onions are tender, stirring frequently. Add water and reduce heat to low, cover, and cook for 15 minutes or until sweet potatoes are tender. Stir occasionally while cooking and add water in small amounts, if necessary, to prevent sticking.

4 servings

Ask for Faith to Conquer Your Fears

September 24

The Word of God to Guide Your Soul

"While He was still speaking, some came from the ruler of the synagogue's house who said, 'Your daughter is dead. Why trouble the Teacher any further?' As soon as Jesus heard the word that was spoken, He said to the ruler of the synagogue, 'Do not be afraid; only believe'" (Mark 5:35-36).

> *Dear Lord, I love You and thank You for reassuring me I can have faith in the plans You have for my life. Send Your Holy Spirit to greatly increase my faith so it conquers all my fears. Lead me to someone today who needs Your love and reassurance. Speak through me to share Your words of wisdom —'Do not be afraid; only believe." Amen.*

Music to Inspire Your Mind

- Contemporary Christian "I Choose to Believe" by Dan Dean, Don Poythress, and Tony Wood, performed by Phillips, Craig, and Dean.
- Vocal "I Will Have Faith in You" by Sarah Hart and Sam Mizell, performed by Sarah Hart.

- Hymn "I Know Who Holds Tomorrow"—Text and Music: Ira F. Stanphill, performed by The Petersens.
- Your music choice: _____

Nutrition to Strengthen Your Body

Vegetable Frittata

- 1½ cup fresh mushrooms, sliced, or 1 can (8 ounces) sliced mushrooms, drained
- 1 cup sweet onions, chopped
- 1 clove garlic, minced, or ⅛ teaspoon dried, minced garlic
- 2 tablespoons olive oil
- 5 eggs or 1¼ cup egg substitute
- 1 package (10 ounces) frozen spinach, thawed and drained
- 1 jar (6 ounces) marinated artichoke hearts, drained
- 1 cup (4 ounces) reduced-fat, sharp Cheddar cheese, grated
- Salt-free seasoning and pepper to taste
- Nonstick olive oil cooking spray

Preheat oven to 350 degrees. In a large skillet, heat oil over medium heat and saute mushrooms, onion, and garlic until tender, for about 5-7 minutes. In a medium bowl, beat eggs lightly. Add vegetables and remaining ingredients to eggs; blend until mixed. Spray a 1½-quart casserole dish with cooking spray and pour in egg mixture. Bake for 45 minutes or until firm.   8 servings

Walk as a Child of the Light

September 25

The Word of God to Guide Your Soul

"For you were once darkness, but now you are light in the Lord. Walk as children of light (for the fruit of the Spirit is in all goodness, righteousness, and truth), finding out what is acceptable to the Lord" (Ephesians 5:8-10).

> *Dear Lord, I love You and thank You for saving me and making me a child of Your heavenly family. Send Your Holy Spirit to help me live in a way that is acceptable to You and makes You pleased and joyful. Never let me slip back into darkness but grant me the grace to produce "all goodness, righteousness, and truth." Let those I encounter today recognize the light of Your love in my words and deeds. Amen.*

Music to Inspire Your Mind

- Contemporary Christian "We Are" by James Tealy, Chuck Butler, Hillary McBride, and Ed Cash, performed by Kari Jobe.

- Vocal "The Light in Me" by Brandon Health and Dan Muckala, performed by Brandon Heath.
- Hymn "Song for the Nations"—Text and Music: Chris Christensen, performed by Chris Christensen.
- Your music choice: _____

Nutrition to Strengthen Your Body

Veggie Quesadillas and Salad

- 4 whole wheat flour tortillas
- 4 ounces (1 cup) reduced-fat Mexican cheese blend, shredded
- 4 tablespoons salsa
- 1 cup green pepper, chopped
- 1 package lettuce and vegetable blend salad
- Light salad dressing (your choice)

Place ¼ cup of cheese in the center of each tortilla. Add 1 tablespoon salsa and ¼ cup chopped green pepper to each tortilla as well. Fold in the sides on each and roll up. Place on a microwavable dish, cover with a paper towel, and microwave on high for 1-2 minutes. Serve with salad and dressing of choice. 4 servings

Watch and Pray to Resist Temptations

September 26

The Word of God to Guide Your Soul
"Watch and pray, lest you enter into temptation. The spirit indeed is willing, but the flesh is weak" (Matthew 26:41).

> *Dear Lord, I love You and thank You for this reminder to always be on guard against every temptation by consistently watching and praying. Send Your Holy Spirit to grant me discernment when evil is present and then to be strong against it. I know I can't always be perfect, and I thank You for Your forgiveness but help me to live a virtuous life that reflects who I am—a follower of Jesus and a child of my heavenly Father. Amen.*

Music to Inspire Your Mind
- Contemporary Christian "When My Flesh Is Weak (Watching and Praying)" by Joel Payne, performed by Resound Worship.
- Vocal "The Spirit Is Willing (But the Flesh Is Weak)" by Babbie Mason.

- Hymn "Rise, My Soul, to Watch and Pray"—Text: Johann B. Freystein, translated by Catherine Winkworth, Music and additional chorus: Lori Sealy, performed by Lori Sealy.
- Your music choice: _____

Nutrition to Strengthen Your Body

Green Bean Casserole

- 1 package (16 ounces) frozen French-style green beans
- ½ cup fresh mushrooms, chopped, or 1 can (4 ounces) pieces and stems mushrooms, drained and chopped
- 1 cup sweet onion, chopped
- 1 can (10.5 ounces) cream of mushroom soup (reduced fat and sodium)
- 1 teaspoon salt-free seasoning
- 1 tablespoon black pepper
- ¼ teaspoon garlic powder
- 1 cup seasoned salad croutons, crushed

Preheat oven to 350 degrees. Prepare green beans according to package directions and drain. In a large bowl, mix green beans, mushrooms, onion, and cream of mushroom soup. Add salt-free seasoning, pepper, and garlic powder. Pour into a 2-quart casserole dish and bake, covered, for 20 minutes. Top with crushed salad croutons. Bake, uncovered, for an additional 5-10 minutes.   6 servings

Trust in the Lord's Loving Care

September 27

The Word of God to Guide Your Soul

"Therefore humble yourselves under the mighty hand of God, that He may exalt you in due time, casting all your care upon Him, for He cares for you" (1 Peter 5:6-7).

> *Dear Lord, I love You and thank You for how much You care for me. Send Your Holy Spirit to help me trust in Your love and cast all my cares upon You. Grant me the grace of a childlike faith that has perfect confidence in You and never worries about what tomorrow may bring. Let me inspire others with my total trust in Your plans for my life. Amen.*

Music to Inspire Your Mind

- Contemporary Christian "Sinking Deep" by Joel Davies and Aodhan King, performed by Hillsong Young and Free.
- Vocal "Trust in You" by Lauren Daigle, Michael Farren, and Paul Mabury, performed by Lauren Daigle.
- Hymn "No One Ever Cared for Me like Jesus"—Text and Music: Charles F. Weigle, performed by Sandi Patty.
- Your music choice: _____

Nutrition to Strengthen Your Body

Open-Face Broiled Bean, Cheese, and Tomato Sandwich

- 4 slices whole wheat bread or buns
- 1 can (16 ounces) vegetarian baked beans, drained
- 4 slices reduced-fat Swiss or American cheese
- 4 large slices of fresh tomato

Preheat the oven broiler. Place bread on a baking sheet lined with foil. Toast one side of bread under the broiler. Remove from oven, turn over bread, and spread beans on the untoasted side and top with cheese. Lay slice of tomato on top. Return to the broiler for a few minutes until cheese melts and beans are heated through. 4 servings

Rest in God's Promise to Supply All Your Needs

September 28

The Word of God to Guide Your Soul

"And my God shall supply all your need according to His riches in glory by Christ Jesus. Now to our God and Father be glory forever and ever. Amen" (Philippians 4:19-20).

> *Dear Lord, I love You and thank You for supplying all my needs, both physically and spiritually. Send Your Holy Spirit to help me rest in Your promise that You will provide for myself and my family, in accord with Your "riches in glory by Christ Jesus." Inspire me to follow Your example and be generous with those in need. Amen.*

Music to Inspire Your Mind

- Contemporary Christian "Miracle" by Tauren Wells.
- Vocal "Jesus, Strong and Kind" by Jonny Robinson, Rich Thompson, Michael Farren, and Colin Buchanan, performed by CityAlight, featuring Colin Buchanan.
- Hymn "Jesus, I Am Resting, Resting"—Text: Jean Sophia Pigott, Music: David Hampton, performed by Steve Green.

- Your music choice: _____

Nutrition to Strengthen Your Body

Layered Veggie Italian Pasta Bake

- 8 ounces whole grain macaroni or other favorite pasta
- 1 medium sweet onion, chopped
- 4 celery ribs, chopped
- 2 tablespoons olive oil
- 1 package (16 ounces) frozen mixed vegetables, thawed
- Salt-free seasoning and pepper, to taste
- 1 jar (24 ounces) pasta sauce with basil and garlic
- 1 cup reduced-fat mozzarella cheese, shredded
- Nonstick olive oil cooking spray

Preheat oven to 350 degrees. Prepare pasta according to package directions and drain. (Reduce cooking time by 2-3 minutes, as pasta will cook more when baked.) In a large skillet, saute onion and celery in olive oil over medium-high heat. Reduce heat to low and add thawed mixed vegetables and seasonings. Cover and heat through. Spray a 9x13-inch baking pan with nonstick cooking spray; place ½ jar of spaghetti sauce on bottom, ½ of cooked pasta, ½ of vegetable mixture, and ½ cup of mozzarella cheese. Repeat for another layer. Bake for 30 minutes. Let sit for 5 minutes before serving. 6-8 servings

Praise the Lord for His Protection

September 29

The Word of God to Guide Your Soul

"The LORD is my strength and my shield; my heart trusted in Him, and I am helped; therefore my heart greatly rejoices, and with my song I will praise Him" (Psalm 28:7).

> *Dear Lord, I love You and thank You for protecting me and being "my strength and my shield." Send Your Holy Spirit to grant me the grace to always entrust my heart to Your keeping. Help me truly rejoice in You this day, no matter what circumstances may come my way, and let my joy inspire others to seek Your help and protection. Amen.*

Music to Inspire Your Mind

- Contemporary Christian "Strong God" by Jon Egan, Jason Ingram, and Meredith Andrews, performed by Meredith Andrews.
- Vocal "There Is None like You" by Lenny LeBlanc.
- Hymn "Awesome Power"—Text and Music: John G. Elliott, performed by John G. Elliott.

- Your music choice: _____

Nutrition to Strengthen Your Body

Garden Stuffed Pepper Tomato Soup

- 4 medium green peppers
- 1 can (15 ounces) red kidney beans, drained and rinsed
- 1 package (10 ounces) frozen, chopped broccoli, thawed
- 8 ounces reduced-fat Muenster, Monterey Jack, or mozzarella cheese, shredded
- 1 can condensed tomato soup (lower fat and sodium)
- ½ cup low-fat milk

Cut each green pepper lengthwise in half and remove seeds. In a large skillet, place pepper halves cut-side up in ½-inch of water; heat to boiling over high heat. Reduce heat to low; cover and simmer for 5 minutes or until peppers are tender-crisp. Meanwhile, in a medium bowl, combine beans, broccoli, and cheese. Toss to mix well. Remove peppers from skillet. Fill each pepper half with some bean mixture. Discard water in skillet. In the same skillet, stir condensed tomato soup and milk until blended. Carefully place stuffed peppers in the soup mixture; heat to boiling over high heat. Reduce heat to low; cover and simmer for 10-15 minutes until vegetable mixture is heated through and cheese is melted. Serve in a bowl and ladle soup over peppers.

4 servings

Live a Healthy Life to Glorify God

September 30

The Word of God to Guide Your Soul

"Or do you not know that your body is the temple of the Holy Spirit who is in you, whom you have from God, and you are not your own? For you were bought at a price; therefore glorify God in your body and in your spirit, which are God's" (1 Corinthians 6:19-20).

> *Dear Lord, I love You and thank You for making my body a temple in which You dwell. Send Your Holy Spirit to grant me the virtues of temperance and self-control, so, in gratitude, I take good care of this body You have graciously given me. Let me be a witness to others through living a healthy life and glorifying You in all I do. Amen.*

Music to Inspire Your Mind

- Contemporary Christian "Christ in Me" by Jeremy Camp and Bernie Herms, performed by Jeremy Camp.
- Vocal "Be Glorified" by Don Moen, performed by Don Moen and Integrity's Hosanna! Music.

- Hymn "Take Time to Be Holy"—Text: William D. Longstaff, Music: George C. Stebbins, performed by David and Steven Au.
- Your music choice: _____

Nutrition to Strengthen Your Body

Carrot and Spinach Orzo

- 2 teaspoons margarine (olive-oil based)
- 2 cloves garlic, finely chopped, or ¼ teaspoon dried, minced garlic
- 1 cup carrots, coarsely shredded or diced
- 4 cups vegetable broth
- 2 cups orzo pasta
- 1 package (10 ounces) frozen chopped spinach, thawed and squeezed to drain
- ¼ cup Parmesan cheese, grated
- 1 teaspoon dried basil leaves
- Salt-free seasoning and pepper to taste

In a 2-quart saucepan, melt margarine over medium heat. Add garlic and carrots; cook for several minutes, stirring occasionally, until carrot is tender. Stir in broth, orzo, and spinach. Heat to boiling. Reduce heat to medium-low and simmer for 15-20 minutes, or until broth is absorbed. Stir in Parmesan cheese, basil, and seasonings before serving.

8 servings

Listen to Jesus and Be at Peace

October 1

The Word of God to Guide Your Soul

"These things I have spoken to you, that in Me you may have peace. In the world you will have tribulation; but be of good cheer, I have overcome the world" (John 16:33).

> *Dear Lord, I love You and thank You for overcoming the world and all the trials it brings. Send Your Holy Spirit to help me listen to Your words of peace and praise You in every difficulty, as I remember all You have sacrificed to bring me Your peace and love. Show me how to help those around me who are restless and anxious to understand the only way to find peace is to trust in You. Amen.*

Music to Inspire Your Mind

- Contemporary Christian "Praise You in This Storm" by Bernie Herms and Mark Hall, performed by Casting Crowns.
- Vocal "Restless" by Audrey Assad and Matt Maher, performed by Audrey Assad.

- Hymn "Dear Lord and Father of Mankind"—Text: John Greenleaf Whittier, Music: Sir Charles Hubert Hastings Parry, performed by Katherine Jenkins.
- Your music choice: _____

Nutrition to Strengthen Your Body

Colorful Autumn Succotash

- 2 tablespoons olive oil
- 1 medium sweet onion, diced
- 2 garlic cloves, finely chopped, or ¼ teaspoon dried, minced garlic
- 1 package (10 ounces) frozen lima beans, thawed
- 1 package (10 ounces) frozen yellow sweet corn, thawed
- 1 green bell pepper, diced
- 1 pint grape tomatoes, halved lengthwise
- Salt-free seasoning and pepper to taste
- 2 tablespoons fresh parsley, coarsely chopped, or 1 tablespoon dried parsley (other options: sage, thyme or rosemary)

In a large skillet over medium-high heat, saute onion and garlic in olive oil for 2 minutes. Add the rest of the ingredients, except parsley, and mix well. Cook and stir often until vegetables are tender, for about 10 minutes. Stir in parsley or other herbs of choice and serve. 6 servings

Thank the Lord for Your Guardian Angel

October 2

The Word of God to Guide Your Soul
"No evil shall befall you, nor shall any plague come near your dwelling; for He shall give His angels charge over you, to keep you in all your ways. In their hands they shall bear you up, lest you dash your foot against a stone" (Psalm 91:10-12).

Dear Lord, I love You and thank You for my Guardian Angel. Thank You for every time my angel has protected me from spiritual and physical harm. Thank You for the moments I have received an encouraging word of hope from a kind "stranger" who has helped me to carry on. Send Your Holy Spirit to help me be an "angel" to others today as they journey through this life toward their heavenly home. Amen.

Music to Inspire Your Mind
- Contemporary Christian "Angels among Us" by Becky Hobbs and Don Goodman, performed by Alabama.
- Choral "Angel" by Robert Prizeman, performed by Libera.

- Hymn "Guardian Angel" by Marilla Ness.
- Your music choice: _____

Nutrition to Strengthen Your Body

Peach-Berry Trifle

- 1 angel food cake, cut into cubes
- 1 carton (8 ounces) low-fat peach yogurt (or other favorite flavor)
- 1 carton (8 ounces) frozen light whipped dessert topping, thawed
- 3 cups mixed fresh or frozen berries, thawed (raspberries, blueberries, and sliced strawberries)

Place angel food cake cubes in a large serving bowl (preferably glass). In a small bowl, stir together the yogurt and ¼ of the carton of whipped topping. Spoon over cake cubes. Top with berries. Garnish with additional light whipped dessert topping, as desired. 6 servings

Praise God for His Unconditional Love

October 3

The Word of God to Guide Your Soul
"But God demonstrates His own love toward us, in that while we were still sinners, Christ died for us" (Romans 5:8).

> *Dear Lord, I love You and thank You for Your unconditional love. Send Your Holy Spirit to increase the virtue of charity and love in my life so I may reflect Your loving heart to all I meet. I'm so sorry for the times I haven't loved You or others as I should. Help me show love, especially to those most difficult to love. Amen.*

Music to Inspire Your Mind
- Contemporary Christian "More" by Kenny Greenberg, Jason Houser, and Matthew West, performed by Matthew West.
- Vocal "See How He Loves Us" by Marc Willerton and Jon Althoff, performed by Sovereign Grace.
- Hymn "Lamb of God"—Text and Music: Twila Paris, performed by The Maranatha Singers.

- Your music choice: _____

Nutrition to Strengthen Your Body

Tasty Vegetarian Baked Beans

- 2 cans (16 ounces each) vegetarian baked beans
- ¼ cup brown sugar
- 2 tablespoons catsup
- 1 tablespoon prepared mustard
- 2 tablespoons maple syrup or honey
- ½ small sweet onion, chopped
- 1 teaspoon cinnamon
- ¼ teaspoon cloves

In a large bowl, mix all ingredients together. Pour into a 1½-quart casserole dish. Cover and microwave on high for 5 minutes, stir, and microwave for an additional 5 minutes.

6 servings

Appreciate the Lord's Work in the Beauty of Nature

October 4

The Word of God to Guide Your Soul

"O LORD, how manifold are your works! In wisdom You have made them all. The earth is full of Your possessions. You send forth Your Spirit, they are created; and You renew the face of the earth. May the glory of the LORD endure forever; may the LORD rejoice in His works" (Psalm 104:24, 30-31).

> *Dear Lord, I love You and thank You for all of the beauty You have created in nature. Send Your Holy Spirit to open my eyes to Your wonders surrounding me every day of my life, as in a fluttering butterfly or a rainbow after a storm. Today, help me proclaim, as Saint Francis did, Your greatness and goodness to all who are struggling to find You. Amen.*

Music to Inspire Your Mind

- Contemporary Christian "Great Are You Lord" by Jason Ingram, Leslie Jordan, and David Leonard, performed by Casting Crowns.

- Vocal "Prayer of St. Francis" by St. Francis of Assisi and Sebastian Temple, performed by Susan Boyle.
- Hymn "All Creatures of Our God and King"—Text: St. Francis of Assisi; translated by William H. Draper, Music: Geistliche Kirchengesange, Cologne, 1623, performed by Fernando Ortega.
- Your music choice: _____

Nutrition to Strengthen Your Body

Crustless Vegetable Pot Pie

- 1 medium sweet onion, sliced
- 1 tablespoon olive oil
- 2 cups peeled, cubed potatoes
- 2 medium stalks celery, sliced
- 1 package (10 ounces) frozen mixed vegetables
- 1 teaspoon salt-free seasoning
- ½ teaspoon paprika
- Dash pepper
- 1 tablespoon cornstarch

In a large skillet, saute onion in olive oil over medium heat for 5 minutes, stirring occasionally. Add potatoes and celery; cook for 5 minutes more. Stir in mixed vegetables, salt-free seasoning, paprika, and pepper. Cover, reduce heat to low, and cook for 20 minutes, stirring occasionally and separating frozen vegetables. In a cup, mix cornstarch with ⅓ cup cold water. Gradually add to vegetable mixture; cook, stirring constantly, until thickened. Serve over rice or noodles.

6 servings

Enter Salvation Through Jesus, the Door, and Good Shepherd

October 5

The Word of God to Guide Your Soul

"Then Jesus said to them again, 'Most assuredly, I say to you, I am the door of the sheep. All who ever came before Me are thieves and robbers, but the sheep did not hear them. I am the door. If anyone enters by Me, he will be saved, and will go in and out and find pasture'" (John 10:7-9).

> *Dear Lord, I love You and thank You for saving my soul and leading me to heavenly pastures. Send Your Holy Spirit to securely keep me with Your flock and never let me wander off. Grant me the grace to always make You the Shepherd of my heart. I pray for the courage today to help someone understand that You are the door to salvation and eternal life. Amen.*

Music to Inspire Your Mind

- Contemporary Christian "Jesus" by Chris Tomlin and Ed Cash, performed by Chris Tomlin.

- Vocal "Shepherd of My Heart" by Mark Baldwin and Dick Tunney, performed by Sandi Patty.
- Hymn "Pastures of the Lord"—Text and Music: Curtis Stephan, performed by Curtis Stephan.
- Your music choice: _____

Nutrition to Strengthen Your Body

French Toasted Cheese and Tomato Sandwiches

- Margarine, to taste
- Prepared mustard to taste
- 8 slices oatmeal or whole grain bread
- 4 slices reduced-fat Muenster cheese
- 4 slices reduced-fat Cheddar cheese
- 4 slices tomato
- 2 eggs, beaten, or ½ cup egg substitute
- ½ cup low-fat milk
- ¼ teaspoon salt-free seasoning
- Applesauce, as desired (optional)

Spread margarine on each slice of bread on one side. For each sandwich, spread bottom slice (buttered side down) with mustard, 1 slice of Muenster cheese, 1 slice of tomato, 1 slice of Cheddar cheese, and a second slice of bread, buttered on the outside and mustard on the inside. In a medium bowl, blend together eggs, milk, and salt-free seasoning. Dip sandwiches in egg mixture, coating both sides well. In a large skillet, sprayed with nonstick cooking spray, brown both sides on medium heat. Cover and cook on low just until cheese begins to melt and sandwiches are heated through. To serve, slice sandwiches in half diagonally and top each half with applesauce, as desired.

4 servings

Spend Daily Quiet Time with God

October 6

The Word of God to Guide Your Soul
"Draw near to God and He will draw near to you" (James 4:8a).

> *Dear Lord, I love You and thank You for drawing near to me when I take the time to draw near to You. Send Your Holy Spirit to remind me of the importance of spending a daily quiet time with You. I'm sorry for the days I have let the busyness of life keep me from taking the time to just be with You and enjoy our friendship. Help me to do better and share with others as well the value of resting in Your presence. Amen.*

Music to Inspire Your Mind
- Contemporary Christian "Just Be Held" by Mark Hall, Bernie Herms, and Matthew West, performed by Casting Crowns.
- Vocal "Draw Me Close" by Kelly Carpenter, performed by Michael W. Smith.

- Hymn "Nearer, My God, to Thee"—Text: Sarah F. Adams, Music: Lowell Mason, performed by BYU Vocal Point, featuring BYU Men's Chorus.
- Your music choice: _____

Nutrition to Strengthen Your Body

Snow Pea Pods and Angel Hair Pasta

- 1 package (10 ounces) frozen snow pea pods
- 4 ounces angel hair pasta
- ¼ cup plus 2 tablespoons low-fat sour cream
- 3 tablespoons lemon juice
- 2 tablespoons prepared yellow or Dijon mustard
- 2 tablespoons olive oil
- ½ cup sweet onion, diced
- 1 jar (2 ounces) sliced pimiento, drained

Prepare snow pea pods according to package directions; drain and set aside. Meanwhile, cook pasta according to package directions; drain and set aside. In a small bowl, combine sour cream, lemon juice, and mustard. In a large skillet, heat olive oil over medium-high heat. Saute onion for 2-3 minutes or until tender. Add snow peas, sour cream mixture, pasta, and pimiento. Cook, stirring constantly, 2-3 minutes or until heated through. Serve immediately.   6 servings

Ask, Seek, and Knock

October 7

The Word of God to Guide Your Soul
"Ask, and it will be given to you; seek, and you will find; knock, and it will be opened to you. For everyone who asks receives, and he who seeks finds, and to him who knocks it will be opened" (Matthew 7:7-8).

> *Dear Lord, I love You and thank You for your promise to answer when I sincerely ask, seek, and knock in accordance with Your will. Send Your Holy Spirit to make me constantly aware of how You are helping and encouraging me. Lead me to someone today who is searching for You and needs to be encouraged to ask, seek, and knock. Amen.*

Music to Inspire Your Mind
- Contemporary Christian "Right in Front Of Me" by Josh Wilson, Jeff Pardo, and Steve Wilson, performed by Josh Wilson.
- Vocal "The Lord's Prayer" by Ben Fielding, Benjamin Hastings, Reuben Morgan, and Marty Sampson, performed by Hillsong Worship.

- Hymn "Seek Ye First"—Text and Music: Karen Lafferty, performed by Maranatha! Music.
- Your music choice: _____

Nutrition to Strengthen Your Body

Broccoli Florets with Almond Topping

- 1 package (16 ounces) frozen broccoli florets
- 2 tablespoons olive oil
- 1 small sweet onion, chopped
- 1 medium red bell pepper, diced into ½-inch pieces
- ¼ teaspoon dried, minced garlic
- ⅓ cup sliced almonds
- Salt-free seasoning and pepper to taste

In a medium skillet, saute onions in olive oil for 3-4 minutes over medium heat. Stir in diced pepper, garlic, and almonds. Increase heat to medium-high. Cook, stirring constantly, for 2 minutes. Cover and keep warm over low heat. Prepare broccoli according to package directions. Drain and place into a serving dish. Season with salt-free seasoning and pepper, as desired. Pour almond mixture over top of broccoli and serve.   6 servings

Embrace the Grace of a Holy Life

October 8

The Word of God to Guide Your Soul
"Therefore do not be ashamed of the testimony of our Lord, nor of me His prisoner, but share with me in the sufferings for the gospel according to the power of God, who has saved us and called us with a holy calling, not according to our works, but according to His own purpose and grace which was given us in Christ Jesus before time began" (2 Timothy 1:8-9).

> *Dear Lord, I love You and thank You for the grace to live a life empowered by Your love, a grace given "before time began." Send Your Holy Spirit to grant me confidence and faith, always looking to You to help me live a holy life, according to Your own design. Let my life today inspire others to walk with You and embrace the grace of a holy life. Amen.*

Music to Inspire Your Mind
- Contemporary Christian "Confidence" by Matt Armstrong, Chris Rohman, Dustin Lolli, and Ethan Hulse, performed by Sanctus Real.

- Vocal "You Say" by Lauren Daigle, Jason Ingram, and Paul Mabury, performed by Lauren Daigle.
- Hymn "O Master, Let Me Walk with Thee"—Text: Washington Gladden, Music: H. Percy Smith, Arranged by Vince Gill, John Hobbs, and Brown Bannister, performed by Amy Grant.
- Your music choice: _____

Nutrition to Strengthen Your Body

Pan-fried Zucchini Chips

- 2 medium zucchini, thinly sliced (about ½-inch thick)
- 2 large eggs, beaten, or ½ cup egg substitute
- 1 sleeve multigrain crackers, crushed
- ¼ teaspoon garlic powder
- 2 tablespoons olive oil
- Salt-free seasoning and pepper, to taste

Place crushed crackers in a medium bowl and add garlic powder. Mix well. Prepare each zucchini slice by dipping in eggs, them pressing into cracker crumbs. Place each slice onto a plate, but do not stack. In a large skillet, heat olive oil over medium heat. Pan fry each zucchini slice until coating browns and zucchini softens, for about 3 minutes each side. Season with salt-free seasoning and pepper, as desired.   4 servings

Give Thanks to the Lord for His Love and Faithfulness

October 9

The Word of God to Guide Your Soul
"It is good to give thanks to the LORD, and to sing praises to Your name, O Most High; to declare Your lovingkindness in the morning, and Your faithfulness every night" (Psalm 92:1-2).

> *Dear Lord, I love You and thank You for Your unconditional love and unwavering faithfulness. Send Your Holy Spirit to grant me an attitude of gratitude, no matter what circumstances may come my way. For whatever happens to me, I am still Your child and an heir to Your heavenly kingdom. Let my thanksgiving be evident and brighten someone's day. Amen.*

Music to Inspire Your Mind
- Contemporary Christian "Forever" by Chris Tomlin.
- Vocal "Hosanna (Praise Is Rising)" by Brenton Brown and Paul Baloche, performed by Paul Baloche.

- Hymn "We Praise Thee, O God, Our Redeemer"—Text: Julia Cady Cory, Music: Netherlands folk song, performed by Altar of Praise Chorale.
- Your music choice: _____

Nutrition to Strengthen Your Body

Slow Cooker Vegetable Paella

- 2 tablespoons olive oil
- 1 medium sweet onion, chopped
- 1 medium red pepper, chopped
- 2 garlic cloves, minced, or ¼ teaspoon dried, minced garlic
- 1 cup uncooked brown rice
- 1 can (14.5 ounces) stewed tomatoes
- 1 can (14.5 ounces) vegetable broth
- 2 medium carrots, chopped
- 1 small zucchini, cut into 1-inch cubes
- Seasonings: 1 teaspoon paprika, 2 teaspoons Italian seasoning, ⅛ teaspoon pepper
- 1 jar (6.5 ounces) marinated artichoke hearts, drained and chopped
- ½ cup frozen peas, thawed
- ¼ cup chopped fresh parsley or 1 tablespoon dried parsley

In a large skillet, saute onions in olive oil over medium heat until translucent and tender, about 6-8 minutes. Transfer onions to a slow cooker and stir in uncooked brown rice. Add

593

the rest of the ingredients except artichokes, peas, and parsley. Cover and cook on low for 4-6 hours or on high for 2-3 hours, until liquid is absorbed. Stir in artichokes, peas, and parsley. Cover and cook for another 20 minutes on low or until heated through.   8 servings

Lose the World and Gain Christ

October 10

The Word of God to Guide Your Soul

"But what things were gain to me, these I have counted loss for Christ. Yet indeed I also count all things loss for the excellence of the knowledge of Christ Jesus my Lord, for whom I have suffered the loss of all things, and count them as rubbish, that I may gain Christ and be found in Him" (Philippians 3:7-9a).

> *Dear Lord, I love You and thank You for the indescribable loss You suffered by purchasing my salvation with Your precious blood. Send Your Holy Spirit to grant me the same courage You had so I may lose all this world has to offer to gain a beautiful life with You, now and forever. Help me be an example to others of what it looks like to be "found" in You and serve only You. Amen.*

Music to Inspire Your Mind

- Contemporary Christian "Enough" by Louie Giglio and Chris Tomlin, performed by Jeremy Camp.
- Vocal "Jesus, My Everything" by Matt Maher.

- Hymn "Jesus, All for Jesus"—Text and Music: Robin Mark and Jennifer Atkinson, performed by Robin Mark.
- Your music choice: _____

Nutrition to Strengthen Your Body

Pumpkin Cupcakes

- 1 box spice cake mix
- ½ cup water
- ⅓ cup vegetable oil
- 1 cup canned pumpkin
- 4 eggs or 1 cup egg substitute
- 2 teaspoons cinnamon
- 1 teaspoon pumpkin pie spice
- Light whipped cream (optional)

Preheat oven to 325 degrees. Place cupcake liners in muffin pan. In a large mixing bowl, combine all ingredients. Mix on medium for two minutes. Fill cupcake liners with batter, approximately ⅔ of the way full. Bake for 17-22 minutes. Remove and let cool, then top with a dollop of light whipped cream, if desired.   24 cupcakes

Lift Up Your Soul to Receive Abundant Mercy

October 11

The Word of God to Guide Your Soul
"Rejoice the soul of Your servant, for to You, O Lord, I lift up my soul. For You, Lord, are good, and ready to forgive, and abundant in mercy to all those who call upon You" (Psalm 86:4-5).

> *Dear Lord, I love You and thank You for Your abundant forgiveness and mercy. Send Your Holy Spirit to lift up my soul when I'm struggling or feeling down. Gladden me with a deep sense of Your presence, as I call upon Your name. Grant me an opportunity today to share Your miraculous mercy with someone who needs to know how kind and forgiving You are "to all those who call upon You." Amen.*

Music to Inspire Your Mind
- Contemporary Christian "Who You Are to Me" by Hillary Scott, Charles Kelley, Dave Haywood, and Chris Tomlin, performed by Chris Tomlin and Lady A.
- Vocal "Till I Met You" by Bryan Fowler, Chris Stevens, and Laura Story, performed by Laura Story.

- Hymn "Unto Thee, O Lord"—Text and Music: Charles F. Monroe, Performed by Maranatha Singers.
- Your music choice: _____

Nutrition to Strengthen Your Body

Harvest Vegetable Stew

- 2 tablespoons olive oil
- 2 pounds butternut squash, peeled and chopped into ½-inch chunks
- 1 large sweet onion, coarsely chopped
- 2 cloves garlic or ¼ teaspoon dried, minced garlic
- 1 can (14 ounces) tomatoes, diced
- 1 green bell pepper, seeded and chopped
- 1 package (16 ounces) frozen corn, cooked and drained
- ½ teaspoon oregano
- ½ teaspoon basil
- Salt-free seasoning and pepper to taste

In a large skillet, heat oil over medium heat. Saute squash, onion, and garlic for 5 minutes. Add tomatoes (with liquid) and green pepper; bring to boil over medium heat. Reduce heat to medium-low and cover; simmer for 15 minutes. Meanwhile, prepare corn according to package directions and drain. Add corn and seasonings to the skillet. Simmer, covered, for 5 more minutes or until squash is tender. Uncover and increase heat to medium-high. Cook for 5 minutes or until the liquid is reduced to desired amount. 6 servings

Be Assured That Jesus Never Changes and He Will Love You Forever

October 12

The Word of God to Guide Your Soul
"Jesus Christ is the same yesterday, today, and forever" (Hebrews 13:8).

> *Dear Lord, I love You and thank You for never changing and always loving me. Send Your Holy Spirit to strengthen my faith in You. Never let me falter or forget the tremendous sacrifice You made to attain my salvation. Protect me from being deceived by this world and all the temptations it offers. Grant me the wisdom and courage today to help others discover Your unchanging love. Amen.*

Music to Inspire Your Mind
- Contemporary Christian "God of All My Days" by John Mark Hall and Jason Ingram, performed by Casting Crowns.
- Vocal "Always the Same" by Ron Hamilton, performed by the Hamilton Family.

- Hymn "Of the Father's Love Begotten"—Text: Marcus Aurelius and C. Prudentius, 4th century, Music: Plainsong, 13th century, arranged by Lloyd Larson, performed by Hope Publishing Choir.
- Your music choice: _____

Nutrition to Strengthen Your Body

Herbed Carrot Coins

- 1 bag (16 ounces) crinkle cut carrot coins
- 2 tablespoons olive oil
- ½ teaspoon thyme or basil
- ½ teaspoon dried dill weed
- Salt-free seasoning and pepper to taste

In a large skillet, heat oil over medium heat. Add carrots; cover and cook for 4 minutes. Uncover and cook for 3-4 minutes, stirring. Add the herbs, salt-free seasoning, and pepper; stir to blend. (Be creative and experiment with different herbs!)

4 servings

Sing Endless Praise to the Goodness of God

October 13

The Word of God to Guide Your Soul

"You have turned for me my mourning into dancing; You have put off my sackcloth and clothed me with gladness, to the end that my glory may sing praise to You and not be silent. O LORD my God, I will give thanks to You forever" (Psalm 30:11-12).

> *Dear Lord, I love You and thank You for bringing joy into my life and clothing me with gladness. Send Your Holy Spirit to keep my mind focused on Your goodness and how You have saved me in the past. Help me be an inspiring example to others of how the joy I have in knowing You does not change with my circumstances. Let me sing forever to You, giving thanks for Your love and mercy. Amen.*

Music to Inspire Your Mind

- Contemporary Christian "Goodness of God" by Jenn Johnson, Brian Johnson, Jason Ingram, Ed Cash, and Ben Fielding, performed by Jason Ingram, featuring Vertical Worship.

- Vocal "Sing" by Corey Crowder, Cary Barlowe, Chris Tomlin, and Florida Georgia Line, performed by Chris Tomlin, featuring Russell Dickerson and Florida Georgia Line.
- Hymn "Sing Praise to God Who Reigns Above"—Text: Johann J. Schutz, Music: Bohemian Brethren's Kirchengesange, Berlin, 1566, performed by Krista Stolarski.
- Your music choice: _____

Nutrition to Strengthen Your Body

Fall Bounty Salad

- 1 bag (16 ounces) of favorite salad blend
- 2 red Gala or McIntosh apples (rough chop with peel on, sprinkled with lemon juice)
- 4 ounces (1 cup) reduced-fat mozzarella cheese, shredded (or other favorite cheese)
- ½ cup cashews or sunflower seeds
- 1 bag (4-5 ounces) dried cherries or cranberries
- Apple cider vinaigrette dressing, as desired

In a large salad bowl, mix together the first 5 ingredients. Fold in dressing, a little at a time. Toss salad right before serving.

4 servings

Rejoice in Jesus' Great Sacrifice for Your Salvation

October 14

The Word of God to Guide Your Soul
"For God did not send His Son into the world to condemn the world, but that the world through Him might be saved" (John 3:17).

> *Dear Lord, I love You and thank You for coming to bring salvation to the world and to me. Send Your Holy Spirit to make me forever grateful and in awe of the great sacrifice You made by giving up Your most precious blood. When I get frustrated with my life or complain about anything, help me remember all You have done for me and how fortunate I am to be a child of God. Let me share that good news with someone I meet today. Amen.*

Music to Inspire Your Mind
- Contemporary Christian "Man of Sorrows" by Matt Crocker and Brooke Ligertwood, performed by Hillsong.
- Vocal "Mercy" by Matt Redman and Jonas Myrin, performed by Matt Redman.

- Hymn "In the Cross of Christ I Glory"—Text: John Bowring, Music: Jim Spencer, performed by Kelvedon Green Music.
- Your music choice: _____

Nutrition to Strengthen Your Body

Baked Cinnamon Pears

- 4 ripe pears
- ½ cup melted margarine
- 1 tablespoon cinnamon sugar (use ready-made or make your own*)
- 1 cup old-fashioned rolled oats
- ½ cup finely chopped almonds
- ⅓ cup brown sugar
- 1 teaspoon ground cinnamon
- Pinch of salt
- Nonstick cooking spray
- Light vanilla ice cream (optional)

Preheat oven to 400 degrees. Wash and halve pears lengthwise; scoop out some of the center to make space for the oatmeal mixture. Spray a 9x13-inch baking pan with cooking spray and place pears in the pan. Brush the insides of the pears with 2 tablespoons melted margarine and sprinkle with cinnamon sugar. In a medium bowl, combine the remaining ingredients. Pour the rest of the melted margarine into the bowl and combine all ingredients until fully coated and crumbly. Spoon into pear halves. Bake until pears are soft, for about 35-40 minutes. If desired, top with a small scoop of vanilla ice cream and serve warm. *(Recipe for homemade cinnamon sugar: ¼ cup granulated sugar mixed with 1 tablespoon cinnamon.)

8 servings

Be Still and Listen for God's Voice

October 15

The Word of God to Guide Your Soul

"And after the earthquake a fire, but the LORD was not in the fire; and after the fire a still small voice. So it was, when Elijah heard it, that he wrapped his face in his mantle and went out and stood in the entrance of the cave. Suddenly a voice came to him, and said, 'What are you doing here, Elijah?'" (1 Kings 19:12-13).

> *Dear Lord, I love You and thank You for always being there to give me guidance if I would but listen. Send Your Holy Spirit to enable me to hear Your still, small voice. Then help me to be obedient and follow Your will for my life so others may know and follow You as well. Amen.*

Music to Inspire Your Mind

- Contemporary Christian "Song of My Father" by Jordan Frye, performed by Urban Rescue.
- Vocal "Still Small Voice" by Cherie Call.

- Hymn "Still Small Voice"—Text and Music: Brian Doerksen, performed by Brian Doerksen and Vineyard Café.
- Your music choice: _____

Nutrition to Strengthen Your Body

Greek Vegetarian Pastitsio

- 1 large eggplant, peeled and cubed
- 1 medium red pepper, seeded and diced
- 1 medium green pepper, seeded and diced
- 8 ounces small pasta shells
- 16 ounces meatless spaghetti sauce (your choice of seasonings, e.g. onion and garlic)
- ¼ teaspoon ground cinnamon
- 12 ounces low-fat cottage cheese
- 8 ounces plain, non-fat yogurt
- 1 tablespoon all-purpose flour
- Seasonings: 1 teaspoon dried oregano, ½ teaspoon salt-free seasoning, ¼ teaspoon pepper
- ¼ cup Parmesan cheese, grated

Preheat oven to 400 degrees. Microwave peeled and cubed eggplant by placing on a plate with two sheets of paper towels. Cook on high for 5 minutes. Place diced peppers in a casserole dish with 2 tablespoons of water and microwave on high for 4 minutes, stirring once after 2 minutes. Meanwhile, prepare pasta according to package directions and drain. Place pasta in the bottom of a 9x13-inch baking dish. Stir together spaghetti sauce and cinnamon and spoon over pasta. Then spoon eggplant and peppers on top of sauce. In a medium bowl, combine the remaining ingredients (using only 2 tablespoons of Parmesan cheese) and stir until well blended. Spread over top of mixture in the baking dish. Bake, covered, for 40 minutes. Uncover and sprinkle with remaining Parmesan cheese. Bake for another 15 minutes until the top is golden brown.   6 servings

Serve the Lord by Serving Others

October 16

The Word of God to Guide Your Soul

"So when He had washed their feet, taken His garments, and sat down again, He said to them, 'Do you know what I have done to you? You call Me Teacher and Lord, and you say well, for so I am. If I then, your Lord and Teacher, have washed your feet, you also ought to wash one another's feet. For I have given you an example, that you should do as I have done to you'" (John 13:12-15).

> *Dear Lord, I love You and thank You for giving me a model to follow of what it means to be a humble servant. Send Your Holy Spirit to open my eyes to the needs of all those around me. Grant me the grace to see how the smallest kindness can make the biggest difference in someone's life. Help me today to serve You by serving and helping someone in need. Amen.*

Music to Inspire Your Mind

- Contemporary Christian "Dream Small" by Josh Wilson.

- Choral "Song of a Faithful Servant" by Don Besig and Nancy Price.
- Hymn "Something for Thee"—Text: Ira B. Wilson, Music: Robert Lowry, arranged and performed by Kai McQueen.
- Your music choice: _____

Nutrition to Strengthen Your Body

Flavor-filled Lima Beans

- 2 tablespoons olive oil
- ½ medium sweet onion, finely chopped
- 1½ cups vegetable broth
- 1 package (16 ounces) frozen lima beans

In a large saucepan, saute onions in olive oil over medium heat for 4-5 minutes until soft and translucent. Stir in broth and bring to a boil. Add lima beans and enough water, if needed, just to cover. Bring to a boil. Decrease heat to low, cover, and simmer for 30 minutes.   4 servings

Find Comfort in God's Love and Mercy

October 17

The Word of God to Guide Your Soul

"For as the heavens are high above the earth, so great is His mercy toward those who fear Him; as far as the east is from the west, so far has He removed our transgressions from us. As a father pities his children, so the LORD pities those who fear Him" (Psalm 103:11-13).

> *Dear Lord, I love You and thank You for reassuring me of Your fatherly love and mercy. Send Your Holy Spirit to grant me the wisdom to run to You, find comfort in Your arms, and remember I am Your child. Let Your love and mercy shine through me so all those who are part of my life now may also be part of my forever family someday. Amen.*

Music to Inspire Your Mind
- Contemporary Christian "Every Time I Breathe" by Michael Farren, Andy Cloninger, and Mike Weaver, performed by Big Daddy Weave.
- Vocal "Love like This" by McKendree Tucker, Hope Darst, and Andrew Holt, performed by Hope Darst.

- Hymn "In the Arms of God"—Text and Music: Tony Alonso, performed by Tony Alonso and Choir.
- Your music choice: _____

Nutrition to Strengthen Your Body

Tostado Casserole

- 1 package (12 ounces) of frozen veggie crumbles (used in place of ground beef)
- 1 tablespoon olive oil
- 1 can (15 ounces) tomato sauce
- 1 envelope taco seasoning mix
- 2½ cups corn chips
- 1 can (16 ounces) pinto beans, drained and rinsed
- 4 ounces reduced-fat Cheddar cheese, shredded

Preheat oven to 375 degrees. In a large skillet, prepare veggie crumbles according to package directions, using olive oil. Add ½ cup tomato sauce and taco seasoning mix to cooked veggie crumbles; mix well. Place 2 cups of corn chips in a plastic bag and coarsely crush. Line bottom of 8-inch square baking dish with crushed chips. Crush remaining corn chips and set aside. In a medium bowl, combine the remaining tomato sauce and beans. Spread veggie crumble mixture over chips, then spoon bean mixture over veggie crumbles. Bake for 25 minutes. Sprinkle cheese and reserved corn chips on top. Bake for an additional 5 minutes.   6 servings

Measure Your Value Through God's Eyes

October 18

The Word of God to Guide Your Soul

"Are not five sparrows sold for two copper coins? And not one of them is forgotten before God. But the very hairs of your head are all numbered. Do not fear therefore; you are of more value than many sparrows" (Luke 12:6-7).

> *Dear Lord, I love You and thank You for seeing me as worthy of Your love in spite of the many times I have failed You. Send Your Holy Spirit to grant me the grace to see my self-worth through Your eyes of love and mercy. When others make me feel small or unimportant, remind me that I am Your child and heir to Your kingdom. Today, help me build up someone who is feeling down by sharing how much You love them and want to be with them forever. Amen.*

Music to Inspire Your Mind

- Contemporary Christian "Beloved" by Paul Duncan, Jordan Feliz, and Colby Wedgeworth, performed by Jordon Feliz.

- Vocal "Through Heaven's Eyes" by Stephen Schwartz, performed by Brian Stokes Mitchell and Tabernacle Choir.
- Hymn "His Eye Is on the Sparrow"—Text: Civilla D. Martin, Music: Charles H. Gabriel, performed by Sandi Patty.
- Your music choice: _____

Nutrition to Strengthen Your Body

Hawaiian Sugar Snap Peas

- 1 package (10 ounces) frozen sugar snap peas, thawed
- 1 can (15 ounces) pineapple tidbits in juice
- 1 red pepper, seeded and cut into small strips
- 1 tablespoon plus 1 teaspoon cider vinegar
- 1 tablespoon reduced-sodium soy sauce
- 2½ teaspoons cornstarch
- 2 teaspoons sugar

Drain pineapple, reserving ½ cup juice. In a large skillet, combine juice, vinegar, soy sauce, cornstarch, and sugar. Cook over medium heat, stirring constantly, until thickened and bubbly. Add sugar snap peas, pineapple, and red pepper to sauce, mixing gently. Cook over medium heat for 5 minutes or until thoroughly heated. Serve immediately.   8 servings

Make Known to All the Lord's Mighty Acts

October 19

The Word of God to Guide Your Soul

"All your works shall praise You, O LORD, and your saints shall bless you. They shall speak of the glory of Your kingdom, and talk of Your power, to make known to the sons of men His mighty acts, and the glorious majesty of His kingdom" (Psalm 145:10-12).

> *Dear Lord, I love You and thank You for the "glorious majesty" of Your kingdom, both here on earth and someday in heaven. Send Your Holy Spirit to bring me back to childlike awe and wonder at every aspect of Your awesome creation. Grant me courage to make known to all Your "mighty acts" so they can love You and become part of "the glory of Your kingdom." Amen.*

Music to Inspire Your Mind

- Contemporary Christian "Overwhelmed" by Michael Weaver and Phil Wickham, performed by Big Daddy Weave.

- Vocal "God of Wonders" by Steve Hindalong and Marc Byrd, performed by Third Day.
- Hymn "Awesome God"—Text and Music: Rich Mullins, performed by Rich Mullins.
- Your music choice: _____

Nutrition to Strengthen Your Body

Cauliflower and Tomato Cheese Casserole

- 1 package (16 ounces) frozen cauliflower florets
- 2 medium tomatoes, cut in wedges
- Salt-free seasoning and pepper to taste
- ¼ teaspoon nutmeg (optional)
- 4 ounces (1 cup) reduced-fat Cheddar cheese, shredded (or other favorite cheese)
- 2 tablespoons fresh, chopped parsley or 2 teaspoons dried parsley
- Nonstick olive oil cooking spray

Preheat oven to 400 degrees. Prepare frozen cauliflower according to package directions and drain. Spray a 2-quart casserole with cooking spray. Place cauliflower in the casserole and surround with tomato wedges. Sprinkle with salt-free seasoning, pepper, and nutmeg, if desired. Bake for 5 minutes, sprinkle with cheese, and bake for an additional 5 minutes or until cheese is slightly melted. Serve garnished with parsley.

6 servings

Be Rooted and Grounded in the Passionate Love of Christ

October 20

The Word of God to Guide Your Soul

"That you, being rooted and grounded in love, may be able to comprehend with all the saints what is the width and length and depth and height—to know the love of Christ which surpasses knowledge; that you may be filled with all the fullness of God" (Ephesians 3:17b-19).

> *Dear Lord, I love You and thank You for Your love that surpasses all understanding. Send Your Holy Spirit to grant me the grace to be "rooted and grounded in love" so I may be "filled with all the fullness of God" in everything I do and say. Today, help me be a witness to the passionate love of Christ to everyone I meet. Amen.*

Music to Inspire Your Mind

- Contemporary Christian "No Greater Love" by Matt Maher, Chris Tomlin, and Audrey Assad, performed by Matt Maher.
- Vocal "See How He Loves Us" by Marc Willerton and Jon Althoff, performed by Sovereign Grace Music.

- Hymn "Jesus, My Jesus"—Text and Music: Carol Cymbala, performed by Brooklyn Tabernacle Choir.
- Your music choice: _____

Nutrition to Strengthen Your Body

Egg and Vegetable Bake

- 1 package (32 ounces) frozen, diced hash brown potatoes
- 2 tablespoons olive oil
- 1 package (10 ounces) frozen, chopped broccoli florets, thawed or 2 cups fresh, chopped
- 1 medium red bell pepper, chopped
- 1 medium sweet onion, chopped
- 2 cups sliced fresh mushrooms or 1 can (8 ounces) sliced mushrooms, drained
- 8 large eggs or 2 cups egg substitute
- ¼ cup low-fat milk
- Seasonings: ¼ teaspoon garlic powder, ¾ teaspoon salt-free seasoning, ½ teaspoon black pepper
- Nonstick olive oil cooking spray
- Grated Parmesan cheese, as desired

Preheat oven to 350 degrees. In a large skillet, heat olive oil over medium-high heat. Add potatoes, broccoli, bell pepper, and onion. Cook for 10 minutes, or until potatoes start to brown, stirring occasionally. Add the mushrooms and cook for 5 minutes or until tender. In a medium bowl, beat together the eggs, milk, and seasonings. Spray a 9x13-inch baking pan with cooking spray and place the skillet vegetable mixture in the pan. Pour the egg mixture over the vegetables and sprinkle Parmesan cheese on top. Bake for 10-12 minutes.   6-8 servings

Receive Unwavering Peace from the Lord of Peace

October 21

The Word of God to Guide Your Soul
"Now may the Lord of peace Himself give you peace always in every way. The Lord be with you all" (2 Thessalonians 3:16).

> *Dear Lord, I love You and thank You for blessing me with Your unwavering peace "always in every way." Send Your Holy Spirit to help me turn to You in every situation so I may never lose that peace by turning away from Your love and mercy. Enable me to pass Your supernatural peace along to others at every opportunity this day brings. Amen.*

Music to Inspire Your Mind
- Contemporary Christian "Peace" by Josh Baldwin, Bobby Strand, and Anthony Skinner, performed by Josh Baldwin.
- Vocal "I'll Give You Peace"—by Dawn Thomas Yarbrough and Tom Yarbrough, performed by Sandi Patty.
- Hymn "May the Peace of God"—Text and Music: Keith Getty and Stuart Townend, performed by Kristyn Getty, Margaret Becker, and Joanne Hogg.

- Your music choice: _____

Nutrition to Strengthen Your Body

Kidney Beans and Rice Skillet Dish

- ¾ cup sweet onion, chopped
- ½ cup celery, chopped
- ¼ teaspoon dried, minced garlic
- 2 tablespoons olive oil
- 1 can (16 ounces) kidney beans, drained and rinsed
- 2 cups cooked brown or wild rice
- 2 tablespoons chopped fresh parsley or 1½ teaspoon dried parsley
- ⅛ teaspoon pepper

Prepare rice according to package directions. In a large skillet, heat olive oil over medium heat. Saute onion, celery, and garlic in oil until tender, for about 5-7 minutes. Reduce heat to low and add remaining ingredients. Cover and simmer together for about 5 minutes to blend flavors and heat through.

4-6 servings

Believe You Are a New Creation in Christ

October 22

The Word of God to Guide Your Soul
"Therefore, if anyone is in Christ, he is a new creation; old things have passed away; behold, all things have become new. Now all things are of God, who has reconciled us to Himself through Jesus Christ, and has given us the ministry of reconciliation" (2 Corinthians 5:17-18).

> *Dear Lord, I love You and thank You for making me a new creation through Your sacrifice on the cross. Send Your Holy Spirit to help me truly change and give up anything that is displeasing to You. Let my life be a testimony to the fact that I am reconciled to You, and old habits and ways are gone. Grant me the grace today to inspire my family, friends, and all I meet with the new things I am saying and doing. Amen.*

Music to Inspire Your Mind
- Contemporary Christian "Believer" by Rhett Walker, Mitch Wong, and Bryan Fowler, performed by Rhett Walker.

- Vocal "All Things New" by Travis Greene.
- Hymn "O for a Heart to Praise My God"—Text: Charles Wesley, Music: Simon Goodall, performed by Simon Goodall.
- Your music choice: _____

Nutrition to Strengthen Your Body

Spinach with Crunchy Croutons

- 2 packages (10 ounces) frozen spinach
- 2 cups garlic seasoned croutons (or choose your favorite)

Prepare spinach according to package directions. Drain thoroughly and toss with croutons. (Add croutons to any vegetable dish to give some extra flavor and crunch.) 4 servings

Be Joyful in Knowing the Lord is Always with You

October 23

The Word of God to Guide Your Soul

"You have hedged me behind and before, and laid Your hand upon me. Such knowledge is too wonderful for me; it is high, I cannot attain it. If I take the wings of the morning, and dwell in the uttermost parts of the sea, even there Your hand shall lead me, and Your right hand shall hold me" (Psalm 139:5-6, 9-10).

> *Dear Lord, I love You and thank You for being with me at all times and in all places. Send Your Holy Spirit to bring me constant joy in knowing You are always at my side, guiding me and ultimately bringing me home to You. Inspire me to share that joy with someone who needs an encouraging word today. Amen.*

Music to Inspire Your Mind
- Contemporary Christian "Abide With Me" by Matt Maher, Matt Redman, Jason Ingram, and David Crowder, performed by Matt Maher.

- Vocal "Psalm 139 (Far Too Wonderful)" by Sean Carter and Shane Barnard, performed by Shane & Shane.
- Hymn "You Are Near"—Text and Music: Dan Schutte, performed by Kitty Cleveland.
- Your music choice: _____

Nutrition to Strengthen Your Body

Beet and Cucumber Salad

- 1 can (15 ounces) sliced beets, cut into ½-inch pieces
- 1 medium cucumber, peeled, halved lengthwise, and thinly sliced
- 4 ounces reduced-fat Feta cheese, crumbled
- 1 tablespoon dried dill weed
- ½ cup balsamic vinaigrette dressing

In a large bowl, combine beets and ¼ cup of dressing. Right before serving, add cucumber, cheese, dill, and the remaining dressing. Gently toss together.   4 servings

Accept the Healing That Jesus Offers

October 24

The Word of God to Guide Your Soul
"Who Himself bore our sins in His own body on the tree, that we, having died to sins, might live for righteousness—by whose stripes you were healed" (1 Peter 2:24).

> *Dear Lord, I love You and thank You for bearing my sins on the cross so that I may be healed—spiritually, physically, and mentally. Send Your Holy Spirit to increase my faith so that I accept Your healing and trust in You for all my needs. Work through me today to extend Your healing touch to others so they may rejoice and overcome their trials. Amen.*

Music to Inspire Your Mind
- Contemporary Christian "Healing Hands" by Josh Blakesley.
- Vocal "Gentle Healer" by Michael Card, performed by Selah.
- Hymn "I Am the God That Healeth Thee"—Text and Music: Don Moen, performed by Don Moen.
- Your music choice: _____

Nutrition to Strengthen Your Body

Red Potato Vegetable Bake

- 4 medium red potatoes, cut in chunks (leave skin on)
- 1 small sweet onion, chopped into medium-sized pieces
- 1 small green pepper, seeded and cut into medium-sized pieces
- ⅛ teaspoon garlic powder
- ⅛ teaspoon pepper
- ¼ teaspoon salt-free seasoning
- 1 tablespoon margarine, melted
- Nonstick olive oil cooking spray
- Low-fat sour cream (optional)

Preheat oven to 375 degrees. Lightly coat the bottom of an 8-inch square baking dish with nonstick spray. In a large bowl, combine all ingredients, except margarine and sour cream, and transfer to a baking dish. Drizzle margarine over potato mixture. Cook for 30-45 minutes or until a fork inserts easily into potato chunks. Serve with low-fat sour cream, if desired.

4 servings

Walk in Christ's Love

October 25

The Word of God to Guide Your Soul
"And walk in love, as Christ also has loved us and given Himself for us, an offering and a sacrifice to God for a sweet-smelling aroma" (Ephesians 5:2).

> *Dear Lord, I love You and thank You so much for handing Yourself over as a sacrificial offering so that I might walk in Your love and grace. Send Your Holy Spirit to keep me devoted to You and let Your beautiful love lift me high above this world's sin and strife. Let my life be a reflection of Your love to all I meet today and grant me the opportunity to help lift others up to be saved by Your love. Amen.*

Music to Inspire Your Mind
- Contemporary Christian "Let It Be Jesus" by Chris Tomlin, Matt Redman, and Jonas Myrin, performed by Passion, featuring Christy Nockels.
- Vocal "How Beautiful" by Twila Paris.
- Hymn "Love Lifted Me"—Text: James Rowe, Music: Howard E. Smith, performed by Encounter Music.

- Your music choice: _____

Nutrition to Strengthen Your Body

Sweet Potato Pudding with Pecan Topping

- 1 can (29 ounces) sweet potatoes, drained
- 2 large eggs, slightly beaten, or ½ cup egg substitute
- 1 cup packed brown sugar, separated into ½ cups
- 1 cup low-fat milk
- ¼ cup melted margarine
- 2 teaspoons lemon juice
- ¼ teaspoon ground ginger
- ¼ teaspoon ground cloves
- ½ teaspoon ground cinnamon
- 1 cup pecan halves
- 1 teaspoon vanilla extract, separated into ½ teaspoons
- Nonstick cooking spray

Preheat oven to 350 degrees. Spray an 8-inch square baking dish or 1½-quart casserole dish with cooking spray. In a large bowl, beat together all ingredients, except pecans, ½ cup brown sugar, and ½ teaspoon vanilla extract. Pour into prepared dish. Arrange the pecan halves on top of the pudding and top with ½ cup of brown sugar. Sprinkle ½ teaspoon of vanilla extract by small droplets over the brown sugar. Bake until the top is browned, for about 30-45 minutes. 6 servings

Seek the Lord and Share Your Heart

October 26

The Word of God to Guide Your Soul
"I love those who love me, and those who seek me diligently will find me" (Proverbs 8:17).

> *Dear Lord, I love You and thank You for loving me and always being there for me when I diligently seek You. Send Your Holy Spirit to strengthen my relationship with You and teach me to share everything that is in my heart, as I would my best friend. Grant me the grace to be a guiding light to others who seek You and long to know You better. Amen.*

Music to Inspire Your Mind
- Contemporary Christian "First" by Hank Bentley, Lauren Daigle, Mia Fieldes, Jason Ingram, and Paul Mabury, performed by Lauren Daigle.
- Vocal "The More I Seek You" by Zach Neese, performed by Kari Jobe.

- Hymn "Take the World, But Give Me Jesus"—Text: Fanny J. Crosby, Music: John R. Sweney, performed by Fountainview Academy Choir.
- Your music choice: _____

Nutrition to Strengthen Your Body

Roasted Garlic Couscous with Edamame, Tomato, and Garbanzo Beans

- 1 tablespoon olive oil
- 1 cup fresh or frozen shelled edamame (soybeans)
- 1 cup red pepper, chopped
- 1½ cups water, divided
- ¼ cup chopped fresh basil or 1 tablespoon dried basil
- 1 can (16 ounces) garbanzo beans, drained and rinsed
- 1 can (14.5 ounces) diced tomatoes, undrained
- 1 package (5.8 ounces) uncooked, roasted garlic couscous
- 1 cup coarsely chopped red onions
- 1 cup reduced-fat Feta cheese, crumbled

In a large skillet, heat olive oil over medium heat. Saute edamame and red pepper for 3 minutes, stirring frequently. Stir in ½ cup water, basil, garbanzo beans, and tomatoes; simmer for 15 minutes. Add 1 cup water and seasoning packet from couscous package; bring to a boil. Gradually stir in couscous. Remove from heat. Cover and let stand for 5 minutes. Stir in onions and Feta cheese; toss well. (This is also good as a salad the next day.)   4 servings

Remember You Do Not Belong to This World

October 27

The Word of God to Guide Your Soul

"I [Jesus] do not pray that You should take them out of the world, but that You should keep them from the evil one. They are not of the world, just as I am not of the world. Sanctify them by Your truth. Your word is truth" (John 17:15-17, brackets added for clarity).

> *Dear Lord, I love You and thank You for keeping me safe in this world until I come home to You. Send Your Holy Spirit to sanctify me "by Your truth" so I stay devoted to You and accomplish Your will for my life. Help me share Your word with others so they will understand their true home is in heaven with the family of God. Amen.*

Music to Inspire Your Mind

- Contemporary Christian "Where I Belong" by Jason Ingram and Jason Roy, performed by Building 429.
- Vocal "Goin' Home" by Anne Herring, performed by The Second Chapter of Acts.

- Hymn "I'll Fly Away"—Text and Music: Albert E. Brumley, performed by Alison Krauss and Gillian Welsh.
- Your music choice: _____

Nutrition to Strengthen Your Body

Peas in Tomato Sauce

- 1 package (15 ounces) frozen sweet peas
- 1 tablespoon olive oil
- 1 medium sweet onion, chopped fine
- 1 can (8 ounces) tomato sauce
- 2 tablespoons flour
- 2 bay leaves
- Pepper to taste

Microwave peas according to package directions; do not drain. In a large nonstick skillet, heat oil over medium heat and saute onions until transparent and slightly soft (for 4-5 minutes). Add peas and liquid. Pour in tomato sauce and stir. Sprinkle flour into the mixture and continue stirring until the mixture is thickened. Add bay leaves and pepper. Simmer on low heat for 15 minutes.   4 servings

Ask God for Patience and Wisdom

October 28

The Word of God to Guide Your Soul
"My brethren, count it all joy when you fall into various trials, knowing that the testing of your faith produces patience. But let patience have its perfect work, that you may be perfect and complete, lacking nothing. If any of you lacks wisdom, let him ask of God, who gives to all liberally and without reproach, and it will be given to him" (James 1:2-5).

> *Dear Lord, I love You and thank You for reminding me about the importance of persevering in trials and relying on You for wisdom. Send Your Holy Spirit to help me grow in both of these virtues. Grant me clarity and discernment so I may never be deceived by this world's "wisdom." Work through me to lead others to the wisdom of Your plan for salvation. Amen.*

Music to Inspire Your Mind
- Contemporary Christian "Who I'm Meant to Be" by Caleb Andrew Grimm, Joey Stamper, Rob Hawkins,

Nikita Odnoralov, Yan Odnoralov, and Alina Odnoralov, performed by Anthem Lights.

- Vocal "God, I Look to You" by Jenn Johnson and Ian McIntosh, performed by Francesca Battistelli.
- Hymn "Immortal, Invisible, God Only Wise"—Text: Walter Chalmers Smith, Music: Traditional Welsh Hymn melody, Additional music, and lyrics by David Hamilton and Steve Green, performed by Steve Green.
- Your music choice: _____

Nutrition to Strengthen Your Body

CST Sandwiches (Cucumber, Sprouts, and Tomato)

- 4 slices whole-grain bread
- 4 tablespoons softened light cream cheese
- Coarse ground or regular Dijon mustard, to taste
- ½ large cucumber, peeled and sliced
- 1 cup alfalfa sprouts
- 1 medium tomato, sliced and dried on paper towels
- ½ medium sweet or red onion, thinly sliced
- Salt-free seasoning and pepper to taste (optional)

Spread two slices of bread with the softened cream cheese. Spread the mustard over the other two slices of bread. Arrange the sliced onion over the cream cheese, then the cucumbers and tomatoes. Sprinkle tomatoes lightly with salt-free seasoning and pepper, if desired. Top tomatoes with sprouts and the remaining slice of bread, mustard side down. Gently press sandwich and slice in half. 2 sandwiches

Call Upon the Beautiful Name of Jesus

October 29

The Word of God to Guide Your Soul
"Therefore God also has highly exalted Him and given Him the name which is above every name, that at the name of Jesus every knee should bow, of those in heaven, and of those on earth, and of those under the earth, and that every tongue should confess that Jesus Christ is Lord, to the glory of God the Father" (Philippians 2:9-11).

> *Dear Lord, I love You and thank You for humbling Yourself and coming to earth to save me through Your life, death, and resurrection. Send Your Holy Spirit to remind me to call upon Your beautiful name, morning, noon, and night. Let me be an example to others today of showing respect and honor at all times to Your holy name. Amen.*

Music to Inspire Your Mind
- Contemporary Christian "The Name of Jesus" by Chris Tomlin, Jesse Reeves, Matt Redman, Daniel Carson, Kristian Stanfill, and Ed Cash, performed by Chris Tomlin.

- Vocal "What a Beautiful Name" by Ben Fielding and Brooke Ligertwood, performed by Hillsong Worship.
- Hymn "At the Name of Jesus"—Text and Music: Cindy Berry, performed by Singing Men of Texas North Central.
- Your music choice: _____

Nutrition to Strengthen Your Body

Sweet and Spicy Carrots

- 2 tablespoons olive oil
- 1 package (10 ounces) matchstick carrots
- ⅔ cup pineapple juice
- 2 tablespoons water
- 1 tablespoon cornstarch
- 1 tablespoon reduced-sodium soy sauce
- ⅛ teaspoon ground cinnamon
- ⅛ teaspoon ground nutmeg

In a large nonstick skillet, heat oil over medium heat. Add carrots and saute, stirring frequently, for 10 minutes or until carrots are tender-crisp and starting to brown. In a small bowl, combine the remaining ingredients. Stir enough to dissolve cornstarch. Add slowly to carrots and cook, stirring constantly, for 1 minute or until sauce is thick and carrots are coated.

4 servings

Trust Your Heavenly Father and Seek First His Kingdom

October 30

The Word of God to Guide Your Soul
"And do not seek what you should eat or what you should drink, nor have an anxious mind. For all these things nations of the world seek after, and your Father knows that you need these things. But seek the kingdom of God, and all these things shall be added to you" (Luke 12:29-31).

> *Dear Lord, I love You and thank You for Your promise to provide for all my needs. Send Your Holy Spirit to keep me focused on seeking Your kingdom rather than worrying about material things. Let me be an example to others today and show them how much I trust You to help me in all aspects of my life, spiritually, physically, and emotionally. Amen.*

Music to Inspire Your Mind
- Contemporary Christian "Seek First" by Ben Smith and Jason Upton, performed by Housefires, featuring Pat Barrett.

- Vocal "No Other" by Donna Douglas and Margaret Becker, performed by Susan Ashton, Margaret Becker, and Christine Dente.
- Hymn "Give Me Jesus"—Text: Fanny J. Crosby, Music: Ernie Haase, Joel Lindsey, and Wayne Haun, performed by Ernie Haase and Signature Sound.
- Your music choice: _____

Nutrition to Strengthen Your Body

Vegetable Cheese Pie

- 2 tablespoons olive oil
- 1 cup fresh mushrooms, sliced, or 1 can (4 ounces) sliced mushrooms, drained
- 1 small zucchini, peeled and chopped
- 1 small green pepper, chopped
- 1 carton (16 ounces) low-fat cottage cheese
- 1 cup (4 ounces) reduced-fat Cheddar cheese, shredded
- 3 eggs, beaten, or ¾ cup egg substitute
- 1 package (10 ounces) frozen, chopped spinach, thawed and drained well
- 1 teaspoon dried dill weed
- ¼ teaspoon garlic powder
- Salt-free seasoning and pepper, to taste

Preheat oven to 350 degrees. In a large skillet, heat olive oil on medium-high heat. Add mushrooms, zucchini, and green pepper. Saute for about 5 minutes or until soft. Drain any excess liquid and cool to lukewarm. In a large bowl, combine the remaining ingredients with a mushroom mixture. Lightly spray a 9-inch pie baking dish with nonstick cooking spray and place the mixture in the baking dish. Bake for about 45-50 minutes, or until knife comes out clean when inserted into the center of the pie. Remove from oven and let stand for 5 minutes before serving.   6 servings

Seek the Lord with Your Whole Heart

October 31

The Word of God to Guide Your Soul

"Glory in His holy name; let the hearts of those rejoice who seek the LORD! Seek the LORD and His strength; seek His face evermore" (1 Chronicles 16:10-11).

> *Dear Lord, I love You and thank You for giving me the strength and will to seek You with my whole heart. Send Your Holy Spirit to fill me with the grace to make a daily commitment to You and Your will for my life. Show me how I might serve You today and help those I encounter to seek You with all their heart and soul. Amen.*

Music to Inspire Your Mind

- Contemporary Christian "Whole Heart" by Brandon Heath.
- Vocal "With All My Heart" by Babbie Mason.
- Hymn "I Give You My Heart—by Reuben Morgan, performed by Hillsong.
- Your music choice: _____

Nutrition to Strengthen Your Body

Pumpkin-Banana Bread

- 1 mashed ripe banana
- 1 can (15 ounces) pumpkin puree
- ¼ cup vegetable oil
- 2 large eggs or ½ cup egg substitute
- 2 cups all-purpose flour
- 1 teaspoon baking powder
- ½ teaspoon baking soda
- ½ teaspoon salt
- ⅔ cup sugar
- ½ teaspoon nutmeg
- ½ teaspoon ginger
- 1 teaspoon cinnamon
- Nonstick cooking spray

Preheat oven to 350 degrees. Spray an 8½ x 4½-inch loaf pan with nonstick cooking spray. In a large bowl, beat mashed banana, pumpkin puree, oil, and eggs with a mixer on low speed. In a medium bowl, place the remaining ingredients and stir with a whisk. Add flour mixture to banana and pumpkin mixture and mix until just moist. Pour batter into loaf pan and bake for 1 hour or until toothpick place in center comes out clean. (Goes great with some steaming hot apple cider!)

12 servings

Rejoice with the Saints and Follow Their Example of Holiness

November 1

The Word of God to Guide Your Soul

"After these things I looked, and behold, a great multitude which no one could number, of all nations, tribes, peoples, and tongues, standing before the throne and before the Lamb, clothed with white robes, with palm branches in their hands, and crying out with a loud voice, saying, 'Salvation belongs to our God who sits on the throne, and to the Lamb!'" (Revelation 7:9-10).

> *Dear Lord, I love You and thank You for the beautiful, holy lives of so many saints who have loved and served You with all of their heart, mind, and soul. Send Your Holy Spirit to help me follow their example and totally dedicate my life to loving and serving You by loving and serving others. Show me how I can best fulfill the purpose You have for my life. Amen.*

Music to Inspire Your Mind

- Contemporary Christian "Salvation Belongs to Our God" by Adrian Howard and Pat Turner, performed by Crystal Lewis.
- Vocal "Take My Life (Holiness)" by Scott Underwood, performed by Micah Stampley.
- Hymn "For All the Saints"—Text: William W. How, Music: Ralph Vaughan Williams, performed by Concordia Publishing House Choir.
- Your music choice: _____

Nutrition to Strengthen Your Body

Hummus Dip and Colorful Snack Platter

- 1 carton (10 ounces) hummus (choose your favorite kind)
- 1 medium green pepper, seeded and cut into strips
- 1 medium red pepper, seeded and cut into strips
- Carrot sticks
- Broccoli florets
- Cherry tomatoes
- 6 reduced-fat cheese sticks
- Paprika

On a large serving platter, place hummus in the middle and sprinkle with paprika. Wash and prepare vegetables and arrange on a platter. Cut cheese sticks in half crosswise and arrange on a platter with vegetables. (Be creative and use whatever veggies or snacks you have on hand.)   6 servings

Trust in Jesus' Promise of Resurrection and Everlasting Life

November 2

The Word of God to Guide Your Soul

"And this is the will of Him who sent Me, that everyone who sees the Son and believes in Him may have everlasting life; and I will raise him up at the last day" (John 6:40).

> *Dear Lord, I love You and thank You for Your promise of resurrection and everlasting life. I can never thank you enough for all You have done to save me and give me hope. Send Your Holy Spirit to increase my faith and trust in You with each day I live on this earth. Help others to be inspired by both my words and actions so they will believe You have conquered death and prepared an eternal home for them in heaven. Amen.*

Music to Inspire Your Mind

- Contemporary Christian "Resurrecting" by Chris Brown, Steven Furtick, Wade Joye, Matthews Ntlele, and Mack Brock, performed by Elevation Worship.

- Vocal "I Will Rise" by Chris Tomlin, Jesse Reeves, Louie Giglio, and Matt Maher, performed by Chris Tomlin.
- Hymn "I am the Bread of Life"—Text and Music: Suzanne Toolan, performed by Jaime Thietten.
- Your music choice: _____

Nutrition to Strengthen Your Body

Dressed-Up Tomato Soup

- 1 can (10.75 ounces) tomato soup (lower in sodium and fat)
- 1 can (14.5 ounces) diced tomatoes with basil, garlic, and oregano, drain and reserve liquid
- Low-fat milk, if needed, to add to reserved tomato juice to make one soup can of liquid (Use less liquid if you would like a thicker soup.)
- 1 bay leaf
- ½ cup pumpkin seeds
- Croutons or goldfish crackers, as desired
- 1 cup (4 ounces) reduced-fat sharp Cheddar cheese, shredded, or Parmesan cheese to taste

In a large saucepan, combine tomato soup, diced tomatoes, one soup can of tomato juice/milk, and bay leaf. Simmer on medium-low heat for about 15-20 minutes. Stir in pumpkin seeds and remove bay leaf. Pour into serving bowls and top with croutons or goldfish crackers and sprinkle with desired cheese.   4 servings

Find Joy in the Little Things

November 3

The Word of God to Guide Your Soul
"Make a joyful shout to the LORD, all you lands! Serve the LORD with gladness; come before His presence with singing" (Psalm 100:1-2).

> *Dear Lord, I love You and thank You for bringing so much joy to my life. Send Your Holy Spirit to make me aware of all the blessings You send my way. When I get down and distracted with worldly things, give me a nudge to wake up and be grateful for Your gifts that are seen and unseen. Grant me the grace to have a joyful attitude today and pass along Your love and joy to others. Amen.*

Music to Inspire Your Mind
- Contemporary Christian "Smile" by Ben McDonald, David Frey, Josh Bronleewe, and Hannah Ellis, performed by Sidewalk Prophets.
- Gospel "Joy, Joy, Joy" by Tommy Walker, performed by Maranatha! Gospel Choir.

- Hymn "Joy! Joy! Down in My Heart"—Text and Music: George W. Cooke, performed by Jeremy Riddle and Bethel Music. (Maranatha Kids is a good children's version.)
- Your music choice: _____

Nutrition to Strengthen Your Body

Slow Cooker Spiced Pears and Apples

- ¼ cup margarine
- 1 teaspoon vanilla extract
- 1 cup packed brown sugar
- ½ cup water
- 3 tablespoons of lemon juice
- ½ teaspoon ground cinnamon
- ½ teaspoon ground cloves
- 5 Bartlett, Bosc, or Anjou pears, cored and quartered
- 5 Granny Smith or Honeycrisp apples, cored and quartered

In a medium saucepan, melt margarine over medium heat. Add all ingredients to the saucepan, except pears and apples. Bring to a boil and stir for one minute. Remove from heat. Spray slow cooker with nonstick cooking spray and put in pears and apples. Pour mixture in the saucepan over fruit and mix well. Cover and cook on low 3½ to 4 hours or on high for 2 hours. Stir fruit every 45 minutes to ensure even cooking. Serve alone or over angel food cake or light ice cream.   6 servings

Share the Love of Jesus with Your Neighbor

November 4

The Word of God to Guide Your Soul

"For you, brethren, have been called to liberty; only do not use liberty as an opportunity for the flesh, but through love serve one another. For all the law is fulfilled in one word, even in this: 'You shall love your neighbor as yourself'" (Galatians 5:13-14).

> *Dear Lord, I love You and thank You for showing me how to serve others through love. Your life was such a beautiful example of total love for others, to the point of sacrificing Your life so Your followers can live with You forever. Send Your Holy Spirit to increase my love for my neighbor and all who are in need. Let Your love shine through me to every person I encounter today, and grant me courage to share how they can be embraced by Your love as well. Amen.*

Music to Inspire Your Mind

- Contemporary Christian "The Proof of Your Love" by Joel Smallbone, Fred Williams, Luke Smallbone, Jonathan Lee,

Ben Glover, and Mia Fieldes, performed by For King & Country.

- Vocal "Love God Love People" by Danny Gokey, Colby Wedgeworth, and Ben Glover, performed by Danny Gokey, featuring Michael W. Smith.
- Hymn "People Need the Lord"—Text and Music: Greg Nelson and Phill McHugh, performed by Avalon.
- Your music choice: _____

Nutrition to Strengthen Your Body

Fall Vegetable Saute

- 2 tablespoons olive oil
- 1 package (10 ounces) frozen sweet corn, thawed
- 1 medium zucchini, thinly sliced
- ½ cup sweet onions, chopped
- ½ cup green pepper, chopped
- 1 cup tomato, peeled and chopped
- ½ teaspoon dried basil
- ½ teaspoon dried oregano
- 1 teaspoon sugar
- ¼ teaspoon salt-free seasoning
- ¼ teaspoon lemon-pepper seasoning

In a large skillet, heat oil over medium heat. Add corn, zucchini, onions, and green pepper. Saute vegetables for 5 minutes. Add tomato, herbs, sugar, and seasonings; mix well. Cover and cook over medium-low heat until vegetables are tender, stirring frequently. 8 servings

Conquer Any Trial Through the Ever-Present Love of Christ

November 5

The Word of God to Guide Your Soul
"Who shall separate us from the love of Christ? Shall tribulation, or distress, or persecution, or famine, or nakedness, or peril, or sword? Yet in all these things we are more than conquerors through Him who loved us" (Romans 8:35, 37).

> *Dear Lord, I love You and thank You for Your unconditional, ever-present love. Send Your Holy Spirit to remind me I am never separated from You, whether my moments are filled with trials or joy. Help me to persevere and have faith that You will provide a way through every problem I may face. Let others be inspired by our friendship, Lord, and desire to know more about Your love that never fails. Amen.*

Music to Inspire Your Mind
- Contemporary Christian "He Still Does (Miracles)" by Jason Ingram, Jonathan Steingard, Johan Asgarde, and Oliver Lundstrom, performed by Hawk Nelson.

- Vocal "Greater Than All My Regrets" by Mike Donehey, Jeff Owen, and David Leonard, performed by Tenth Avenue North.
- Hymn "Jesus Is All the World to Me"—Text and Music: Will L. Thompson, performed by Mercy's Well.
- Your music choice: _____

Nutrition to Strengthen Your Body

Brussels Sprouts with a Lemon-Dill Twist

- 2 packages (10 ounces each) frozen Brussels sprouts
- 1 tablespoon margarine
- 2 tablespoons lemon juice
- 2 teaspoons dill weed
- Salt-free seasoning and pepper, to taste

In a large saucepan, melt margarine over medium heat. Stir in lemon juice and dill. Meanwhile, microwave Brussels sprouts according to package directions and drain. When Brussels sprouts are cooked to desired tenderness, add to saucepan and mix with lemon-dill sauce. Season with salt-free seasoning and pepper, as desired.   6 servings

Be Fearless and Courageous

November 6

The Word of God to Guide Your Soul
"Yea, though I walk through the valley of the shadow of death, I will fear no evil; for You are with me; Your rod and Your staff, they comfort me" (Psalm 23:4).

> *Dear Lord, I love You and thank You for being by my side at all times and in all places. Send Your Holy Spirit to grant me courage, strength, and faith when I am walking through a dark valley in my life. Help me hold tight to Your powerful Word and study it daily so I never forget how much greater You are than all the evil forces in the world combined. Let others see how fearless and courageous I can be when I put my trust in You. Amen.*

Music to Inspire Your Mind
- Contemporary Christian "Fear Not" by Chris Tomlin and Ed Cash, performed by Chris Tomlin.
- Vocal "Greater Is He" by Blanca Reyes, Casey Brown, and Jason Ingram, performed by Blanca.

- Hymn "The Lord's My Shepherd"—Text: Based on Psalm 23, Music: Stuart Townend, performed by Stuart Townend and the Stoneleigh Worship Band.
- Your music choice: _____

Nutrition to Strengthen Your Body

Vegetable Spaghetti Platter

- 4 ounces spaghetti, linguine or fettucine
- 1 package (10 ounces) frozen cauliflower, baby carrots, and pea pods
- ⅔ cup low-fat milk
- 1 tablespoon all-purpose flour
- ¼ teaspoon dried thyme
- ¼ teaspoon lemon-pepper seasoning
- ¼ teaspoon salt-free seasoning
- ½ cup (2 ounces) reduced-fat Swiss cheese, shredded
- Parmesan cheese, as desired

In a large saucepan, cook pasta in a large amount of boiling water for 8 minutes. Add vegetables and return to boiling. Cook for 1-2 minutes more or until pasta is just tender. Drain and return to saucepan. Cover to keep warm. In a small saucepan, stir together the remaining ingredients, except for cheeses. Cook and stir over medium heat until thickened and bubbly. Cook and stir for 1 more minute. Add Swiss cheese and stir until melted. Transfer pasta and vegetables to a warm serving platter and top with sauce. Toss gently to coat. Sprinkle with

Parmesan cheese, if desired, and serve immediately. (You can also use your favorite spaghetti sauce instead of the white sauce if desired.) 4 servings

Forgive Others and Yourself

November 7

The Word of God to Guide Your Soul
"Then Peter came to Him and said, 'Lord, how often shall my brother sin against me, and I forgive him? Up to seven times?' Jesus said to him, 'I do not say to you, up to seven times, but up to seventy times seven'" (Matthew 18:21-22).

> *Dear Lord, I love You and thank You for teaching Peter (and myself) that forgiving those who have wronged us is not an option but a requirement for all those who follow You. Send Your Holy Spirit to grant me the grace of mercy when I feel hurt by someone else's words or actions. Help me to forgive myself as well when I dwell on hurtful things I have said or done. Thank you for the complete forgiveness You obtained for me at the cross, and show me how I can pass that unconditional forgiveness along to someone today. Amen.*

Music to Inspire Your Mind
- Contemporary Christian "Forgiven" by Chris Rohman, Dan Gartley, Mark Graalman, Matt Hammitt, and Peter Prevost, performed by Sanctus Real.

- Vocal "Losing" by Mike Donehey, Jeff Owen, and Ruben Juarez, performed by Tenth Avenue North.
- Hymn "We Are Called"—Text and Music: David Haas, performed by St. Paul Young Adult Choir and Ensemble (Virtual Choir).
- Your music choice: _____

Nutrition to Strengthen Your Body

Stuffed Tomatoes

- 6 medium tomatoes
- 1 package (10 ounces) frozen chopped broccoli
- ¼ cup sweet onion, chopped
- ½ cup uncooked oats (quick or old fashioned)
- ⅓ cup low-fat cottage cheese
- ¼ teaspoon basil
- ⅛ teaspoon garlic powder
- 1½ tablespoons grated Parmesan cheese
- Nonstick olive oil cooking spray

Preheat oven to 350 degrees. Slice ¼ inch from the stem end of each tomato. Scoop out pulp and seeds and place tomatoes in a 1½-quart casserole dish, sprayed with cooking spray. Cook broccoli together with onions according to package directions; drain. Stir in remaining ingredients, except Parmesan cheese, and mix well. Fill tomatoes with broccoli mixture and sprinkle with Parmesan cheese. Bake for 20-25 minutes or until heated through. 6 servings

Find Your Safety and Security in the Lord

November 8

The Word of God to Guide Your Soul
"You shall hide them in the secret place of Your presence from the plots of man; You shall keep them secretly in a pavilion from the strife of tongues. Blessed be the LORD, for He has shown me His marvelous kindness in a strong city!" (Psalm 31:20-21).

> *Dear Lord, I love You and thank You for being my stronghold and keeping me safe. Send Your Holy Spirit to increase my trust in Your provision for the needs and safety of my family and friends. Whenever I feel uncertain or afraid, bring to mind the times You have helped me in the past. Let me be Your strength for others and help someone today who needs to find safety and security in Your strong and loving arms. Amen.*

Music to Inspire Your Mind
- Contemporary Christian "Our God" by Chris Tomlin, Jesse Reeves, Matt Redman, and Jonas Myrin, performed by Chris Tomlin.

- Vocal "Safe" by Justin Gray, Juan Winans, Moira Dela Torre, and Lee Simon Brown, performed by Victory Worship.
- Hymn "Only in God"—Text and Music: John Michael Talbot, performed by Wendy and Mary.
- Your music choice: _____

Nutrition to Strengthen Your Body

Savory Cut Italian Green Beans

- 1 package (15-16 ounces) frozen Italian cut or Pole cut green beans
- 1 can (8 ounces) tomato sauce
- ¼ cup sweet onions, chopped
- ¼ teaspoon dried oregano
- ¼ teaspoon dried basil
- ⅛ teaspoon garlic powder
- ½ cup reduced-fat mozzarella cheese, shredded, or 2 tablespoons grated Parmesan cheese
- Italian style bread crumbs, as desired (optional)

Prepare green beans according to package directions and drain. In a medium saucepan, combine remaining ingredients, except cheese and bread crumbs. Heat through over medium heat, stirring occasionally. Add green beans to tomato sauce mixture and reduce heat to low. Cover and let simmer for about 10 minutes. Transfer to serving dish and top with cheese and bread crumbs, if desired.   4 servings

Cling to What is Good

November 9

The Word of God to Guide Your Soul
"Let love be without hypocrisy. Abhor what is evil. Cling to what is good. Be kindly affectionate to one another with brotherly love, in honor giving preference to one another" (Romans 12:9-10).

> *Dear Lord, I love You and thank You for Your amazing love and goodness. Send Your Holy Spirit to fill me with love and grant me the grace to focus on all that is good and true. When I get discouraged, remind me to count my blessings and remember that I am Your child and will be with You and my heavenly family forever. Let me be an uplifting and positive example today, fulfilling what Your word instructs in today's Scripture verses. Amen.*

Music to Inspire Your Mind
- Contemporary Christian "Love Lifting Me" by Keith Smith, Ross King, Jordan Sapp, and Tasha Smith, performed by Tasha Layton.

- Vocal "Truth I'm Standing On" by Leanna Crawford, Matthew West, and Andrew Pruis, performed by Leanna Crawford, featuring Matthew West.
- Hymn "God, You're So Good"—Text and Music: Traditional, additional music and text by Brooke Ligertwood, Scott Ligertwood, Kristian Stanfill, and Brett Younker, performed by Kristian Stanfill and Melodie Malone.
- Your music choice: _____

Nutrition to Strengthen Your Body

Banana Pumpkin Smoothie

- 1 cup low-fat vanilla yogurt
- ¾ cup canned pumpkin, chilled
- ½ cup ice cubes
- ⅓ cup orange juice
- 1 tablespoon brown sugar
- ½ teaspoon ground cinnamon
- ⅛ teaspoon ground nutmeg
- Dash of ground cloves (optional)
- 1 ripe banana, sliced and frozen

Combine all ingredients in a blender and process until smooth. Garnish with a dash of ground cinnamon, if desired. Serve immediately. 2 servings

Be a Good and Faithful Servant of the Lord

November 10

The Word of God to Guide Your Soul
"His lord said to him, 'Well done, good and faithful servant; you were faithful over a few things, I will make you ruler over many things. Enter into the joy of your lord'" (Matthew 25:21).

> *Dear Lord, I love You and thank You for encouraging me to be a "good and faithful servant." Send Your Holy Spirit to constantly help me in all situations to be faithful to You and Your will for my life. Let me be completely surrendered to You rather than to this world and the false idols it offers. As I go through this day, show me how to help others open their hearts to You so they can one day hear You say to them in heaven, "Well done, good and faithful servant." Amen.*

Music to Inspire Your Mind
- Contemporary Christian "Surrender" by Marc James, performed by Lincoln Brewster.
- Vocal "I Pledge Allegiance to the Lamb" by Ray Boltz.

- Hymn "Guide Me, O Thou Great Jehovah"—Text: William Williams, Music: John Hughes, performed by Stuart Townend and Robin Mark. (Fountainview Academy Orchestra and Choir is another good version.)
- Your music choice: _____

Nutrition to Strengthen Your Body

Vegetarian Taco Bean Bake

- 1 cup baking mix (lower in fat version)
- 1 cup salsa (divided into ¼ cup and ¾ cup)
- 1 can (16 ounces) vegetarian refried beans
- ½ medium green pepper, chopped
- 1 cup (4 ounces) reduced-fat sharp Cheddar cheese, shredded
- ½ cup low-fat sour cream
- 1 cup lettuce, shredded
- 1 small tomato, chopped
- Nonstick olive oil cooking spray

Preheat oven to 375 degrees. Spray an 8-inch square baking dish with cooking spray. In a medium bowl, combine baking mix, ¼ cup salsa, refried beans, and green pepper. Spread in the baking dish. Top with ¾ cup salsa and cheese. Bake, uncovered, about 30 minutes or until set. Let rest for five minutes. Spread sour cream on baked mixture and top with lettuce and tomato before serving.   4 servings

Trust in the Lord to Protect You

November 11

The Word of God to Guide Your Soul
"Though an army may encamp against me, my heart shall not fear; though war may rise against me, in this I will be confident" (Psalm 27:3).

> *Dear Lord, I love You and thank You for protecting me against the army of evil that roams this earth. Send Your Holy Spirit to give me a spirit of courage and trust as I battle against the devil and his forces. Thank you for all of the veterans who have fought to protect me from those who would take away my freedom and safety. Grant all veterans physical, emotional, and spiritual healing. Help me show my gratitude in some way today as we recognize our veterans and all they have done. Amen.*

Music to Inspire Your Mind
- Contemporary Christian "Greater" by Bart Millard, Mike Scheuchzer, Nathan Cochran, Rob Shaffer, Barry Graul, David Garcia, and Ben Glover, performed by MercyMe.

- Vocal "Whom Shall I Fear (God of Angel Armies)" by Chris Tomlin, Ed Cash and Scott Cash, performed by Chris Tomlin.
- Hymn "God of Our Fathers"—Text: Daniel C. Roberts, Music: George W. Warren, performed by the Tabernacle Choir.
- Your music choice: _____

Nutrition to Strengthen Your Body

Vegetable-Rice Medley

- 1 tablespoon olive oil
- Chopped vegetables: 1 small sweet onion, 1 carrot, 1 celery rib, and ½ red pepper (or substitute 3 cups of frozen vegetables, thawed)
- 1 can (14.5 ounces) vegetable broth
- 1½ cups instant brown rice, uncooked
- 1 cup frozen peas
- Lower sodium soy sauce (optional)
- Fresh or dried parsley (optional)

In a large skillet, heat oil over medium heat. Add onion, carrot, celery, and red pepper. Saute for about five minutes or until tender. Add vegetable broth and bring to a boil. Stir in rice and peas. (If using frozen vegetables instead of fresh, add at this time.) Cover and simmer for 5 minutes. Remove from heat and let stand for 5 minutes. Sprinkle with soy sauce and parsley, if desired. 4 servings

Give with Generosity and Cheerfulness

November 12

The Word of God to Guide Your Soul

"But this I say: He who sows sparingly will also reap sparingly, and he who sows bountifully will also reap bountifully. So let each one give as he purposes in his heart, not grudgingly or of necessity; for God loves a cheerful giver" (2 Corinthians 9:6-7).

Dear Lord, I love You and thank You for reminding me how much You love a cheerful giver. Thank you for being an example of what that looks like, especially in giving Your life so that I might live in joy and peace with You eternally. Send Your Holy Spirit to help me be detached from material things, remembering everything I have is on loan from You. Grant me discernment in knowing when and how much to give to do the greatest good. As I go through my day, help me give of my time, talent, and treasure with generosity and cheerfulness. Amen.

Music to Inspire Your Mind

- Contemporary Christian "Give It Away" by Michael W. Smith, Amy Grant, and Wayne Kirkpatrick, performed by Michael W. Smith.
- Choral "A Generous Heart" by Chris de Silva, performed by Chris de Silva and Choir.
- Hymn "Cheerful Giver"—Text and Music: Ross Jutsum, performed by Ross Jutsum.
- Your music choice: _____

Nutrition to Strengthen Your Body

Potato Pancakes and Applesauce

- ½ cup grated Parmesan cheese
- 2 tablespoons chopped fresh chives or 2 teaspoons dried chives
- 1 large egg or ¼ cup egg substitute
- 2 cups cold mashed potatoes
- ½ cup all-purpose flour, divided
- 2 tablespoons olive oil, divided
- Applesauce, for serving

In a large bowl, combine Parmesan cheese, chives, and egg. Lightly beat together with a fork. Add mashed potatoes and ¼ cup of flour. Stir to combine. Refrigerate mixture for 10 minutes. Place the remaining flour in a shallow bowl or dish. Divide the potato mixture into 8 portions (about ¼ cup each). Shape each portion into a patty about 3 inches wide. Dredge the patty in the flour on both sides, shaking off excess. Set aside on a large plate. Heat 1 tablespoon of olive oil in a large skillet over medium-high heat. Tilt the pan so the oil covers the bottom. Using a wide, flat spatula, gently transfer 4 of the patties into the frying pan. Cook until golden brown, flipping once, for about 3 minutes for each side. Repeat with the remaining 1 tablespoon oil and 4 patties. Serve warm with applesauce.

4 servings

Keep Your Mind Stayed on the Lord

November 13

The Word of God to Guide Your Soul

"You will keep him in perfect peace, whose mind is stayed on You, because he trusts in You" (Isaiah 26:3).

> *Dear Lord, I love You and thank You for promising "perfect peace" if I but trust in You. Send Your Holy Spirit to keep my mind stayed on You and to stand strong on everything You have taught me in Your Word. Let my faith shine through and inspire all those I encounter today to desire a deep, personal relationship with You so they can also stay in "perfect peace." Amen.*

Music to Inspire Your Mind

- Contemporary Christian "I Will" by Jeff Pardo and Ben Calhoun, performed by Citizen Way.
- Vocal "I Will Rest in You" by Bryan Brown, Brett Younker, Nathan Nockels, and Christy Nockels, performed by Worship Together.

- Hymn "Almighty"—Text and Music: Wayne Watson, performed by Wayne Watson and Choir.
- Your music choice: _____

Nutrition to Strengthen Your Body

Slow Cooker African Vegetable Soup

- 1 medium sweet onion, peeled and chopped
- 1 stalk celery, washed and chopped
- 1 medium sweet potato, peeled and cubed ½-inch
- ¼ cup chopped fresh parsley or 2 teaspoons dried parsley
- 3 cups water
- 1 can (28 ounces) diced tomatoes, undrained
- Seasonings: 1 teaspoon salt, 1 teaspoon turmeric, ½ teaspoon ground cumin, ½ teaspoon dried thyme, ⅛ teaspoon cinnamon, ⅛ teaspoon pepper, and 1 bay leaf
- 1 small zucchini, sliced ¼-inch thick
- 1 can (15 ounces) garbanzo beans, rinsed and drained
- 4 ounces (1 cup) uncooked elbow macaroni

Combine all ingredients in a slow cooker. Stir to mix evenly. Cover and cook on low for 6-8 hours or on high for 3-4 hours. Remove and discard bay leaf before serving.   8-10 servings

Call on the Spirit to Help You Live a Righteous Life

November 14

The Word of God to Guide Your Soul

"Stand fast therefore in the liberty by which Christ has made us free, and do not be entangled again with a yoke of bondage. For we through the Spirit eagerly wait for the hope of righteousness by faith" (Galatians 5:1, 5).

> *Dear Lord, I love You and thank You for setting me free from the yoke of bondage to sin. Send Your Holy Spirit to prevent me from submitting again to any sin and doubt. Let me always be filled with gratitude for Your great sacrifice on the cross that redeems me and gives me the "hope of righteousness." Help me to be a light to someone today who is struggling under a yoke of sin and needs encouragement to stand fast in their faith. Amen.*

Music to Inspire Your Mind

- Contemporary Christian "Redeemed" by Benji Cowart and Mike Weaver, performed by Big Daddy Weave.

- Vocal "I See God in You" by Josh Wilson and Jeff Pardo, performed by Josh Wilson.
- Hymn "Holy Spirit, Light Divine"—Text: Andrew Reed and Anne-Marie Strohman, Music: Anne-Marie Strohman, performed by Anne-Marie Strohman.
- Your music choice: _____

Nutrition to Strengthen Your Body

Fresh Fruit Trifle

- 1 prepared angel food cake
- 1½ cups low-fat milk
- ½ cup low-fat strawberry or peach yogurt
- 1 teaspoon grated orange peel
- 1 box (3.4 ounces) vanilla instant pudding mix
- 4 cups assorted fresh fruit (sliced strawberries, blueberries, grapes, oranges, and/or pineapple)

Tear cake into bite-size pieces. In a medium bowl, combine milk, yogurt, and orange peel. Add pudding mix and beat until well blended. Let stand for 5 minutes. In a large serving bowl (glass, if possible), layer half of the cake pieces, ⅓ of the fruit, and half of the pudding mixture. Repeat layers. Arrange remaining fruit on top. Cover and refrigerate for at least 2 hours.   10 servings

Commit Your Way to the Lord

November 15

The Word of God to Guide Your Soul
"Commit your way to the LORD, trust also in Him, and He shall bring it to pass" (Psalm 37:5).

> *Dear Lord, I love You and thank You for Your faithfulness. Send Your Holy Spirit to grant me perseverance and firm commitment in following Your will for my life, so I trust You no matter what circumstances may befall me. Help me be strong in my witness to others about Your love. Amen.*

Music to Inspire Your Mind
- Contemporary Christian "No Matter What" by Kerrie Roberts, Chuck Butler, and Tony Wood, performed by Kerrie Roberts.
- Vocal "Always" by Jason Ingram and Kristian Stanfill, performed by Kristian Stanfill.
- Hymn "Be Strong in the Lord"—Text: Linda Lee Johnson, Music: Tom Fettke, performed by Witnessing Sound and Alumni Virtual Choir.
- Your music choice: _____

Nutrition to Strengthen Your Body

Mushroom Moussaka

- 1 pound fresh mushrooms, rinsed, trimmed, and sliced
- 1 small sweet onion, chopped
- 1 clove garlic, minced, or ⅓ teaspoon minced garlic
- 2 tablespoons olive oil
- 1 package (10 ounces) frozen succotash
- 3 tablespoons all-purpose flour
- ¼ teaspoon dried oregano
- 1 can (8 ounces) tomato sauce
- 3 eggs or ¾ cup egg substitute
- 1 carton (12 ounces) low-fat cottage cheese
- 2 tablespoons chopped parsley
- ½ teaspoon salt-free seasoning
- Paprika

Preheat oven to 350 degrees. In a large skillet, saute mushrooms, onions, and garlic in olive oil over medium-high heat for 3 minutes. Add frozen succotash to the skillet and break up as it thaws. Reduce heat to medium and cover. Cook for 5 minutes. Sprinkle flour over the vegetable mixture. Stir in oregano and tomato sauce. Continue cooking and stirring until mixture thickens and boils for 1 minute; spoon into a 2-quart casserole dish, sprayed with nonstick cooking spray. In a medium bowl, beat eggs until blended. Beat in cheese, parsley, and salt-free seasoning. Spoon in an even layer over vegetable mixture in the dish. Sprinkle paprika lightly over the top. Bake for 45 minutes or until topping is set. Let stand for 10 minutes before serving.

4 servings

Stay Close and Connected with Jesus

November 16

The Word of God to Guide Your Soul
"Abide in Me, and I in you. As the branch cannot bear fruit of itself, unless it abides in the vine, neither can you, unless you abide in Me" (John 15:4).

> *Dear Lord, I love You and thank You for being my nourishing "vine" and source of all true love and joy. Send Your Holy Spirit to keep me close and connected to You in every moment. Grant me the grace to abide in You, as You abide in me so I can be fruitful and fulfill Your purpose for my life. As I go through this day, show me how I can share Your fruit with all those I meet so they can realize how much they need a deep, personal relationship with their Savior. Amen.*

Music to Inspire Your Mind
- Contemporary Christian "Jesus I Need You" by Reuben Morgan, Brooke Ligertwood, Scott Ligertwood, and Jarred Rogers, performed by Hillsong Worship.

- Vocal "Grace Flows Down" by Louie Giglio, David Bell, and Rod Padgett, performed by Christy Nockels.
- Hymn "I Need Thee Every Hour"—Text: Annie S. Hawks and Robert Lowry (Refrain), Music: Robert Lowry, performed by Fernando Ortega.
- Your music choice: _____

Nutrition to Strengthen Your Body

Salsa Zucchini Boats

- 4 small to medium zucchini
- 1 can (15.5 ounces) black beans, rinsed and drained
- 2 tablespoons olive oil
- ½ cup chives, chopped, or 2 tablespoons dried chives or parsley
- 2 carrots, peeled and diced
- 1 jar (16-24 ounces) salsa, divided
- 1 teaspoon taco seasoning
- 8 ounces reduced-fat Mexican-blend cheese, shredded (or your favorite cheese)
- Nonstick olive oil cooking spray
- Garnish: chopped tomatoes, shredded lettuce

Preheat oven to 400 degrees. Cut the zucchini in half lengthwise, scoop out the centers, and set aside. Chop the scooped-out zucchini. In a large skillet, heat oil over medium-high heat and saute the chives or parsley, carrots, and scooped-out zucchini for about 5 minutes or until tender. Reduce heat to medium. Add the black beans and heat through. Stir in 1 cup of the salsa and the taco seasoning. Spray a 9x13-inch baking pan with nonstick olive oil spray and place zucchini halves in the pan. Spoon the skillet mixture into the zucchini and bake for 30 minutes. Sprinkle with shredded cheese and bake for a few more minutes until cheese melts. Garnish with tomatoes and lettuce and serve immediately. 4 servings

Rejoice in God's Love, Protection, and Guidance

November 17

The Word of God to Guide Your Soul
"Preserve me, O God, for in You I put my trust. You will show me the path of life; in Your presence is fullness of joy; at Your right hand are pleasures forevermore" (Psalm 16:1, 11).

> *Dear Lord, I love You and thank You for Your love, protection, and guidance. Send Your Holy Spirit to fill my soul with joy, delight, and gratitude at all You are and all You have done for me. Help me not to get so caught up in this world that I lose sight of the glory of heaven. Let my joy shine for all to see, today and always. Amen.*

Music to Inspire Your Mind
- Contemporary Christian "You Are I Am" by Daniel Muckala, Jason Ingram, Seth Mosley, Robby Shaffer, Barry Graul, Jim Bryson, Bart Millard, Mike Scheuchzer, and Nathan Cochran, performed by MercyMe.
- Vocal "More than Wonderful" by Lanny Wolfe, performed by Sandi Patty and Larnelle Harris.

- Hymn "Center of My Life"—Text and Music: Paul Inwood, performed by Journeysongs Choir.
- Your music choice: _____

Nutrition to Strengthen Your Body

Asian Salad

- ¾ cup Asian sesame dressing with ginger and soy
- ¼ cup margarine
- 2 packages ramen noodles, less the broth mix
- ½ cup sunflower seeds
- 1 package (8 ounces) broccoli slaw
- 1 package (8 ounces) red cabbage slaw
- 2 green onions, sliced

In a medium skillet, melt margarine over medium heat. Crumble ramen noodles and add to skillet, along with sunflower seeds. Saute seeds and noodles until golden brown, being careful not to burn noodles. Remove from heat. In a large mixing bowl, mix noodles and seeds with the remaining ingredients. Mix well with dressing.   4-6 servings

Consider Your Sufferings from an Eternal Perspective

November 18

The Word of God to Guide Your Soul
"For I consider that the sufferings of this present time are not worthy to be compared with the glory which shall be revealed in us" (Romans 8:18).

> *Dear Lord, I love You and thank You for the hope You give when I think of sharing heaven with You forever. Send Your Holy Spirit to grant me an eternal perspective when I am going through trials and sufferings so I don't give in to despair. Remind me that my earthly strife lasts but a moment compared with the eternal joy that awaits me. Let me be an encouragement to someone today who is going through a hard time of suffering so I may pass along the hope only You can give. Amen.*

Music to Inspire Your Mind
- Contemporary Christian "There Will Be a Day" by Jeremy Camp.

- Vocal "Your Presence Is Heaven" by Micah Massey and Israel Houghton, performed by Free Chapel.
- Hymn "O That Will Be Glory"—Text and Music: Charles H. Gabriel, performed by Marshall Hall.
- Your music choice: _____

Nutrition to Strengthen Your Body

Seasoned Potato Bake

- 2 medium Yukon Gold or Russet potatoes, washed and thinly sliced (with or without skin)
- 1 cup fresh mushrooms, washed and sliced, or 1 can (4 ounces) sliced mushrooms, drained
- ½ medium sweet onion, thinly sliced
- 1½ cups vegetable broth
- ½ teaspoon garlic powder
- ¼ teaspoon dried thyme
- 1 teaspoon salt-free seasoning
- ⅛ teaspoon pepper
- Nonstick olive oil cooking spray

Preheat oven to 350 degrees. Spray a 2-quart casserole dish with cooking spray. In a casserole dish, combine potatoes, mushrooms, and onions. In a medium bowl, combine broth, garlic powder, thyme, salt-free seasoning, and pepper. Pour over the potato mixture. Cover and bake for 30 minutes. Uncover and bake for 15 minutes more or until vegetables are tender. 4 servings

Follow Jesus with Your Whole Heart

November 19

The Word of God to Guide Your Soul
"Then He [Jesus] said to them, 'Follow Me, and I will make you fishers of men.' They immediately left their nets and followed Him" (Matthew 4:19-20, brackets added for clarity).

> *Dear Lord, I love You and thank You for choosing me to be one of Your followers. Send Your Holy Spirit to grant me true devotion to You so I follow You with my whole heart. Let Your love be shown to others through me so they will want to follow You as well. Help me always be a worthy ambassador and shining example of what it means to be a Christian and follow You. Amen.*

Music to Inspire Your Mind
- Contemporary Christian "Here With Me" by Brad Russell, Bart Millard, Michael Scheuchzer, James Bryson, Robin Shaffer, Nathan Cochran, Barry Graul, Dan Muckala, and Pete Kipley, performed by MercyMe.

- Vocal "I Will Follow Him" Music by J.W. Stole and Del Roma, English Lyric by Norman Gimbel and Arthur Altman, Original Lyric by Jacques Plante, performed by Sister Act Choir.
- Hymn "The Summons"—Text: John L. Bell, Music: Traditional Scottish melody, performed by Robert Kochis.
- Your music choice: _____

Nutrition to Strengthen Your Body

Harvest Stuffed Peppers

- 4 large green bell peppers
- 1 cup uncooked brown rice
- 1 package (10 ounces) frozen corn, thawed
- 1 can (15 ounces) tomato sauce, divided
- ⅛ teaspoon garlic powder
- ½ teaspoon salt-free seasoning
- ¼ teaspoon pepper
- Grated Parmesan cheese, to taste
- Nonstick olive oil cooking spray

Preheat oven to 350 degrees. Cut an opening from the top of each pepper, scoop out the insides, and rinse. Place peppers upright in a 2-quart casserole dish, cover with plastic wrap, and microwave on high for 3-4 minutes to soften. Remove from microwave and let cool. In a large saucepan, cook rice according to package directions. Add remaining ingredients, except cheese, into the rice mixture, using 1 cup of tomato sauce, and spoon into pepper shells. Spray shallow baking pan with cooking spray. Place peppers in the pan and pour remaining sauce over peppers. Cover with foil and bake for 30 minutes. Uncover and cook for an additional 15 minutes. Remove from oven and sprinkle with Parmesan cheese.

4 servings

Hold Fast to the Hope that Lies Before You

November 20

The Word of God to Guide Your Soul

"This hope we have as an anchor of the soul, both sure and steadfast, and which enters the Presence behind the veil, where the forerunner has entered for us, even Jesus having become High Priest forever to the order of Melchizedek" (Hebrews 6:19-20).

> *Dear Lord, I love You and thank You for being the hope and anchor of my soul. Send Your Holy Spirit to grant me faith to hold fast to that hope. Thank you, Jesus, for Your sacrifice on my behalf that makes it possible for me to look forward to everlasting joy and peace in heaven with You. As I go through this day, let my faith be evident to all so others are encouraged to also make You the anchor of their soul. Amen.*

Music to Inspire Your Mind

- Contemporary Christian "This We Know" by Kristian Stanfill and Jason Ingram, performed by Vertical Worship Band.

- Vocal "I Have This Hope" by Jason Ingram, Michael Donehey, and Jeff Owen, performed by Tenth Avenue North.
- Hymn "My Life Is in You, Lord"—Text and Music: Daniel Gardner, performed by Joseph Garlington and Integrity's Hosanna! Choir.
- Your music choice: _____

Nutrition to Strengthen Your Body

Layered Spinach and Tomato Casserole

- 1 package (10 ounces) frozen chopped spinach
- 1 cup reduced-fat ricotta or cottage cheese
- ½ teaspoon garlic powder
- ¼ teaspoon nutmeg
- Salt-free seasoning and pepper to taste
- 2 tomatoes, thinly sliced
- 1 cup reduced-fat mozzarella cheese, shredded
- 1 tablespoon Parmesan cheese, grated
- Nonstick olive oil cooking spray

Preheat oven to 350 degrees. Microwave spinach according to package directions and drain. In a large bowl, combine the spinach, ricotta or cottage cheese, and seasonings. Spray a 2-quart casserole dish with cooking spray. Spread ½ of spinach mixture in the casserole dish. Cover with ½ of tomato slices and sprinkle with ½ of mozzarella cheese. Repeat layering. Sprinkle with Parmesan cheese. Bake for 30 minutes.

4-6 servings

Believe in the Power of the Trinity—Father, Son, and Holy Spirit

November 21

The Word of God to Guide Your Soul
"That your faith should not be in the wisdom of men but in the power of God. Now we have received, not the spirit of the world, but the Spirit who is from God, that we might know the things that have been freely given to us by God" (1 Corinthians 2:5, 12).

Dear Lord, I love You and thank You for this reminder to stay focused on Your Trinitarian wisdom and power rather than on human wisdom or the "spirit of the world." Send Your Holy Spirit to grant me a strong faith that is not swayed by worldly forces. Help me to always desire You above all things. As I go through this day, grant me an opportunity to witness to someone how faith in the Trinity brings true wisdom and understanding. Amen.

Music to Inspire Your Mind

- Contemporary Christian "How Glorious" by Kyle Lee, Mark Harris, and Tony Wood, performed by Gateway Worship, featuring Anna Byrd.
- Vocal "That's What Faith Must Be" by Michael Card.
- Hymn "I Will Call upon the Lord"—Text and Music: Michael O'Shields, performed by Divine Hymns Choir.
- Your music choice: _____

Nutrition to Strengthen Your Body

Sweet Potato Casserole

- 2 cans (15 ounces each) sweet potatoes, drained
- ¼ cup orange juice
- ¼ cup chopped almonds or pecans, dry-roasted
- ¼ teaspoon nutmeg
- ¼ teaspoon cinnamon
- Nonstick olive oil cooking spray

Preheat oven to 375 degrees. Lightly spray a 1½-quart casserole dish with cooking spray. In a large bowl, mash the potatoes. Stir in remaining ingredients until well mixed. Transfer to the casserole dish. Bake, uncovered, for 25 minutes or until heated through.   6 servings

Run to Your Heavenly Father and Take Refuge in His Strong Tower

November 22

The Word of God to Guide Your Soul

"The name of the Lord is a strong tower; the righteous run to it and are safe" (Proverbs 18:10).

> *Dear Lord, I love You and thank You for promising that You will always keep me safe and secure in Your strong tower of love and mercy. Send Your Holy Spirit to replace my worry and anxiety with confidence in Your unfailing help. When I get caught up in regret about the past or panic about the future, help me run to You and leave all those negative thoughts at the foot of Your cross. Let all those I encounter today be inspired by how I put my complete trust in You and rely on You for everything. Amen.*

Music to Inspire Your Mind

- Contemporary Christian "Strong Tower" by Marc Byrd, Mark Lee, Jon Micah Sumrall, and Aaron Sprinkle, performed by Kutless.

- Vocal "Run to the Father" by Matt Maher, Ran Jackson, and Cody Carnes, performed by Matt Maher.
- Hymn "God Is Our Strength and Refuge"—Text: Joe Tyrpak, Music: Samuel Wesley, performed by Paul Keew and Church Works Media.
- Your music choice: _____

Nutrition to Strengthen Your Body

Autumn Cauliflower and Rice

- 1 package (10 ounces) frozen cauliflower florets
- 1 package (8.8 ounces) ready to microwave long grain and wild rice
- ⅓ cup chopped carrots
- 2 tablespoons silvered almonds
- ¼ teaspoon dried thyme leaves
- ¼ teaspoon dried basil or oregano

Combine cauliflower and carrots in a 2-quart casserole dish and microwave according to package directions and drain. Microwave rice according to package directions. Add rice and the rest of the ingredients to cauliflower and carrots and mix well. Cover and microwave on high for 2-3 minutes, just enough to heat through for serving.   4 servings

Remember You Are Chosen and Cherished by the Lord

November 23

The Word of God to Guide Your Soul
"You did not choose Me, but I chose you and appointed you that you should go and bear fruit, and that your fruit should remain, that whatever you ask the Father in My name He may give you. These things I command you, that you love one another" (John 15:16-17).

> *Dear Lord, I love You and thank You for choosing me to love and serve You with all my heart, mind, body, and soul. Send Your Holy Spirit to remind me that I am cherished by You, even when I feel rejected by others. Thank You for thinking of me even before time began. Today, show me a way to let others know how special they are in Your eyes. Amen.*

Music to Inspire Your Mind
- Contemporary Christian "Chosen" by Ben McDonald, Dave Frey, Seth Mosley, and Tommy Iceland, performed by Sidewalk Prophets.

- Vocal "Chosen and Beloved" by Karethe Opitz and Buddy Coblentz, performed by Buddy Coblentz and Active Christianity.
- Hymn "He Knows My Name"—Text and Music: Tommy Walker, performed by Maranatha Singers.
- Your music choice: _____

Nutrition to Strengthen Your Body

Slow Cooker Bean and Vegetable Medley

- 2 tablespoons olive oil
- 2 cups celery, sliced
- 2 cups sweet onion, chopped
- 1 tablespoon finely chopped fresh garlic or ¼ teaspoon dried, minced garlic
- 6 cans beans, drained and rinsed (15-16 ounces each) of the following: pinto, black, lima, kidney, garbanzo, and wax
- 1 can (14.5 ounces) stewed tomatoes
- 1½ cups vegetable broth
- 1 can (6 ounces) tomato paste
- ⅓ cup firmly packed brown sugar
- ⅓ cup molasses, honey, or maple syrup
- ¼ cup Dijon-style mustard
- 1 tablespoon paprika
- ¼ teaspoon pepper

In a large skillet, heat olive oil over medium heat and add celery, onions, and garlic. Saute until vegetables are softened (for 8-10 minutes). Add to a slow cooker, along with remaining ingredients. Stir to blend. Cover and cook on low for 5-6 hours.

12 servings

Overflow with Thanksgiving for the Abundant Grace of God

November 24

The Word of God to Guide Your Soul
"Knowing that He who raised up the Lord Jesus will also raise us up with Jesus, and will present us with you. For all things are for your sakes, that grace, spread through the many, may cause thanksgiving to abound to the glory of God" (2 Corinthians 4:14-15).

> *Dear Lord, I love You and thank You for Your abundant grace that forgives my sins and opens the door to an eternity in Your presence. Send Your Holy Spirit to make me ever thankful in knowing that the One who "raised up the Lord Jesus will also raise us up with Jesus." Let my joy overflow to others today so they will seek Your amazing grace and follow the path to salvation. Amen.*

Music to Inspire Your Mind
- Contemporary Christian "Grace to Grace" by Chris Davenport and Joel Houston, performed by Hillsong Worship.

- Vocal "Grace for All" by Holly Starr and David Moffitt, performed by Holly Starr.
- Hymn "What Grace Is Mine"—Text: Kristyn Getty, Music: Londonderry Air (traditional Irish melody), performed by Kristyn Getty.
- Your music choice: _____

Nutrition to Strengthen Your Body

Pumpkin Pudding

- 1 package (5.1 ounces) vanilla instant pudding and pie filling mix
- 1 can (12 ounces) evaporated 2 percent milk
- 1 can (15 ounces) 100 percent pure pumpkin
- 1 teaspoon pumpkin pie spice
- Light whipped topping (optional)
- Cinnamon, to taste (optional)

In a large bowl, beat the pudding mix and evaporated milk, according to package directions. Refrigerate for 5 minutes. Add pumpkin and pumpkin pie spice and mix well. Spoon into dessert dishes. Refrigerate for 10 minutes or until ready to serve. Top with whipped topping and sprinkle with cinnamon, if desired.   7 servings

Worship Christ Your Lord and King

November 25

The Word of God to Guide Your Soul
"When the Son of Man comes in His glory, and all the holy angels with Him, then He will sit on the throne of His glory. All the nations will be gathered before Him, and He will separate them one from another, as a shepherd divides his sheep from the goats. Then the King will say to those on His right hand, 'Come, you blessed of My Father, inherit the kingdom prepared for you from the foundation of the world'" (Matthew 25: 31-32, 34).

> *Dear Lord, I love You and thank You for being the Lord and King of my life, both now and for all eternity. Send Your Holy Spirit to help me worship You in truth, beauty, and goodness. Thank You for Your promise that You are coming again in glory and will take me home to the kingdom You have already prepared for all who love You. Grant me the opportunity today to help someone come to know You as their Savior, Lord, and King. Amen.*

Music to Inspire Your Mind

- Contemporary Christian "Almighty" by Chris Tomlin, Ed Cash, and Jared Anderson, performed by Chris Tomlin.
- Vocal "The King Shall Come" by Trevor Thomson.
- Hymn "Crown Him with Many Crowns"—Text: Matthew Bridges, Music: George J. Elvey, performed by Kingsway Music.
- Your music choice: _____

Nutrition to Strengthen Your Body

Royal Greek Salad Mini Subs

- 6 King's Hawaiian mini sub rolls (may also use hamburger buns, hot dog buns, or pita bread)
- 3 cups (about ½ of a 9-ounce package) romaine garden salad mix
- ¾ cup light Greek vinaigrette salad dressing
- 4 ounces reduced-fat Feta cheese, crumbled
- 3 small tomatoes, cut into wedges
- ½ cup black olives, sliced
- 1 cucumber, peeled and chopped

In a large bowl, mix salad with Greek dressing to coat. Stir in the cheese, tomatoes, olives, and cucumber. Distribute evenly into mini-sub rolls or buns. Best if served very cold.   6 servings

Give Thanks to the Lord for His Steadfast Mercy

November 26

The Word of God to Guide Your Soul

"Oh, give thanks to the LORD, for He is good! For His mercy endures forever. To Him who alone does great wonders, for His mercy endures forever" (Psalm 136:1, 4).

> *Dear Lord, I love You and thank You for Your mercy that "endures forever." Send Your Holy Spirit to remind me often how much You love me and want me to find joy in following You. Grant me the grace to always be thankful for Your many blessings, even when trials and hardships come. Make my life an inspiration to others so they desire to seek Your mercy and goodness for themselves. Amen.*

Music to Inspire Your Mind
- Contemporary Christian "Thank You, Jesus" by Jeff Pardo, Ben McDonald, David Frey, Cal Joslin, Blake Bratton, and Dan Macal, performed by Sidewalk Prophets.

- Choral "All Good Gifts" by Stephen Schwartz and Matthias Claudius, translated by Jane M. Campbell, performed by Hal Leonard and Shawnee Press Choir.
- Hymn "Now Thank We All Our God"—Text: Martin Rinkart, translated by Catherine Winkworth, Music: Johann Cruger, performed by Marie Osmond.
- Your music choice: _____

Nutrition to Strengthen Your Body

Sesame Sauce Vegetables and Pasta

- 1 package (16 ounces) frozen cauliflower, broccoli, and carrots
- 1 package (10 ounces) frozen cut green beans
- 8 ounces ziti or other pasta, uncooked
- 1 tablespoon margarine
- 2 tablespoons flour
- 1 cup vegetable broth
- 3 tablespoons sesame seeds
- 1 tablespoon Dijon mustard
- 1 teaspoon salt-free seasoning
- ¼ teaspoon garlic powder

Prepare vegetables and pasta according to package directions and drain. Meanwhile, melt margarine in a 1-quart saucepan over low heat; add flour and stir until smooth. Cook and stir for 1 minute. Gradually add broth and cook over medium heat, stirring constantly, until thick and bubbly. Stir in sesame seeds, mustard, salt-free seasoning, and garlic powder. Simmer for 1 minute, stirring constantly. In a large bowl, combine vegetables, pasta, and sesame sauce. Toss until all ingredients are evenly coated.   6 servings

Be Ready for the Lord's Return

November 27

The Word of God to Guide Your Soul
"Watch, therefore, for you do not know what hour your Lord is coming. But know this, that if the master of the house had known what hour the thief would come, he would have watched and not allowed his house to be broken into. Therefore you also must be ready, for the Son of Man is coming at an hour you do not expect" (Matthew 24:42-44).

> *Dear Lord, I love You and thank You for Your promise that You will return to take those who love You to our heavenly home. Send Your Holy Spirit to help me be watchful and ready for the day You come again. Never let me forget I am really a citizen of heaven, not of earth. Grant me the grace to help my family, friends, and all I encounter be ready for Your return as well. Amen.*

Music to Inspire Your Mind
- Contemporary Christian "Come, Lord Jesus (Even So, Come)" by Chris Tomlin, Jess Cates, and Jason Ingram, performed by Chris Tomlin.

- Vocal "Come, Lord Jesus" by Marc Willerton, performed by Sovereign Grace Music.
- Hymn "O Come, O Come Emmanuel"—Text: Latin Hymn, translated by John M. Neale and Henry S. Coffin, Music: Adapted from Plainsong by Thomas Helmore, performed by David Archuleta.
- Your music choice: _____

Nutrition to Strengthen Your Body

Cornbread Veggie Bake

- 1 can (10.75 ounces) condensed cream of mushroom or celery soup (lower in sodium and fat)
- 1 cup low-fat milk, divided
- 1 package (10.8 ounces) frozen mixed vegetables, thawed and chopped into bite-size pieces
- 1 package (8.5 ounces) corn muffin mix
- 1 large egg, lightly beaten, or ¼ cup egg substitute
- Nonstick olive oil cooking spray

Preheat oven to 350 degrees. In a large bowl, combine the soup, ⅔ cup milk, and vegetables. Transfer to an 11x7-inch baking dish sprayed with cooking spray. In a medium bowl, combine the corn muffin mix, egg, and remaining milk, just until blended. Carefully spread over vegetable mixture. Bake for 25-30 minutes or until lightly browned and a toothpick inserted in the center comes out clean.   6 servings

Shine the Light of Christ for All to See

November 28

The Word of God to Guide Your Soul

"You are the light of the world. A city that is set on a hill cannot be hidden. Nor do they light a lamp and put it under a basket, but on a lampstand, and it gives light to all who are in the house" (Matthew 5:14-15).

> *Dear Lord, I love You and thank You for shining the light of Your love and mercy into my life. Send Your Holy Spirit to grant me strength and boldness in sharing Your light and helping others to see that You are the way, the truth, and the life. When I get timid and want to hide "under a basket," remind me of Your courage and the great sacrifice that opened the door to salvation and living in Your glorious light forever. Amen.*

Music to Inspire Your Mind

- Contemporary Christian "Be a Light" by Thomas Rhett, Josh Miller, Josh Thompson, and Matthew Dragstrem, performed by Thomas Rhett, featuring Keith Urban, Chris Tomlin, Hillary Scott, and Reba McEntire.

- Vocal "Light a Candle" by Joel Lindsay and Wayne Haun, performed by Avalon.
- Hymn "Come, Thou Long-Expected Jesus"—Text: Charles Wesley, Music: Rowland H. Prichard, arranged by Meredith Andrews and Jacob Sooter, performed by Meredith Andrews.
- Your music choice: _____

Nutrition to Strengthen Your Body

Lima Bean Medley

- 1 package (16 ounces) frozen lima beans
- 1 cup fresh, sliced mushrooms or 1 can (8 ounces) canned, sliced mushrooms, drained
- ½ cup sweet onions, chopped
- 2 tablespoons olive oil
- 1 teaspoon oregano
- ¼ teaspoon garlic powder
- Salt-free seasoning and pepper, to taste

In a medium skillet, saute mushrooms and onions over medium-high heat in olive oil to desired tenderness. Stir in oregano, garlic powder, salt-free seasoning, and pepper. Meanwhile, microwave lima beans according to package directions and drain. Transfer lima beans to serving dish and add mushroom and onion mixture. Stir lightly to mix.

4 servings

Use Your Gifts for Good Works This Advent and Christmas

November 29

The Word of God to Guide Your Soul

"For we are His workmanship, created in Christ Jesus for good works, which God prepared beforehand that we should walk in them" (Ephesians 2:10).

> *Dear Lord, I love You and thank You for creating me as part of Your glorious workmanship. Send Your Holy Spirit to help me fulfill the plan You have for my life that You "prepared beforehand." Grant me the courage to follow that plan and accomplish the good works You need to do through me. Make me Your hands and feet for the poor and needy, both spiritually and materially, especially during this beautiful season of Advent and Christmas. Amen.*

Music to Inspire Your Mind
- Contemporary Christian "Give Me Your Eyes" by Jason Ingram and Brandon Heath, performed by Brandon Heath.
- Vocal "Follow You" by Leeland Mooring, Jack Mooring, and Ed Cash, performed by Leeland.

- Hymn "O Come, Divine Messiah"—Text: Abbe Simon-Joseph Pellegrin, translated by Sr. Mary of St. Philip, Music: Traditional French Carol, performed by Passionist Sacred Music.
- Your music choice: _____

Nutrition to Strengthen Your Body

Vegetable Rice Surprise

- 1 package (6.3 ounces) wild mushroom and herb, rice pilaf mix (or other favorite rice mix)
- 1 package (10 ounces) frozen mixed vegetables
- ¼ teaspoon garlic powder
- ¼ cup low-fat sour cream or plain yogurt

Prepare rice according to package directions. Meanwhile, microwave vegetables according to package directions and drain. Cut vegetables into bite-size pieces and sprinkle with garlic powder. Add vegetables to rice during the last 5 minutes of cooking. Just before serving, stir in sour cream or yogurt.

6 servings

Await with Hope and Peace the Renewal of Heaven and Earth

November 30

The Word of God to Guide Your Soul

"Nevertheless we, according to His promise, look for new heavens and a new earth in which righteousness dwells. Therefore, beloved, looking forward to these things, be diligent to be found by Him in peace, without spot and blameless" (2 Peter 3:13-14).

> *Dear Lord, I love You and thank You for the promise of "new heavens and a new earth in which righteousness dwells." Send Your Holy Spirit to grant me the grace "to be found without spot and blameless" when that eagerly awaited time comes. Help me to be a bold witness to someone today who needs to hear Your promise of hope and renewal in the salvation story of Jesus' birth, death, and resurrection. Amen.*

Music to Inspire Your Mind

- Contemporary Christian "Glory (Let There Be Peace)" by Matt Maher, Rachel Taylor Popadic and Chris Stevens, performed by Matt Maher.

- Vocal "Immanuel" by Michael Card.
- Hymn "I Wonder as I Wander"—Text and Music: John Jacob Niles, performed by Vanessa Williams.
- Your music choice: _____

Nutrition to Strengthen Your Body

Baked Sugar Snap Peas

- 2 tablespoons sweet onion, chopped
- ⅛ teaspoon minced garlic or garlic powder
- 1 tablespoon fresh basil, chopped, or ⅓ teaspoon dried basil
- 1 pound fresh sugar snap peas or frozen, thawed
- 1 tablespoon olive oil

Preheat oven to 400 degrees. Layer peas on a nonstick or foil-lined baking sheet; top with onions, garlic, and basil. Drizzle with olive oil. Bake for 8-10 minutes or until desired tenderness.

4 servings

Be Mindful of Jesus' Constant Presence and Love

December 1

The Word of God to Guide Your Soul
"Behold, the virgin shall be with child, and bear a Son, and they shall call His name Immanuel," which is translated, 'God with us'" (Matthew 1:23).

> *Dear Lord, I love You and thank You for being my closest and dearest friend who is always there for me. Send Your Holy Spirit to keep me ever mindful of Your presence and love. Help others to see Your light shine through me in every circumstance I may encounter on this day. Amen.*

Music to Inspire Your Mind
- Contemporary Christian "Our God Is With Us" by David Binion, Nicole Binion, and Rita Springer, performed by Rita Springer and Nicole Binion.
- Vocal "Breath of Heaven (Mary's Song)" by Amy Grant and Chris Eaton, performed by Amy Grant.

- Hymn "Lo! How a Rose E'er Blooming"—Text and Music: German Carol, performed by Charlotte Church.
- Your music choice: _____

Nutrition to Strengthen Your Body

Snow-capped Potato and Broccoli Casserole

- 4 large Yukon Gold or Russet potatoes
- 1 package (10 ounces) broccoli florets
- 1 cup plain low-fat yogurt
- 1 cup low-fat cottage cheese
- ¼ cup chopped chives
- 1 teaspoon salt-free seasoning
- ⅛ teaspoon black pepper
- ⅛ teaspoon garlic powder
- Nonstick olive oil cooking spray

Preheat oven to 350 degrees. Scrub and poke potatoes with a fork tine several times. Place on a paper towel in microwave and space evenly. Microwave on high for 4 minutes. Turn and microwave for an additional 4 minutes. Wrap in a paper towel and set aside. Next, microwave broccoli florets according to package directions and drain. Cut potatoes into cubes and broccoli into bite-size pieces. In a large mixing bowl, combine all ingredients and transfer to a 2-quart casserole dish, sprayed with cooking spray. Bake for 30 minutes or until hot and bubbly.

8 servings

Rest in the Arms of Jesus

December 2

The Word of God to Guide Your Soul
"Come to Me, all you who labor and are heavy laden, and I will give you rest. Take My yoke upon you and learn from Me, for I am gentle and lowly in heart, and you will find rest for your souls. For My yoke is easy and My burden is light" (Matthew 11:28-30).

> *Dear Lord, I love You and thank You for encouraging me to come to You for rest and comfort when life gets difficult. Send Your Holy Spirit to grant me guidance and wisdom in sharing life's burdens with You so they become easy and light. Forgive me for all the times I haven't trusted You and tried to carry my burdens on my own. Today, grant me an opportunity to help make someone else's burden lighter. Amen.*

Music to Inspire Your Mind
- Contemporary Christian "Rest in the Arms" by Aaron Shust, Jason Ingram, Doug McKelvey, and Matthew West, performed by Aaron Shust.

- Vocal "Arms of Love" by Amy Grant, Michael W. Smith and Gary Chapman, performed by Amy Grant.
- Hymn "What Child Is This?"—Text: William C. Dix, Music: Traditional English melody, 16th century, performed by Josh Groban.
- Your music choice: _____

Nutrition to Strengthen Your Body

Mixed Veggie Egg Muffins

- 1 bag (24 ounces) frozen mixed vegetables, thawed
- ½ cup sweet onions, chopped
- 1 tablespoon olive oil
- 1 cup (4 ounces) reduced-fat Cheddar cheese, shredded
- ¼ cup Parmesan cheese, grated
- 12 large eggs or 3 cups egg substitute
- ¼ cup low-fat milk
- Seasonings: salt-free seasoning to taste, ½ teaspoon each of mustard powder, dried dill weed, and black pepper
- Nonstick olive oil cooking spray

Preheat oven to 350 degrees. Coat a 12-well muffin tin with cooking spray or use a nonstick muffin tin. In a large skillet, heat oil over medium heat; saute onions and vegetables until tender crisp. Divide the vegetables and cheeses over the 12 wells. In a large mixing bowl, combine eggs, milk, and seasonings. Mix well. Pour egg mixture evenly over each well. Bake for 22-25 minutes or until set. Remove from muffin tin and serve immediately.   12 muffins

Rejoice that God Makes All Things New

December 3

The Word of God to Guide Your Soul

"And God will wipe away every tear from their eyes; there shall be no more death, nor sorrow, nor crying. There shall be no more pain, for the former things have passed away. Then He who sat on the throne said, 'Behold, I make all things new'" (Revelation 21:4-5a).

> *Dear Lord, I love You and thank You for Your promise of life, instead of death; joy, instead of sorrow; laughing, instead of crying. Send Your Holy Spirit to make me aware of how You are making all things new, even now, as I offer more and more of my life to Your will. During this Advent and Christmas, show me how I can help others have a stronger relationship with You so they can also rejoice in being renewed and restored in Your love. Amen.*

Music to Inspire Your Mind

- Contemporary Christian "All Things New" by Ben Fielding and Dean Ussher, performed by Hillsong.

- Vocal "Grown-Up Christmas List" by David Foster and Linda Thompson Jenner, performed by Kelly Clarkson.
- Hymn "How Great Our Joy"—Text and Music: Traditional German Carol, performed by Discover Worship Choir.
- Your music choice: _____

Nutrition to Strengthen Your Body

Apple Ginger Dessert

- 1 box (14.5 ounces) gingerbread mix
- ½ cup water
- 2 cups peeled apple slices (2 to 3 apples)
- Topping:
- ⅓ cup firmly packed brown sugar
- ⅓ cup chopped nuts
- 2 tablespoons margarine, melted
- Nonstick cooking spray

Preheat oven to 375 degrees. In a medium mixing bowl, combine gingerbread mix and water. Blend at low speed, then beat 2 minutes at medium speed. Stir in apple slices. Coat an 8 or 9-inch square baking pan with cooking spray. Pour in batter. In a small mixing bowl, combine topping ingredients and crumble over batter. Bake for 25-30 minutes or until top springs back when lightly touched in center. Serve warm or cool.   6-8 servings

Open Your Heart Completely to God's Love

December 4

The Word of God to Guide Your Soul

"'But the Lord is faithful, who will establish you and guard you from the evil one. Now may the Lord direct your hearts into the love of God and into the patience of Christ' (2 Thessalonians 3:3, 5).

> *Dear Lord, I love You and thank You for being faithful, giving me strength, and guarding me from the evil one. Send Your Holy Spirit to direct my heart and mind always toward You rather than toward worldly pursuits and pleasures. Show me the best way today to help others open their hearts to Your love and surrender all to follow You. Amen.*

Music to Inspire Your Mind
- Contemporary Christian "Make Room" by Mark Hall and Matt Maher, performed by Casting Crowns, featuring Matt Maher.
- Vocal "My Heart Belongs to You" by Tom Booth.

- Hymn "Open the Eyes of My Heart"—Text and Music: Paul Baloche, performed by Michael W. Smith.
- Your music choice: _____

Nutrition to Strengthen Your Body

Tomato, Green Pepper, and Couscous Salad

- 1 box (5.8 ounces) roasted garlic and olive oil couscous mix (or another favorite mix)
- 1¼ cups vegetable broth or water
- ½ cup sweet onions, chopped
- 1 cup plum tomatoes, diced and seeded
- ½ cup green pepper, chopped
- 1 can (4.25 ounces) chopped black olives, drained (optional)
- ⅓ cup fresh basil, chopped, or 1 tablespoon dried basil
- ¾ cup balsamic vinaigrette dressing (or other favorite dressing)
- Black pepper to taste
- Cherry tomatoes, cut in halves

Prepare couscous according to package directions, substituting broth for water, if desired. Remove from heat and let stand for five minutes. Transfer to a large mixing bowl, fluff with a fork, and let cool. Mix the remaining ingredients with couscous, except cherry tomatoes. Chill for at least 2 hours or overnight. Garnish with cherry tomato halves before serving.   4 servings

Share the Hope of Christmas

December 5

The Word of God to Guide Your Soul

"Blessed is the man who trusts in the LORD, and whose hope is the LORD. For he shall be like a tree planted by the waters, which spreads out its roots by the river, and will not fear when heat comes; but its leaf will be green, and will not be anxious in the year of drought, nor will cease from yielding fruit" (Jeremiah 17:7-8).

> *Dear Lord, I love You and thank You for giving me the hope of Christmas. Send Your Holy Spirit to help me always bear His fruit, even when my times are filled with heat and drought. Let me pass along Your message today that there is hope for everyone in the birth, life, death, and resurrection of Jesus. Amen.*

Music to Inspire Your Mind

- Contemporary Christian "Hope for Everyone" by Jason Ingram and Matt Maher, performed by Matt Maher.
- Vocal "The Hope of Christmas" by Matthew West and Andrew Pruis, performed by Matthew West.
- Hymn "Infant Holy, Infant Lowly"—Text and Music: Traditional Polish Carol, performed by Cara Dillon.

- Your music choice: _____

Nutrition to Strengthen Your Body

Veggie Hummus Grilled Cheese Sandwich

- 8 slices whole grain bread
- 8 tablespoons hummus, any flavor
- Margarine (olive-oil based), to taste
- 1 tablespoon olive oil
- Vegetables: 1 small zucchini, peeled and thinly sliced, ½ red bell pepper, seeded and thinly sliced, 1 small sweet onion, thinly sliced, 4 large, fresh mushrooms, washed and thinly sliced
- 4 slices reduced-fat mozzarella or other favorite cheese
- Fresh or dried basil, to taste

Prepare each slice of bread by spreading 1 tablespoon of hummus on one side and margarine on the other. In a large skillet, heat 1 tablespoon olive oil over medium heat. Add zucchini, red bell pepper, onion, and mushrooms; saute for 4-5 minutes or until soft. Remove vegetables to a plate and reduce heat to low. Place four slices of bread in the skillet, hummus side up. Divide sauteed vegetables between the four slices of bread. Top vegetables with 1 slice of cheese and basil, as desired. Top each sandwich with another slice of bread, hummus side down. Cook until the bottom slice is toasted, flip, and continue cooking until cheese is melted and the other half is toasted. Cut in half and serve immediately.   4 sandwiches

Give with a Heart Overflowing with Love

December 6

The Word of God to Guide Your Soul
"Give, and it will be given to you: good measure, pressed down, shaken together, and running over will be put into your bosom. For with the same measure that you use, it will be measured back to you" (Luke 6:38).

> *Dear Lord, I love You and thank You for all of the countless ways You have blessed my life. Send Your Holy Spirit to make my heart overflow with love and generosity so I share those blessings with all who are in need. As You gave Your life for me, I give my life and possessions as an offering to You and in gratitude for leaving Your heavenly home and coming to earth to redeem us. Amen.*

Music to Inspire Your Mind
- Contemporary Christian "Christmas Offering" by Paul Baloche, performed by Casting Crowns.
- Vocal "The Gift Goes On" by Claire Cloninger and Ron Harris, performed by Sandi Patty and Children's Choir.

- Hymn "O Little Town of Bethlehem"—Text: Phillips Brooks, Music: Lewis H. Redner, performed by Gaither Vocal Band. (For a contemporary version, try "O Little Town (The Glory of Christmas)" by Matt Redman.)
- Your music choice: _____

Nutrition to Strengthen Your Body

Baked Vegetarian Spaghetti

- 8 ounces vegetable spaghetti pasta
- 1 package (10 ounces) frozen, chopped spinach, cooked and drained
- 1 cup sweet onions, diced
- ¼ cup green bell pepper, diced
- 3 large eggs or ¾ cup egg substitute
- Seasonings: 1 teaspoon dried oregano, 1 teaspoon salt-free seasoning, ½ teaspoon garlic powder
- 2 cups reduced-fat Italian-blend cheese, shredded and divided
- 1 jar (24-26 ounces) tomato basil spaghetti sauce

Preheat oven to 400 degrees. Cook pasta according to package directions. Meanwhile, in a large bowl, combine spinach, onions, bell pepper, 1 egg, and seasonings until blended. Spread mixture evenly in a 9x13-inch baking dish, sprayed with nonstick olive oil cooking spray. Drain pasta thoroughly, but do not rinse. In a medium bowl, whisk the remaining 2 eggs and stir in ½ cup cheese. Add pasta and toss to coat. Spread pasta evenly over vegetable mixture in the baking dish. Pour pasta sauce over the top. Sprinkle with the remaining 1½ cups of cheese. Bake for 30-35 minutes. Let stand for 5 minutes before serving. 8 servings

Dwell in the Secret Place of the Almighty

December 7

The Word of God to Guide Your Soul
"He who dwells in the secret place of the Most High shall abide under the shadow of the Almighty. I will say of the LORD, 'He is my refuge and my fortress; my God, in Him I will trust'" (Psalm 91:1-2).

> *Dear Lord, I love You and thank You for being my refuge and fortress. Send Your Holy Spirit to help me always trust and take shelter in Your loving arms. Whenever things look bleak, grant me the grace of strong, consistent faith, knowing that You will work all things out for my good. As I go about my day, let others see that I am abiding in the love, light, and peace You brought to the world on Christmas Day. Amen.*

Music to Inspire Your Mind
- Contemporary Christian "Light of the World" by Lauren Daigle, Paul Duncan, and Paul Mabury, performed by Marc Martel.

- Vocal "In the Bleak Midwinter" by Gustav Holst, performed by Susan Boyle and Libera.
- Hymn "Hark! The Herald Angels Sing"—Text: Charles Wesley, altered by George Whitefield, Music: Felix Mendelssohn, arranged by William H. Cummings, performed by Phil Wickham.
- Your music choice: _____

Nutrition to Strengthen Your Body

Festive Split Pea Soup

- 2 cans (19 ounces each) green split pea soup
- 1 cup frozen peas, thawed
- 1 small sweet onion, chopped
- 1 cup celery, chopped
- 1 cup carrots, shredded
- 1 cup red pepper, chopped
- ¼ teaspoon black pepper
- ¼ teaspoon dried, minced garlic
- 1 teaspoon dried thyme
- 1 teaspoon dried dill weed
- Croutons (optional)

Combine all the ingredients, except croutons, in a large saucepan. Bring to a boil, cover, and simmer on low for at least 30-60 minutes. Top with your favorite croutons before serving, if desired.   4 servings

Be Open to God's Plan for Your Life

December 8

The Word of God to Guide Your Soul
"Then the angel said to her, 'Do not be afraid, Mary, for you have found favor with God. And behold, you will conceive in your womb and bring forth a Son, and shall call His name JESUS.' Then Mary said, 'Behold the maidservant of the Lord! Let it be to me according to your word.' And the angel departed from her" (Luke 1:30-31, 38).

> *Dear Lord, I love You and thank You for sharing Your Mother Mary's example of complete obedience to Your will and plan for her life. Send Your Holy Spirit to fill me with the same level of trust and faith. Help me say with Mary, "Let it be to me according to your word." Grant me the opportunity today to introduce You to someone who is searching for the true meaning of Christmas, as Mary introduced You to a dark and struggling world of sin. Amen.*

Music to Inspire Your Mind
- Contemporary Christian "Let It Be Done" by Chris Muglia.

- Classical "Ave Maria" by Franz Schubert, performed by Andre Rieu and Mirusia.
- Hymn "Mary, Did You Know?"—Text and Music: Mark Lowry and Buddy Greene, performed by One Voice Children's Choir.
- Your music choice: _____

Nutrition to Strengthen Your Body

Bethlehem Bean Salad

- 2 cans (16 ounces each) beans of choice, drained and rinsed
- ½ cup red onion, diced
- 1 large tomato, seeded and diced
- 1 medium cucumber, seeded and diced
- ½ cup fresh parsley, chopped, or 2 tablespoons dried
- 1 tablespoon fresh mint, chopped, or 1 teaspoon dried
- ¼ cup lemon juice
- 1 teaspoon cumin (optional)
- ¼ teaspoon each salt-free seasoning and pepper
- ¼ cup olive oil

In a salad bowl, combine beans and the next 5 ingredients. In a small mixing bowl, combine lemon juice with cumin, salt-free seasoning, and pepper. Mix in olive oil. Fold into the salad and chill for several hours for flavors to blend.   6 servings

Endure Trials to Find Eternal Joy

December 9

The Word of God to Guide Your Soul

"Looking unto Jesus, the author and finisher of our faith, who for the joy that was set before Him endured the cross, despising the shame, and has sat down at the right hand of the throne of God. For consider Him who endured such hostility from sinners against Himself, lest you become weary and discouraged in your souls" (Hebrews 12:2-3).

Dear Lord, I love You and thank You for coming to earth and enduring the cross so that I might one day find joy forever with You in heaven. Send Your Holy Spirit to grant me the endurance to not "become weary and discouraged" when life gets difficult, and trials seem to never end. Today, help me be a witness to the hope and joy that is found in knowing You, no matter what my circumstances may be. Amen.

Music to Inspire Your Mind

- Contemporary Christian "Hearts Waiting (Joy to the World)" by Matt Redman, Jonas Myrin, Chris Tomlin, and Beth Redman, performed by Matt Redman.
- Vocal "Comfort and Joy" by Tony Wood, Keith Smith, and Tasha Layton, performed by Tasha Layton.
- Hymn "Hope of the Nations (Christmas Edition)"—Text and Music: Brian Doerksen, performed by Brian Doerksen and Integrity's Hosanna! Music.
- Your music choice: _____

Nutrition to Strengthen Your Body

Cauliflower-Wild Rice Casserole

- 1 package (6 ounces) long grain and wild rice
- 1 package (10.8 ounces) frozen cauliflower florets
- 1 cup vegetable broth
- 1 can (8 ounces) sliced mushrooms, drained
- 1 can (8 ounces) water chestnuts, drained
- ½ cup crushed garlic and cheese croutons
- 1 cup (4 ounces) reduced-fat Cheddar cheese
- 1 teaspoon salt-free seasoning
- Nonstick olive oil cooking spray

Preheat oven to 350 degrees. In a large saucepan, prepare rice according to package directions. Meanwhile, microwave cauliflower as directed on package and drain. Add the cooked cauliflower, mushrooms, water chestnuts, and vegetable broth to the rice mixture. Mix in cheese and salt-free seasoning. Spray a large casserole dish with cooking spray and spoon rice and cauliflower mixture into the dish. Top with crushed croutons. Bake for 30-35 minutes, covered. Remove cover for the last 10 minutes.   8 servings

Rejoice with the Angels That Jesus Has Come to Set Us Free

December 10

The Word of God to Guide Your Soul
"And suddenly there was with the angel a multitude of the heavenly host praising God and saying: 'Glory to God in the highest, and on earth peace, goodwill toward men!'" (Luke 2:13-14).

> *Dear Lord, I love You and thank You for coming to set me free from my fallen nature. Send Your Holy Spirit to grant me the grace of endless joy and peace when I think of the ocean of mercy you offer to forgive all my sins. Show me today how to share that joy, peace, and mercy with all I meet in encouraging words, fervent prayers, and concrete actions. Amen.*

Music to Inspire Your Mind
- Contemporary Christian "Gloria / Angels We Have Heard on High" by Bernie Herms and Mark Hall, performed by Casting Crowns.
- Vocal "Christmas Angels" by Jonas Myrin and Michael W. Smith, performed by Michael W. Smith and Choir.

- Hymn "Angels We Have Heard on High"—Text and Music: Traditional French Carol, arranged by Robert Prizeman, performed by Libera.
- Your music choice: _____

Nutrition to Strengthen Your Body

Veggie-Filled Nachos

- 2 tablespoons olive oil
- 1 sweet onion, chopped
- 1 green bell pepper, chopped
- Salt-free seasoning and pepper, to taste
- 1 bag thick tortilla chips
- 1 can (15 ounces) black beans, drained and rinsed
- 8 ounces (2 cups) reduced-fat, extra sharp Cheddar cheese, shredded
- Toppings: 1 cup diced tomatoes, 1 cup diced avocado, chopped fresh cilantro (optional)

Preheat oven to 400 degrees. In a large skillet, heat olive oil over medium heat. Saute onions and peppers until tender, for about 5 minutes. Turn off heat and season with salt-free seasoning and pepper to taste. Line a baking sheet with aluminum foil. Spread the chips out on the baking sheet and spoon on the beans, cooked onions, and peppers. Sprinkle cheese on top. Bake for 10-12 minutes. Add additional toppings, as desired. Serve immediately.   6 servings

Gaze on the Lord's Beauty and Spend Quiet Time with Him Daily

December 11

The Word of God to Guide Your Soul

"One thing I have desired of the LORD, that will I seek: that I may dwell in the house of the LORD all the days of my life, to behold the beauty of the LORD, and to inquire in His temple. For in the time of trouble He shall hide me in His pavilion; in the secret place of His tabernacle He shall hide me; He shall set me high upon a rock" (Psalm 27:4-5).

> *Dear Lord, I love You and thank You for Your beauty, truth, and goodness. Send Your Holy Spirit to fill me with the desire to spend quiet time with You every day and seek Your guidance and shelter in good times and in bad. Thank you so much for never letting me go, and grant me the grace today to never give up on my family and friends who still need to open their hearts to Your beauty and love. Amen.*

Music to Inspire Your Mind

- Contemporary Christian "Psalm 27 (One Thing)" by Shane Barnard, performed by Shane and Shane.

- Vocal "Emmanuel" by Reuben Morgan, performed by Hillsong Worship.
- Hymn "It Came upon the Midnight Clear"—Text: Edmund H. Sears, Music: Richard S. Willis, performed by Steven Curtis Chapman.
- Your music choice: _____

Nutrition to Strengthen Your Body

Zesty Pasta with Broccoli and Carrots

- 8 ounces uncooked pasta (your choice)
- 2 tablespoons olive oil
- 3 tablespoons red wine vinegar
- 1½ teaspoons dried oregano leaves or 2 tablespoons fresh, chopped
- ¼ teaspoon salt-free seasoning
- ½ teaspoon crushed red pepper
- 2 cloves garlic, crushed, or ¼ teaspoon dried, minced garlic
- 2 tablespoons sliced pimiento-stuffed olives
- 2 tablespoons sliced ripe olives
- 1 package (10 ounces) frozen broccoli flowerets, thawed
- 1 can (14 ounces) sliced carrots, drained, or 1 package (10 ounces) frozen sliced carrots, thawed
- Parmesan cheese, grated (as desired)

Prepare pasta according to package directions and drain. While pasta is cooking, in a large skillet, heat olive oil over medium heat. Add vinegar, oregano, salt-free seasoning, red pepper, and garlic; mix well. Next, add olives, broccoli, and carrots to the skillet. Reduce heat to medium-low, cover, and cook for 10-12 minutes, stirring occasionally, until mixture is heated through and vegetables are crisp-tender. Serve over pasta and sprinkle with Parmesan cheese.   4 servings

Pray for Endurance to Do the Will of God

December 12

The Word of God to Guide Your Soul
"For you have need of endurance, so that after you have done the will of God, you may receive the promise: 'For yet a little while, and He who is coming will come and will not tarry'" (Hebrews 10:36-37).

> *Dear Lord, I love You and thank You for Your promise of coming back to earth again to bring all who love You to our heavenly home. Send Your Holy Spirit to grant me the endurance and patience to do Your will to the end so I may receive the fulfillment of this beautiful promise. Help me discern today how I can share Your love and the promise of Your Second Coming with someone in need of hope and salvation. Amen.*

Music to Inspire Your Mind
- Contemporary Christian "Day After Day" by Kristian Stanfill, Tim Gibson, and Jason Ingram, performed by Kristian Stanfill.

- Vocal "Son of God" by Michael W. Smith, Tony Wood, and David Hamilton, performed by Michael W. Smith and choir.
- Hymn "That Beautiful Name"—Text: Jean Perry, Music: Mabel Johnston Camp, performed by The Stevens Family.
- Your music choice: _____

Nutrition to Strengthen Your Body

Asian Wrap Sandwiches

- 4 cups (8 ounces) shredded coleslaw mix
- ½ cup green onions, sliced
- 1 package (12 ounces) frozen veggie crumbles
- ¼ cup bottled stir fry sauce
- 2 tablespoons hoisin sauce or 1 tablespoon reduced-sodium soy sauce
- Garlic powder, to taste
- 4 (8-inch) flour tortillas
- Nonstick olive oil cooking spray

Coat a large skillet with cooking spray. Place over medium heat. Add coleslaw and green onions and cook for 4 minutes, stirring constantly. Add veggie crumbles, stir fry sauce, Hoisin or soy sauce, and garlic powder. Reduce heat to low and cook for 3-4 minutes. Meanwhile, put flour tortillas on a microwavable plate and cover them with a damp paper towel. Microwave in 30-second bursts until they are warmed through. Place 1 cup of cabbage mixture on each tortilla. Fold in sides and roll up (like a burrito). Cut in half and serve.   4 servings

Give Thanks for the Father's Love

December 13

The Word of God to Guide Your Soul
"For the Father Himself loves you, because you have loved Me, and have believed that I came forth from God" (John 16:27).

> *Dear Lord, I love You and thank You for Your unconditional, everlasting love. Thank You so much for bringing Your love to earth as a baby, then growing and experiencing all the struggles of our humanity. Send Your Holy Spirit to increase my love and faith in You more with each new day, as I understand all You gave up to save me. Grant me the courage to share Your amazing love with someone in need today, and let that person be inspired to seek You more, especially during this special time of Advent and Christmas. Amen.*

Music to Inspire Your Mind
- Contemporary Christian "Love Has Come" by Matt Maher.
- Choral "When Love Was Born" by Mark Schultz, performed by One Voice Children's Choir.

- Hymn "Love Came Down at Christmas"—Text: Christina G. Rossetti, Music: Traditional Irish melody, performed by Ali Matthews.
- Your music choice: _____

Nutrition to Strengthen Your Body

Nutty Lime Asparagus

- 1 package (16 ounces) frozen asparagus cuts and tips, thawed
- 2 tablespoons olive oil
- 2 tablespoons lime juice
- ¼ cup slivered blanched almonds
- ⅛ teaspoon garlic powder
- Salt-free seasoning and pepper to taste

Toast almonds by placing nuts in a dry skillet. Heat over medium heat for 4-5 minutes until golden and fragrant. Constantly stir and monitor, as nuts can burn easily. Heat olive oil in a large skillet over medium-high heat. Add asparagus and saute for 3-4 minutes. Add lime juice, cover, reduce heat to low, and simmer for 2-3 minutes. Add almonds, garlic powder, salt-free seasoning, and pepper, tossing gently.   6 servings

Celebrate the Promise of Everlasting Joy

December 14

The Word of God to Guide Your Soul

"So the ransomed of the Lord shall return, and come to Zion with singing, with everlasting joy on their heads. They shall obtain joy and gladness; sorrow and sighing shall flee away" (Isaiah 51:11).

> *Dear Lord, I love You and thank You for Your promise of everlasting joy for those whom You have ransomed. Send Your Holy Spirit to remind me of Your promise when I feel sad or discouraged. Help me look up to You and whisper Your name, which makes dark forces flee and restores my joy and gladness in Your saving mercy once again. Let those I meet today see how my life is a celebration of Your love. Amen.*

Music to Inspire Your Mind

- Contemporary Christian "Joy" by Bart Millard, Barry Graul, Mike Scheuchzer, Nathan Cochran, Robby Shaffer, Ben

Shive, Brown Bannister, Isaac Watts, and George Frederick Handel, performed by MercyMe.

- Vocal "Joy Has Dawned" by Stuart Townend and Keith Getty, performed by Kristyn Getty.
- Hymn "Mary's Little Boy Child" Text and Music: Jester Hairston, performed by Mandisa.
- Your music choice: _____

Nutrition to Strengthen Your Body

Sauteed Vegetables and Beans over Rice

- 1 cup uncooked brown rice
- ½ cup sweet onion, chopped
- 2 garlic cloves, minced, or ¼ teaspoon dried, minced garlic
- 2 tablespoons olive oil
- 1 medium zucchini, coarsely chopped
- 1 medium green pepper, chopped
- ½ teaspoon oregano leaves
- ¼ teaspoon salt-free seasoning
- ⅛ teaspoon pepper
- 2 medium tomatoes, peeled and coarsely chopped
- 1 can (16 ounces) kidney beans, rinsed and drained
- 4 ounces (1 cup) reduced-fat Cheddar cheese, shredded

Prepare rice according to package directions. In a large skillet, saute onion and garlic in olive oil over medium heat for about 5-7 minutes, or until onion is tender. Add zucchini, green pepper, oregano, salt-free seasoning, and pepper. Cook for about 5 minutes, or until vegetables are crisp-tender. Add tomatoes and beans; cover, reduce heat to low, and simmer for about 10 minutes or until thoroughly heated. Spoon hot rice onto the serving platter. Top rice with vegetable mixture and sprinkle with cheese.

6 servings

Seek the Wisdom of Peace

December 15

The Word of God to Guide Your Soul

"But the wisdom that is from above is first pure, then peaceable, gentle, willing to yield, full of mercy and good fruits, without partiality and without hypocrisy. Now the fruit of righteousness is sown in peace by those who make peace" (James 3:17-18).

> *Dear Lord, I love You and thank You for the incomparable wisdom Your word provides to guide my life. Send Your Holy Spirit to grant me an increase of peace, gentleness, and kindness as I grow to understand Your will and how to be Your faithful disciple. Show me the best way to spread Your merciful love to my family, friends, and all I encounter today. In this crazy world of strife and division, help me always be the one to "make peace." Amen.*

Music to Inspire Your Mind

- Contemporary Christian "Peace Has Come" by Ben Hastings, Seth Simmons, and Ben Fielding, performed by Hillsong Worship.
- Vocal "Let There Be Peace" by Chris DeStefano, Carrie Underwood, and Brett James, performed by Carrie Underwood.

- Hymn "Let There Be Peace on Earth (Let It Begin with Me)"—Text and Music: Sy Miller and Jill Jackson, performed by the Harlem Boys' Choir.
- Your music choice: _____

Nutrition to Strengthen Your Body

Slow Cooker Apple Crisp

- 6 medium apples, peeled and thinly sliced (Golden Delicious, Granny Smith, or Honeycrisp)
- 2 teaspoons lemon juice
- 1 ⅓ cups quick-cooking oats
- ½ cup all-purpose flour
- ½ cup packed light brown sugar
- ½ teaspoon ground cinnamon
- ¼ teaspoon ground ginger
- Pinch ground nutmeg
- ¼ cup (4 tablespoons) cold margarine
- Nonstick cooking spray

Coat slow cooker with cooking spray. Place apples in a slow cooker and sprinkle with lemon juice. Toss well. In a medium mixing bowl, combine remaining ingredients, except margarine. Cut in margarine with a pastry cutter or two knives until the mixture resembles coarse crumbs. Pour oat mixture into slow cooker over apples and smooth out the top. Cover and cook on high for about 2 hours or low for about 4 hours.

6 servings

Grow in the Grace and Truth Freely Given Through Jesus

December 16

The Word of God to Guide Your Soul

"And the Word became flesh and dwelt among us, and we beheld His glory, the glory as of the only begotten of the Father, full of grace and truth. And of His fullness we have all received, and grace for grace. For the law was given through Moses, but grace and truth came through Jesus Christ" (John 1:14, 16-17).

> *Dear Lord, I love You and thank You for giving up Your glorious home in heaven to bring me Your grace and truth. Send Your Holy Spirit to open my mind, heart, and soul to all of the mercy, grace, and truth You long to reveal to me. Work through me today to help others receive Your "grace for grace" and come to know the joy of living with You now and forever. Amen.*

Music to Inspire Your Mind

- Contemporary Christian "Christmas Changes Everything" by Josh Wilson and Jeff Pardo, performed by Josh Wilson.
- Vocal "The Final Word" by Michael Card.

743

- Hymn "Christmas Grace"—Text and Music: Ruth Elaine Schram, performed by The Lorenz Corporation Choir.
- Your music choice: _____

Nutrition to Strengthen Your Body

Greek Scrambled Eggs

- ½ medium red onion, thinly sliced
- 1 sweet red pepper, seeded and thinly sliced into 2-inch strips
- 2 tablespoons olive oil
- 1 large tomato, peeled and chopped
- 6 eggs or 1½ cups egg substitute
- Salt-free seasoning and pepper, to taste
- ¼ cup fresh parsley or 1 tablespoon dried parsley
- ½ cup reduced-fat Feta cheese, crumbled

In a large skillet, heat olive oil over medium heat. Add onion and pepper; saute until tender, for about 5-7 minutes, stirring often. Add the tomatoes and simmer on medium-low heat for 3-4 minutes. Meanwhile, beat the eggs with the seasonings and add to the vegetables in the skillet. Sprinkle with parsley and Feta cheese, blending everything together. Cook over medium-low heat until the eggs begin to set, gently stirring to scramble until desired consistency. Serve immediately.   4 servings

Obey God's Voice and Cling to Him

December 17

The Word of God to Guide Your Soul

"Therefore choose life, that both you and your descendants may live; that you may love the LORD your God, that you may obey His voice, and that you may cling to Him, for He is your life and the length of your days" (Deuteronomy 30:19b-20a).

> *Dear Lord, I love You and thank You for coming to earth as an infant King, choosing to embrace humanity and experience our struggles and temptations. Send Your Holy Spirit to grant me perseverance in listening to Your voice, obeying Your will, and clinging to You in all situations. Lead me in how best to help others choose You and the beautiful life You offer. Amen.*

Music to Inspire Your Mind

- Contemporary Christian "Away in a Manger (Forever Amen)" by James R. Murray, Jonathan Smith and Phil Wickham, performed by Phil Wickham.

- Vocal "Do You Hear What I Hear" by Noel Regney and Gloria Shayne, performed by Martina McBride.
- Hymn "Sing Lullaby (Infant King)" by Rev. Sabine Baring-Gould, performed by Libera.
- Your music choice: _____

Nutrition to Strengthen Your Body

Vegetarian Chili Burritos

- 1 can (14 ounces) fat-free refried beans
- 1 teaspoon chili powder
- ½ teaspoon ground cumin
- ½ teaspoon dried oregano
- ⅛ teaspoon garlic powder
- 1 package (8.8 ounces) whole grain brown rice, ready to microwave
- 1 cup (8 ounces) reduced-fat Cheddar cheese or Mexican cheese blend, shredded
- Salsa (your flavor choice), as desired
- 1 package (10 counts) whole wheat soft tortilla wraps
- Suggested Toppings: Chopped tomatoes, shredded lettuce, sliced black olives, sliced scallions, sliced jalapeno, low-fat sour cream, and guacamole

Place beans in a 2-quart casserole dish. Stir in the next 4 ingredients. Microwave on medium power for 3 minutes, stirring once halfway through. (Add extra water if the mixture becomes too thick.) Microwave rice according to package directions; add to bean mixture. Heat tortillas one at a time in a dry skillet over medium heat for about 20-30 seconds per side. Place about ⅓ cup bean mixture in each tortilla, add cheese, salsa, and desired toppings. Roll up and serve.   6 burritos

Cling to What is Good

December 18

The Word of God to Guide Your Soul
"Let love be without hypocrisy. Abhor what is evil. Cling to what is good. Be kindly affectionate to one another with brotherly love, in honor giving preference to one another" (Romans 12:9-10).

> *Dear Lord, I love You and thank You for Your example of sincere love for all nations and peoples. Send Your Holy Spirit to grant me the grace to love and honor others, as You have loved me. Help me "cling to what is good" and meditate often on Your amazing love. Show me how to be an encouragement to someone today so they can also experience the miracle of Your kindness and goodness. Amen.*

Music to Inspire Your Mind
- Contemporary Christian "Miracle of Love" by Chris Tomlin, Ed Cash, and Ashley Gorley, performed by Chris Tomlin.
- Vocal "Think about His Love" by Walt Harrah, performed by Don Moen.

- Hymn "Angels, from the Realms of Glory"—Text: James Montgomery, Music: Henry T. Smart, performed by The Piano Guys, Peter Hollens, and David Archuleta.
- Your music choice: _____

Nutrition to Strengthen Your Body

Italian Macaroni and Cheese

- 2 cups cubed reduced-fat Cheddar cheese
- 1 cup fat-free evaporated milk
- 1 tablespoon Dijon mustard
- 10 ounces dry elbow macaroni (to make about 2½ cups, cooked)
- ½ teaspoon dried basil
- 1 can (16 ounces) diced, plum tomatoes, with liquid
- 1-2 tablespoons Italian-style bread crumbs
- Nonstick olive oil cooking spray

Preheat oven to 350 degrees. Cook pasta according to package directions to al dente firmness and drain. Meanwhile, in a medium saucepan, combine cheese, milk, and mustard. Cook over low heat, stirring constantly, until cheese melts. Add cooked pasta and mix well. In a medium mixing bowl, add basil to tomatoes. In a 9x13-inch baking dish, lightly coated with cooking spray, layer ⅓ of the macaroni and cheese; top with ⅓ of the tomato mixture. Repeat layers, ending with macaroni and cheese but reserving a generous spoonful of tomatoes to put in the center of the top layer. Sprinkle with bread crumbs. Bake, covered, for 30 minutes or until mixture is hot and bubbly.   6 servings

Sanctify Christ as Lord in Your Heart

December 19

The Word of God to Guide Your Soul

"But even if you should suffer for righteousness' sake, you are blessed. 'And do not be afraid of their threats, nor be troubled.' But sanctify the Lord God in your hearts, and always be ready to give a defense to everyone who asks you a reason for the hope that is in you, with meekness and fear" (1 Peter 3:14-15).

Dear Lord, I love You and thank You for Your comforting words of encouragement. Send Your Holy Spirit to grant me the right words to say when I'm asked about my faith and why my hope is in Your love and forgiveness. Help me to always sanctify and consecrate my life to Your will. Let everyone know, without a doubt, that You are the love and Lord of my heart. Amen.

Music to Inspire Your Mind
- Contemporary Christian "Hope Was Born This Night" by Dave Frey, performed by Sidewalk Prophets.

- Vocal "Here's My Heart" by Chris Tomlin, Jason Ingram, and Louie Giglio, performed by Lauren Daigle.
- Hymn "O Come All Ye Faithful"—Text: Latin Hymn, Music: John Francis Wade, performed by Carrie Underwood.
- Your music choice: _____

Nutrition to Strengthen Your Body

Meatless Shepherd's Pie

- Vegetable mixture: 1 package (16 ounces) frozen peas and carrots, thawed, 1 cup sweet onion, chopped, 1 cup green pepper, chopped, 2 teaspoons dried thyme, 2 teaspoons paprika
- 2 tablespoons olive oil
- 4 cups (8 ounces) frozen shredded hash brown potatoes, thawed (or 4 cups mashed potatoes)
- ⅔ cup reduced-fat ricotta or cottage cheese
- ½ teaspoon salt-free seasoning, divided
- Bean mixture: 1 can (15 ounces) black beans, drained and rinsed, 1 cup tomato, diced, 1 can (8 ounces) tomato sauce, 2 teaspoons Worcestershire sauce
- Nonstick olive oil cooking spray

Preheat oven to 350 degrees. In a large skillet, heat olive oil over medium heat. Saute onion and green pepper until tender. Add peas and carrots, thyme, and paprika. Reduce heat to low and cook, covered, for 10-15 minutes. Meanwhile, in a large saucepan, cook hash browns in boiling water to cover for 10 minutes or until tender. Drain and mash. Stir in ricotta or cottage cheese and ¼ teaspoon salt-free seasoning. Set aside. In a large mixing bowl, combine vegetable mixture, bean mixture, and ¼ teaspoon salt-free seasoning. Coat a 9x13-inch baking dish with cooking spray and add vegetable/bean mixture. Spoon hash brown or mashed potato mixture in a border around edge of the dish and a large dollop in the center. Sprinkle paprika over the top. Bake, uncovered, for 20 minutes.

6 servings

Turn to the Lord for His Blessing of Peace

December 20

The Word of God to Guide Your Soul
"The LORD bless you and keep you; the LORD make His face shine upon you, and be gracious to you; the LORD lift up His countenance upon you, and give you peace" (Numbers 6:24-26).

> *Dear Lord, I love You and thank You for watching over me and blessing me with Your kindness and peace. Send Your Holy Spirit to make me truly grateful for all You have done to save me and make me part of Your heavenly family. Grant me an opportunity today to be a blessing to someone and share Your gracious love and peace so they will be encouraged to seek You and know You better. Amen.*

Music to Inspire Your Mind
- Contemporary Christian "Glory (Let There Be Peace)" by Matt Maher, Rachel Taylor Popadic, and Chris Stevens, performed by Matt Maher.
- Vocal "Peace on Earth" by Austin French, Jake Henry, and Jeff Pardo, performed by Austin French.

- Hymn "While Shepherds Watched Their Flocks"—Text: Nahum Tate, Music: George Frederick Handel, performed by Hymn Charts. (For a beautiful choral arrangement by Craig Courtney, listen to the Atlanta Master Chorale.)
- Your music choice: _____

Nutrition to Strengthen Your Body

Pan Roasted Vegetables

- ⅓ cup margarine
- ½ teaspoon dried thyme
- ¼ teaspoon salt-free seasoning
- ¼ teaspoon pepper
- 1 package (10.8 ounces) frozen cauliflower florets, thawed
- 1 package (10.8 ounces) frozen broccoli florets, thawed
- 1 package (12 ounces) carrot sticks
- 2 small sweet onions, quartered

Preheat oven to 400 degrees. In a 9x13-inch baking pan, melt margarine in the oven. Stir in thyme, salt-free seasoning, and pepper. Add vegetables and toss to coat. Cover with aluminum foil and bake for 25 minutes or to desired tenderness. (Be creative and try different vegetables.) 6 servings

Delight in Knowing that God Rejoices Over You

December 21

The Word of God to Guide Your Soul

"The LORD your God in your midst, the Mighty One, will save; He will rejoice over you with gladness, He will quiet you with His love, He will rejoice over you with singing" (Zephaniah 3:17).

Dear Lord, I love You and thank You for rejoicing over me with gladness and quieting me with Your love. Send Your Holy Spirit to grant me unquenchable happiness and delight when I think of You singing joyfully because You created me. Whenever I get discouraged, as I journey on through this life toward my heavenly home, remind me of this promise in Your word and show me how I can share this beautiful news with all my family and friends. Amen.

Music to Inspire Your Mind

- Contemporary Christian "Isn't He (This Jesus)" by Natalie Grant, Mia Fieldes, Andrew Holt, and Seth Mosley, performed by The Belonging Company, featuring Natalie Grant.

- Vocal "Somewhere in Your Silent Night" by Mark Hall, Bernie Herms, and Matthew West, performed by Casting Crowns.
- Hymn "We Will Glorify"—Text and Music: Twila Paris, performed by Twila Paris.
- Your music choice: _____

Nutrition to Strengthen Your Body

Three-Bean Casserole

- 1 can (15 ounces) kidney beans, drained and rinsed
- 1 can (15 ounces) butter beans, drained and rinsed
- 1 can (15 ounces) vegetarian baked beans
- 2 tablespoons olive oil
- 1 large sweet onion, chopped
- ½ cup ketchup
- 1 teaspoon prepared mustard
- ½ cup brown sugar
- Nonstick olive oil cooking spray

Preheat oven to 300 degrees. In a large mixing bowl, mix together all of the beans. In a medium skillet, heat olive oil over medium-high heat and saute onion until tender (for 5-7 minutes). Combine all the remaining ingredients and onions with a bean mixture. Transfer to a large casserole dish sprayed with cooking spray. Bake for 2 hours, uncovered.   8 servings

Magnify the Lord with Mary

December 22

The Word of God to Guide Your Soul

"And Mary said: 'My soul magnifies the Lord, and my spirit has rejoiced in God my Savior. For He who is mighty has done great things for me, and holy is His name'" (Luke 1:46-47, 49).

Dear Lord, I love You and thank You for doing "great things for me." Thank You for the example of Your mother, Mary, and her willingness to joyfully say yes to all You asked of her. Send Your Holy Spirit to grant me that same willingness and boldness in proclaiming Your mercy and salvation. Let those I encounter today see my joy in living for You and serving those around me. Amen.

Music to Inspire Your Mind

- Contemporary Christian "My Soul Magnifies the Lord" by Chris Tomlin and Daniel Carson, performed by Chris Tomlin.
- Vocal "Almost There" by Michael W. Smith, Wes King, and Amy Grant, performed by Michael W. Smith, featuring Amy Grant.

- Hymn "Magnficat (with Wexford Carol)"—Text and Music: Keith and Kristyn Getty and Stuart Townend (based on Luke 1:46-55), performed by Keith and Kristyn Getty
- Your music choice: _____

Nutrition to Strengthen Your Body

Broiled Open-face Tomato and Cottage Cheese Toast

- 1 cup reduced-fat cottage cheese (plain, cucumber, garden vegetable, or other favorite flavors)
- 2 tablespoons green onions, chopped
- ¾ teaspoon salt-free seasoning
- ⅛ teaspoon pepper
- 4 slices whole-grain bread, toasted
- 2-3 medium tomatoes, thickly sliced

Preheat the oven broiler. Place toast on a baking sheet lined with aluminum foil. In a small mixing bowl, combine the cottage cheese, onions, salt-free seasoning, and pepper. Spread ¼ cup of the cheese mixture over each slice of toast. Top with tomato slices. Broil for 1-2 minutes or until cheese is melted. (You may also serve this cold if preferred.)   4 servings

Welcome the Dayspring from on High into Your Life

December 23

The Word of God to Guide Your Soul

"Now his [John the Baptist's] father Zacharias was filled with the Holy Spirit, and prophesied, saying: 'Through the tender mercy of our God, with which the Dayspring from on high has visited us; to give light to those who sit in darkness and the shadow of death, to guide our feet into the way of peace'" (Luke 1:67, 78-79, brackets added for clarity).

> *Dear Lord, I love You and thank You for coming as a tiny babe and shining Your light into the darkness of this world. Thank you also for Your promise of everlasting life and light in Your heavenly kingdom. Send Your Holy Spirit to grant me an open and welcoming mind and heart to the light of Your truth and wisdom. Let me be Your instrument to lead others "into the way of peace." Amen.*

Music to Inspire Your Mind

- Contemporary Christian "Joy Unto the World" by Matt Fuqua, Joshua Havens, Dan Ostebo, Jordan Mohilowski, and Ethan Hulse, performed by The Afters.

- Vocal "Song of Zechariah" by David LaChance, Jr.
- Hymn "The King Shall Come" Text: Greek, translated by John Brownlie, Music: Trevor Thomson, performed by Trevor Thomson.
- Your music choice: _____

Nutrition to Strengthen Your Body

Stuffed Sweet Potatoes

- 2 large sweet potatoes
- ½ cup crushed pineapple, drained
- ¼ cup raisins
- 2 tablespoons margarine, melted
- ½ teaspoon pumpkin pie spice

Preheat oven to 400 degrees. Wash sweet potatoes and pierce 3-4 times with a fork. Place potatoes on a microwave-safe plate and microwave for 5 minutes, turning halfway through. Check to see if they are fork-tender. If not, continue microwaving at 30-second intervals. Cool and halve lengthwise. Scoop out the pulp from potato halves into a mixing bowl, leaving ¼-inch shells. Mash pulp and reserve shells. Add remaining ingredients to potato pulp and stir to combine. Spoon potato mixture evenly into reserved shells. Place on a baking sheet lined with aluminum foil. Bake until heated through, for about 10 minutes. 4 servings

Rejoice with the Angels on This Holy Night

December 24

The Word of God to Guide Your Soul

"Now there were in the same country shepherds living out in the fields, keeping watch over their flock by night. And behold, an angel of the Lord stood before them, and the glory of the Lord shone around them, and they were greatly afraid. Then the angel said to them, 'Do not be afraid, for behold, I bring you good tidings of great joy which will be to all people. For there is born to you this day in the city of David a Savior, who is Christ the Lord'" (Luke 2:8-11).

> *Dear Lord, I love You and thank You for coming to be my Savior, Messiah, and Lord. Send Your Holy Spirit to grant me "great joy" and cast out all fear when I meditate on this wondrous event. Show me how to share the same message the angels proclaimed to the shepherds with all those I know who are in need of salvation, love, and hope. Amen.*

Music to Inspire Your Mind

- Contemporary Christian "These Christmas Lights" by Matt Redman, Nick Herbert, and Sam Bailey, performed by Matt Redman.
- Vocal "O Holy Night" by Placide Cappeau, John S. Dwight, and Adolphe Adam, performed by Josh Groban.
- Hymn "Night of Silence/Silent Night"—Text: Daniel Kantor/Joseph Mohr, Music: Daniel Kantor/Franz X. Gruber, performed by St. Olaf Choir in Minnesota.
- Your music choice: _____

Nutrition to Strengthen Your Body

Mini Vegetarian Pot Pies

- 1 package (8-count) of reduced-fat crescent rolls
- 1 package (10 ounces) frozen mixed vegetables (corn, carrots, peas, and green beans), thawed
- 1 package vegetarian brown gravy mix
- 2 tablespoons red wine vinegar (optional)
- Nonstick olive oil spray

Preheat oven to 375 degrees. Spray 8 wells of a muffin tin with nonstick spray and line each with a crescent roll, leaving enough to enclose the veggie mixture. Prepare gravy according to package directions and add veggies and vinegar (if desired). Cook for 5 minutes. Spoon the gravy vegetable mixture into the dough triangles and wrap the dough over the top. Bake for 10-12 minutes until golden. Remove from oven and let sit for 5 minutes to firm up.   4 servings

Adore the Baby Jesus with All of Creation

December 25

The Word of God to Guide Your Soul
"For unto us a Child is born, unto us a Son is given; and the government will be upon His shoulder. And His name will be called Wonderful, Counselor, Mighty God, Everlasting Father, Prince of Peace. Of the increase of His government and peace there will be no end" (Isaiah 9:6-7a).

> *Dear Lord, I love You and thank You for bringing joy and peace to all of creation through Your humble birth, selfless life, sacrificial death, and miraculous resurrection. From the wood of the manger to the wood of the cross, You were faithful and obeyed the Father's will. Send Your Holy Spirit to help me adore You and love You with my whole heart at Christmas and all year through. Amen.*

Music to Inspire Your Mind
- Contemporary Christian "Adore" by Graham Kendrick and Martin Chalk, performed by Chris Tomlin.
- Vocal "Someday" by Rick Vale, performed by Sandi Patty.

- Hymn "Joy to the World"—Text: Isaac Watts, Music: George Frederick Handel, performed by Celtic Woman (live at the Helix in Dublin, Ireland).
- Your music choice: _____

Nutrition to Strengthen Your Body

Christmas Cranberry Delight Gelatin Salad

- 1 can (20 ounces) crushed pineapple in juice
- 1 package (6 ounces) strawberry gelatin
- 1 cup water
- 1 can (14 ounces) whole berry cranberry sauce
- 3 tablespoons fresh lemon juice
- 1 tablespoon lemon peel, grated
- ¼ teaspoon ground nutmeg
- 2 cups light sour cream or plain yogurt
- ½ cup walnuts or pecans, chopped
- Nonstick cooking spray

Drain pineapple well, reserving all juice. In a 2-quart saucepan, combine pineapple juice with gelatin. Stir in water. Heat to boiling while stirring to dissolve gelatin. Remove from heat. Blend in cranberry sauce. Add lemon juice, peel, and nutmeg. Chill until the mixture slightly thickens. Blend sour cream or yogurt into gelatin mixture. Fold in pineapple and nuts. Lightly spray mold or Bundt pan with cooking spray. Pour gelatin mixture into mold dish and chill overnight or until firm. Unmold onto serving platter.   10-12 servings

Show the Lord Your Love by Keeping His Commandments

December 26

The Word of God to Guide Your Soul
"He who has My commandments and keeps them, it is he who loves Me. And he who loves Me will be loved by My Father, and I will love him and manifest Myself to him" (John 14:21).

> *Dear Lord, I love You and thank You for Your Word that teaches me how to live a life pleasing to You. Thank you for Your beautiful promise to manifest Yourself to me as I learn to love and obey You more each day. Send Your Holy Spirit to grant me the perseverance to consistently keep Your commandments and follow Your will for my life. Help me to love others, as You have loved me. Amen.*

Music to Inspire Your Mind
- Contemporary Christian "Your Word" by Chris Davenport, performed by Hillsong Worship.
- Vocal "This Baby" by Steven Curtis Chapman.
- Hymn "Speak, O Lord"—Text and Music: Stuart Townend and Keith Getty, performed by Keith and Kristyn Getty.

- Your music choice: _____

Nutrition to Strengthen Your Body

Lemon-Dill Carrot Coins

- 1 package (16 ounces) crinkle cut carrot coins or baby carrots cut in half
- ⅓ cup, plus 3 tablespoons water
- 1 teaspoon cornstarch
- 1 teaspoon margarine
- ½ teaspoon dried dill weed
- ¼ teaspoon grated lemon rind
- ¼ teaspoon salt-free seasoning

In a 1½-quart casserole dish, add carrots and 3 tablespoons of water. Cover and microwave on high for 10-12 minutes, stirring occasionally, until tender. Drain. Meanwhile, in a small saucepan, combine cornstarch and lemon juice, stirring until smooth. Add ⅓ cup water and cook over medium heat, stirring constantly until thickened. Stir in margarine, dill weed, lemon rind, and salt-free seasoning. Cook, stirring constantly, until margarine melts. Pour lemon juice mixture over carrots and toss gently. 6 servings

Share the Light of Christ and Praise His Holy Name

December 27

The Word of God to Guide Your Soul
"Light is sown for the righteous, and gladness for the upright in heart. Rejoice in the Lord, you righteous, and give thanks at the remembrance of His holy name" (Psalm 97:11-12).

> *Dear Lord, I love You and thank You for bringing Your saving light to this dark world of sin. Send Your Holy Spirit to help me truly rejoice and praise Your holy name every day, even when times are difficult. Grant me the grace to always remember You are my King, and I am an heir to Your kingdom. Let others see my joy and the light of Your glory and love in my eyes. Amen.*

Music to Inspire Your Mind
- Contemporary Christian "A King Like This" by Chris Tomlin, Matt Redman, and Jonas Myrin, performed by Chris Tomlin.
- Vocal "Ding Dong! Merrily on High" by Traditional French Carol, performed by Jackie Evancho.

- Hymn "Arise, Shine/Great Is the Lord"—Text and Music: Rita Baloche and Jamie Harvill/Chris Christensen, performed by Chris Christensen and Integrity's Hosanna! Music.
- Your music choice: _____

Nutrition to Strengthen Your Body

Spinach Mushroom Casserole

- 1 package (10 ounces) frozen, chopped spinach
- 1 can (4 ounces) sliced mushrooms, drained
- 1 teaspoon dried, minced onion
- 1 teaspoon dried, minced garlic
- 1 teaspoon salt-free seasoning
- Dash of pepper
- ⅓ cup light sour cream

In a 2-quart casserole dish, prepare spinach in the microwave according to package directions. Drain well. Combine with remaining ingredients in a casserole dish. Microwave for an additional 2-3 minutes or until hot. Serve immediately.

4 servings

Bring All Your Sins and Brokenness to Jesus

December 28

The Word of God to Guide Your Soul
"My little children, these things I write to you, so that you may not sin. And if anyone sins, we have an Advocate with the Father, Jesus Christ the righteous. And He Himself is the propitiation for our sins, and not for ours only but also for the whole world" (1 John 2:1-2).

> *Dear Lord, I love You and thank You for being my Advocate with the Father. Send Your Holy Spirit to make me aware of my sins and grant me the grace to overcome them. When I'm feeling broken because I have failed You, help me remember that You died to provide "propitiation" for my sins and "also for the whole world." Let my life be a reflection of Your saving love and forgiveness. You are truly mighty to save! Amen.*

Music to Inspire Your Mind
- Contemporary Christian "Cry of the Broken" by Darlene Zschech, performed by Hillsong.

- Vocal "Help from Heaven" by Matt Redman and Jonas Myrin, performed by Matt Redman, featuring Natasha Bedingfield.
- Hymn "Mighty to Save"—Text and Music: Reuben Morgan and Ben Fielding, performed by Michael W. Smith.
- Your music choice: _____

Nutrition to Strengthen Your Body

Slow Cooker Sweet Potatoes

- 4 sweet potatoes
- 2 teaspoons olive oil
- Toppings (as desired): 1) margarine, salt-free seasoning, and pepper; 2) margarine, brown sugar, and cinnamon; 3) margarine, maple syrup, and chopped pecans or other nuts; 4) light sour cream or plain yogurt, chives, salt-free seasoning, and pepper

Scrub each sweet potato and dry completely. With a fork, pierce each potato several times. Prepare individual sheets of aluminum foil for each potato. Place potatoes on aluminum foil and drizzle each with olive oil. Rub completely over all of the potatoes. Wrap in foil and place in a slow cooker. Cook on high for 2-3 hours or low for 7-9 hours or until soft and tender. Carefully remove potatoes from the slow cooker with tongs or potholders. Add toppings as desired.   4 servings

Rest in the Lord's Light and Love

December 29

The Word of God to Guide Your Soul
"The sun shall no longer be your light by day, nor for brightness shall the moon give light to you; but the Lord will be to you an everlasting light, and your God your glory" (Isaiah 60:19).

> *Dear Lord, I love You and thank You for bringing Your light and glory to every aspect of my life. Send Your Holy Spirit to help me dwell in Your light and love every moment of every day. When I am anxious or worried, let me rest in Your arms and trust that all is well with You by my side. Show me how to be an encouragement to someone today who is seeking a way out of the darkness of this world into the light of Your love. Amen.*

Music to Inspire Your Mind
- Contemporary Christian "Rest in the Arms" by Aaron Shust, Jason Ingram, Doug McKelvey, and Matthew West, performed by Aaron Shust.

- Vocal "All Is Well" by Michael W. Smith and Wayne Kirkpatrick, performed by Jordan Smith, featuring Michael W. Smith.
- Hymn "Still, Still, Still"—Text and Music: Traditional Austrian Carol, performed by Mannheim Steamroller and Choir.
- Your music choice: _____

Nutrition to Strengthen Your Body

Cauliflower with Celery Cheese Sauce

- 1 package (16 ounces) frozen cauliflower florets
- 1 can (10.5 ounces) cream of celery soup (lower sodium and fat)
- ⅓ cup low-fat milk
- ½ cup reduced-fat sharp Cheddar cheese, shredded

Microwave cauliflower according to package directions and drain. In a medium saucepan, combine soup, milk, and cheese. Cook over low heat, stirring occasionally, until cheese is melted and the sauce has heated through. Serve over cauliflower.

4 servings

Follow the Lord's Plan for Your Life Like Joseph

December 30

The Word of God to Guide Your Soul

"Now when they [the Magi] had departed, behold, an angel of the Lord appeared to Joseph in a dream, saying, 'Arise, take the young Child and His mother, flee to Egypt, and stay there until I bring you word; for Herod will seek the young Child to destroy Him.' When he arose, he took the young Child and His mother by night and departed for Egypt" (Matthew 2:13-14, brackets added for clarity).

Dear Lord, I love You and thank You for the example of Joseph in following Your will obediently and quickly. Send Your Holy Spirit to help me discern Your voice and grant me faith to follow Your plan, as did both Joseph and Mary. Remind me each and every day to spend time in silence and prayer so I can hear Your voice above all the noise of this world. Let me also be an example to others of the beauty, truth, and goodness that is found in a life dedicated to following You. Amen.

Music to Inspire Your Mind

- Contemporary Christian "Joseph's Lullaby" by Bart Millard and Brown Bannister, performed by MercyMe.
- Vocal "Joseph's Song" by Michael Card.
- Hymn "Once in Royal David's City"—Text: Cecil F. Alexander, Music: Henry J. Gauntlett, performed by Celtic Woman featuring the Orchestra of Ireland.
- Your music choice: _____

Nutrition to Strengthen Your Body

Warm Three-Bean Salad

- 1 package (10 ounces) frozen cut green beans
- ½ cup sweet onion, thinly sliced
- 1 clove garlic, minced, or ⅛ teaspoon dried, minced garlic
- ⅓ cup light Italian dressing
- 1 can (15 ounces) pinto beans, rinsed and drained
- 1 can (15 ounces) butter beans, rinsed and drained

In a 2-quart casserole dish, combine green beans, onion, garlic, and Italian dressing. Cover and microwave on high for 6-8 minutes, stirring halfway through. Add the remaining ingredients, cover, and microwave on high for an additional 3-6 minutes or until bean salad is heated through.   8 servings

Be Faithful to the Lord as He is Faithful to You

December 31

The Word of God to Guide Your Soul
"Therefore know that the LORD your God, He is God, the faithful God who keeps covenant and mercy for a thousand generations with those who love Him and keep His commandments" (Deuteronomy 7:9).

> *Dear Lord, I love You and thank You for Your faithfulness throughout my life. Thank you for this past year and all of the blessings and struggles You brought me through. Send Your Holy Spirit to keep me always faithful to You, no matter what the New Year might bring my way. Show me how to best serve You and others so I can be Your instrument to spread Your love and faithfulness. Amen.*

Music to Inspire Your Mind
- Contemporary Christian "Great Things" by Jonas Myrin and Phil Wickham, performed by Phil Wickham.
- Vocal "Faithful God" by Laura Story.

- Hymn "Forever"—Text and Music: Chris Tomlin, performed by Michael W. Smith.
- Your music choice: _____

Nutrition to Strengthen Your Body

Broccoli, Lemon, and Cheese Quesadillas

- 1 package (10 ounces) frozen broccoli florets
- ½ cup sweet onion, finely chopped
- 1 cup reduced-fat cottage cheese
- 1 cup reduced-fat Cheddar cheese, shredded
- 1 tablespoon of lemon juice
- 1 teaspoon of dried parsley or thyme
- ½ teaspoon of garlic powder
- 1 egg or ¼ cup egg substitute
- Nonstick olive oil cooking spray
- 4 whole wheat tortillas
- Alfalfa sprouts, as desired

Microwave broccoli according to package directions and drain well. Roughly chop florets. In a mixing bowl, combine broccoli, onion, cheeses, lemon juice, seasonings, and egg. Lightly spray a large skillet with cooking spray. Place one tortilla in the pan, then spread with half the broccoli mixture. Top with a second tortilla. Over medium heat, cook for 4 minutes or until the base is golden. Turn over and cook for another 3 minutes or until golden. Cover and reduce heat to low. Cook for 5 minutes or until cheese is melted. Remove from the pan. Repeat with remaining tortillas and broccoli mixture. Cut into wedges and top with alfalfa sprouts to serve.   4 servings

About the Author

Cathy has worked as a clinical dietitian and a public health nutritionist. She has also been an editor and writer of small-group Bible studies for Serendipity, LifeWay, and Standard Publishing. She enjoys singing, playing piano and guitar, and serving in the music ministry at church. She lives in sunny Oviedo, Florida, with her husband, Gil.